Truth, Errors, and Lies

Truth, Errors, and Lies

POLITICS AND ECONOMICS
IN A VOLATILE WORLD

GRZEGORZ W. KOLODKO

Translated from the Polish by William R. Brand

COLUMBIA UNIVERSITY PRESS   NEW YORK

This publication has been funded by The Book Institute–The ©POLAND
Translation Program.

Columbia University Press
Publishers Since 1893
New York   Chichester, West Sussex
Copyright © 2008 Grzegorz W. Kolodko
Translation copyright © 2011 Columbia University Press
All rights reserved
Library of Congress Cataloging-in-Publication Data

Kolodko, Grzegorz W.
[Wedrujacy swiat. English]
Truth, errors, and lies : politics and economics in a volatile world / Grzegorz
W. Kolodko ; translated from the Polish by William R. Brand.
p.   cm.
Includes bibliographical references and index.
ISBN 978-0-231-15068-2 (cloth : alk. paper) — ISBN 978-0-231-52156-7 (ebook)
1. Economic geography.   2. Economic development.   3. Economic policy.
4. Economic history.   5. Economic forecasting.   I. Brand, William R.
II. Title.
HF1025.K58413   2011
330 — dc22   2010033569

Columbia University Press books are printed on permanent and durable acid-free
paper.
This book is printed on paper with recycled content.
Printed in the United States of America

c 10 9 8 7 6 5 4 3 2 1

References to Internet Web sites (URLs) were accurate at the time of writing.
Neither the author nor Columbia University Press is responsible for URLs that
may have expired or changed since the manuscript was prepared.

To Everyone

Contents

The Navigator

www.volatileworld.net

THIS BOOK is deliberately free of tables, graphs, and maps, in order to make it easier and more attractive to read. Nor is there a traditional bibliography in alphabetical order, because all the cited sources are described in the endnotes. Instead, there is a special apparatus: the Navigator. The Navigator is a website, www.volatileworld.net, especially prepared for interested readers. It contains a vast amount of statistical information connected with the material presented on these pages. You can find tables, graphs, and maps that illustrate many of the phenomena and processes that I discuss. There are also my own photographs showing various corners of our wandering world, and places discussed in this book.

Moreover, the data presented in this unique virtual annex is updated regularly, on a quarterly, semi-annual, or annual basis so that the reader can quickly find the latest information.

Of course, the Navigator is only for those who wish to explore the statistics and performance indexes in greater depth, who enjoy charts, trends, and the shapes and colors of maps and photographs. The Navigator is more than essential background and statistical information to supplement the book. Years from now, users of the Navigator will still be able to keep up to date with the themes that I discuss. Scholarly interpretation, facts, and logic will still hold true, but the statistical background keeps changing.

The Navigator also includes an extensive bibliography of the works I consulted while working on the issues examined in the book. This is not a complete scholarly bibliography—something that would be nearly unthinkable, given the broad, interdisciplinary scope. Nevertheless, it will enable the inquisitive to delve far more profoundly into issues of humankind and the economy, the world and development, and the past and the future. The bibliography features many original sources along with links to them, so that a single click often serves to open up important source documents. This should be an aid to both researchers and students.

Finally, the Navigator includes a blog where the unending debate about the international community, the global economy, and the human fate can continue to unfold—including our own place in all of this and our own outlook. In this way, the reader can stay in intellectual contact with me and with others who find these matters fascinating.

Our Navigator is thus a splendid instrument to aid and enhance our great, unique journey through time and space—the journey of our "Wandering World" in its search for a better future.

With the Navigator in hand, or rather under the reader's fingers, it might be a little easier to find the right way.

Truth, Errors, and Lies

CHAPTER ONE

The World, Words, and Meaning

*Where Truth, Errors, and Lies in Economics and
Politics Come from and What to Do to
Make Truth Come First*

Difficult economics is best explained through simple,
meaningful words.

ECONOMISTS are supposed to describe and explain what's happening. The best ones know what's going on and can convince us. Problems begin to crop up when they

- Know, but cannot convince us.
- Don't know but try to convince us anyway.
- Know that things are different from what they are trying to convince us of.

In the first case, there is nothing to do except to try to help them get the message across. Appearances notwithstanding, this is no easy task. The effort needs to be supported by publications, informational programs, teaching, the independent media, progressive nongovernmental organizations, and people of good will—who are never in short supply. First, however, they need to know how things stand.

In the second case, when people don't know how things really stand but try to convince us of their concept, they're just plain wrong. Then it's necessary to argue calmly with them and to pay attention to the other side, because anyone can be wrong—including us. We can tell that the people propounding the mistaken views have good intentions. As they see it, they are trying to get at the truth and to share it with others. Therefore, they are allies in the struggle for truth, and all it takes to bring them (or ourselves) into line is to make them aware of their mistakes and work out a common position.

The worst case is the third one, when people deliberately proclaim falsehoods. In politics, this is an everyday occurrence—politics is about results, not truth. Evading the latter sometimes serves the former, which is why veracity and lying are treated instrumentally in politics. This explains why many of the economists who enter politics become enmeshed in falsehood. Truth is a fine thing at a scientific conference, but not at political rallies, which, in our day, usually take place in front of the spotlights and the TV cameras. After all, it would have been unthinkable in Polish government policy at the turn of 1989–90 to announce that the national income would fall by almost 20 percent over the next two years and that there would be 3 million unemployed within four years. The public would not have accepted such policies, or those responsible for them. Honest economists issued warnings,[1] only to be shouted down by their more obeisant colleagues. In Russia, similarly, it would have been political suicide to declare in 1992 that neoliberal policies would lead to seven lean years in which production fell by more than half and a vast part of the population would face social exclusion.

It is too easy to dodge the truth in economics, and the tolerance for prevarication—despite its evident harmfulness—is much greater than in other branches of knowledge. Another reason for this is that it is easier to hoodwink people in economics and to convince them of relationships that do not actually exist in economic processes like saving, accumulation, investment, production, trade, and finance. When economists make statements that sooner or later turn out to be false, we are left facing a dilemma: Were they wrong, or lying? There are no other possibilities, except perhaps that they were partially wrong and partially lying. These arguments and examples—and it is not difficult to find more of them on the basis of the experience of many countries in many different periods—should help in understanding why bad things are sometimes read as good, and should provide some of the material needed to avoid mistakes.

In the struggle for truth in real science, with a capital S, it is necessary to cultivate a critical attitude. The approach to the truth also often requires an honest public debate, despite the frequent risk that the distinction between truth and untruth is sometimes impossible to attain in common discourse. Nevertheless, this is a way to win allies for the truth. In the social sciences, including economics, this is very important, because the dissemination and popularization of research results are important in implementing them. People were occasionally burned at the stake for defending the scientific truth in public, because a conservative and brutal Inquisition wanted it that way. Nowadays, portions of the media willingly stand in for that physical, psychological, and political terror which, we should remind ourselves, was cruel in the short term but ineffective in the long term.

Public debate and its instrument, the media, constitute a two-edged sword. On the one hand, it is impossible to pass the torch of knowledge to a wider audience without them. On the other, they enable demagogues and liars to reach that same audience. There is no alternative but to pick up the cudgels and swing the sword—the word—so as to deliver blows while suffering as few as possible oneself. This is not easy by any means.

The best way to fight is to call things by their proper names. One must understand the essence of irrationality—its sources, mechanisms, and dynamics—in order to proceed rationally. This can sometimes be more difficult than surrendering to intellectual laziness and going along with the arguments of charlatans or simple fools. Carl Sagan wrote that "one of the saddest lessons of history is this: If we've been bamboozled long enough, we tend to reject any evidence of the bamboozle. We're no longer interested in finding out the truth. The bamboozle has captured us. It is simply too painful to acknowledge—even to ourselves—that we've been so credulous."[2] This kind of deception can influence important processes that affect great numbers of people. Much has been written about how people are led astray in science and how they can persist in error for long periods, placing their trust in nonsense, falsehoods, pseudoscience, myths, and demagogy.[3] Seldom is the subject written about in economics, unfortunately.

In his book *How Mumbo-Jumbo Conquered the World*,[4] Francis Wheen writes somewhat mockingly, somewhat ironically, and above all insightfully about this. Perhaps mumbo-jumbo should be treated as a special category in sociology and political science; it plays no small role in economics.

The recipe for economic mumbo-jumbo is an easy one: First, simplify as much as possible, and then exaggerate. For example: If you privatize everything, then everything will improve rapidly. Or the converse: Nationalize everything, and then everything will get better and better. It all depends on the epoch in which the mumbo-jumbo is intended to addle our brains. Wheen refers to the far-reaching consequences (or the nonsensical interpretations) of such statements as the neoliberal Thatcherite TINA ("There Is No Alternative") or Fukuyama's "the end of history"[5]—although in the latter case there was a great deal of misinterpretation of Fukuyama's original thought.

It is a truism that there was no shortage of alternative paths to development even when neoliberal Thatcherism was flourishing and refused to notice or accept any alternatives to its dream of hegemony. Nor is there any shortage of them now, when neoliberalism is beginning to wither away. As for history, it goes on, as does humanity with all the problems that, even on the historical scale, remain abundant.

Another example of mumbo-jumbo is the slogan "Innovate or Die!" Recently, this has been a popular credo in management schools. Although no reasonable person would doubt the enormous significance of innovation both for increased productivity and for economic progress in general, we know that growth has been possible for whole centuries without any particular innovative capacities. Even today the majority of countries (national economies) and the great majority of companies are hardly dying from a lack of innovative talent. They do quite well and earn a decent living, thanks to imitation.

The ones that die are not those incapable of thinking and acting innovatively in terms of introducing new production methods and products, but rather those incapable of competing. It is perfectly possible to compete without innovation. The repetition of such an empty slogan by the media, governments, business leaders, business school professors, consultants of all kinds, and management gurus encourages mistakes by diverting attention from the authentic requirements for and sources of success in business.[6] Innovation is for those who are good at innovating, but not for everyone.

Unfortunately, these and other examples of mumbo-jumbo have done immeasurable harm, in material as well as intellectual terms. After all, we exist in a world not only of words, but also of actions, including erroneous and harmful actions. Many of them are irreversible. The costs and the damage have already been suffered, and the possibility of any gains belongs to the past. Time is always a factor. Even if some good finally comes out of the sacrifices made and the burdens borne, the generational process is such that many of those who paid the price will already be in the next world.

In the postsocialist world, older people remember the effort at making them happy through the forced collectivization of agriculture, while the young still bear the burden of the naïve and injurious neoliberal *idée fixe* known as "shock therapy." The failed efforts to carry it out led to enormous costs that could have been avoided, and yielded far fewer therapeutic benefits than could have been achieved by choosing changes of a different kind.[7] The fact that some people prefer to forget such rubbish as "shock therapy" (or would like to convince themselves and others that it somehow succeeded) makes it necessary to get to the heart of the matter—just as in the case of the unfortunate collectivization of two-and-a-half generations earlier. This necessity has to do not only with historical truth—always badly falsified in regard to eras that have just ended—and the facile accuracy of economic interpretation in hindsight. It also has significance before the fact, because the historical process of development is at different stages in various parts of the world, and it is still not too late to avoid many mistakes. All that is needed is to draw the appropriate conclusions from other people's experiences, and the lessons of accomplishments and failures in other countries.[8]

Iran is now attempting to implement a program called "Justice Shares," which consists of the distribution for free of part of the state assets to the poorest segment of the populace. It would be far better to sell these assets for the highest possible price on the capital markets and use the income from denationalization for responsibly targeted social programs to limit the causes and symptoms of poverty. The Iranians had a chance to avoid the mistake of economically senseless, ideologically motivated free distribution—a mistake that was not avoided in some postsocialist countries.

In Poland, we also had an experience with mumbo-jumbo in the form of the "Universal Privatization Program," a term that once dominated the front pages, especially the front page of one particular newspaper. When it later became clear to everyone that the economic payoff was not worth the ideological exertion, we had already entered the domain of consequences. Neither the goal of microeconomic transformation nor the social aim of the accelerated formation of a middle class was achieved. The ambitions of the instigators of this and similar programs were satisfied, as were the hardly inconsiderable interests of the financial and legal intermediaries who profited handsomely.

In Poland, we now have a chance to avoid another bad idea—the so-called flat tax. Some of our neighbors have put the notion into practice, where economic mumbo-jumbo has triumphed over common sense. At some point, they will have to reverse themselves, if for no other reason than because they will be unable to maintain the aging segment of their societies without a progressive tax. With a growing proportion of retirees, the working part of the society will have to pay higher taxes than the retirees and disability recipients, because otherwise the social support system will be unbalanced. Wealthier people must pay higher taxes, because otherwise the social system suffers from disequilibrium. The flat tax is not as simple as claimed by its advocates (and potential beneficiaries). Rather, it is indecently simplistic enough to seduce large numbers of people. Classical mumbo-jumbo on the basis of a classic recipe: a simple and overhyped panacea for something that seems to upset many people. Who likes paying taxes? In fact, it is a matter of accommodating the few. Some people have already been taken in, and naïvely place their trust in a concept that is intrinsically harmful to them. That's the purpose of this kind of economic rubbish—deceiving some to the benefit of others.

Economics is like a path through the woods: It's easy to get lost. When you turn around and go back, what seems to be the same path is in fact not the same. The process of change in economic relations is something natural and completely obvious, at least past a certain level in the development of civilization. Change is an economic category unto itself, and it can be very profound, extending far into the substance of the phenomena or processes being described. Sometimes change occurs very rapidly on the historical scale—even more quickly than the change from one generation of economists to the next. This is one of the reasons that they sometimes find themselves unable to keep up. They cannot get a theoretically accurate grip on the present because they are looking at it through yesterday's eyes. Even worse, they are sometimes peering at an image of times already past, different from the here and now. When they cling too tightly to their obsolete interpretations, they begin getting things wrong. They don't know what the truth is—and how can they proclaim the truth if they don't know it? It has faded away, along with the times in which it was adequate. Times change. Views must change.

Unfortunately, instead of adjusting to change, economists often turn to more advanced countries with different cultures, superior technologies, and more mature institutions. They borrow interpretations, elements of theory, and even whole schools of thought that they then have trouble adapting to local conditions, because the adaptations fit their own conditions like two left shoes. This has become especially prevalent in recent years under the influence of domination by a single way of thinking—neoliberalism, which has been imposed on others by the most powerful interest groups connected with big international capital. More than one country has paid a high price for disdaining regional and national differences under the widely proclaimed but naïve neoliberal slogan "one size fits all," which is a call for ignoring local differences in the application of economic policy. Even when countries pay a high price, however, it is always good business for someone.

A fixation on the most developed economies leads to the uncritical importing of the ideologies that are popular and regarded as mainstream social science there. In economics, this is an epidemic. If they shine at all, local analysts and commentators shine with a reflected light. No one demands that they shine like the sun, but let them at least have a decent lamp, or even a candle, of their own.

It is a real event when a Nobel Prize winner who is an outstanding economist (the two do not always go hand in hand) singles out a local economist for praise. This is what happened when Joseph E. Stiglitz of Columbia, perhaps the most cited authority in the field, referred to theories advanced by a Polish economist who had obtained positive real-world results.[9] What happened? The facts of the matter notwithstanding, the Polish economist's local adversaries were infuriated. An ideological activist of neoliberal tendencies with pretensions to an academic career attempted to discredit the Nobel Prize winner and called for a boycott (*sic!*) of his works, all because he quoted the innovative, proven views of a Polish economist who is unpopular with the neoliberal extremists. The strident advocate of the "party line" (where do we know that from?) wrote that

the fact that it is not worth paying attention to Stiglitz may be shown from the passage in his book *Globalization and Its Discontents* devoted to Poland: "Poland introduced a gradualist privatization policy, while at the same time building the basic institutions of a market economy, such as banks that actually lend money, and a legal system that demands respect for contracts and honest bankruptcy proceedings." Quoting Grzegorz W. Kolodko as an authority, [Stiglitz] states that our country "did not engage in rapid privatization and did not place the lowering of inflation above other macroeconomic considerations. Instead, it emphasized such matters as achieving democratically expressed support for reform, which resulted in efforts to keep unemployment low . . . and to create the institutional infrastructure needed for the functioning of a market economy." . . . it is hard to resist the impression that these lovely words must be about some other country. This is why Stiglitz and what he writes about other countries and their problems cannot be taken seriously.[10]

As can be seen, there is no limit to folly—or to destructive emotions.

Simply transcribing from the *lingua franca* of contemporary science—English—into the local idiom, whatever it may be, is a widespread practice. This is understandable in view of the fact that the science of economics is most highly developed in the English-speaking countries, and especially in the United States and Great Britain. The problem is that the things that are true there might also be true here—but not necessarily, for the simple reason that a vast part of economics refers to the changing conditions under which people make lives for themselves and enter into group interactions. As a science, economics must fit reality, and that reality differs over time and space. Over there, it might be tomorrow, whereas here it's still today, and somewhere else it's yesterday.

I regard economics as a science that not only explains the working of the mechanisms that govern economic processes—production and consumption, saving and investment, buying and selling, the flow of streams and resources—and the social interactions that occur in the course of these processes, but that also serves as a basis for the formulation and realization of effective strategies for long-term development. Good economics is both a descriptive science that depicts things as they are and a normative science that issues pointers and prompts about the way things should be. That is, it should not only formulate detached, passive forecasts about the future, but also serve as a starting point for working out and implementing an active development program.

The problem is that, as opposed to physics, medicine, structural engineering, or agronomy, economics is basically not an experimental science. There are no laboratories where you can take a hypothesis and carry out some procedure that verifies its accuracy. Usually, the hypothesis is first proclaimed, and only subsequently demonstrated to be correct—or not—on the living organism of the economy and society. Following this path to truth has turned out, on more than one historical occasion, to be extremely costly. In our part of the world in particular, we have experienced this by way of the historical verification of hypotheses about the utility and effectiveness of central planning, which helped to solve many problems in the initial phase of socialism but ended up becoming an institution that weighed down the economy and impaired its capacity for adaptation. As if this were not enough, in many postsocialist countries, this was followed immediately by the deleterious effects of a neoliberal policy of systemic transformation.

In opting for pragmatic economics—resting on the confirmation of scientific hypotheses in practice, in action, in real economic processes— it is therefore necessary to demand skill in carrying out applied economics, because people are not guinea pigs to be experimented on.

Science is powerful, then, but there are sometimes occasions when it has insufficient power to succeed. Unfortunately, scientific truth often comes second. Pseudoscientists or downright ignoramuses, with a greater affinity for simplistic interpretations than for complicated scientific proofs, sometimes get the upper hand. A British literary critic summed it up splendidly, writing that "we all have our idiots. . . . The main failings we have in common would seem to be that we are willing to believe the most utter nonsense if it can be made to fit our oversimplistic, preconceived, overidealized or self-serving views of the world; and that we naïvely assume that those whose myths, language, money and power control or would control our lives and minds have our best interests at heart. The idiots need not be political leaders—they can be the media, the multinational corporations, other economic powers, cultural movements, systems of belief, ideologues and ideologies of all varieties."[11]

Idiots are best avoided, and idiocy unheeded. First of all, we need to know how to distinguish it from things that are comprehensible and reasonable. This is by no means easy, in economics or in the other social sciences. In the general view, after all, "eminent economist" is a synonym for "well-known economist." Yet the well-known ones are not those who discover important phenomena and processes, but those who appear on television and write in the newspapers. What they write there is less important. A high profile is everything. Banking analysts with blinkered views, working on commission from their sponsors, have been built up into opinion-shaping "independent" economists. Scraps of nonsense published in newspapers have print runs in the hundreds of thousands, or sometimes even millions, whereas the more elaborated truths in scientific books appear in the hundreds of copies. Professors stalk newspapers (more often), and newspapers stalk professors (more rarely). They feed on each other, and in the process they feed others as well. The grain is milled, the chaff remains, and the wheat is lost.

It is clear that the best antidotes for stupidity and arrogance are wisdom and knowledge. This is what makes verbal combat worthwhile. In other words: Read a great deal, listen to others, write a little, and talk to those who are willing to listen—but most of all: think. Struggling to master her own words, the poet asks:

> Why did I take bad things
> for good ones
> and what would it take
> to keep from doing it again?[12]

Although a pinch of imagination and brilliance never hurts, there is no room in science for poetry. This makes it all the more imperative to concentrate on a fundamental, real problem that, strangely enough, is often overlooked: truth and lying in economics and economic policy. This is more than a matter of who is right and who is wrong. It is possible to make mistakes by starting from false assumptions, using the wrong information base, applying statistics inaccurately, or drawing the wrong conclusions. People can also fall under the sway of dubious ideologies, only to discover afterward that there are other ideologies that are no worse, and are perhaps even better. All of this is morally excusable. Humans err, and this includes economists.

Policy and economic thought meander along various paths. The trails they blaze can inspire acknowledgment and approval or, at other times, distaste and negation. There is always a political context, and it is always important who is making the judgments, who is being judged, and when. Two extreme attitudes, stemming from completely different motivations and explained by different psychological factors, can be distinguished. On the one hand, we encounter conservative views, held with greater obstinacy than they deserve, which manifest themselves in an irrational loyalty to received canons, a doctrinaire stance that could just as well be termed dogmatism. On the other hand, there is the facile swing to the opposite flank, the radical shift of views that jumps from apologetics to criticism of the views held earlier. Old ideas and perspectives undergo revision.

When Jeffrey D. Sachs, a master of public relations among economists, published a book titled *The End of Poverty: How We Can Make It Happen in Our Lifetime*[13] in 2005, he ceased forever to be revered as the man who transplanted radical liberalism to Poland in the early 1990s, and tried to transplant it to the neighboring countries. The influential British-American weekly *The Economist* tagged him a "leftist," a term of invective in the Anglo-Saxon countries. He had simply looked the facts in the eye and realized that things had taken a different turn from the proclamations of neoliberal theory from which he had gradually distanced himself.

This type of evolution—rather than radical change and the zealous rejection of one's own earlier convictions, which may have been appropriate, in part, in a different historical and political context—need not be unseemly or blameworthy. Only cows never change their views; doing so is becoming of enlightened economics professors, as long as they do not go overboard and, like religious converts, denounce their own previous views on principle.

It can be assumed with a degree of probability approximating certainty that, had the Soviet Union existed a decade longer—not something that is difficult to imagine—almost all the prominent post-Soviet leaders and influential politicians of the 1990s would have been high-ranking party or government officials in the structure of the communist state. Almost all the stars of the social sciences would have argued completely differently in their publications and lectures than they began doing enthusiastically—or overenthusiastically—in 1991. It would have been the same in Romania, Bulgaria, or the former Czechoslovakia, although not in Poland, Hungary, or the former Yugoslavia, because of the earlier quasi-democratic and pro-market reforms implemented in the latter countries in the 1970s and 1980s. These reforms, aiming for partial political and economic liberalization, had already introduced a certain intellectual unorthodoxy and new thinking under the socialist regime. These are only examples. More can be found all over the world.

As opposed to the evolutionary and smooth transition from Marxist revisionism to theories favoring a social market economy, or from market fundamentalism to a more pragmatic, pro-development orientation, some jumped from one extreme to another. Whether influencing opinion formation through the media or quasi-scientific manipulation, or doing serious harm to economic practice, they made a significant impact. Books on postsocialist adaptation sometimes borrowed their cover designs from far different works of a bygone era, as long as they featured the ubiquitous title *Economic Problems of the Transformation Period*, with gold letters on a red background. Someone quipped that socialism is the difficult transition period between capitalism and capitalism.

The animus typical of recent religious converts is no rarity in the social sciences or the political sphere, particularly when popularity or money is at stake. Many former Marxists have became apologists for neocapitalism, with some vaulting at the first opportunity from the left to the right (in the past, people jumped in the opposite direction). Proponents of free markets have become advocates of state interventionism. Liberals have grown infatuated with populism and populists have become liberals. Members of the labor party have gone over to conservatism. Militarists have become pacifists. Backers of the civilizing mission of colonialism have become warriors in nationalist sociopolitical movements. Agnostics and secular intellectuals have been born again as religious thinkers. Black has become white and white has become black, as if there were no other colors of the rainbow. Psychologically, extremism of this sort can be explained by the desire, sometimes even subconscious, to compensate for past sins, including those that were never committed. Given the fact that there is nothing we can do to make our past selves any better, we resolve to be veritable saints in the future. In real terms, it's often enough to make you cringe, not that the neophytes or those cheering them on ever notice.

Let's be honest: This isn't the biggest problem. The worst thing is the lying in the so-called science of economics. I add the *so-called* because this is the moment when it turns into pseudoscience. The intentional propagation of falsehood is, in its essence, the opposite of science. Montaigne wrote that, "If falsehood had, like truth, but one face only, we should be upon better terms; for we should then take for certain the contrary to what the liar says: but the reverse of truth has a hundred thousand forms, and a field indefinite, without bound or limit."[14]

The thing about economics—as with perhaps all the social sciences—is that the play of the true and the false (in epistemological categories) or of candor and lying (in ethical categories) is very subtle. Unfortunately, we still know very little about this subject. We frequently find ourselves in the fervor of what seems to be a scientific debate, when in fact we are up to our ears in an ideological dispute about differing values, or a political discourse that in fact revolves around competing interests, except that its actual intentions lie concealed behind lovely words about ostensible public goals.

It is understandable that scientists have views, including political ones. After all, they are citizens. But it is not good when, out of ideological motivations or, even worse, as a result of being hired to perform tendentious paid work, they use science as a political weapon. The worst thing of all is when scientists allow themselves to be drawn into the whirlpool of endless political conflicts and permit their science to reflect the structure of political interests. If everything boiled down to right and left, then we should have right-wing and left-wing economists and ecologists. However, the political scene is far more complicated than such a dichotomy, and this fact is reflected in science when it serves political ends. Even if it seems to people that they are fighting for the truth and following objective scientific procedures, they have in fact been drawn into the political struggle. That struggle is about interest groups, and not about the truth.

The pressure can flow in the opposite direction. Making use of the popular media without which nothing can be accomplished these days, politics disturbs the scientific process by attacking nonpartisan scholars engaged in the pursuit of truth. If these scholars' discoveries and theories could lead to rational actions that would be disadvantageous to the interest groups, then those interest groups denounce the scholars and accuse them of error. Things become embarrassing when other scientists allow themselves to be dragged in. Egged on at first from outside, often without even being aware of the fact, and then later following their own impulses, they fight like gladiators, or rats. This is the reason that so many debates and disputes bearing on the most important theoretical questions are carried out not in professional journals, but in mass-market newspapers and the electronic media.

Economics is thus political in the sense that some economists simply lie, out of various motivations that are often related to doctrinal or ideological zealotry. Or they may do so out of their political sympathies, or even for the trivial reason that it pays. Furthermore, inertia comes into play at a certain point. It is easier to keep clawing through a thicket of untruth than to admit to having been wrong, as if sticking to a position can make it right.

When learned economists err in what they say and write, we can continue the discussion on substantive grounds. However, we have a major problem when they know how the facts stand but nevertheless publicly say and write something different because it serves certain ideas shared by narrow elites, or because they are paid by interest groups to enunciate theories, decked out in pseudoscientific trappings, that they know to be false. The problem is also an ethical one.

Despite the fact that psychology in particular has a great deal to say about the essence of lying,[15] we often cannot tell whether someone is merely consistently mistaken or lying outright. Even when we know that someone is simply lying rather than continuing to be wrong, it can be impossible to prove. If the person is deliberately lying, we are wasting our time in attempting to persuade him that he is wrong.

It is difficult to find a better recent example than the pseudoscientific debate about the previously mentioned flat tax, which is all about cutting taxes for a narrow group of beneficiaries and shifting the cost of the operation onto low-income taxpayers (the real aim), while claiming—or, in this case, lying, unless someone is in fact persistently wrong because he cannot understand what is going on—that it is all a matter of creating better conditions for capital formation and investment (the declared aim).

This syndrome explains the impossibility of convincing some adversaries, who otherwise seem to be enlightened economists, of views that are correct and at times obvious. They understand that these views are reasonable, but they voice different views. What can be done? At the very least, enough to convince others—listeners, viewers, and above all readers—that our interlocutor is wrong. The audience will have the impression that the opponent is in error, which is no small accomplishment. In other words, when it is impossible to demonstrate that someone is deliberately misleading others, it is at least worthwhile proving publicly that they are wrong.

There are pseudoscientific debates in which it is impossible to arrive at intellectual agreement because the differences inhere not in the officially expressed views, but in the intentions. This occurs more frequently in politics than in science, although we should be under no illusions about the latter field. For understandable reasons (the pressure of conflicting interests), economic science is particularly vulnerable to this, but the danger exists in other disciplines. Pharmacology, medicine, and ecology—the science of the natural environment of humans—should be mentioned. Disputes about the effectiveness of some drug or the current debate about the causes and effects of global warming are the best examples. For money—for big money in some cases, and for next to nothing in others—it is possible to purchase whole institutes, or think tanks, that will prove whatever the customer wants. Why shouldn't it be the same in economics? Sometimes it is.

Of course, it costs money to hire intellects—often not inconsiderable ones—that are ready to argue in pseudoscientific categories in favor of the viewpoints desired by the sponsors. Aside from hiring politicians, this is a profitable form of investment in a unique form of "human capital." It is also possible to hire people who simply think in a useful way and, with the best of intentions and in line with their own convictions, say things that, although untrue, are advantageous for a given interest group. These people will find sponsors interested in supporting such convenient research and propagating its results.

Following this principle, many departments of economics and social sciences at universities—especially American ones—went over to neoliberal positions in the 1980s and 1990s. With few exceptions, the business schools opened in this period took on a similar coloration. The importance of these changes should not be underestimated. The eminent American anthropologist David Harvey observes that "the eventuality of the prevalent ideas being imposed by the ruling elites is overlooked, even though there is clear evidence of the mass intervention of business elites and financial interest groups in the creation of ideas and ideologies through investment in research centers, the education of technocrats, and control of the media."[16] It is worth noting, by the way, that each and every one of the 247 newspapers in Rupert Murdoch's media empire supported the invasion and occupation of Iraq.

Nor is it strange that neoliberal research centers, analytical organizations, and institutes that support the special interests of big money and its influential leaders are especially active, in view of the financing available. In the United States, where "liberalism" denotes a socially progressive orientation, they are sometimes referred to as "neoconservative." They proclaim the apotheosis of the unfettered market and private property while fighting against the state and demanding the far-reaching curtailment of its economic intervention, budgetary redistribution, and social policy. They use such concepts as freedom and entrepreneurship, or choice and the law, even as they manipulate the meaning of these terms and subordinate the processes associated with them to special interests. Neoliberalism—as opposed to authentic, sincere liberalism, which correctly promotes such values—has nothing to do with genuine democratic politics, economic effectiveness, or social rationality beyond exploiting these beautiful ideas to serve the needs of a narrow elite at the cost of the rest of the population. Unfortunately, it must be admitted that neoliberalism does this skillfully and adroitly.

Around the world, and especially in the Anglo-Saxon countries, there is no lack of analytical-research centers that make up a well-developed network supporting the neoliberal tendency. Along the way, they also produce many valuable publications. An attractive name is essential for these centers. In Washington, aside from the libertarian Cato Institute (founded in 1977, with an annual budget of more than $20 million), we can thus find the influential American Enterprise Institute and the quintessentially neoconservative Heritage Foundation. London has its Institute of Economic Affairs; Sweden, its Center for Business and Policy Studies (SNS); and Italy its Istituto Bruno Leoni. The Institute for the Economy in Transition is doing very well in Moscow, along with numerous branches of British and American centers. There are a few in Warsaw, where the Adam Smith Center has a particularly high profile. Naming this extremist neoliberal center after the great figure universally regarded as the creator of classical liberal economics is an intellectual abuse.

After a time, the committed economists and other researchers fall victim to their own zeal, and their work becomes doctrinaire and perfunctory. They start believing the things they say, and the media connected with the same ideologies and interest groups cheer them aggressively on. This is more a matter of faith than of knowledge, more ideology than science. From this point, some might even be inclined to carry on the fight for free, for the sake of the ideal. It would be strange if they voluntarily showed as much dedication in the name of the socially excluded poor, unemployed, and homeless, or the struggling labor unions, or simply in the name of the majority of the population and the cause of development—but there are no commissions from such sources. Such research, if done at all, must either be what is known as "private scholarship" or be state financed, and the state is neoliberalism's enemy number 1.

In the fervor of the unending public debate, big money and its lobby need professional-sounding, persuasive voices to convince wider audiences of the supposed superiority of some solutions (those that favor the minority and special interests) over others (that favor the majority and the general interest). Such voices are especially important in democratic societies, because they must drown out whatever parts of the media remain authentically independent, refusing to be servile and uncritical toward the egoistic interests of big capital—no matter how hard it is to resist the lucrative inducements to do so. In the final analysis, big money not only sponsors the market, but also inundates it with a mass of well-paid advertising. Advertising space is either sold or not; everybody needs to make a living, and not necessarily at poverty level.

The media are in an especially comfortable position, because they can always make themselves heard and can outshout everyone else. Paradoxically, although everyone knows who they are, the media enjoy a kind of anonymity. When the media and journalists are criticized in general, it is never clear exactly who is being condemned. This resembles the situation regarding complaints about politics and politicians. The media, as opposed to politicians, can resort to the effective tactic used by thieves who shout "Stop! Thief!" Almost everyone has bitter words to say about the media—almost everyone, because self-critical is the one thing that the media are not. There is also an unwritten law that one media outlet never criticizes another. They criticize politicians, but not all politicians, and not all the time. They do it selectively. Often they fail to criticize precisely the ones who deserve it, and instead criticize those they are paid to criticize. The criticism may be ideological and it may be personal. Its true intent is always camouflaged.

The political world fears the media and attempts to manipulate them (that's politics), but often finds itself in the position of the dog being wagged by its tail. The media manipulate politics effectively, and certainly forcefully, not so much by expressing public opinion, with which politicians must reckon, as by shaping it. The fear of the media is so great that accusations against them are usually expressed in general terms. It is a rarity to carry out the needed research and publish the results, and in any case, the media themselves must be used to deliver those results to a wider audience. Always knowing best and knowing "how things really are," the media delight in undermining such skeptical findings.

Accusations about media bias flow from various, often opposing political corners and areas of public life. In the United States, both the Republicans and the Democrats complain, although the latter should do so less, because the media seem to favor them. When news comes out in America about the growth of the GDP, the Republicans receive from 16 to 24 percent less favorable ratings than the Democrats. The spread ranges from 0 to 21 percent on news about unemployment. The *New York Times* has carried fewer positive economic stories when the Republicans are in office. On the west coast, the situation at the *Los Angeles Times* is precisely the opposite.[17]

Interestingly, researchers have discovered that it is not true that bad news sells best, at least when it has to do with economic processes. In the United States, because it is impossible to generalize, good news produces more follow-up stories on the same issue, and these follow-ups are also much better written. They offer coverage that is broader and more in-depth. The Democrats would surely charge the authors of this research with bowing to manipulation by Republican interest groups and make accusations of bias against media that cover Democratic successes objectively.

The degree of disinformation, distortion, and tendentiousness depends on the nature of the story being covered. I saw this from the inside on the two occasions when I was in charge of the Polish economy (1994–1997 and 2002–2003), and I have consistently seen it from the outside at all other times. When the growth in production plummeted under neoliberal governments, the neoliberal press, radio, and television "reported" that the situation was improving. When the rate of growth accelerated under a pragmatic center-left administration, the same media "reported" that it was accelerating either too slowly or too rapidly, and the populist-oriented press complained the whole time that the growth was too slow, and, of course, that it was inequitable.

Let's sum up. This summary may serve my audience—viewers, listeners, and especially readers—as a kind of methodological guide for skillfully moving through the thickets of unceasing economic debate, and especially the public debate fought out in the media and politics. Someone—an ideological formation, a party, a research institute, a newspaper, or an individual—states a view—for instance, that limiting the role of the state (i.e., the government) and weakening its position as an economic player favors economic growth. Now what? Should we agree or not? Should we believe it or not? I am not talking about a situation where people understand nothing, believe no one, and are happy with that. They're to be envied! To evaluate this view—to agree with it or reject it—already requires knowing a great deal about the subject. Those who have too little knowledge to understand the issue have only the alternatives of believing or not. It is better, of course, to know than to believe.

In accepting or rejecting someone's point of view, it is worth considering the fact that its proponents can be in three hypothetical situations:

- They believe what they say and regard it as the truth.
- They regard what they say as the truth and feel that it reflects the way things are.
- They know that what they say is not the truth.

In the first variant—they believe what they say and regard it as the truth—we are dealing with a kind of profession of faith, with ideology rather than science and with doctrine rather than a desire for objectivity. Rational arguments are of little use on this level. Using them may be fruitless, particularly in conducting polemics with the demagogues who abound in the pages of history, and especially in hard times or periods of great change. Doctrinaire stances of this kind are hardly a rarity in economics and economic policy. In real economic processes and the application of economic policy, they can constitute a grave danger. Of particular danger are situations where two false ideologies and their doctrinaire proponents face each other, as is the case at present when neoliberalism comes up against populism.

In the second case—they regard what they say as the truth and feel that it reflects the way things are—we face two alternatives:

- They're right.
- They're wrong.

If they're right, then all we can do is to understand things as well as we can, and share this knowledge and the lessons to be drawn from it with others. If they're wrong, then we should conduct a substantive polemic in which we present a different concept supported by rational arguments. We should add that a calm, frank, substantive polemic against the opposing point of view is within the abilities of everyone who is not doctrinaire or mendacious. We can recognize the latter—some of the time—by the fact that they are reluctant to enter into frank polemics, or downright refuse to do so. They would rather talk than listen. On the other hand, those who are convinced that they are speaking the truth and understand the essence of the issue betray neither doctrinaire zeal nor the cynicism of liars. They are open to polemics and attempt to convince others while also listening to their arguments. They listen as well as talk.

In the third case—they know that what they say is not the truth—they proclaim a false point of view with premeditation. It may be wrapped in pseudoscientific rhetoric, but its proponents know better than anyone that they are spreading falsehoods. They are not wrong, as may occur in one of the variants in the second case. They are deliberately leading their audience into error. Liars are not wrong. You can be wrong involuntarily, but you have to want to lie. Why? There are three reasons:

- They are deliberately proclaiming false views because it pays to do so in terms of group or personal interests.
- They are advancing false theories and concepts for ideological reasons. This is not the same as the doctrinaire attitude in the first case, because here we are not talking about deep faith, but about cynicism. They know that the ideology they are presenting does not serve the officially proclaimed ends. For instance, neoliberalism does not serve the aim of social justice, and populism does not favor economic effectiveness.
- They might only be wrong at first but stick so doggedly to their views that, given the belligerence prominent in economic debates and a misguided concept of professional prestige, they begin deliberately defending false views and become guilty of intellectual opportunism. People, and economists in particular, hate to be wrong, and even more to admit it—especially in public. By defending false

arguments, they stop being wrong and start deliberately leading others into error.

We should add that there are different ethical dimensions to deliberately misleading people. The latter situation in particular is less morally suspect than the two preceding ones. Nevertheless, regardless of the motivation, they are all equally harmful in practice.

Deliberate deception often relies on methods that are organized and financed in particularly sophisticated ways, and is done by highly skilled professionals. Sometimes only the sponsors are aware of this for years on end, because the deceivers themselves might not know exactly who they are working for. They are hired guns. The audience is completely unaware. At best, they might become suspicious, but the discretion of the procedures applied leaves them unable to prove anything. The cold war is over, but not the psychological war. The conflicts of interests go on, together with the accompanying struggles. On our own, we are incapable of knowing when we are under fire on the front line. This time around, the weapons are words. By the time we find this out, if we ever do, it will be history.

It would be the height of naïveté to assume that the placement of carefully crafted material in the media is not practiced in the global political and economic game, during the unending pursuit of domination in terms of ideas and political and economic interests. Intelligence services interested in penetrating a given region or country plant articles, books, and radio and TV programs. The purpose is not only to manipulate general public opinion, but also to exert pressure on opinion leaders and ruling elites. Sometimes this succeeds. The game goes on all the time. The future is at stake—or, as some would have it, new worlds. And also a place in this one and only world, where there is less and less space and more and more inequality.

When following the main threads of the debate and the placement of accents, it is impossible not to notice the particular activity of certain influential global ("Western") media and specialized research centers bent on discrediting China around the turn of the century and Russia in recent years. In the case of China, the country's crushing economic success (which not everyone wished them, but from which everyone is trying to profit) has changed this, but Russia is still under attack—if for no other reason than to prevent that vast land from repeating the

Chinese success. These two countries have been quick to respond by using their own special channels to place material in the media, including the Western media. To a large degree, the Islamic and some of the Western Hemisphere Hispanic countries are painted in predominantly dark colors. There is no lack of further examples.

This is not a matter of accident or ignorance, or of a purely doctrinaire attitude. Decades ago, there was nothing accidental about the way the intelligence wing of the KGB, the Soviet secret service, effectively planted stories in the media of countries (from the Third World to the First World, and even including the United States) that were crucial in any given phase of the great game of the day.[18] In turn, the CIA did not stand idly by, but replied in kind in those same countries, and in others as well. The difference is that although the CIA remains shrouded in secrecy in the interests of national security, the archives in the postsocialist countries have been opened, or the information has been leaked in other ways, and not necessarily with the national interest in mind.

It is possible to get lost in this matrix of truth, sincerity, ignorance, error, falsehood, and lies. We can all use our awareness of our own journeys through time and space to try to find out where we stand. Some people deliberately go on speaking falsehood so long that they become slaves to it, and end up simply believing it. Beginning as liars, they become doctrinaire. This happens rather often in economics. There are also times when people's principles lead them to go over to a position of honest science and concern for the truth. It can happen. Such cases occurred, for instance, during the epoch of orthodox central planning in the socialist economies, when there were those capable of tearing themselves away—some sooner, and others later—from the dogma of the time. They went over to a scientific position without falling into the other, antisocialist extreme. The most outstanding contemporary economist from this part of the world, János Kornai, evocatively describes his own experiences of this kind in his most recent book, *By Force of Thought*.[19]

All this is also very important in the reception of what we read and hear, and above all in polemics. It is necessary to argue in one way with someone who is scientifically honest but with whom we disagree, or whom we do not fully understand because we cannot keep up with thinking that is ahead of its time. With a doctrinaire liar or scientific or media hack, we must argue in a completely different way. As a rule, such problems do not exist in genuine science, where we find only an authentic desire to get to the bottom of things and understand the rules governing the processes that interest us. In public life—including the pseudoscientific kind—and during political debates, we frequently find ourselves dealing with the three other possibilities: doctrinaire, mistaken, or lying.

So now we return to the example of the view that limiting the role of the state and undermining its position in the economic process favors growth. This is clearly not the case, as we will show in our further considerations. It has, furthermore, been proven irrefutably in the literature on the subject,[20] but a handful of other arguments are still worth citing. Let us emphasize at once that the opposite assumption, that increasing the role of the state and strengthening its position in the economic process favors growth, is also false. Nor is a simple averaging out of these two hypotheses—that leaving the role of the state and its position in the economic process unchanged favors growth—true. These issues are far more complicated, and all that we shall say for the moment is that the state has a significant role to play in the process of economic growth, and its position in this matter is far from inconsiderable, but in concrete terms this depends on still other factors that are completely excluded from these statements. If the view in question is incorrect, we must now answer the question, "Are those who proclaim it doctrinaire, mistaken, or lying?" No other alternatives exist, unless we take into account some additional variants that combine these three. It should now be easier to resolve this kind of dilemma, because we know what to look for, how to ask the questions, and how to formulate the criteria. The rest remains entangled in the thickets of the beautiful science of economics.

It is still possible to write in an accessible way about highly complicated economic problems and the philosophical, cultural, social, and political issues that inevitably accompany them. Perhaps it is necessary to do so, because that is the way to hit home, to reach a broader audience. This does not at all mean that it is possible to indulge in such lazy and slippery thinking as to pronounce banalities and generalities about the necessity of privatizing almost everything, cutting taxes, reducing social expenditure, and limiting the role of the state in the economy. Such naïve neoliberalism has already done enough damage.

When writing in a simple way, we must still observe the requirements of scientific rigor while avoiding the opposite extreme. Argumentation that strains to "sound scientific" is all too common but is only ostensibly scientific. Overblown vocabulary, exaggeratedly formalized proofs, and flowery writing where a few clear words suffice cannot add conceptual weight or scholarly authority to the argumentation, but can make it needlessly obscure. It is therefore necessary to oppose both academic vulgarity and mannerism.

In science and when writing for a general audience, precision never does any harm—far from it. The methods and language of mathematics have also added a great deal to economics. Although economics is a social science by its nature, mathematical precision enables those who know how to use it to understand many complicated relationships. It is hardly surprising that "mathematical economics" has been marked off as a separate branch, using a completely different language from sociopolitical economics.[21] There are also great categories, phenomena, and processes—such as the world, globalization, development, progress, transformation, institutions, regulation, and above all humanity—that do not fit into the precision of mathematical formulas in any sensible way.

A friend advised me to write a superbook, highly academic, with a multitude of formulas, so that no one would understand anything. I took this valuable advice to heart—and decided to do the opposite: to include not a single formula and to write so that everyone, or almost everyone, would understand everything. I don't know which is more difficult.

Mathematics can be used in economics, but it is not unavoidable, the way that it is in physics. It can and should be used in research. But it need not and ought not be imposed on the readers to whom the results of the research are presented, so that they can take things in more easily. The important thing is for the message to be scientific but, at the same time, more or less universally comprehensible. In the sciences—including economics—it is necessary to think about difficult matters in a complicated way, but to talk and write about them as simply as possible, and not the other way around. We economists are fortunate that, although this is not easy, it can be done. Others are not so lucky. Yet this never prevented the greatest of them from achieving renown.

When Albert Einstein visited the United States for the second time in 1931, before settling there a year later, he asked for a chance to meet another great twentieth-century figure, Charlie Chaplin. After the premiere of *City Lights*, the audience applauded the two outstanding figures, and Chaplin said, "They cheer me because they all understand me, and they cheer you because no one understands you."[22] Economics steers a course between fiction, as in the movies, and precision, as in the pure sciences. The closer to the latter, the better—and best of all when it is as precise as mathematics and as interesting as a film.

On another occasion, Einstein himself said, "Physics should be as simple as possible, but not simpler." This could be paraphrased and applied to economics, which far more people find interesting and comprehensible, in their own subjective belief, than physics.

Economics should be as simple as possible—but not simpler.

CHAPTER TWO

How Things Happen

*Economic Processes—What Science, Policy,
and Happenstance Have to Do with Them
and Who Set It Up This Way*

Things happen the way they happen
because many things happen at the same time.

THE FORMULATION in the sentence above, as trivial as it sounds, is the key to explaining history that is more or less ancient, as well as what's happening around us now. More important, it is a basic guide for looking into the future.

The term *futurology* suggests that there is a science of the future, but it is in essence only an intellectual exercise. Usually making use of the extrapolation method and the continuation of trends from the past into the future, it consists of drawing up scenarios that could come true. This is not "hard" science. Much more promising than simple extrapolation is future studies, an interdisciplinary approach to issues now present in their rudimentary stages, or characterized by especially dynamic tendencies. Future studies can also anticipate the appearance of completely new phenomena and processes that are unmistakably indicated through the recognition of trends in scientific-technological progress, or through the inevitability of cultural and social evolution. The creative blending of knowledge and the imagination is of crucial importance.

Attempts to extend tendencies from the past into the future can sometimes turn out to be accurate, but they are usually wrong. At the end of the nineteenth century Parisians were warned that if the growth in the number of horse-drawn cabs continued, the city would turn into one vast stable. Understandably, it is easier to credit such doomsaying when looking at Camille Pissaro's lovely painting, in the Hermitage in St. Petersburg, of hackney coaches jamming the streets of Montmartre. The car came along and turned the horse-drawn carriage into a technological relic and a tourist attraction, and Parisians today have nightmares about traffic jams of a different kind.

It is a fact that numerous phenomena and processes—not only technological, but especially economic, social, and political—were never predicted, but only recognized in hindsight, to the point that we regard them as indisputable, or even trivial. This holds true in science, and even in science fiction. In an early *Star Trek* episode from the mid-1960s, there is a scene showing the control room on the *Enterprise*—with an ashtray on every console! Everybody's smoking. The producers never dreamed that within a generation not only athletes and astronauts, but even those in New York City bars would be nonsmokers. To see a film star enveloped in a cloud of bluish smoke, we can borrow the DVDs of Humphrey Bogart in *The African Queen* (1951) or Krystyna Janda in *Man of Marble* (1977).

It's worth asking whether *Star Trek* got it so wrong because of insufficient knowledge or because of insufficient imagination. The answer is, "Both." The writers and producers failed to understand the essence of the maxim that things happen the way they do because many things occur at the same time. Technological methods change, but so do cultural values and social preferences. As a result, the standards of measurement change as well. External factors, both close at hand and more remote, also come into play. The parties involved might not even be aware of this at the moment that change is occurring. What happens far away, increasingly, has just as much effect as what happens "here." "Afterward," when it's all over, everything seems clear, even though there was no clarity at the time—"then," or rather "now."

More than a century and a half ago, for instance, the northern part of the U.S. Midwest was in the middle of an economic boom resulting from the flourishing trade in furs and other goods imported from nearby Canada. Over time, this commerce was superseded—not without economic and social disturbances, and political consequences—by the increasing cultivation of grain, and its processing on a grand industrial scale at water-powered mills built at the cataracts of the Mississippi in Minneapolis and the vicinity. The last of these mills closed not so long ago, in 1965. Few believed then that a new Ford pickup factory would provide employment for the laid-off flour mill workers (who had to be retrained in automotive assembly). But it did—for more than four decades, until the Ford assembly line shut down in 2007 for the simple reason that competition from Toyota made it unprofitable. The time had come for the shift to high-level electronics and growth in the knowledge-based telecommunications, education, and research-and-development sectors. Now, none of the truck-factory workers retraining for the Internet and financial sectors of the service economy imagine that their companies will be closed around 2050 as obsolescent and replaced by jobs, ways of working, and types of production unknown today. This is most likely to happen as a result of advances in the biological sciences but it is still too early to say exactly what those advances will be. We don't know yet. Many things will have to happen at the same time— and they will, in their own time. There's a time for everything: hunting poor fur-bearing animals, grinding flour in water mills, assembling Ford pickups, and running on-line financial services. In the future, there will be time for biotechnology, for example.

This is worth remembering. It is sometimes impossible to keep up with the interpretation of a variety of facts, because some essential link in the chain of reasoning is missing. You can notice a lot of what's going on, but overlooking a single important element can lead to dubious conclusions.

The main thing is to avoid confusing scientific knowledge with superficial interpretations, and imagination with delusions. The imagination can rub up against dreams that motivate actions and set them in motion, and also against nightmares that should warn of potential mistakes.

Literary fiction can stimulate the imagination and lead to questions about whether things must always be the way they are. By a strange coincidence, two writers, the British novelist Jim Crace in *The Pesthouse*[1] and the American Cormac McCarthy in *The Road*,[2] published grim visions of the total collapse of the United States at the same time. What follows in both cases is an exodus. In a mirror image of the romantic conquest of the Wild West, people head for the East Coast. From there, a new migration across the Atlantic takes place, except that the goal this time is Europe. Living in America has become impossible, so people decide to get out, en masse. Fantasy? Of course it is. However, this sort of literary fiction shows that certain combinations of cata-strophic circumstances can change the course of history, as has already happened.

It is intriguing to think that the new great migration could be a re-turn to Europe. In a period of unprecedented transatlantic rivalry, this might sound optimistic to Europeans living in constant fear of higher American productivity. Yet panic would follow immediately—where are we supposed to put all these Americans, and how are we supposed to feed them? For now, things are still better in the United States than in what we so grandly refer to as Europe. According to some estimates, the European Union remains no fewer than two decades in arrears.[3] Whether it's really twenty years, and whether it's really "no fewer," is a subject to which we shall return.

The director Sylvestre Amoussou, from Benin, has filmed a highly original vision of the future. At Fespaco, The Panafrican Film and Television Festival of Ouagadougou,[4] the capital of Burkina Faso, he showed his 2006 movie *Afrique Paradis,* in which Africa has become an earthly paradise. People from the Western countries that used to be more developed and that exploited Africa for centuries now long to move there. Doing so is not easy, however. Africa is the land of milk and honey, whereas back home there is only stench, filth, misery, and poverty.

Is this a fantasy? Certainly it is, especially in the short term. It is worth remembering, however, that if we had told the people who were kidnapped, enslaved, and dragged to America from the coast of West Africa—from today's Benin and Ghana, then known as Dahomey and The Gold Coast—that, 200 years in the future, people from their home-lands would risk their lives trying to escape, praying to get to the places where their forebears were brutally transported in slavery, it would have struck them as preposterous. In the same way, the slave merchants—English, Portuguese, French, Dutch, Swedish, and Danish—would have thought it incredible that their countries would someday have crowds of Africans trying, of their own free will, to get in.

So is Amoussou's film a fantasy? It may be fantastic, at least in terms of a future that can be predicted (and shaped). Yet it would also have seemed like a fantasy not so long ago that an artistic event of the mag-nitude of Fespaco could occur in Upper Volta—the name, sounding absurd in some ears, under which white colonists all too recently bru-tally administered Burkina Faso. For Americans and Europeans to emigrate there on a mass scale in the future, many things would have to happen at the same time. For now it may not look likely, but it is always better to know which events depend on which causes. In this particular case, the poetic license of writers and filmmakers notwithstanding, what conditions of stagnation and growth, and what other things would have to happen "at the same time" for Africa, even if it did not become an earthly paradise, to break free of stagnation and start down the path of development? What things would have to happen "at the same time" to prevent Americans from fleeing to Europe in the future, and Europeans to Africa? Or, sticking closer to reality and the present, what would have to happen, and how, for Africans not to emigrate en masse from their Eldorado to Europe and America? Or for hundreds of thousands of Poles, especially young ones, not to move to Ireland, or for large numbers of Ukrainians not to be forced by economic and political pressures to cross the River Bug into Poland, or for Polynesians not to attempt at any cost to reach the shores of Australia, or for Mexicans not to sneak across the Rio Grande under cover of night?

This is not at all about fantasy. It is about awakening the creative imagination, and above all about making use of knowledge—theoretical science and practical experience—to explain what determines stagnation and growth. Why do some peoples, countries, and regions manage to sprint ahead while others trudge along in their wake or become completely bogged down? How is it possible that some—the few—live in abundance, or even wallow in affluence, while others—the many—exist in poverty, suffer hunger, and sometimes starve to death?

It is not necessary to cast the memory all that far backward. Two centuries ago, in 1807, Britain officially ended slavery. Yet it is also a fact that, barely two generations ago, Louis Armstrong sang:

How would it end. . .
I ain't got a friend
My only sin. . .
Is in my skin. . .
What did I do. . .
To be so black and blue?[5]

It is also true that a half a century ago the "Brown II" ruling by the U.S. Supreme Court, which some are too young to remember and others prefer to forget, left the door open for states to maintain de facto educational segregation. At the very time when Ghana was becoming the first African country to break free of British colonialism, the White House deployed military units to Little Rock to enforce desegregation against the resistance of a racist local administration. Today others are being lectured—sometimes still with the use of force—about what democracy is and how to observe human rights.

Bill Clinton comes from Arkansas. Clinton was only nine when the army came to Arkansas to hold back the hostile students. The idea that Clinton would become the forty-second president would have seemed improbable at the time, but it would have seemed far more unlikely that, within two generations, another Democrat, Barack Obama, would become the first president of African heritage. His foster-grandmother, Sarah Anyango Obama, still lives in the Kenyan village of Kogela and has clear memories of the colonial era,[6] while Barack Obama holds the highest office in the United States and the most powerful post in the world.

It was also half a century ago that the European Union (E.U.), or rather its predecessor, the European Economic Community (E.E.C.), came into existence on the strength of the Treaty of Rome, signed by Belgium, France, The Netherlands, Luxembourg, Germany (the Federal Republic), and Italy. The E.E.C., in turn, grew out of the European Coal and Steel Community (E.C.S.C.), set up in 1951 by these same Western European countries, which only six years earlier had been involved in a murderous, destructive war. The E.E.C. arose, even though it need not necessarily have done so. Also playing a role in its birth was a combination of political and economic circumstances, including a specific configuration of phenomena and processes associated with overcoming the consequences of the recently concluded war. There were layers of nationalistic and patriotic resentments, a need to coordinate policies in rebuilding war-ravaged heavy industry, the lengthening shadow of the Cold War between East and West, and the political implications of the impending decolonization of Africa, as exemplified by the political-military crisis over the Suez Canal.

The evolution of the Community and its development during the next half-century, now concluded, exceeded the boldest expectations. At present, the E.U. accounts for nearly 8 percent of the world population (515 million people), and 20 percent of world output. (The GDP of the twenty-seven E.U. countries, calculated according to Purchasing Power Parity,[7] was $13.4 billion in 2007.) Having long ago forgotten its foundations of coal and steel, the E.U. is now attempting, within the time frame of the years following 2010, to realize its vision of becoming "the most competitive and dynamic knowledge-based economy" on the planet. The so-called Lisbon Agenda at the turn of the century, which set 2010 as the year for attaining this goal, now turns out to have been illusory and overambitious.

What next? What will the next half-century look like, and what will the E.U. be like in the mid-twenty-first century? No one knows. We can, however, predict with a high degree of probability that, for a long time—reckoned in decades rather than years—the United States will remain the leader in competitiveness and the use of intellect and knowledge as direct productive forces. The distance separating these two locomotives of the world economy will continue to shrink, but the distance separating the two of them from the third—and fastest-moving—locomotive, the Chinese economy, will shrink even more.

Furthermore, we know that many things that should have been done were not done, for political reasons. As the prime minister of Luxembourg, Jean-Claude Juncker, suggestively remarked, "We all know what to do, but we do not know how to be re-elected after we do it." The problem is that it is not true that "we all know." Many do not—and, even worse, they do not even know that they do not know.

What we do know is the three thorniest questions facing the European Union after half a century. Aside from the issue of the so-called constitution and the fate of the common currency, the euro, the problem of the future boundaries of the Union is and will continue to be fundamental. Aside from more thorough integration, there will be further expansion—beyond Croatia, where membership is already expected.

The United States is fortunate not to have such problems. If it did— for instance, through full integration with Mexico, a populous (108 million) and less-developed neighbor with a GDP about 24 percent that of the United States—we would immediately note a relative slowing of the rate of growth, because the focus of politics and business would have to turn away from other major priorities in maintaining the high competitiveness of American companies and the economy. Over time, it is true, growth would accelerate because of the benefits of integration in terms of the size of the market and production costs, but that is a different matter. For now, the Americas—from Alaska to Tierra del Fuego—already face sufficient problems with the slow pace of trade liberalization and the creation of a single American free market. Because of reasons like this, the E.U. remains about as far behind the United States as the Americas as a whole are behind the E.U.

Within the European Union itself, it is necessary either to announce unequivocally that the process of expansion is definitely finished or to answer questions about the aspirations of some other European countries—especially in the Balkans, but also in the post-Soviet areas in the eastern part of the continent and on its borders. Someday it will be necessary to close the door and say, "That's a full house, and there won't be any new members." That will happen. Today we should have no doubts that it is also in the long-term interests of the Union itself for countries from the two areas I have mentioned to join. This will happen when they meet the criteria and when the political situation makes it possible for them to join. Leaving aside Macedonia, which began accession negotiations in early 2008, this will occur in the decade between 2021 and 2030.

Today, however, is too soon to rule anything out, since we do not even know how many countries there will be in the vicinity, or what kind of countries they will be. Kosovo will be independent, but what will happen to Bosnia and Herzegovina? Will the "and" mean that it is still a single country, or will it be two, or even three? What about Transnistria, as the Romanians call it, which is also known as Transdniestria, and which the Russians call Pridnestrovie, which de facto is no longer a part of Moldova, yet remains a part of Europe?

On the fiftieth anniversary of the European Union, *The Economist* conducted a provocative exercise in which it gave rein to fantasy and suggested what the E.U. might—or might not—look like on its one-hundredth birthday.[8] By then, not only Turkey, but also Ukraine will have been a member for a quarter of a century. The first North African country, the former French colony of Morocco, will have been a member since the early 2030s. What is more, the forty-ninth and fiftieth members will be Israel and Palestine. This will have been made all the more possible by the fact that, in the 2020s, the only way to reunify Cyprus (divided since the 1970s) will be to bring it under the political, economic, and social mechanisms of the Union. Against this background, America too will have to come to the conclusion that the only way to resolve the otherwise intractable Middle East problem is membership in the E.U. for both of these countries—all the more so because having both of them become States of the Union will be out of the question. One of them might want to join the United States, but the other—never.

———————

Yes, things really do happen, processes unfold, the world changes, history goes on, and the future is a question mark. Someday perhaps, with the greatest enthusiasm but not necessarily traveling by *kibitka*, the sort of horse-drawn boxcar used to transport Tsarist exiles, we will move to a flourishing, ecologically friendly Siberia. Or the president of Poland could be Chinese. Why not, since a woman of African heritage from Dominique has already been crowned Miss France? Perhaps Poland will have to restrict immigration when too many Germans want to move here, attracted by the high standard of living on the banks of the Vistula, and the Swiss will rush to make deposits in Polish banks.

You should already be getting rid of dollars and buying yuan and rubles. Today it is easier to imagine this changing again than it was even a dozen or so years ago to imagine that there would be trends in which the Chinese currency appreciates and the American depreciates. It is understood that the reason for selling dollars and yen in order to buy yuan and rubles is not that the economies of China and Russia are more sound than those of the U.S. and the E.U., because this is surely not yet the case (although it could be someday). It is rather because many concrete circumstances are coinciding that result in changes to relative currency values. In this part of the real world as well, events occur as they do because many things happen at the same time. All that's needed is to know why these things happen and what combination of circumstances they depend on.

The old curse "May you live in interesting times!" has come true, in spades. Things keep getting more and more interesting. The events we have lived through are shocking enough, but what awaits us is even more so. The problem is that, despite appearances and the passage of time, what has already happened is by no means behind us. William Faulkner wrote, "The past is never dead. It's not even past."[9] In all sorts of ways, we are up to our necks in the past, failing to understand it, interpreting various aspects of it in contradictory ways, or deliberately falsifying it. It weighs on our assessment of the present, making it impossible for us to answer the apparently simple question, "What are things like?" Furthermore, it has colossal and frequently unappreciated implications for the future. To make progress, it is necessary to see the past as well looming ahead of us—if only to avoid making its mistakes in the future. It's worth delving into the past, as long as we don't sink into it.

It also turns out sometimes that the influence of the past on the future is exaggerated. This takes place when there is too much reliance on cultural, systemic, political, and material continuities when interpreting various phenomena and processes. As a result, we attribute too much importance to these influences on the present and future course of events. Of course, it is possible to claim that, if not everything, then at least a great deal is a product of the past. This, to an overwhelming degree, is the way we think. Moving forward forces us to follow paths that are determined at least to a degree by continuity. This is known as path dependence. Such interpretations are sometimes forced. Conditions change and, above all, the learning process goes on all the time. Sometimes—especially in periods of great change, as at present—learning is very rapid.

To take an example, the interpretation according to which the postcolonial countries would be incapable of governing themselves, because they were used to being administered by others, turned out to be mistaken. It is erroneous to attempt to explain the contemporary economic and political processes in Russia by pointing to the presence among the populace, especially among the decision-making elite, of mental, behavioral, or bureaucratic baggage carried over from the Tsarist period. In Poland in the early twenty-first century it is an exaggeration to attribute the lower level of entrepreneurship in Polesie as compared with the Lubusz region to the fact that the former was ruled by the Russians and the latter by the Prussians in the nineteenth century. It was widely assumed in the 1990s that the countries involved in the postsocialist transformation, even those like Poland, Hungary, and the former Yugoslavia, which had already carried out far-reaching pro-market reforms in the socialist period, would prove incapable of producing a professional, effective managerial class; this proved profoundly wrong. The assumption apparently made strategic foreign investors essential, since only they would presumably know how to change the way firms were run so as to guarantee international competitiveness and a pro-growth attitude. It very quickly became apparent that locally hired experts were more than up to the challenge.

When path dependence actually does emerge in the real historical process of development, it can sometimes be difficult to overcome.

Breaking this dependence, where it hampers the desired evolutionary trends and slows down growth, requires a wide range of efforts, from education to politics, and from structural renovation to institutional change. When the right blend of such actions is achieved, an "economic miracle" occurs. This is what happened when the United States over-came the Great Depression by introducing a New Deal based on Keynes-ian economics in the 1930s, or when West Germany rebuilt itself quickly and created the "social market economy" after defeat in World War II, or in Southeast Asia in the last quarter of the twentieth century. This is also what happened when the post-Soviet Baltic republics became the part of the European Union with the most rapid economic develop-ment in the first decade of the present century. Above all, it is what has been going on for thirty years in China, which in a single generation has improved the basic living conditions for a larger population than has ever been done anywhere.

Similar "economic miracles" cannot be ruled out in the future, even in some Islamic countries, or in Latin America. Future development there, after all, is only partially determined by what has happened in the past and by what is happening now. Far more important is what will happen, and what could happen. For example, Dubai and Senegal or Costa Rica and Chile have been able to perceive this and interpret it in their policies, to the benefit of their development. On the other hand, Kuwait and Sudan or Honduras and Columbia have perceived it less clearly, and done worse.

In the real developmental process, we are dealing with the unceasing interpenetration of continuity and change. Continuity dominates at one moment and change at another. The whole time, these apparent contradictions are in contact with each other. Evolution goes on, and revolutions sometimes occur. Many of them still lie before us, although we do not know exactly where and when each of them will break out, or which of them—like the French or the October—will be regarded by history as epochal. Yet it is worth at least knowing why they break out. Break out they will, and epochal they will be.

Evolution is a permanent process, and its consequences sometimes seem predictable. Charles Darwin (1809–1882) found that it was not the strongest or the most intelligent species that survived the great changes occurring in history, but rather those that could adapt to chang-ing conditions. As much as I distance myself from "social Darwinism," his findings are highly useful in economic analysis. The only guarantee for long-term—or longer—survival is the ability to make adaptations to objectively changing conditions.

This is why socialism fell. It fell because it could not adapt to the contemporary phase of the scientific-cultural revolution, and this was exacerbated by several other phenomena and processes, including systemic supply shortages and factors of a political or international nature, about which we will have more to say later. Neoliberal economic fundamentalism will fall because the values it proclaims prevent it from adapting to a changing social environment and the evolution in the way people think in the twenty-first century.

Evolution goes on. Some products vanish from the market and others appear; obsolescent technologies give way to more modern ones; old buildings come down to be replaced by new ones; important systems wither and different ones arise; values fade away as new ones take hold. All of this keeps happening in this same old world of ours, even if it may seem to have expanded somewhat of late due to the creation of additional cultural and economic space thanks to the Internet. Things keep spinning around, but a good many of them spin in place, idling in neutral. So it is at times with the world economy, especially in some regions where stagnation gains the upper hand over development. This is the way it is, but it need not be so.

There are universal expectations that, in the conditions of globalization, changes in the economic system should bear the fruit of lasting, rapid economic development. Structural reforms and institutional changes should favor increases in the effectiveness of capital and better use of human, financial, and natural resources. This, in turn, should lead to growing competitiveness and a relatively faster rate of economic growth. In the actual mechanisms of the real economy, this often fails to occur.

Sometimes whole social groups or geographic regions are simply shoved to the margins of the economic process. Such incidents are hardly pathological or "exceptions that prove the rule," but rather relatively permanent characteristics of the system, connected with the way it functions within "the new reality."

Fundamental questions arise: Why do things happen this way? What determines the makeup of the blend of conditions—not only strictly economic (finance, investment, commerce, and organization) but also cultural, institutional, political, and social—that make the difference between, on the one hand, economic success and recovery from developmental backwardness or, on the other, failure, being left behind, and falling even farther behind?

In the real process of development (or stagnation), change (or the lack of it) occurs in a certain way rather than another (it is always necessary to investigate, understand, and interpret it in a scholarly way and sometimes to evaluate it and locate it in a hierarchy), since these processes are conditioned by a whole complicated structure of other events, and chains of happenstances that are not only economical and financial in nature, but also political and cultural. The role of political and cultural factors and determinants is very important and, significantly, increasingly so. The importance of this role must therefore be better understood in theory, and utilized in practice.

After several decades in which structural reforms have been carried out in various ways, qualitatively changing the way the economy works and the rules that apply, it can already clearly be seen that in many cases there is a "missing link" in economic growth and social progress, or at least that these things do not occur on the scale of social expectations or political declarations. What is more, real progress (growth and development) or its absence (stagnation and inertia) seem not to confirm the assumptions of numerous theories of economic growth or, more broadly speaking, socioeconomic development. At times, indeed, so-called socioeconomic practice stands in actual contradiction to the correctness of some elements of such theories.

It suffices to mention the disappointment that many countries—or specific social and occupational groups within them—once experienced through nationalization and centrally administered economies, or more recently through trade liberalization, or through privatization, or through the excessive limitation of the role of the state in the economy. At that point, counterarguments are raised against the structural reforms associated with these endeavors, whereas the problem lies elsewhere.

The doubts arise in such regions of the world, as different as they may be in terms of competitiveness and the level of development, as Africa (which continues to strive unsuccessfully to escape from civilizational disadvantages) and the European Union, with its high level (but not the highest level) of development, which has so far been unable to meet the American challenge and which is unable to carry out the Lisbon Agenda that it imposed on itself. This also applies to economies undergoing postsocialist transformation, where, regardless of great regional differentiation, it should have been possible in the past to achieve far more.

In many cases—in various places and times—full advantage is not taken of the existing developmental potential.

Therefore, to understand what is happening in the global economy, or why some regions flourish while others lag or wither, it is necessary to move unceasingly among three dimensions: the geographical, the historical, and the interdisciplinary. Even if we fail to understand everything—which is impossible, after all—we will surely see more. That's something. When we add comparative studies to these three dimensions for research and analysis, we can accomplish a great deal. Nothing is more educational than comparison, applying the techniques characteristic of different sciences in the spatial, temporal, and interdisciplinary dimensions. Comparing and contrasting brings out important things, so that we perceive various aspects of the phenomena and processes that, in a different case, we might overlook.

———————

To compare is to know.

CHAPTER THREE

A Brief History of the World and What We Can Learn from It

Why Some Countries Are Wealthy and Others Poor and Whether It Must Always Be So

Nothing happens outside of time.

THERE IS NO WAY to understand development issues without expanding the temporal context within which we perform the analysis. We are talking about time frames, extending from one point to another, and not merely about the shape of a single vector that disappears into the future. To look forward in any sensible way, we must be good at glancing backward. Everything that was once new becomes old and can disappear entirely over time. This applies to great civilizations and whole empires, as well as to events that may start out being cultural or technological breakthroughs, before being marginalized and, in the end, made irrelevant. When the first telegram was sent across the Atlantic, from Great Britain to the United States, in 1858, no one dreamed that the last telegram would also be dispatched someday. Yet this is what happened in 2007. Will the last e-mail ever be sent? Perhaps. Today we need not occupy our minds with this, but many serious and important matters exist that are worth asking about. Those who don't ask the questions never learn the answers.

A retrospective glance back along the trail of time, and recognition of the mechanisms that formed the course of economic history, is not only absorbing in itself, but also useful in catching a glimpse of the future. As for these glimpses, to the degree that we wish to attach any hopes to them, it is worth bearing some cautions in mind:

- We don't know what's going to happen in the future.
- We analyze what could happen.
- The only thing we know (although not all of us, or always) are the things we want to happen.

The methodological and substantive accuracy (no small matter) of analyses and prognoses about development requires the broadest dimensions possible and the extension of the temporal perspective in both directions—above all forward, but also backward. It's like hiking: While walking, people see most when they look around at the whole surrounding view, and not only at the line of the horizon ahead of them.

When we look backward into the distance—no matter how much we admire the present time and respect the accomplishments of humankind—which is only twenty times more numerous today than 1,000 years ago yet produces as much in a single working shift as in a whole year back then—we note at once that humanity has been wasting its time throughout most of its history, in terms of economic development, and thus the production of ever-increasing quantities of goods and services, and improvements in the quality of life. Not everyone, not always, and not everywhere, but in overall terms, unfortunately, that's the way it's been. This statement applies to some civilizations, to whole epochs, and to centuries or generations, not to mention years and days. The eminent Polish sociologist Zygmunt Bauman writes about this with his own brand of sarcasm: "Purchasing the worthless bundled with the valuable, absurdity bundled with sense, and fear bundled with hope is probably the best business that humanity has done throughout its entire history."[1] This is surely the case, because it would have been possible to do worse, and to buy worthlessness, absurdity, and fear all by themselves. We shall see what this depends on and whether we can manage in the future to purchase the valuable, the sensible, and hope by themselves.

If the road zigzags, then it is necessary to trace it every step of the way, and not to limit oneself to the milestones alone. I think that when we see things not from the position of the historian, but from the perspective of the needs of development economics, we can perceive, even on a road that is so uneven in terms of time and space, certain phenomena and processes that can be generalized. Observations made against this background can be significant for interpretations arrived at within the framework of development economics. Unquestionably, more can be derived from recent history, but the lessons stemming from even the hoariest pages should not be ignored.

There can be no doubt that it would have been possible to achieve better results in the past in relation to the investment made, or to achieve the same results as were actually achieved with less investment. For the economist, the implications of this statement are as far-reaching as possible, because they are an assessment of the scale of the rationality of the actions that were taken—and economics is nothing if not the science of rational action. This lack or inadequacy of rationality is something that should never be lost sight of. The fact is that even more time could have been wasted, and, naturally, even less achieved than was the case. In other words, for as long as civilization has been in existence, things could always have turned out differently. They could have been better or worse than they were, and than they are.

What does this depend on? What is it that determined that we are where we are and that we followed the path that we followed? It was certainly a particular derivative of the unceasing struggle of wisdom with stupidity, and of creativity with destruction. When reason and creativity prevailed, humanity moved forward, and science, art, and the economy flourished. When stupidity and destruction held the upper hand, there was an abundance not only of obscurantism and misery, but also often of bloodshed. For better or for worse—and it was usually worse—these latter periods were decidedly more frequent and, in total, lasted longer. Few people ask "What if?" aside from the practitioners of alternative history,[2] who show us how much of what has happened in our history was simply the result, more or less lucky, of chains of coincidences. Things happened the way they did because many events occurred at the same time. More than one historical process could have unfolded very differently, and the economic consequences would have been far from trivial.

Had things turned out differently, humankind could have been at a far higher level of civilization—on the condition that truth and knowledge had spread more quickly and that governments and policy had worked for peace and development. Today we can say the same thing about tomorrow and the day after. Unfortunately, in the course of the combinations of factors that make up the historical process, we will also fail to achieve in the future everything that, beforehand, seems possible. Stupidity, falsehood, destructiveness, and greed must be combated, but they can never be completely eradicated.

Aside from geography, war and politics have determined the appearance of the map of the world throughout most of history. At present, it is peace, business, and science that decide its outlines to an increasing degree. "In the brief intervals of lucidity, when stupidity and violence stop calling the tune, flowers bloom on the dung heap," remarks Jacques Attali in describing the great turning point of some five centuries ago.[3] He correctly regards the year 1492—usually taken to mark the discovery of America by Columbus, or more precisely, the arrival of his first expedition at several islands in the Antilles, as crucial to the epochal changes that lasted for generations before and after that date. After all, much more was happening then besides the adventures of the flotilla flying the flag of Castille—the *Nina*, the *Pinta*, and the *Santa Maria*, followed later by other sailing ships. The discoveries that followed Columbus's expedition like an avalanche had incalculable consequences for economic development, including the ubiquitous globalization of our own day.

Yet there is much more to the 1492 temporal boundary. It marks the true birth of the modern period, with all the cultural implications for the following centuries. A breakthrough discovery with a revolutionary impact on culture, the printing press—the fifth great invention of mankind—emerged in those years. In the mid-fifteenth century, the largest library collections contained a maximum of 600 volumes, fewer than many of us have in a single room today. The total number of books in Europe was about 100,000. By 1500, there were more than 9 million books. Those years represented a new chance for Europe and its influence around the world. The most interesting thing is that this only became clearly visible from the distant perspective of the passing centuries.

There were few turning points when so much—in methods of thinking and doing things, in the hierarchy of values and culture, and in technology and administration—changed in such a short time. Five centuries earlier came the turning point around the year 962, when the Holy Roman Empire of the Germans arose under Otto I. The political foundations for the shape of Europe over the coming centuries were in place. This is when the institutions of the state formed. Denmark,

Hungary, Bohemia, England—and Poland, too—emerged as states with national economies. At the same time, without any connection to the European changes, China was developing, as was the remote Khmer empire in the lands that are Cambodia, Laos, and Thailand today. On the far side of the world, other civilizations flourished in the pre-Inca cultures in what are today Peru and Ecuador, and the culture of the Maya (in the early postclassical period) in Mexico, Belize, Guatemala, and Honduras.

Three and a half centuries after 1492, in turn, came the remarkable year 1848, the culmination of the Spring of Nations. The French Revolution and the end of the eighteenth century preceded it by two generations. This is a period that had great significance for the process of qualitative economic changes. This is when Great Britain attained world economic ascendancy for a time. Also in the year 1848, Marx and Engels published the *Communist Manifesto*. The Austrian Empire abolished serfdom and gave peasants in Galicia the right to own land. (In Austria itself, this had already been done during the reforms of Joseph and Theresa at the end of the eighteenth century.) Both the American and the Prussian models of agrarian capitalism were achieving success. The process of industrialization and modernization, following either the British or the continental model of transformation, was gathering pace in Europe. The first technological revolution was picking up speed, accompanied by maritime transport, railroads, and the spread of the telegraph. Industry was accelerating and the cities were growing in population. The cultural landmarks of the time remain popular today, especially in literature and music. Victor Hugo and Adam Mickiewicz were writing their masterpieces. This is when Hector Berlioz was composing his *Te Deum*, and Richard Wagner was conducting the opera in Dresden and writing *Lohengrin*. Frédéric Chopin was still giving concerts. The economic expansion of America, and later of Japan, was under way. The modern period seemed to be starting all over again, except that its scale was intercontinental this time, tentatively reaching out toward Australia and New Zealand in the Antipodes, and more boldly toward a Latin America that was freeing itself from colonialism. As a result of general technical, economic, and political progress, it became much easier from the mid-nineteenth century for new ideas and a range of merchandise to penetrate to the farthest corners of the world.

Perhaps we, too, are lucky, because there are many indications that the epoch we are living in—extending one generation back and one generation into the future—is also a turning point. In a few hundred years, or perhaps a few decades, could there be a book titled *1989*? Then it will turn out that, as the popular Polish singer Maryla Rodowicz had it,

How lucky I am
That at this very time I can
Live my life
In the country on the Vistula
How lucky I am
Living in this happy land,
Lovely and real . . .[4]

The year 1989, with all the circumstances of the time, had breakthrough significance for the course of history, including economic history. It was in Poland that the collective common sense emanating from the Round Table agreements in the spring of 1989 brought down the Berlin Wall, which fell that autumn. The positive aspects of this great turning point included the end of the Cold War and the beginnings of the Internet; the fall of dictatorial regimes in Chile, South Africa, Romania, and South Korea, and the Soviet withdrawal from Afghanistan; the opening of scores of countries to international free trade and the flow of capital; breakthroughs in genetics and the explosion of wireless communication; nanotechnology and satellite television; space flight beyond the solar system and mass international tourism; and the start of the international coordination of climate-protection measures and the expansion of socially committed global nongovernmental organizations (NGOs).

Yet history is, unfortunately, also made up of things that are evil, and even very evil. The Tiananmen tragedy occurred in Beijing when government security forces brutally dispersed the demonstrating students. In Tehran, the Iranian spiritual leader Ayatollah Khomeini imposed a fatwa, or Islamic anathema, on the British writer Salman Rushdie, and the reverberations are still being felt two decades later.[5] New diseases, abnormalities, and pathologies emerged. What is worse, unpredictable ones continue to appear today—just as, in that breakthrough year of 1989, even the most prominent futurologists[6] failed to forecast the scale of international terrorism or the cataclysm associated with the spread of HIV-AIDS. The Inquisition and slavery are gone, but the dung heap remains.

———————

Surveying the history of the universe, we can say that we haven't been running things for long. As humankind, in general, we have existed for a very short time, and some might even feel tempted to say that we have accomplished a great deal in the recent stages of history, considering the slow rate of progress during the whole epochs preceding the last couple of thousand years. Fifteen billion years have passed since the Big Bang, but humans have existed for only about 3 million years. If all of time were a single day, then we would have been around for only the last seventeen seconds. Or perhaps thirty-five, since, in the end—or rather, perhaps, from the beginning—we do not know how long we have been in existence. Evolution has been under way all the time.

The traces of the presence of the earliest hominids reach back 7 million years. The oldest *Australopithecus* was already wandering the earth then, and the first *Homo* arrived 2.6 million years ago. That is when primordial, primitive tools appeared, which have been found in the Olduvai Gorge. (The so-called Olduvai culture on the Serengeti plain, now in Tanzania, has been dated to about 2.1 million years ago.) The earliest vestiges of *Homo erectus,* dating from about 1.4 million years ago, have been found in Southwest Asia. Later, in the Lower Paleolithic period, the Acheulean culture developed in the Middle East and became widespread about 700,000 to 300,000 years ago. *Homo sapiens,* which is more familiar, is only 250,000 to 300,000 years old, and its European branch is about 180,000. We are very modern, but the first long-ago *Homo sapiens* was archaic, before the later Cro-Magnon humans, who were quite close to us (about 45,000 years ago). For a short time, Cro-Magnon humans lived alongside Neanderthals, who died out in Europe about 30,000 years ago. During their fifteen millennia of coexistence, they had enough time (and sufficient opportunities) to swap genes. The encounters must have been fascinating.

If the few seconds—or rather the 3 million years—that have passed since the appearance of humans were to be treated as a twenty-four-hour day, then our economy has existed for the last seven minutes. Conscious human economic activity has been around for some 15,000 years. Against this background, contemporary globalization is like the blink of an eye compared with a whole lifespan. But we are the ones doing the blinking, so the time counts differently for us.

Those 15,000 years refer to settled economic activity, although opinions are divided about this. Early humans followed a wandering life, with an existence based on hunting, fishing, and gathering, although some embryonic forms of economic activity began to appear 40,000 to 45,000 years ago, during the so-called Upper Paleolithic Revolution. We note burials, and thus the first traces of religion, about 100,000 years ago. A little bit later, 35,000 to 30,000 years ago, the first works of art (or at least the earliest ones to be preserved so that we know about them) began to appear in the form of cave paintings.

First, however, *Homo erectus* emerged in the slow course of evolution: one of our forebears stood up straight, looked around, and came to the conclusion that the view was better up there—all the way to the horizon. It is precisely this that may have been the greatest invention in the history of mankind. It was, of course, a long-term evolutionary process. To get an idea of how great this change was, all you have to do is get down on all fours for a moment, take a look around, and then stand up and look around again.

Homo sapiens wandered and traded tools. The dating of the origins of exchange continues to evoke controversy among archaeologists and historians, but there is agreement that it began much earlier than was once supposed. There are signs of it from as early as 50,000 years ago, but it could have begun even earlier. *Homo sapiens* used seeds, and stored them in holes dug especially for this purpose. Elements of human spiritual culture can also be noted. Makeshift calendar notations, showing the ability to observe the lunar cycle, go back 30,000 years. Humans already wanted to know how time passed. This must have influenced their attitude to the struggle for life, which turned into economic activity over the following centuries.

Settled life developed as a result of the so-called Neolithic Revolution of 12,000 to 14,000 years ago. This occurred first in the valleys of the Euphrates and the Tigris—where the Americans are now teaching democracy to the Iraqis. In those days before the Sunni and the Shi'a culture and economics developed, the Natufian people (named for the archaeological excavations in the Shuqba cave in Wadi an-Natuf) inhabited the land. The Natufians (who are defined in the historical terminology as a Mesoneolithic society or, as others would have it, Epipaleolithic) were the first to domesticate certain animals. This was a turning point leading from hunting to husbandry (goats and sheep). This was also when humans—probably independently in northern Europe and the Near Middle East—domesticated the dog, which was one of the best ideas in history.

Man made the initial attempts at cultivating plants. This first happened in semiarid Mesopotamia, about 10,000 years ago. Irrigation began, and this led to a changeover from gathering to growing barley and wheat. In Southeast Asia about 8,500 years ago, farming arose from the ability to plant rice. In Central America, corn and pumpkins appeared in small growing plots somewhere between 10,000 and 7,000 years ago. It is interesting that, among the approximately 450,000 species of plants that exist in nature, man cultivates only about 200 for purposes of food, and the basic part of our nutrition comes from twenty crops in only eight plant groups. Paradoxically, after the passage of several thousand years some of them are being genetically modified, and varieties of the seeds originating in Mesopotamia will be legally and commercially manipulated.

Later—not more than about 6,500 years ago—the first cities arose. Stone-built dwellings and cemeteries appeared. In other, less populated regions of the world, hunting and gathering continued all this time. There are places where it remains dominant today—for example, in some of the mountain valleys of New Guinea, in southeastern Namibia, and the part of western Botswana where the San people, better known as the bushmen, live.

Historians assume that at least two processes result from conscious human economic activity: trade and accumulation. They trace their origins to the Upper Paleolithic Revolution, which preceded the Neolithic by about 20,000 to 30,000 years. Trade was the first sign and result of the division of labor. Next came something that would be defined many thousands of years later as specialization. However, it was so simple that it had little influence on the efficacy of work. For whole epochs, civilization functioned in principle within the framework of simple reproduction, involving the repetition of a static production cycle and its replication at an unchanging level. This was stagnation. However, even stagnation required the gathering of supplies and stores. This meant the emergence of accumulation, which led to the planning of the production cycle and the deferral of some of the results of production, especially crops, for the future. When it later turned out that a surplus remained, the bright idea arose that it could be exchanged with others for the surplus of their own production. Exchange intensified. At first, it took the form of barter—goods for goods—and only later did common equivalents—or money—emerge. This was the fourth great human "invention"—after standing erect, fire, and the wheel. I put it in quotation marks because money—just like contemporary globalization—was not thought up by anyone. It arose on its own in the course of the long process of the development of exchange. This is how trade was born.

The universal appearance of money, in the course of the seventh century BCE, is connected with the economic activity of the Phoenicians. Their mobility contributed a great deal to economic development, mostly through the expansion of trade, in which they were the leaders in their time. In this way, they inspired the division of labor over significant areas, and this made labor more effective. Voyaging and trade accelerated the dissemination of knowledge of technology, and this was an indisputable stimulus of economic growth. From their cities of Byblos, Sidon, Tyre, and Ugarit, which were already flourishing 3,500 years ago, they traded with the entire known world—known to them and their contemporaries. In this way, they set in motion the process of the development of the goods-and-money economy, which no one since has ever been able to bring to a halt (although some have tried, and not so very long ago).

In all of this, money emerged independently in different places on earth that did not necessarily have any links with each other. In some regions, countable and divisible goods became money. In extreme cases, this included even cattle, which was certainly easy to count but harder to divide. More commonly, it was metal: first bronze, then silver, gold, and a variety of alloys. Shells were also frequent, in widely separated places like the islands of Micronesia or the Bissagos Archipelago off the coast of what is now Guinea-Bissau. Today, life on the Ilha de Rubane or the Ilha de Joao Vieira is similar to what it was thousands of years ago, and the inhabitants, in addition to barter, still use mussels in exchange transactions involving freshly caught fish from the blue Atlantic for copra from the green coconut palms. As necessary, they also use the regional currency CFA in contacts with the outside world, and do not turn up their noses at dollars or euros.

For whole millennia, when people were already wandering across the face of the earth, little happened from the point of view of development. *Homo sapiens* expanded slowly—farther and farther, from today's Africa and Southwest Asia to Europe and the rest of Asia, and from there in a northeast direction to America, and to Oceania in the southeast. The number of people remained relatively stable. If it rose somewhat, then tribal combat and wars, epidemics, and famine thinned it out. Over time, various cultures began to appear, evolve, and develop. In the vast majority of cases, they did not know of each other's existence. Technological progress advanced at a rate of more or less 5 to 10 kilometers per year. This means that a given method of irrigation or manufacturing tools that was used in one place spread 1,000 kilometers into adjacent lands in the course of 100 to 200 years.

In the meantime, during the last few millennia before our era, several great civilizations rose and fell. We admire their material vestiges to this day: the temple of Ipet-sut in Thebes and the pyramids in Giza in today's Egypt, Persepolis, the Wall of China, the Acropolis in Athens, Pergamon and Troy on the western coast of Turkey, the Roman Forum Magnum, and Jerusalem. Other masterpieces—the Colossus of Rhodes and all the rest of the five wonders of the ancient world, aside from the Egyptian pyramids—are lost. The first games were held at Olympus in Greece in 776 BCE. The economies and cultures of China and of India were flourishing splendidly at the turn of the sixth and fifth centuries BCE—just as, at the turn of the twentieth and twenty-first centuries of our era, these countries are increasingly astounding the rest of the world. Back then, two and a half millennia ago, the Buddha also appeared (563–483 BCE), followed two and a half centuries later by the great Greek philosophers. We draw on their intellectual achievements to this day, just as the Chinese continue to benefit from the teachings of the Buddha's contemporary, Confucius (551–479 BCE). It was also then that Darius I, the Achmenid ruler of the Persians, began in 518 BCE to erect the glorious city of Pars, later known as Persepolis. It was there, in the northeastern part of today's Iran and the Turkmenistan borderlands, that Zarathustra created one of the oldest monotheistic religions. We do not know whether he lived from 660 to 583 BCE, as some researchers suggest on the basis of interpretations of his own immortal works, the *Gathas* (a part of the holy scripture of the Avesta), or several centuries earlier, at the turn of the eleventh and tenth centuries BCE.

Unfortunately, we also know little about the dynamics of production of the first millennium before the new era, but production was higher than in the first millennium of our era. In the preceding centuries, a great deal was happening in the Mediterranean cultural area, the

Middle East, the territory of today's Pakistan and India, and China, and very little in sparsely populated America and Africa. The majority of Oceania remained uninhabited. In overall terms, however, we were dealing with economic growth and, more broadly, with development, since that growth was connected with structural and social changes. Against this background, culture also flourished.

At the most, 300 million people were alive in the world at the beginning of the new era, when Christianity arose and, in 70 CE, the army of the Roman emperor Titus sacked Jerusalem—fewer than live in the United States today or eight times as many as in Poland. Together, they produced only a small fraction of what we can produce today. It is hard to believe, but, from the point of view of value, the entire world at that time produced only a third of what the Poles produce today. In material terms, of course, it was a completely different kind of production. We can estimate that the per capita value of the goods and services in the most highly developed parts of the ancient world was not more than $800 in present-day terms.[7] This is as much as in the poorest countries in today's world. Outside the Mediterranean basin and some of the more advanced Asian civilizations, including parts of India and China, it must have been significantly less.

Income disparities were markedly smaller than at present. If we compare the average levels across large territories, the differences become completely insignificant. The highest income level was in what is called Western Europe and Asia excluding Japan—about $450 in 1990 terms, or almost $800 today's terms). At $425 ($755 today), Africa was better off than America or Eastern Europe and the areas now referred to as "the former Soviet Union." The average for the world as a whole was $455 ($790) per capita. While incomes in North America and Africa were equally low (and lower than those in Western Europe and the more economically advanced parts of Asia) at the beginning of our era, incomes in America today are twenty times greater than those in Africa.

Incomes and property were relatively more dispersed in the most highly developed Mediterranean civilizations. Inequality was significant there, if for no other reason than the fact that the few aristocrats of the time had much and the more numerous slaves had practically nothing. Elsewhere—in remote regions of the world with which the Roman Empire had no contact—primeval communities predominated in most cases, existing at a low level of output and consumption. Things were different (already) in China, which resembled Rome in some ways and primitive communities in others, but with less income inequality than at the present day.

Little changed over the subsequent 1,000 years. Deeper change came only at the turn of the fifth and sixth centuries, when the Roman Empire fell. This was cascading change, while the other transformations followed a peaceful evolutionary path. Technological progress was feeble, culture at a low level, wars unceasing, and the economy stagnant. Over scores of succeeding generations, the human population remained more or less the same as at the time of Christ, when the most splendid center of civilization was Alexandria, with its renowned lighthouse, one of the seven wonders of ancient architecture. In the year 1000, the epicenter of world culture was Córdoba, with its universities and dozens of public libraries. About 310 million people then lived in the world. After another millennium, when New York, with its unprecedented concentration of capital and intellect, took the place of Alexandria and Córdoba, there were 6.5 billion of us. Which city will be known as the most splendid in the year 3000? Perhaps it does not exist yet. After Africa, Europe, and America, it may well be the turn of Asia. We can draw a more or less straight line from Alexandria through Córdoba to New York. If we extend it to the northwest, we arrive somewhere in northeastern Siberia.

In the year 1000, the value of the output of all humanity was the same as 1,000 years earlier. Since the population had grown slightly, the per capita income was a bit lower. The western part of Europe, to the west of the Elbe and also including southern Europe (a part of the Continent that is regarded as including the Czech lands but not Hungary), was not much more wealthy than the eastern part—about $400 ($710 in today's terms) in both. This was a lower figure than in Africa, where the average was $415 ($740), a figure weighted by the relatively higher level in North Africa, which was under the influence of the highly developed Islamic culture, as opposed to the less populated and relatively less developed sub-Saharan remainder of the Continent. Regions along the coastline of the Mediterranean, already containing strong elements of urban economies and cultures, were particularly developed. The wealthiest were the Apennines, the French-speaking countries, Lombardy, and Galicia. Byzantium was rich. Scandinavia was impoverished. If the European Union had existed then, Turkey would long have been a member state, because Byzantium and its dependent territories would have been one of the glories of the E.U.—and there would probably have been strong opposition to the accession of the poor economies of northern Europe.

All of humanity, including the privileged strata that we now refer to as the elites, was probably unaware that throughout the first millennium, and especially in the second half of that millennium, after the fifth century, it was living in stagnation. This, rather than development, was the norm. People were perfectly well aware that some years were less abundant (or rather more poverty-stricken) than the preceding ones. The rulers had a rough idea about the economic situation, since they knew that the treasury was less full and there was less money for war. However, they did not connect such observations with a need for the deliberate stimulation of economic growth or for combating stagnation. There was more praying for good crops than thinking about ways of systematically increasing them. Empty coffers were an impulse for new raids and plunder, rather than a signal that there was a need to increase production. Inertia prevailed. Pro-development thinking was born in the pangs of stagnation and was quite slow to gain the upper hand over the temptations of greed and possessiveness. Creative economic thinking emerged and spread even more slowly than technological advances.

We can see that, although much has happened throughout history—by definition—little was happening in the fields of economic development for whole millennia and centuries. Change was inconsiderable, and at times nonexistent. Stagnation: it affected both populations and output, which are connected in well-known ways. For there to be more people, they must know how to produce more—starting with food and other products essential for life and procreation. The lack of the appropriate changes in production methods ruled this out during the overwhelming majority of the time that we have been here. Leaving aside the splendid periods of antiquity (not splendid for everyone, such as the slaves and the gladiators), full-blown change emerges only with the onset of the modern period. It is true that change did not shift into top gear until the Renaissance, but many elements of the modern began appearing successively in the first half of the last millennium. It was between the years 1000 and 1500 that there was a noticeable modification of farming technology to the east of the Elbe and the north of the Carpathians. The urban network and the road system developed considerably in those centuries. The level of education improved, if we measure it by the ability to read and write. The first universities were founded. The first banks and the first "European" currency came into being. The Gothic flourished in this period, and erecting so many wonderful edifices in this style required a great deal of knowledge and advanced building techniques.

However, economic changes have only recently taken on sufficient dynamism to permit the rapid expansion of output and the population. Even 200 years ago, there were fewer than a billion people—fewer than there are Hindus today.[8] A century later, there were 1.65 billion people, and half a century after that, 2.5 billion. It took another 50 years to reach 6 billion. In 2050, there will be about 9 billion of us—ten times more than at the time of the French Revolution or the final partition of Poland. How many of us will there be in the year 3000—more, or fewer? There will probably be fewer of us.

Therefore, while the world population barely increased during the first millennium of our era,[9] it has increased by a factor of 20 since then. While the earth's per capita income changed hardly at all in that first millennium, and may even have fallen slightly, it has grown to a level thirteen times higher in the millennium that followed. As a result, the total world GDP is 300 times greater than it was 1,000 years ago. Output grew at a snail's pace between 1000 and 1820—at an average of 0.05 percent per year, a pace that was completely imperceptible for generations at a time. In the course of more than 800 years, the world per capita GDP grew by a puny 50 percent—the same as the percentage increase in China during the last five years!

Only after 1820, when our great-great-great-great-grandparents were alive,[10] did world economic growth take off. In the course of less than two full centuries, per capita GDP has risen by a factor of 8, while the number of those earning it has more than quintupled. Compared with previous human history, this is a veritable explosion. Understandably, the growth during this period has followed varying trajectories in different regions, and this has led to larger inequalities in the material situation of the inhabitants of the globe. In 1820, per capita income in Western Europe, North America, Japan, Australia, and New Zealand was twice as high as that in the rest of the world. Now the proportion is 7:1.

Stagnation also characterized the structure of employment and production for whole centuries, and greater changes occurred only over the last two centuries. Data from the United States provide an especially clear illustration of this. Two hundred years ago, about 85 percent of Americans worked in agriculture and mining (mostly in agriculture), and no more than 4 percent in the service sector. Today the figures are 3 percent and 79 percent, respectively (with the other approximately 18 percent employed in the world's most productive manufacturing sector).

In view of the low overall level of development and the universal lack of rudimentary health services, the average lifespan in the year 1000 was, shockingly, 24 years. The very high rate of infant mortality was the major factor. One out of every three infants failed to survive the first year. Famine and epidemics were the order of the day, and there was little improvement until the turn of the eighteenth and nineteenth centuries. Incredible as it may seem, estimates based on the fragmentary available sources indicate that the average life expectancy at birth in England at the beginning of the fourteenth century was still twenty-four years. Three hundred years later, this figure had increased to almost forty-one years—and had not quite reached thirty-nine in France. Two hundred years ago, in the times of Byron and Stendhal, infant mortality in the two countries was 144 and 181 per thousand live births, respectively. This matches the current figures in the poorest countries of Africa, which are also those worst affected by HIV-AIDS. Is 200 years a longer or a shorter time span than one might have expected?

Afterward, the changes were thoroughgoing. Today a newborn citizen of this world can, in statistical terms, expect to live to be 66. In concrete cases, the deviations from this norm are considerable—15 years more in the wealthiest countries, like Japan or Canada, and as much as 30 years less in the poorest, such as Swaziland or Tanzania.

———

Although I have used the term *revolution* several times here, one of the first obvious lessons to be drawn from this cursory overview of history, and one that has no small consequences for peering into the future, is the statement that the changes that take place in human history and the history of civilization are of the cascading variety. This is neither the monotonous uniformity of tiny changes until, whole epochs later, "quantity becomes quality" nor (with certain exceptions) the alternation of periods of total stagnation with spectacular leaps of a revolutionary kind. Changes build up, accumulating and overlapping—just like a cascade—and send the wheel of history jolting down the bumpy path, sometimes faster, sometimes slower, and sometimes—this is when we see change most clearly—in a cumulative way, as a cascade. So it will be in the future as well. It's already that way, since we have spent our lives negotiating a series of these cascades.

A brief excursion through time shows clearly that, without a critical attitude, there is no progress, and this also applies to economic development. This is the second obvious lesson. The ability to make a critical evaluation of the situation is an essential condition for diagnosing the way things are and an irreplaceable condition for defining the right corrective action. After the fall of ancient civilization, the capacity for criticism dwindled almost to nothing. This led to the ten centuries of the Middle Ages. In that epoch, somehow or other—from the fall of the Roman Empire in the fifth century to the start of the Renaissance in the fourteenth—outstanding Islamic thinkers fostered critical thinking and carried on the postclassical philosophical tradition. The fact that this happened came down to the differing circumstances in the two neighboring civilizations. In what had previously been the most highly developed part of the world, ancient culture died out and the economy entered a period of stagnation as a result of institutional weakness, multiple conflicts, the shortsightedness and stupidity of the rulers, and the mental rot and conservatism that resulted from the dominance of the dogmas of the Christian religion. The need for critical thinking developed precisely where craftsmanship and trade were flourishing— among the Arabs and the Persians. More precisely, a feedback mechanism came into being: the pulsating economy stimulated creative thinking, which in turn spurred economic activity. Religion was also less of a hindrance to the creative transfer of ideas, perhaps even less than it is in certain areas of Islamic culture today.

The way things turned out is that, when religious dogma—stifling curiosity and the desire to search for objective scientific truth that leads to new discoveries, ideas, and applications—gained the upper hand in the Christian world, it was fortunately the other way around with Islam. There was stagnation, on the one hand, and development, on the other, particularly under the influence of enlightened leaders who did not shy away from science and art and did not permit religion to dominate life. The dogmatic Christianity of the Middle Ages repressed the need for the ability to think and act creatively. People, including rulers, had few possessions, and what they had, in both cultural and economic terms, came only from God. In Islamic circles at the same time, on the other hand, critical and creative thinking, glorying in and advancing mathematics and astronomy, brought in their train the development of physics. The side effect of this was to rescue some of the achievements of antiquity from oblivion and carry them over into the modern era. As early as the first century BCE, the Greeks had been capable of creating the amazingly refined and accurate Antikythera Mechanism, regarded by some as the first computer, which in fact is a complex machine for measuring cosmic and earthly time. A similar machine appeared in the sixth century and then, at least as far as we know today, only in the thirteenth century, on the Iberian Peninsula, which was still flourishing under the influence of Islamic culture.

The demand for critical and ingenious thinking created a supply. The concrete interactions between culture and the economy were already crucial to maintaining developmental tendencies. Those who could make a contribution rose to the top. After a time, beginning in the thirteenth century, for reasons similar to the mix of favorable and unfavorable circumstances of 1,000 years earlier—the tables turned again. The Reformation dawned in Europe, and the loosening of religious dogmatism freed the desire to search for new things through knowledge rather than faith. Before this happened, the Arabs and Persians rescued civilization—not only when Hafiz of Shiraz, the great fourteenth-century Persian poet who is revered to this day in Iran, wrote beautifully about the love of a hummingbird for a rose, but above all when they safeguarded the capacity for critical thinking throughout the long centuries preceding the Renaissance.

For centuries, the thought of Islamic philosophers, scholars, artists, and politicians far exceeded the capabilities of the Christian thinkers of the time. Many of these intellects left an indelible mark on the ages. Here it is worth mentioning Ibn Sina (980–1037) and Ibn Rushd (1126–1198). The first—a great scholar, philosopher, and physician, better known as Avicenna—was Persian, and Iranians are still proud of him. The second, known as Averroes, was an Arab philosopher and physician. It is interesting to note that outstanding thinkers were physicians at that time, just as they are economists or other social scientists today. It was these two men, Avicenna in Persia and Averroes in Andalusia, whose commentary on Aristotle (384–322 BCE) saved Greek philosophy from being completely lost during the European Middle Ages.

Bearing all this in mind, we must look skeptically upon the contemporary cultural and political split that some have termed the "Clash of

Civilizations." The phrase became common in 1993, when Samuel P. Huntington published an article under that title in *Foreign Affairs*. The article was Huntington's riposte to Francis Fukuyama's *The End of History*, which came out a year earlier. In 1998 Huntington elaborated on his theses in a book in which he argues that world politics will be shaped by confrontation and hostility among the major civilizations of the contemporary world.[11] International conflicts will stem not from incompatible economic interests, but from cultural differences, especially those with a religious underpinning. It is significant that the cover of the original version of a book with this title should feature two graceful colonnades, different but complementary, one Arabic and the other Greek. When the Polish version came out, however, the cover illustration depicted two warriors—from different civilizations, we were to understand—hacking away at each other. It should be added that the term *Clash of Civilizations* has taken on pejorative connotations as yet another example of mumbo jumbo, since it is evidently exaggerated. Its use is apparently intended to cause disputes, despite the fact that it does not require great expertise to know that it is harmony that is constructive.

Therefore, although differences in the level of development were small and the level of development itself was low 1,000 or 2,000 years ago, the differentiated rate of growth has led to a situation in which the present average per capita output in North America is more than four times greater than the world average, whereas in Africa it is less than a quarter. The rest of the world is located between these two extremes. These differences have increased significantly over the past two centuries. In the years 1820–2000, the per capita GDP of the West (calculated using the methodology of comparative conditions, or PPP) has grown at an average annual rate of 1.51 percent. The most rapid growth has been in Japan, at 1.93 percent, whereas it has amounted to 1.75 percent in North America and 1.51 percent in Western Europe. During the same period, it has been increasing by 1.22 percent per year in Latin America, by 1.06 percent in the rest of Europe, by 0.86 percent in China by 0.67 percent in Africa, and by 0.92 percent in the rest of Asia.

From today's perspective, these values seem unremarkable, and the minimal differences between them unimportant. This is a gigantic delusion, because the values apply only on the scale of a single year. If we run the numbers for the whole period at compound interest, we find that the level of output in Japan has increased by 3,022 percent, but that of Africa has increased by only 233 percent—an enormous difference! This is the difference between development and stagnation. Even the apparently slight divergence in the average percentage of increase between Western Europe and North America (0.24 percent annually) compounds after six generations to 786 percent, since the rises in income are 1,385 percent and 2,171 percent, respectively. This simple arithmetic illustrates the power of economic growth, which, in the long term, is always the basis for social development. Great artists sometimes find the inspiration for masterpieces in misery and suffering. For its spirit and culture to flourish, however, a society needs the dynamic material basis that can be ensured in the long run only by economic growth. This is the second important lesson that flows from our concise history.

It must be added that the last few years have broken out of the framework of Maddison's fascinating calculations and are characterized by significantly greater dynamism. In the decade from 1998 to 2007, the rate of growth of the world GDP (in real terms, in PPP with the results of inflation removed) has averaged 3.5 percent. Subtracting the 1.3 percent rate of population growth, this still leaves us with 2.2 percent per capita. This is almost twice as high as during the preceding 180 years. Many countries of Asia are growing at a much higher rate of more than 6 percent per year. The GDP in Southeastern Europe is growing faster than average, at 3.6 percent.[12] Output in Africa is growing at 2.1 percent, close to the world rate. In the most advanced economies, including the United States, it is slightly lower, at 2.0 percent, and in Japan it is much slower—1.2 percent.

This period is only a third of a generation. Nevertheless, it is worth remembering that, if Africa maintained its present tempo and output in Western Europe[13] rose during the next 180 years at the same rate as over the last ten—1.8 percent—then in 2187 the per capita GDP in Africa would have increased above the present level by 4,213 percent, and that in Western Europe would have risen by 2,481 percent. Western Europe has been growing sluggishly in the last 5 years, and Africa has grown more rapidly, at annual rates of 1.28 percent and 3.38 percent, respectively. Over the long temporal perspective, each tenth of a percentage point is multiplied many times over. Growth of 1.3 percent per year doubles income in fifty-four years, 1.8 percent in thirty-nine years, 3.4 percent in twenty-one years, and 8.5 percent in eight and a half years. If the rates of 1.3 percent and 3.4 percent were to be maintained over the long term, and assuming that the average African now earns about $3,000 per year and the average European about $32,000, then after six generations (when our great-great-great-great-grandchildren are alive) the per capita GDP in Europe would amount to $2.19 million, an unimaginable sum today, whereas the average African would earn "only" $316,000 per year. Would this be *"Afrique Paradis"*?

It would all be absurd were it not for the case that this is the way history works. The things that were once possible in certain places and that are still occurring in spades in China and a few other cases, will not be possible elsewhere in the future. The things that happened at the same time in the past in the countries that are wealthy today and that are happening now in China, will not happen in those other countries. In China, with one fifth of all human beings, the GDP has doubled every eight and a half years over the last three decades. In 2007, it surpassed $8,300 and, in comparison to 1977, is twelve times higher per capita, despite the fact that there is no shortage of heads to count.

At this point, we need to think about where we are in our journey through time and space. A generation ago, after the death of the doctrinaire Mao Zedong in 1976 and the coming to power a year later of the great reformer and leader Deng Xiaoping, the per capita GDP in China was about $700 in today's money. That's equal to the present per capita income of the poorest of the world's poor countries—Malawi and Burundi. At the same time, it's equal to the average income in the world as a whole, 1,000 or 2,000 years ago. By traveling to another place, therefore, we can travel to another time. Comparisons are necessary. By examining the labor productivity, the effectiveness of production, and the standard of living in those African countries, we can see how things looked a mere generation ago in the China that is advancing today, or 1,000 years ago in the Europe that is now wealthy.

When comparing incomes earlier, we were referring to the western and southern parts of Europe, which then—as now—were far richer than the eastern part. To the degree that Western Europe was then like Burundi today or China when Deng succeeded Mao, Eastern Europe then was at the level of the poorest people in the poorest countries today. Visiting China thirty years ago was a good way to get an idea of what life was like in Poland at the time of Bolesław the Bold. Those who failed to do so can still go to Malawi or Burundi, or even better, to the utterly beautiful Land of the Dogons in Mali, where it is possible to travel one or two millennia backward in time. To get Poland, imagine pigs and cows instead of goats and sheep, and barley instead of millet. The chickens—if the villagers can afford to keep any—are the same.

Today the average Chinese income is half of that in Poland or a fifth of that in America. If China continues to have the same rate of growth in the coming generation that it had in the last, then the GDP thirty years from now will once again have increased by a factor of almost 12. Simple comparisons show that its level in 2037 would be a shocking 140 times greater than in 1977. On the other hand, at about $97,000, it would be 35 percent higher than the highest income in the world today, which is found in tiny Luxembourg (with its population of 480,000 people, 2,750 times smaller than that of China).

China is exceptional not only today. Few people are aware that its position in the world economy was once far stronger than at present. When Europe was slowly lifting itself out of its medieval stagnation and coming to life during the Renaissance, not only the culture but also the economic contribution of China to world output were far more impressive, in relative terms, than today. In the year 1600, China's share of world output was 29 percent. A hundred years later, as a result of the centralization that slowed expansion, and of the conservatism (today we would call this an antireform attitude) of the imperial rulers and their bureaucracy, it had fallen to 22 percent. Later, as a result of the opening up and pro-reform stance of the court in Beijing and its administration, it jumped by ten points and accounted for almost a third of world output in 1820.

Europe and North America were getting under way then, whereas China slowed incredibly. Once again this was due to the central government and the reduction of contact with the outside world. By the time two generations had passed, the Chinese share of world GDP was down to 18 percent in 1870, and on the eve of World War I it was only 9 percent, and only half of that at the moment of the founding of the People's Republic of China in 1949. This unimpressive share in world output of less than 5 percent persisted, generally speaking, throughout the time that Mao Zedong ruled, with output increasing at about the same tempo as the world average. Today the Chinese share of world GDP is again 16 percent, as it was 140 years ago. Then, however, Western Europe, North America, and especially Japan were speeding up, whereas China was slowing down. Why? Could it happen again?

Never again will anyone make as large a withdrawal from the bank of the world's resources as China is making. This is the last transaction on such a scale. Many people advise against using phrases like "never again" or "no one," but I will repeat it: Never again, no one, because the earth will not permit it—not in Africa, or Latin America, or the post-socialist countries of Eastern Europe and Asia. It might still be possible once or twice in small or medium-sized economies, but not on such a broad or even global scale—unless some completely unprecedented new historical epoch arrives in the wake of the sort of pandemonium and great step backward that can only be followed by renewed acceleration— just as the ancient world gave way to the stagnation of the Middle Ages, before the Renaissance flowered. Such things can never be ruled out entirely.

We already know that events occur as they do because many things happen at once. Although formulated in the present tense, this assertion also applies, naturally, to the past. What was it, therefore, that happened in various historical periods to make economic processes function as they did, rather than otherwise? Historical culminations of change—sometimes lasting a dozen or so years, and at other times a whole century or two, resulted in large measure from coincidences. Happenstance prevailed to a very great degree. Nevertheless, the guiding light of the human intellect and carefully considered strategies were capable, in the midst of the general chaos,[14] of steering the course of events, and sometimes even of reversing it. By the same token, unfortunately, unenlightened intellects and the lack of a strategy were capable of helping to bring about complete surrender to the chaos that always may be present in circumstances unfavorable for development. Attractive and repulsive forces commingled, and the derivative of their actions determined the formation of new cultural, economic, and political arrangements and systems. Either stagnation or development followed.

Long-term economic development occurred when five factors came together:

1. Technological progress.
2. The ascendancy of critical thinking and innovation over dogmatism in culture and the economy.
3. Economic awareness and an ability to organize the expansion of production and exchange.
4. Political will on the part of the rulers to carry out essential institutional reforms that set human energy and entrepreneurship free and directed them towards creativity.

5. Openness to external contacts, making possible a broader exchange not only of goods, but also of knowledge, information, and culture.

When any one of these elements was lacking, the economy developed sluggishly or not at all. Europe in the Middle Ages lagged behind the Islamic countries—Arabia and Persia—as well as China, in regard to each of these factors. In turn, the later conservatism of its rulers and the closing of China to the outside world quickly relegated the Middle Kingdom to the periphery of the world. Things could happen the other way, as when the Meiji reforms after 1868 pushed Japan forward at the same time that India was opening up and undergoing integration. Of course, it is almost always possible to find exceptions when development took place despite the absence of one of these factors. For instance, during the rule of the Zhou, the longest-reigning Chinese dynasty (1122–216 BCE), feudalism prospered and the country, while basically closed to outside contact and unreceptive to criticism under the influence of the Legalists, developed more rapidly than Greece. This was one case where the exception proved the rule.

What is more, economic regression has always been possible, both in long historic waves and within the space of recent decades. For at least a generation, this has not occurred in the world economy as a whole, but several individual countries have experienced a reduction in the absolute level of output, sometimes so deep that they have not yet returned to the maximum level of national income that they achieved in the past. One can indicate four groups of countries that have fallen prey to four different cataclysms:

- Countries undergoing systemic transformation from a centrally planned socialist economy to an open-market economy.
- Postcolonial countries in sub-Saharan Africa.
- Latin American countries grappling with the consequences of local conflicts, macroeconomic collapse, and financial crises.
- Economic monocultures, especially in countries reliant on oil exports.

The first case is controversial to the degree that regression in the level of output in postsocialist countries cannot be acknowledged unconditionally as a cataclysm. The scale of the fall in output, especially in the worst affected countries, has been cataclysmic, but this is not necessarily true of the phenomenon as a whole. On the one hand, the transformation recession was unavoidable, but, on the other hand, it had a cathartic effect on some fields, cleansing the economy of structurally ineffective entities that were more of a burden than an asset. However, the scale of the transformation recession was far greater than it need have been. Mistaken economic policies exacerbated the recession. This was not an act of God, but rather a result of human choices.

As a result, it took eighteen years, until 2007, for the twenty-nine postsocialist countries of East-Central Europe and Asia, including all the former Soviet republics and Mongolia, to return as a group to the 1989 output level. The word *level* is important, because the structure is completely different, more modern, and responsive to consumer demand. It delivers quality that, in many cases, enables it to compete in international markets. Only now are Azerbaijan, Bulgaria, and Lithuania equaling their previous maximums. In nine countries (Bosnia and Herzegovina, Montenegro, Georgia, Kyrgyzstan, Macedonia, Moldova, Serbia, Tajikistan, and Ukraine), the level of output remains below the maximums achieved in 1988–1990. In the worst cases, Ukraine and Moldova, it will take until about 2017 to return to the historical maximum level—just in time for the centennial of the Great October Socialist Revolution.

Far more melancholy and disconcerting is the situation in many African countries, to the extent that voices are even heard opining that colonialism was not so bad after all (in general, things were far worse then). Nevertheless, it is a fact that, because of prolonged ethnic conflicts and the recurrence of local wars, the abysmal quality of administration, defective economic policy, underinvestment in human capital, a ruined or nonexistent infrastructure, the devastation of the environment, and cycles of natural disasters from drought through locusts to floods, a dozen or more countries find themselves, at the end of the first decade of the twenty-first century, at the same level of output per capita as in the 1970s. South Africa noted its peak output in 1981; Togo and Namibia, in 1980; Niger and Malawi, in 1979; Gabon, Senegal, and Zambia, in 1976; and the Democratic Republic of the Congo and Madagascar, in 1975.

The situation in the poorest countries of Latin America looks almost as bleak. Armed conflict, failed dictatorial regimes, and submissiveness to exploitation from outside account for the fact that the per capita

GDP in Paraguay and Peru remains lower than in 1981. It is lower than it was in 1979 in Honduras, lower than in 1978 in El Salvador, and lower than in 1977 in Bolivia and Nicaragua. No less than whole decades have been lost to development recently in several of the larger and generally more advanced Latin American countries. Argentina, along with Uruguay, a neighboring country with which it has strong economic ties, remains below its output level from 1998, when it came under frontal assault from an indebtedness, currency, and financial crisis that left a production crisis in its wake. Mexico has still not matched its output figures for the year 2000. Venezuela is in far worse shape. It combines the worst Latin America traits—political instability, a strong populist movement, and feeble macroeconomic management—with those of the oil-producing countries.

The oil producers are a fourth group that, it would seem, should be forging ahead, since they have been so abundantly endowed by nature. However, these blessings do not necessarily include political culture and entrepreneurial flair. Despite their vast, valuable resources, these countries are unable to maintain a steady trajectory of economic growth. When the price of the petroleum they sell is high, output increases rapidly; stabilization or, even worse (for them), a fall in prices plunges them into structural recession and prolonged stagnation. They experienced a boom during the oil crisis (hardly a crisis for them) of the 1970s, but many of these countries have not equaled their earlier output peaks despite the return to higher prices in the current decade. Saudi Arabia remains below its 1978 level, and Kuwait and the United Arab Emirates are below their levels in 1977. This is what happens when several conditions occur at the same time: monoculture, an underdeveloped service sector, reliance on the world price of a single commodity, the lack of a comprehensive development strategy, and a shortage of pragmatism. These sins are paid for by regression from the output levels of bygone decades.

Emphasis should be placed on the complexity of the determinants of long-term growth, because they are not only complementary but also mutually reinforcing. Even with the best intentions of the rulers, the lack of technological progress will never bear the fruit of continuing growth in output. Yet such progress in itself cannot lead to growth without the right kind of support from the state. Even taken together, these two factors will not set the economy rolling if they do not mesh with progress in science and culture, which, by themselves, are also inadequate for maintaining long-term growth. Mathematics and medicine or music and poetry can flourish in passing flashes of brilliance, but not the economy. It takes a synergy of all these factors, accompanied by openness to external contacts and the accumulation of economic experience and knowledge, to ensure outstanding results. This is what we see in Europe in the fifteenth century, and in Western Europe in the nineteenth and again in the second half of the twentieth century. Contemporaries may feel that, from now on, it will always be thus. Perhaps it will be, but not necessarily, and not if one of the links in the chain goes missing.

Technological progress, indisputably, has been the main driving force of growth in output throughout history. At present, we hear endlessly about the "knowledge-based economy," which is intended to emphasize the special role of the intellect in creating new value. However, we note when we take a closer look at history that all periods of significant economic growth were based on knowledge. Growth need not, always and everywhere, result from inventions. It can also—as it was for a long time in Japan and has recently been in China—come simply from innovation and imitation. Whenever the other four processes have been concurrent with technological progress, the economy has moved smartly forward. This coincidence is the best explanation we have of why thriving development and long-term stagnation have occurred at the same time in different places—for example, in Western Europe and Eastern Europe.[15] It also shows why we have seen radically different results in the same place at different times—in the Islamic countries or North America, for instance.

The discovery of great resources—ore or petroleum—has speeded up these processes even more, whereas wars have proved capable of canceling them out. It may sound incredible today, but the Bolivian city of Potosí had about 200,000 inhabitants (and eighty churches) at the turn of the seventeenth and eighteenth centuries, and was one of the richest cities in the world—on a par with New York and Paris—thanks to the staggering wealth of silver mined from the Cerro Rico. To this day, Spanish-speakers talk about *"valer un potosí,"* or being worth a fortune. Yet there have also been cases where the appearance of natural wealth hindered development, as we can see today in many of the Middle Eastern and African oil-exporting states. It is good to have a lot of oil (or other raw materials for which demand is always high) when it is expensive and getting more expensive, but it is not so good when it is cheap and getting cheaper. That is because these countries, for political or cultural reasons, are unable to use the time that nature has given them for the essential institutional reforms and for implementing technological and economic progress. This can be seen particularly starkly in the most populous country in Africa, Nigeria, with its 140 million inhabitants, which is one of the world's largest oil producers (the ninth-largest producer and the sixth-largest exporter), and yet is one of the poorest countries in the world, with a per capita GDP of $1,400.

There have also been cases where war has aided development by bringing about an economic boom—first in the countries that win the war, such as Great Britain during World War I and the United States during World War II, and later in those that lose, such as Germany after both wars. Never, however, has war in itself been a self-sufficient mechanism, and it always requires the assistance of those five crucial factors in development.

It is hardly surprising that the more of us there are in the world and the higher the level of output and trade, the more the complications and diversity, in both time and space—which are, after all, interconnected. If we limit ourselves to the customary division of the world by continents, we find that they can display significant differences in the dynamics of output even within the same historical framework. Each of the continents, moreover, has varied through time. Only recently, and still on a limited scale, have economic phases been synchronized. In light of this, when we deal with the same indicators of the growth rate of world output over decades or centuries, we are in fact seeing the averages of acceleration in some places and slowdowns in others. At present—for instance, let's say, over the last twenty years—the generally dynamic world economy is a derivative of a simultaneous acceleration in China and a slowdown in Europe.

In this regard, the twentieth century was hardly uniform. In calendar terms, it began in 1901 (and not 1900, as is usually stated erroneously), although the nineteenth century is often said not to have ended in political and economic terms until 1913. Those thirteen years have more in common politically, culturally, and economically with the preceding century than with the new one. The years 1900–1913 were a time of significant expansion in the world economy, characterized by the broadening of markets and the growth of international interconnectedness. The world per capita GDP was growing at an average of 1.5 percent annually, compared with only 0.9 percent during the thirty-seven dark years of the two world wars and the Great Depression.

The second half of the twentieth century was not homogeneous either, with 1973 being a special year. The price of oil quadrupled after the latest conflict and crisis in the Middle East, with all the consequences for profitability and the tempo of growth; additionally, and more important, it made pro-productivity structural reforms imperative. These reforms occurred mostly in the developed market economies, although they too suffered as the vigor of the postwar boom petered out and they shifted to the slower growth rate of the last quarter century. The per capita growth rate for the world as a whole from 1951 to 1973 was no less than 2.9 percent annually, whereas it fell between 1974 and 2000 to only 1.4 percent, a slower rate than at the beginning of the century. This was still far higher than the average for the whole millennium that was coming to an end. During the medieval stagnation in the first five centuries of that period, growth was only vestigial, at 0.05 percent. During the last 200 years, as we know, it has been 1.17 percent per year. The average annual growth for the whole last millennium was 0.26 percent annually. Against this background, the years 1951–1973 constitute a veritable boom—as do the years that followed.

For purposes of statistical analysis and comparison, the entire population can be divided into quantitatively equal groups. One fourth of the population is a quartile. In other words, a quartile is 25 percent of the population. If we arrange them according to the average level of income, we obtain a ranked group of quartiles from the lowest to the highest incomes. The average annual income for the poorest 25 percent of the world population at the turn of the nineteenth and twentieth centuries (when about 400 million people comprised each quartile) was slightly above $700—that is, the same as the average for the entire world both 900 and 1900 years earlier. By the turn of the twentieth and twenty-first centuries, this had risen to about $3,100.[16] For the highest quartile, the figures were $6,300 and almost $32,000, respectively. That $3,100, the average income of our 1.6 billion fellow human beings in the year 2000, was about one third more than the income of the third quartile—fairly well-off people—100 years earlier. This shows the great scale of progress.

If a person regarded as wealthy 100 years ago were to visit one of her descendants today—someone who had fallen, in all the vicissitudes of the twentieth century, into the middle class, and perhaps even the lower middle class—she would be shocked at such a high standard of living. She would see things that had not only been lacking in her own home, but that had not even existed, like a refrigerator, washing machine, radio, TV set, computer, cell phone, and a range of other sophisticated devices that had appeared in her own day but that were so rare that only a few people owned them. The majority of her contemporaries would have never even seen them, although they may have heard of them.

She would be amazed by the functionality of the kitchen and bathroom, with all their gadgets and conveniences. She would be impressed by a book collection as numerous as a rabbi's or a pastor's, but what would she think of a home cinema? She wouldn't be able to get over the amount of medication going to waste in the bathroom cabinet, since everyone around her would seem to be so fit and living so long. The young people bustling around the house would have some kind of device plugged into their ears and connected to a little sachet the size of a snuffbox that apparently emitted a cacophony of music; they would inform her that the music came from mp3s (?), before going on to tell her about how an electronic ticket (?) for traveling on a plane (?) had come by e-mail (?), and that they were leaving for a vacation during which they planned to go paragliding (?) along the shores of the Greek island of Rhodes, which they had been dreaming of doing their whole affluent lives, so that they could see the place where the Colossus used to stand, but that they had never been able to afford it until now. What had once been so far away and only for the select few was now close at hand, cheap, and for the many.

Our guest would be convinced that her great-great grandchild had struck it rich and must be some kind of plutocrat—except that she might wonder why he chose to live in such a tiny apartment, or even house, since she had owned a larger one. But she would certainly be agog at the way it was furnished and equipped with conveniences that its occupants treated as completely unremarkable.

Things work the other way around too. If a member of today's middle class liquidated his assets and traveled 100 years back in time, he would find that he could quickly set himself up as a man of wealth. Some would try to tax him and others to rob him, but all would envy him. Whether he would feel rich is an interesting question. Surely not—instead, he would be amazed that it is possible to live on such a basic level, and especially that life is possible at all without a radio, a TV, a car, credit cards, a cell phone, and especially the Internet, that seventh great invention in human history.

This is the result of economic development. The middle class in the early twenty-first century has a higher absolute standard of living than the wealthy of the early 1900s. There are even countries where it took far less than a century to make the leap. In some places, a single lifetime was enough to reach, in old age, a level that was regarded in childhood as wealthy.

We need not look far for examples. I well remember how, during my childhood vacations, I made excursions with my mother to a village near the Bory Tucholskie—as central a part of Central Europe as exists. As we jolted along on a horse-drawn, ladder-type wagon from Gródek to Krąplewice, I would shout, "Look! A brick house!" Now, when I drive through the same outlying suburbs of Warsaw on my way to work at the university, I exclaim to my daughter, "Look! A log cottage!" I have seen the first brick house and the last cottage. Times have changed, although they seem to be the same, because they're ours. How many of us, living in countries with a medium level of development or in highly developed nations in various places around the world, have been affected by similar changes, even if we cannot recognize them—or do not want to?

Today, when the standard of living is far higher, the people who ought to be happy do not feel at all wealthy. This is not only because their aspirations have risen, but also because riches have also been spiraling upward. Subjective wealth is perceived as drawing nearer to the desired level, and not as the objective distance from the lower, and sometimes significantly lower, standard of living in the past.

The poverty line has also been creeping upward, so that in the world's richest countries, like Great Britain or Australia, it is currently at a level of consumption that was once regarded as high. Similarly, contemporary poverty in Eastern Europe, if it could only be transported by time machine or through the memories of the elderly back to the period between World War I and World War II, would strike some as comfortably middle class and still others as affluent.

Being poor and being affluent are prime examples of relative concepts. In this they differ from absolute poverty, which has the same meaning today that it has always had, even in absolute terms. The poverty of Latin American or African rural districts often does not differ from that of decades or centuries ago. Urban poverty differs in the sense that it was once unknown, when today's cities with their hopeless slums did not exist. The poor of contemporary North America or Europe are completely different from the wretches described by Dickens or Hugo.

Someone desirous of seeing what the condition of the English working classes, described 160 years ago in a book of that title by Engels, really looked like could travel to or, even better, live for a time in the Calcutta slum perversely known as the "City of Joy,"[17] and take a good look around. One of the things such a traveler would notice is how many of the people living in extreme poverty are happy. That is because human happiness is not exclusively a function of economic situation—fortunately.

Where great economic progress is under way and, it would seem, where the level of social satisfaction accompanying the unprecedented rise in output should be high, we complain—sometimes a great deal. And we worry, among other things, about how to make ends meet, even when those ends are on a far, far higher level than they once were. So we blame ourselves or others, and count on having more. Is this the right thing to do? That depends on the point of view, and in making value judgments the view both backward and forward is notably shortsighted.

Complaining may well be a part of human nature, but it should never be confused with a critical attitude, which is something to be encouraged. You need some kind of basis for honest criticism, whereas you can complain without the slightest reason. It's just grumbling—or, as in politics, it comes from the need to enhance one's own position by undermining that of one's opponents. That is why the opposition party always and everywhere complains about whatever the government is doing, until they change places and therefore change their outlook. This is like children playing cops and robbers, except that it's for real, and the consequences are far more serious. Those who come to power quickly begin praising the way things are and claiming the credit for all the positives, of which they discover more and more. Those who land in the opposition quickly shift to complaining about the way things are, even if many of the existing shortcomings resulted from their own work. When we talk about whole nations, the rich ones tend to attribute their prosperity mainly to their own wisdom, resourcefulness, and hard work, whereas those left lagging behind prefer to blame others—external forces—for their poverty. They especially blame the wealthy foreigners.

———————

Against the background of our brief history of the world, we need to state the important conclusion that three of the fundamental assumptions of economics are oversimplifications. To put it another way, they are more expressive of our wishes, as economists, than of reality. These three fundamentals are

- The paradigm of the maximization of wealth as the driving force of the economy.
- The statement that rationality is the basis for making economic decisions.
- The belief that the market, with its mechanisms, is in itself a guarantee of effective governance.

In the first place, it is an oversimplification to state unconditionally that the pursuit of the wealth of nations is the driving force of history and, therefore, a stimulant of development. The acceptance of this paradigm lay at the foundations of classical economics, and questions about the sources and the means of increasing wealth became the constituent concerns of economics as a science.[18] In the real-world process, however, it is frequently not the desire for development that lies behind the actions taken and the decisions made, but rather the desire for domination, which can also be achieved through the destruction of others. Other issues are connected with the collision of disparate spiritual values and hostile ideologies, or simply with doctrinaire attitudes. Even if the desire for wealth is the goal of microeconomic activity (at the level of companies, households, and individuals), it need not necessarily be so in the macroeconomic dimension (at the level of states and nations, and especially of the whole global economy). If it were, we would all be rich.

Secondly, another fundamental assumption of economics, that rationality is the basis for decision making, must also be hedged with numerous reservations. It may hold true on the microeconomic scale, although there is often a shortage of rationality even there, as demonstrated by the frequency of bankruptcy. A great many of the decisions taken in companies are irrational not because of the ever-present limitations on or distortion of information, but because of shortsightedness, greed, and ignorance. In economic policy, which along with entrepreneurship is the greatest determinant of development, numerous decisions are far from optimal from the point of view of the processes of reproduction. Macroeconomic decisions are frequently more a function of a peculiar political logic than of pure economic rationality. Political decisions, in turn, are frequently more a function of the dominant ideology or the particular interests of the dominant group than of pragmatic logic. If the ideology is progressive in orientation, forward looking, then it may represent a vision of the world that lies at the basis of pragmatic logic. This is sometimes the case, although not always or everywhere. When it has been possible in some given country and at some given time to bring this logic and rationality together, the scale of economic growth and social progress has risen immediately. Unfortunately, when we look more closely at history—both the long-ago and the completely recent—we are immediately struck by the fact that irrationality is hardly anything exceptional. Sometimes it is downright prevalent. There are beneficiaries and advocates of irrationality. For this reason it is sometimes even presented—up to a point—as rationality.

The third reservation concerns the assumption, often accepted uncritically, that markets, by their essence, are always effective. They are not, although they can be. This happens to markets more frequently and easily to the degree that they are regulated and supplied with the appropriate institutional safeguards by a progressive state. Markets in themselves provide no automatic guarantees of effectiveness and equilibrium, not to mention harmony. Our concise history clearly demonstrates this. Interestingly, Adam Smith (1723–1790) himself pointed this out. Today he must be turning over in his grave, if the little cemetery in Edinburgh can be reached by the neoliberal literature, so remote from the spirit and the letter of his teachings are the attempts to persuade people that the best course is to leave everything—or almost everything—to private capital and the invisible hand of the market. History has turned out best for those who have left to the market only as much as they needed to—no more and no less, both when economies were national and diffuse and when they became ever more susceptible to global influences.

Finally, this brief but fascinating history offers the general lesson that there is no certainty in the long perspective as to "who will be on top" next. Economic historians stress the fact that 1,000 years ago the chances of Europe dominating the world were next to zero.[19] Five centuries later they were about even, and soon afterward they became fact. A thousand years ago the Chinese or Islamic civilizations had far better prospects for expansion and domination. Things turned out differently. Today we know how, and we have a better and better understanding of why. How will they turn out in the future? We do not know. What we do know is that history, like time, flows in only one direction, forward. We also know that the same is true of the direction of the flow in economic history, but that economic history, like physical time, does not progress uniformly or always in a straight line. There have been, and will be, both acceleration and slowing. There have been, and will be, rises and falls. There have been, and will be, development and stagnation. Above all, the processes have proceeded unevenly in time and space. And so it will be in the future.

At present, the chances of Africa dominating the world are close to zero. So it will remain in the foreseeable, or even the conceivable future. Yet it need not always be so. Not long ago, the chances of North America losing its dominant position were negligible. Today they are almost a certainty. The chances are also growing of the world being dominated by Asia—or more precisely, by a part of Asia, as was the case with parts of Europe or America. Development and stagnation, after all, are not contiguous with continental boundaries. This will remain true in the future.

Another reason for this is the fact that, over time—and in the very long term—climatic conditions will play a diminishing role, as was the case with geographical conditions over the preceding 1,000 years. Yet again, what was once unimaginable will, at some point, become doable.

Even when things seem obvious, it is better to make sure that they are. The point is that this historical journey should have begun—and might as well end—by emphasizing the fundamental significance of climatic conditions in growth and development. Silicon Valley could not have sprung up in the Sahara or on Spitsbergen, and not even Swiss cheese or watches could be made there, not to mention the banks. Those are beautiful places, perhaps the most beautiful places in the world, but the agricultural products needed to support a population could not be produced there, nor could the factories that employ people operate there, nor could the postindustrial economy of interchanging services flourish there.

Specific branches of production and services have always arisen where, and only where, they are needed. At the same time, they have arisen only where they were physically—and climatically—possible. Technology is changing this. Whereas banks, for these two reasons, first appeared in Arabian and, later, Italian cities, they could just as well function today in Siberia, servicing transactions all over the world. To the degree that precision industry could arise in Europe and North America, its continuation in the form of electronics, both hardware and software, can now thrive in the parts of southern India that were once "unsuitable for living."

All of this had to come about and ripen in a prolonged process in places where natural conditions permitted (and where there were other favorable factors as well). If we swapped the Germans for the inhabitants of their old colony of Tanganyika (which they "civilized," and how!), we would quickly learn that the Germans were incapable of developing a Ruhr or a Saarland in Africa. However, viewing the exchange from the other perspective, we would learn, equally quickly, that merely changing one climate for another, more amenable to hard work, is still insufficient for economic expansion. If we could, let us say, relocate all the Hutu, Tutsi, and Twa from Rwanda and Burundi to Flanders and Wallonia, then Belgium would not be such a highly developed country. Nor would the Belgians create a highly developed economy on the banks of Lake Kivu and Lake Tanganyika. For the same sorts of reasons, the Boers (mostly originating in Holland, but also in neighboring Flanders) were successful in the far more propitious climate of South Africa.

It is impossible to work efficiently in extreme climatic conditions. To this day, curses are leveled at those who decided to found the city of Phoenix—named for a bird that rises from ashes—in the desert, sentencing future generations to settle there as if there were no alternatives available in what then seemed like the endless tracts of America. To this day, it is impossible not to be staggered by the fact that Timbuktu managed to thrive where it is—it may have a river nearby, but it's still in the middle of the desert. Both of these exceptions show us that great climatic obstacles may sometimes be surmounted—only sometimes, and only partially, and at great cost, as long as it pays to do so at a certain moment.

Often, doing so is not only unprofitable, but also downright impossible. The earth is constructed in such a way that it is possible to live, and to work, only in the places with a "human" climate. Generally speaking, higher levels of technology have steadily expanded this zone over the course of history. I say "generally" because the devastating effect on the natural environment of human economic activity has rendered some previously livable regions intolerable, not only in places where some ancient civilizations, like the Sumerian, flourished, but also where people busily plied their trades even a few decades ago, or less, such as the vicinity of the disappearing Aral Sea on the borders of Uzbekistan and Kazakhstan, or the margins of the Sahel that are undergoing rapid desertification. Similarly, pillaging exploitation has already degraded plots of land in the Amazon that have only just been claimed from the tropical jungle.

Even today it is impossible to work well, and difficult to live, on the greater part of the earth's surface. This was all the more so in the past, with less capital, lower technology, and more limited adaptation strategies. This is why we shouldn't expect economic breakthroughs to take place in locations where they will never take place. We should be full of admiration for the hardiness of the bodies and souls of the Africans from the Hamar tribe who live year round in the sweltering Omo Valley in southern Ethiopia or the Uru Indians who exist on the floating islands of Lake Titicaca in the Andes, as well as for the Tibetans who live and work year round at more than 4,000 meters above sea level, or the Inuit (also known as Eskimos), who live nearly half the year in the darkness of the polar night in the far north of Alaska. One can live anywhere, as I myself have experienced for brief periods in those places—even with great pleasure. Yet it has been impossible—and is still impractical—to carry out economic activity in ways that are possible in other places, where the natural conditions are different.

Productive agriculture, providing the foundations for later industrialization and urbanization, could develop in times gone by in the temperate climate of Europe, but not in the parts of Africa overgrown with tropical jungles, or in equatorial Asia or South America. Manhattan could not have been built in the Gobi or in Greenland, the snow- and ice-covered island that Eric the Red, that jocular Viking, called "Green" 1,000 years ago. New York could, however, have stood, for example, at the mouth of the River Plate, which ended up with nothing more than Buenos Aires and Montevideo, or on the far side of the world, where Sydney was later founded. New York is exactly where it is because of the climate and the winds that blew the enterprising Europeans precisely there, just when they did—which was the right time.

Although physical time passes the same as it did 1,000 or 10,000 years ago, the economic clock is ticking faster than it did a century or even a decade ago.

Time flies in the globalized economy. Times have changed.

CHAPTER FOUR

Globalization—and Then What?

Where Globalization Originated and How to Come Out Ahead in the Era of Worldwide Interdependence

Globalization doesn't have a human face,
but it's worth imagining one.

THIS IS A WAY of expressing the conviction that it is desirable for the functioning and expansion of the world economy to be accompanied by economic good sense, and by authentic concern for the social dimension of governance. It should be read as a suggestion of the direction in which we should move, an emphasis on where we should direct more attention in the future. There can be no doubt that the continuation of globalization following the existing model is impossible. It would lead us into the wilderness, and this would be exceptionally brutal, simply "inhuman," in the case of the world economy. Individuals, or groups of people, or whole regions may stray into the wilderness, but not the whole world.

Before going any further, we should provide sufficiently unambiguous definitions of the concepts we are using. Few words have had such careers as *globalization*. In our lifetime, it is without doubt the most popular term to describe the broadest, worldwide dimension of a rapidly changing reality—not only economic, but also cultural, social, and political. This in itself is a source of various problems. Because the process—and we are talking about a process—affects many areas of human public activity, it falls within the purview of a range of disciplines, from history to political science, from sociology to psychology, from web science to management, and even ecology and theology—as well as, above all and of course, economics. Consequently, globalization has more than one face. It seems different, depending on the angle from which you look at it, which makes the interdisciplinary approach all the more essential to understand it fully.

The most intriguing thing for us is the economic dimension. Here, however, the concept is used rather loosely, if not abused. Particularly irritating in this regard is the frequent appearance, even in scholarly studies, of such expressions as "the globalization of the world economy" or "the globalization of the world." This is pure tautology—using the definition of something to define it. Empty words. "The world" is global by its very essence, which is why it's called "the globe," as well as by definition. "Globalizing the world" makes exactly as much sense as "worldizing the globe."

However, since there is no such verb as "to worldize," we talk about globalizing. Not all that long ago, the word *globalization* and its equivalents in other languages did not exist. The English word *globalization* was probably used for the first time in *The Economist* as long ago as 1959,[1] and it was already in the 1961 *Webster's Dictionary.* Thirty years later, however, when it was already in circulation, it did not merit a place in the dictionary of "contemporary economics" prepared by a stellar team from MIT.[2] Hardly anyone has suggested any origin for the concept outside the English-speaking world, where it indubitably arose. From there, as well, came the processes that were crucial for globalization, and the particular configuration of those processes made it possible to notice that something like "globalization" was taking place.

Back then, in the early 1990s, such concepts as "internationalization" or "transnational" sufficed. At Polish universities, they still taught IER, or "International Economic Relations," and American course catalogues listed "International Economics." Later, this subject began to be called "globalization" or something similar, although there were faculty members who continued to use their old, only slightly updated lecture notes when teaching under the new label. This is a source of interpretative misunderstandings and methodological errors, especially when someone thinks that globalization is merely internationalization on a grander scale. In fact, it is qualitatively new. If you Google "globalization," you get 13.9 million results in 0.17 seconds. A great proportion of them, of course, have nothing to do with globalization.

Most frequently, it is life—real or imagined—that creates concepts; before something gets a name, it is already happening, or at least running around inside our minds. Sometimes, it all happened long ago and managed to fade away into the recesses of history before being described, understood, and named. It has also been true that all of humanity, including the best minds—economists and historians as well—lived in an epoch without knowing what it was called, or rather what it would someday be called. Plato (427–347 BCE) had no idea—although he had ideas about many things—that he was living in antiquity, and Gallus Anonymus never dreamed that he was chronicling Polish history in the Middle Ages. Nor did anyone know that they were living in the era of feudalism. In his letters on the French parliament, published in 1727, Count Henri de Boulainvilliers (1658–1722) was the first to use *feudalism* in its present meaning, as the definition of a socioeconomic system.

In the case of globalization, about which so many of our contemporaries have so much to say and write, the process was accurately named before it was fully understood and described—something we are still a long way from accomplishing. Nor do we know what epoch we are living in. Some go so far as to speak of a special kind of "interepoch," when the old one has ended and the new one has not yet been born, or at least has not yet crystallized. Someday someone will name it so that it becomes universally accepted. It will not be globalization. That word denotes neither a socioeconomic system nor an epoch, but rather a process, or something leading somewhere. We live in times of globalization, just as our forebears lived, for example, in times of colonial conquest or industrialization. Those were only processes that led to qualitatively new systems—in the first case, colonialism, and in the second, capitalism.

The evolution of capitalism led to such advanced productive forces and production relations that, almost 100 years ago, Lenin formulated the theory of imperialism, in which he pointed out several characteristics that distinguished the epoch. He particularly emphasized the following:

1. The rise of monopolies as a result of the centralization and concentration of capital.

2. The birth of oligarchies and finance capital as a result of the fusion of bank and industrial capital.
3. The expansion of the transfer (export) of capital.
4. The creation of supranational corporations that divided up their influence over the world market.
5. The completion of the territorial division of the world among the largest capitalist powers.[3]

It is hard to deny the accuracy of this characterization, or of the analyses of the reality of the time that led to it. Nor is there any way of failing to discern the suitability of some of these characteristics for the analysis of the present. The tremendous difference between then and now had to do with the fact that then, a century ago, nation-states, especially the most powerful ones, with imperial ambitions and interests, dominated the global stage. Then it was the owners of supranational companies and international investors, although they were growing in power, who more frequently cooled their heels in the waiting rooms of politicians, whereas things now tend to be the other way around. At present, as never before in history, international capital has freedom of choice. Nor is this a narrow margin of choice—whether, for instance, to invest in Normandy or colonial Algeria—but rather of where in the whole wide world to invest, often without even taking states and their governments into consideration. The latter have less and less choice. Power belongs to those who have freedom of choice.

However, Lenin, along with many of the others who aspired to power and to a better world, was wrong when he labeled imperialism "the highest stage" and concluded that the inevitable end of the capitalist formation was just around the corner. Originally, in his manuscript in Russian, Lenin titled his work *Imperializm kak novieyshaya stadiya kapitalizma*—and thus not the "highest," but rather the "latest" stage. The term *separate stage* (Russian *otdielnaya stadiya*) also appeared here. However, the confident arguments advanced about it being the final stage, especially after the victory of the Bolshevik revolution, ensured that the book appeared everywhere—in Lenin's lifetime and forever after—with the word *highest* in the title, accentuating what was in fact its main thesis. Words have meaning.

The fact is that capitalism later passed through difficult stages and disenchanted even its greatest proponents—during the crash and depression of 1929–1933; in the rise of aggressive fascism, Nazism, and militarism; during World War II; and during the years of sharp competition when socialism seemed for long periods to have the upper hand. In the end, however, capitalism dragged itself through these decades of setbacks and deviations, and then led the world economy to its present condition. Its visage continues to change, which is precisely because of the influence of globalization.

If Lenin were alive today, he would probably have titled his book *Globalization as the Highest Stage of Imperialism*. All of Lenin's values and categories point in this direction. However, the system and the structures emerging as a result of the process of globalization are not final. They will continue to evolve, in qualitative as well as quantitative terms. Some people already in the past thought that Lenin was wrong. Shortly after Ghana gained independence half a century ago, the great revolutionary leader of this country, Kwame Nkrumah, published a book with the noteworthy title *Neocolonialism: The Last Stage of Imperialism*.[4] Following this line of thought, we now see contributions to the discussion with titles like "Globalization as the Highest Stage of Neocolonialism." Something, someday, should become "The Highest Stage of Globalization." What would it be?

We must be aware that new entities will come into existence in the evolution of the globalization process, the size of the human population, and the world economy. Today we cannot predict what these will be. Instead, what we should predict is the mass of significant problems that globalization will inevitably bring in its wake. Like all the great processes of complex economic transformations in human history so far, it will solve some problems while creating others. When the number of problems being created exceeds the number of problems being solved, the process breaks down, the economy collapses, and the system fades away. The same thing will happen to globalization someday. First, however, a great deal of water will flow under the bridge, because globalization is far from exhausting its potential for expansion.

What, then, is globalization? How can we define it on economic grounds? What gets "globalized" is above all, but not only, the economy and the market. Globalization is a movement aimed at limiting and abolishing limitations in international economic exchange. This applies to overcoming natural and physical barriers, as a result of which fewer and fewer things are "over the hills and far away," and more and more seem to be close at hand. Technical progress plays a large role here. Yet it is not enough, unless a second condition is met—the abolishing of man-made political barriers. Thus, globalization is a historical and spontaneous process of liberalization, along with the accompanying, systematic integration into a single, interdependent global market in goods, capital, technology, information, and—belatedly and on a smaller scale—labor, which previously constituted markets that were isolated or bound by loose functional ties. Three of these words are crucial: *liberalization, integration,* and *interdependence.* Two more—*historical* and *spontaneous*—are important.

In the light of these definitions, we can see at once that globalization is far from complete. Moreover, it is internally uneven to the degree that the most powerful actor on the world stage, capital, has demanded and won far-reaching liberalization for its own movement, whereas labor remains bound in the corset of national restrictions, rather than being able to flow freely around the world. To remain on a purely economic footing—using exclusively economic arguments and applying them with honest consistency—then, in accordance with neoliberal doctrine, labor should have the same freedom of movement as capital. That is, it should be able to move wherever it chooses, without restrictions. To go even further, one might claim that this is one of the basic human rights, endowed by nature—people have a right to move around! After all, it was only after a certain time that some people began prohibiting others from appearing or settling in the bits of territory to which those first people had staked claim—first in small patches of land, but now on the scale of entire continents. Globalization will remain limited and flawed as long as restrictions are applied and people are not allowed to live and seek work wherever they like. Freedom means that there should be free choice in this regard as well. Capital has it, but labor—not in the least.

The completeness of contemporary globalization would therefore require abolishing discrimination in this area, opening the borders to completely untrammeled migration, and refraining from erecting any new fences. We managed to bring the Berlin Wall down, but new fences are still going up—here and there, with even more determination than before, such as on the border dividing the United States from Latin America. The opening of borders to the flow of people—as has already been done for capital—would change the face of the earth in a remarkable way within a generation or two. The mechanism of the global market would suck millions of people out of the poorest regions, especially in Africa and South and Central America. They would enlarge the supply of labor in North America and Europe in an unprecedented way. The increased supply would lead to a fall in its price—that is, in real wages. The wage level, in turn, would rise in the regions from which labor had flowed on a mass scale, because the supply would shrink. The result would be a noticeable diminution of the inequalities in the levels of income between these regions of the world. This is what happened in the eighteenth, and even more so in the nineteenth and twentieth centuries during the great migration from Europe to North America.

Will this ever happen? It is already under way. It is proving exceedingly difficult to restrain the avalanche-like exodus from Africa to Europe and from South America to North America. Democratic and peaceable methods are not working. The only effective preventive measure may be to improve the quality of life in the regions where it is so miserable that people, and especially young people, are ready to do almost anything, even at the risk of their lives, to get out. This would require a fundamentally different approach to long-term development. We would have to find a way to guarantee a clearly higher rate of growth in the poor countries than in the prosperous ones, and then put it into practice, rather than merely proclaiming it on paper and at conferences. This is the only way to close the gap in a visible, tangible way. Otherwise, the pressure for emigration will not only remain strong, but will become even stronger. Unfortunately, this is precisely what globalization has caused over the last quarter century.

Another reason for the incompleteness of globalization is that the liberalization of the agricultural sector is lagging far behind. It is still heavily subsidized in the wealthiest countries, which allocate about $400 billion per year to shore up agricultural production within their borders. This is one fifth more than the GDP of Poland, or nine times the GDP of the Congo, with its population of 66 million. This happens because full liberalization and the opening of agricultural markets to honest international competition would rapidly lead to the marginalization and, in extreme cases, the complete disappearance of agriculture in the most prosperous countries. These countries maintain their agricultural sectors (and the people who work there, and who vote in elections) only thanks to subsidies. This too must change. It is already changing, above all through the systematic but sluggish liberalization of the agricultural market and the modification of the antiproductivity Common Agricultural Policy of the European Union, which is extremely unjust in a global perspective. Much more remains to be done, in the United States and Japan as well as Europe. These countries are going to have to abolish their payments to the farmers who produce cotton or rice. The present discriminatory policies force peasants trying to make ends meet in the small plots of Mali or the rice paddies of Vietnam into poverty.

We must realize in this context that the incompleteness of globalization, which appears mainly—but not only—in the labor and agricultural markets, is going to create increasingly bitter political problems on a world scale. These problems have been looming for years, and the only thing we can expect in the foreseeable future is that they will escalate and perhaps get out of control. Emerging unscathed from the accumulating tensions will require coordinated action on a bilateral and multilateral scale. Political leaders have not yet shown themselves up to the task, and many intellectual and academic circles also seem incapable of understanding its implications fully. These circles prefer to discuss generalized issues in general terms and are far less willing to take up real, practical problems. It's easy to understand this, which is not the same as condoning it, by taking Poland as an example. Here too there are direct payments to agriculture, paid for by taxpayers from all over the European Union, and it is necessary to end them as quickly as possible. They make producers from other parts of the global economy less competitive. Nothing better illustrates the hypocrisy of concern for poor people on the other side of the global fence. The truth is that we worry more about significant improvements to the lot of a few in the middle class at home than about even a minor improvement in the lives of many poor people over there.

———————

So we know that the main attributes of globalization are liberalization, integration, and interdependence.

Liberalization—the process of broadening and deepening the freedom of various economic entities to enter into mutual technological, organizational, production, trade, financial, and investment relationships—is an essential initial condition for developing further, deeper economic ties. Directly connected with freedom and liberty, and sometimes dependent on them, liberalization must be viewed from multiple perspectives. It is a matter, above all, of freedom in the sphere of setting prices—and this includes the supranational perspective—in which the mechanism of the free market is indispensable. Yet this is also a matter of the freedom to enter into mutual relations with partners, especially through purchase and sales agreements for all kinds of goods and services.[5] These contracts must be seen in the broadest possible perspective, because their objects at present may be not only infrastructural capital, but also financial capital in all its forms. This is a matter, finally, of free, liberalized access to the conduct of economic activity—in other words, going freely (which does not mean in an unregulated way) into and out of business, including cases when there is no ability to continue in business (regulated bankruptcy procedures).

Integration—this is the process of combining various fragmentary markets in goods, capital, and, on a smaller scale, labor, into one large market. This is more than a matter of aggregating and mutually opening up local, national, and regional markets in the narrow meaning of the word. It also has to do with supporting this process by developing appropriate market rules for the economic game. This can often be followed up by creating structures that foster liberalization and integration, such as the World Trade Organization (WTO) or the International Labor Organization (ILO), as well as efforts to coordinate policies on a scale that, if not global, is at least international.

Such a market is open to penetration by streams of demand and supply flowing from a wide range of its fragmentary parts. An ideal, complete world market would be the place where one curve indicating aggregate demand for each product intersects the curve indicating aggregate supply. In such a literally uniform market, both of these streams would achieve equilibrium at the balance point indicated by the intersection of these two curves. This point would define a single price that cleaned out the market—everything that was offered would be sold, and everything for which there was a need would be supplied. There would be no superfluous stockpiles of surplus productive capacity; nor would there be unsatisfied demand or intentions of expenditure that could not be actualized. Things are not like this in reality, and never will be. It's pure fiction.

Local farmers' markets can operate this way, and—this is an effect of globalization—so can Internet auctions of the eBay variety; this is as close as we have come so far to a single, integrated, perfectly functioning global market free of asymmetry or information distortion. It's just like in classic mainstream economics textbooks. However, this is not the way real-world markets for the overwhelming majority of products operate. Their prices are formed under the influence of the local realities of supply and demand.

If the equilibrium in some portion of the world market is upset because of a preponderance of demand over supply, then (leaving aside the immediate pressure for an inflationary price rise) goods quickly flow in from other fragments of the same great market. This depends on the assumption, of course, that there is an abundance of them somewhere, or that existing but incompletely utilized productive capacity can immediately be mobilized to increase the supply. If it rains on the North Island of New Zealand and things get muddy, then a factory making galoshes in Warmia, Poland, can add a second and, if it pays, a third shift to increase production. The demand is over there and the supply is here, except that "there" and "here" have now become more or less the same place. If such a relatively large demand, with a tendency to exceed the supply provided by the local productive capacity, is structural and permanent in character, then it is not only the goods that will flow there, but also capital, technology, and—if necessary—qualified labor. The products that are in demand will be manufactured there, on the spot. In our example, if it turns out to be profitable after taking transport costs into account, then a Polish factory making galoshes could be built in the Antipodes. If the Poles don't do it, someone else will—the galoshes have to be there, because there are people who want to buy them.

That's why, instead of shipping Volkswagens from Germany to Brazil, the company built an assembly plant there. Instead of sending Swedish furniture to Italy, a factory was opened there. Instead of carting Mexican beer to the United States, ground was broken for a bottling plant there. Naturally, this trend did not induce Boeing to start producing airliners in Europe. This, however, is not because of a reluctance to add one more flight to the production process, but rather a reflection of concern for group interests, both local and national, as well as of sharp competition and restrictions that are still in effect. Globalization does not eliminate competition; instead it sharpens and changes it. There are more players on a much larger playing field, and they are playing for bigger prizes. This competition is less and less international and more and more global, because capital is increasingly supranational and often pays no mind to so-called national interests, even those of the most powerful nations. Now and then a national party or politician brings them up, but this often has less to do with authentic national interests and more to do with corruption and the protection of private interests.

On an even larger scale, decisions about locating manufacturing facilities abroad have to do with more complete cost accounting, which takes into consideration the costs of local labor and transport. Capital transfer, and especially direct investment, is usually accompanied by technology transfer, and the local political, institutional, and infrastructure conditions that make it possible to open a production line are the same factors that led Japanese, American, and western European companies to locate in Southeast Asia and China. To their pleasant surprise, it quickly emerged that these are also the areas of the most rapidly growing consumer-goods markets, as a result of both an unprecedented economic boom and the continuing demographic growth in that part of the world.

Thus it turns out that two intersecting waves are breaking over an increasingly integrated world market: demand and supply, coming from different directions and combining to make the level of the ocean rise and rise. World output is rising fairly rapidly, and that growth is driven to a large degree by "export." I put that word in quotation marks because one person's export is another's "import," and it's more accurate to speak about "trade exchange," especially when the subject of the analysis is the entire world, indeed the only closed economic zone. Everything else—such subsets as regions or countries—is more or less open.

This ocean is far from pacific. Nor was the ocean placid when the Spanish explorer Vasco Núñez de Balboa first descried it from the western shore of Panama in 1513 and cried out in amazement at how calm the waters were, "*Que pacífico!*" For many years afterward, that name led people into mistakes, because the only calm part of the ocean was what Balboa saw, from the shoreline to the horizon. Further out, there are always frictions and compensatory movements, and sometimes even raging storms, although the moderate, long waves that maintain an increasingly integrated market in relative equilibrium are dominant. It does not overflow its boundaries any more than the Pacific Ocean does. This happens when the mechanisms that balance out its dynamic currents prove inadequate. In the contemporary phase of globalization, these mechanisms function relatively well in regard to the world circulation of merchandise, which integrates within itself what traditional economics referred to as "domestic trade" and "foreign trade."

Just as we should avoid confusing integration with globalization, so should we remember that the progress of economic integration as a constituent part of globalization is nothing more nor less than the coming together of markets as a result of their opening, the raising of political and economic barriers (especially tariffs), the introduction of convertible currencies, and the lowering of the costs of transport and communication. It is also a matter of creating integrated international institutions. The most advanced, and therefore the best example of this in the present-day world is the European Union. However, it represents, at best, "Europeanization," rather than globalization. Furthermore, it is still far from complete; a dozen or more nation-states in Europe and on its periphery remain outside the group, and work also remains to be done inside the twenty-seven member states.

Contemporary European integration is still halfway along the road that was followed in North America, and that has not yet been traveled to the end in South America (although it may be someday). In the North American case, the original thirteen territories of highly varying characteristics, later rising to fifty (some of them former British and French colonies, others seized at gunpoint from the descendants of the Spanish conquistadors, and others still as exotic as the former Russian possession of Alaska or the Polynesian island kingdom of Hawaii that had been colonized by the Americans themselves), were assembled into the United States of America. Farther to the north, Canada came into being when nine provinces and three territories formed an integrated whole.

In the case of South America, the emancipation of the former colonies of Spain and Portugal, along with Guyana, which was divided between the British, the French, and the Dutch, led to the rise of a dozen independent states (French Guyana remains overseas metropolitan territory—in other words, a colony) that have not coalesced into a single continental economic organism. It is true that regional entities, with Mercosur being the largest, have come into being. This common "southern common market," with its rather loose connections and weak institutions, is made up of Argentina, Brazil, Paraguay, Uruguay, and Venezuela, with the remaining Latin countries of Bolivia, Chile, Ecuador, Columbia, and Peru as associate members. However, a sizable chunk of Central America, with a population of 135 million, remains outside its scope. This is the result of a particular set of circumstances, originally political and cultural, but later economic as well.

It is not hard to imagine a different arrangement of circumstances that could have led to the rise of a unified South American market and an atomized North America. The former could have been based on deep cultural ties, a common currency (let us call it the bolivar), and a solid structure resting on the domestic economy of a single state, the United States of South and Central America (USSCE), stretching from Tierra del Fuego to the Rio Grande. On the far bank (or perhaps on the other side of the fence) would lie Spanish-speaking Texas, Arizona, and California, with Florida a little farther away, in addition to French-speaking Louisiana and Missouri, Anglo-Saxon New England along with the northern and eastern states, Russian-speaking Alaska, and Polynesian-speaking Hawaii. It might even have proved possible to preserve some of the indigenous tribes from extermination, so that we could have an independent Dakota where the Sioux still spoke their native language, or perhaps the Omaha would still be at home in Nebraska, which would not have become the thirty-seventh state 140 years ago. Each of these countries would have its own currency, institutions, and interests. The cultural differences among them would be greater than those among the countries of present-day Latin America, because the renowned American ethnic and cultural "melting pot" would never have come about. As a result, there would also be greater or lesser differences in economic policy. The aggregated flows and stocks, and in turn the incomes and national wealth of these countries, would surely be less than today, since that real-world economy is the result of the full integration—in this case, the "Americanization"—of North America.

South America never integrated fully, although some have dreamed of this. They still dream, and if these dreams ever lead to deeds, then something may yet come of it. Almost two centuries ago, the great South American hero Simón Bolívar, *El Libertador*, wanted to create a large state, *Colombia la Grande*, out of the lands liberated from the colonial yoke. Its foundations collapsed like a house of cards because of internal dissension and intrigues. When Bolívar lay dying at the age of 47 in 1830, he said that creating Greater Colombia out of the territory of what today is Panama, Colombia, Venezuela, Ecuador, and parts of Peru and Bolivia, was easy, but keeping it was unimaginably difficult. He added sarcastically: "There have been three great fools in history—Jesus, Don Quixote, and me."

The positive effects of a uniform market—with its structures, institutions, regulations, and intentions—therefore never had the chance to develop. Leaving aside cultural conditions and the unequal level of natural resources, this fact explains the significant differences in levels of development between these regions of the globe. Where there is more integration, there is more prosperity. Full integration means more than a larger market and the resulting benefits in terms of scale of manufacturing, or so-called economies of scale. It also means lower transaction costs and greater predictability in the areas of production and trade relations. Companies in California do not have to worry about unfavorable changes in the rate of exchange in relation to the currency in New York, because they use the same Yankee dollar. Manufacturers in Patagonia have problems with the competitiveness of their exports if the rate of exchange of the Argentine peso falls in relation to the Brazilian real in São Paulo—or vice versa, because exchange rates can go up as well as down. A unified market also means fewer risks of conflict over economic issues. When needed, an arbiter in the shape of the federal government can settle differences in a way that is both pro-growth and fair, as long as we manage to avoid the dangers of excessive red tape, corruption, or the favoring of special interests over the common good.

In the cultural, social, and political dimensions as well, the "Americanization" of North America has been fully successful. There is still no shortage of problems. Nor can we forget that, in the historical perspective, this success is founded on the elimination in a genocidal way of up to 10 million Native Americans, or, according to some estimates, even more. Today, nevertheless, if the world consisted only of North America, we would say that globalization had been completed. This is the best and briefest way of explaining the sense of the process. It is also a basis for pointing out where a hypothetical, centuries-long, historical process of globalization might lead. But it will not lead there. It's too late for that, because there are still too many contradictions that are antagonistic and insoluble under the present system, and they cannot be solved in the American way. Or, from a different perspective, it is still whole centuries too early for that, because these contradictions remain too large.

Yet time keeps passing, and quickly. A hundred and sixty years ago, Marx and Engels published the *Communist Manifesto*.[6] It begins with words that then terrified both the left and the right, but especially the right: "A specter is haunting Europe—the specter of communism." Marx and Engels themselves were hardly terrified, and they ended their manifesto with the exhortation: "Workers of the world, unite!" For decades, the left-wing press, especially the socialist and communist press, had this slogan in their masthead. Although the global proletariat never managed to unite effectively against exploitation by private capital, it was united, in a paradoxical sense, by that very same capital in the global market. It is true that the proletariat has been subordinated, above all, to the interests of those against whom it was supposed to unite, but this is neither the first nor the last time in history that things have turned out the other way around. Progress in the integration of the world economy—and this applies to the labor market as well—is greater now than ever before. Having proved unable to unite on the communist model, workers in all (or almost all) countries have been united by numerous other bonds of interdependence. The supply of labor, and thus the possibilities for employment, or in other words, the price of labor (wages), in any given part of the world is increasingly dependent on what happens elsewhere.

Since Marx and Engels, in a mere six generations, the techniques and technology of production have changed fundamentally, and with them, social relations. The classics of Marxism would tell us that the base (productive capacity and the corresponding relations of production) and the superstructure (political values, institutions, and relations) have undergone a thorough transfiguration. These changes on the scale of generations brought in their wake a fundamental reconstruction of the social structure of the working and nonworking people of the cities and the countryside. There has been a distinct fall in the number of workers or, in broader terms, of wage earners, the hired labor force, or so-called salariat. The middle class has expanded in both relative and absolute terms. Its present membership is more numerous than all of humanity was at the time when Marx and Engels outlined their far-reaching vision on the crest of the Spring of Nations. Then there were 1.25 billion of us. Now we are 6.5 billion—more than five times as many. Thus, in dialectical terms, which are still relevant, there has been a profound change in both quantity and quality. The most intriguing thing in all of this is that the potential for revolution will increase again. It is already doing so—because the original communist unification of the workers was a clear failure, and the unification tailored to the results of globalization is clearly faulty in social terms.

Interdependence—a combination of cause-effect relationships and feedback mechanisms between phenomena and processes occurring at various places in the global space—is the third attribute of globalization. It is fascinating that observations about these kinds of connections were already being made over two millennia ago. Polybius of Megalopolis, a Greek historian and chronicler of Rome who lived between about 200 BCE and 118 BCE, asserted that "earlier events that have occurred in the world were almost never connected with each other, whereas everything is part of a whole now."[7] Multitudes of people have been born since Polybius's "now," and our world has expanded from the Mediterranean to the entire planet—although there seem to be people who hold the opinion that it has ceased to be spherical. Some, like the Anuak people in western Ethiopia, are deeply convinced that, if you trek far enough, you come to the edge of the world and can fall into the abyss; others, like the American journalist Thomas L. Friedman, make the ironic point that the world is once again becoming flat.[8] In all seriousness, it now seems as if the world is complete, at least until the moment when we enter into extraterrestrial relations, which we shall leave out of our considerations for the time being. This is the only world we have.

Interdependence characterizes not only economic, but also cultural and political events. Almost the entirety of humanity can watch the opening ceremonies of the Beijing Olympics or the live broadcast of the terrorist attacks on the World Trade Center. We can speculate about who will win an Oscar or meet in virtual space on the Internet to chat. We can have an influence on elections in Ukraine (democratic, if anyone should ask) or press for the fall of the Mugabe regime in Zimbabwe. In economics, a complex chain of connections among supply, demand, and the prices of goods and services in different fragments of the global market is emerging. Each of these fundamental categories—supply, demand, and price—is so thoroughly connected that it can depend, in part, on things that seem to happen elsewhere. "Seem to," because "elsewhere" increasingly frequently means "here" nowadays, not far away at all. In the long run, in turn, the interaction of demand, supply, and price has an indirect influence on technology, manufacturing, trends in research and education, and models of consumption and behavior.

Interdependence sometimes follows a very winding trail. Occasionally the path is almost completely overlooked in analyses, and therefore is largely unknown. Two centuries ago, imperialist skirmishes and wars between England and France led to a rise in the price of sugar made from cane cut by slaves on plantations in the Caribbean, and this in turn led to the abolition of slavery. It became more profitable in the early nineteenth century to make sugar from sugar beets grown in Eastern Europe. The fall in demand for cane sugar undercut the position and power of the Caribbean plantation owners. At the same time, the abolition movement was growing on both the Caribbean and the British islands. As we know, slavery was abolished in England in 1807. In that phase of globalization, Eastern Europe unintentionally contributed to the end of the shameful institution in the West Indies. In the final analysis, it had nothing to do with the fact that the Polish soldiers sent by Napoleon (1769–1821) in the thousands to Haiti as an expeditionary corps in 1803 realized that they were fighting and dying there not for the sublime ideas of the Revolution, but in defense of the banal interests of Bordeaux merchants. Poles went over to the side of the rebellious General Toussaint L'Ouverture, himself born a slave, who was fighting against the colonists. The son of a man enslaved and abducted in Senegal, Toussaint was a great warrior against slavery, but an even greater contribution to the end of that institution resulted from the supply-demand relationship and the relative profitability of cane and beet sugar. Slavery flourished as a result of transatlantic expansion and global trade, and it began to wither in a specific set of circumstances, when certain things happened at the same time. Polish sugar beets played their part.

Returning to the present, the price of fuel at a gas station in Vienna depends on more than just the supply of petroleum on the market in Rotterdam, in the same way that the price of coffee in the nearest supermarket depends on more than just the size of the crop in Brazil. Today the supply of garments from China determines the level of employment at textile mills in Mexico, wages in the American automobile industry are determined by the numbers of cars rolling off the assembly lines in Japan, and the privatization of mines in Yakutia determines the price of diamonds on Fifth Avenue. The development of whole industries in a given country is a function of the level of demand in other countries. The level of unemployment in Europe depends on the size of the workforce in Asia. Dubliners looking for a place to invest their money fuel the speculative boom in apartment prices in Poland, and people from Warsaw drive up housing prices in Lviv. Then they all join together to put pressure on prices in western Siberia. Decisions by one government affect the economies of other countries. By manipulating interest rates and their reserves, central banks influence the price of money—in other words, the exchange rates in other countries. Although trade unions played no small role in the systemic transformation and the emergence of capitalist market economies in our part of the world, nothing can save them from marginalization as a result of the competitive pressure from other emerging markets, which is felt more sharply than ever before. There is also cheap labor in those places—sometimes far cheaper—and this makes employment both here and there interdependent. We are all riding in the same global vehicle.

The interdependence of the world market is particularly visible in the case of the converging financial markets.[9] The liberalization and deregulation of those markets, followed by the integration resulting from the convertibility of national currencies and the information revolution, led to a chain reaction. To an increasing degree, saving, borrowing, and investing take place in a system of global interconnection. It is by now not only on the scale of national economies, but also on that of the world economy that a dependency obtains under which ex post facto investment always equals savings. Everything that is saved somewhere will be invested somewhere. However, the process of transforming savings into investment has also become global. This means that the financial intermediary agencies in the shape of various segments of the interdependent capital market—banks, markets, investment funds, and a variety of speculators and investors—are globalized.

The financial crisis of the 1990s—with its deleterious effects on the real world in terms of employment levels, output, and consumption, first in the countries of Southeast Asia and later in some other parts of the world, as a result of the spreading wave of its repercussions—was very much a symptom of the operation of a mechanism that adjusts the level of investment ex post facto to the amount of savings. Taking into account the state of financial disequilibrium embodied especially in the enormous budget and trade deficits of the United States, we are facing crises on an even greater scale. There is no longer any way to avoid the consequences, precisely because of the simultaneous antagonistic conflict of interests and the interdependence of phenomena and processes. Because we are all sailing on the same ocean, it makes no difference where the wave comes from—whether it is a storm wave caused by the wind or a tsunami caused by an earthquake. One way or another, the wave breaks and crashes through the interdependent market, with all the consequences.

This does not mean in the least that everything depends on everything else. It doesn't. Nor does it free the governments of states and their independent central banks from the clear responsibility for their own mistakes, just as the boards of directors of corporations and companies cannot use globalization as camouflage for their own managerial incompetence, and especially for failing to adapt to changing economic conditions. Managing in conditions of uncertainty requires skill, and the phenomenon of interdependence raises the bar dramatically. When everything is held to depend on everything else, it can be claimed that nothing depends on us. However, we should pinpoint the reasons for success and failure and not blame our homegrown bumbling on globalization.

Nor does this mean that we can locate the cause of any single phenomenon in some other, completely unconnected phenomenon that merely happens to occur at the same time. Illusory interpretations of interdependence drawn from this kind of erroneous thinking are numerous. This is often a simple post hoc, ergo propter hoc—"subsequent to, and therefore because of"—error in logic. We should avoid searching for interdependences between the contemporary world economy and the ever-changing face of the process of globalization, all the more so because such naïve interpretations seem to be in fashion.

It sometimes seems that even the most blatant nonsense is condoned. For example, the normal oscillations in the exchange rate of the Polish zloty by a few tenths of a percent, undeniably resulting from trivial speculative fluctuations in the market, must somehow be commented upon by the experts in the field, because they are expected to deliver regular doses of pabulum every day—at about 10 in the morning and 4 in the afternoon—that in turn can (or must) be passed on to the innocent readers, listeners, and viewers. The media ask, the analysts reply, the babble flows, and the paper and the ether comply. We come across interpretations of the following variety, as found in Polish news reports on a typical day—March 8, 2007:

The zloty weakened Wednesday morning. . . . According to analysts, our currency could decline further. . . . The weakening of the zloty and other emerging currencies in our region is a result of aversion to risk and the search by investors for safe investments following the incident in the Persian Gulf . . . after reports that the Iranian craft fired on the American ship, the Japanese yen began to strengthen, which had an immediate effect on the emerging markets, from which investors have begun to withdraw.

In the event, the yen did not in fact strengthen, nor did the zloty or any other East-Central European currency flinch in any perceptible way. Soon afterward, the zloty rose. As it turned out, no Iranian ship had even taken aim at the Americans. News stories of this ilk are merely destructive words that obscure reality.

Nevertheless, there is a constant stream of absurd commentaries from these financial analysts and the economists and journalists who serve as a transmission belt for them—all the more so because they can spout off with impunity and, as we know all too well, there is no shortage of demand for such chatter. Just as people are sometimes fooled into purchasing junk merchandise, so they allow themselves to fall for nonsense on the information market. Interestingly, it seems at times that those churning it out are more numerous than those who need protection from it—and all of this in conditions of freedom and democracy. It's as if there were more thieves than police—or perhaps there are. All of this results in myths and misunderstandings about what depends on what, even when the supposed interdependences being foisted on the public do not exist.

Globalization also means that the interdependent functioning of the economy, now worldwide in scale, creates worldwide problems. This applies to many countries and spills over beyond their borders. The vast extent of these problems and their sources, like their mechanisms and consequences, means that single countries or even groups of countries cannot solve them. This even applies to such powerful groupings as the European Union and the Group of Seven. The G-7 consists, in the order of the value of their output, of the United States, Japan, Germany, the United Kingdom, France, Italy, and Canada. For political reasons, Russia was invited to join in the mid-1990s, which gives us the G-8. Although these countries account for 43 percent of world output (the G-7 without Russia amounts to almost 41 percent; Russia has 2.7 percent), they cannot attack some problems effectively. In the political sphere, these problems include international terrorism and organized crime, which has economic consequences of its own.

On the economic level, this is above all a matter of the instability of the flow of speculative finance capital and the associated risks that financial crises could spread like epidemics. We experienced this in the late 1990s, when the wave of financial disturbances that began in Southeast Asia, and especially Thailand and Indonesia, broke all over the world; after Russia and Brazil came the turn of Argentina and Turkey. However, this wave of disturbances was also felt in many other countries on every continent, and in the world economy as a whole.

In the social and humanitarian spheres, there is a growing threat of mass diseases, fast-spreading epidemics, the many refugee crises with their destructive physical and psychological effects, and pornography, especially when it involves minors and children.

The most important of all these threats is climate change and global warming. This is more than an economic phenomenon, because its numerous implications are fundamental to the long-term survival of civilization on earth. This is a case where only coordinated, worldwide action can have the desired results. We already understand this. Unfortunately, we are not yet taking the correct actions on the appropriate global scale. Although the warming of the climate is not in itself caused by globalization, because it is a simple consequence of the expansion of certain methods of production, especially far-reaching industrialization and motorization, it will require a joint effort by all of humanity to slow down and reverse this dangerous tendency. Clearly, the populations of different parts of the world must take different kinds of action. In particular, the greatest burden falls on the G-8, the remaining countries of the European Union, and China and India, but everyone must join the fight for our future existence.

In the economic dimension, globalization means the spread of the capitalist system over increasingly large areas of the globe. A by-product is the continuing integration of local and regional economies in a single global configuration. The world economy consists to a lesser and lesser degree of some 200 national economies; increasingly, those economies are interdependent components. As a result, instead of talking about "domestic" and "foreign," we should speak in terms of "here" and "in other parts of the world economy." The world economy is increasingly "ours," and we function more and more within its framework. "Ours" doesn't mean in the least that we own it. Often more than in the past, the capital that functions in the wide world and circulates at a lightning pace is taken into possession by the powers of this common—or rather, interdependent—world.

However, globalization is not a new process. In the light of our definition, it seems in fact to have been ongoing, with only minor interruptions and setbacks, at least for five centuries. After the globalization of the era of great geographical discoveries that began at the turn of the fifteenth and sixteenth centuries, we had the second wave: the globalization of the era of great scientific-technological discoveries and applications. That phase of globalization culminated in the formation of the system of world capitalism and colonization. The structures and institutions were rules governing connections between the metropolis and the colonies, international trade, and the flow of capital—beginning at the pace of ships. This phase of permanent globalization shuddered to a halt in 1913, in a way that came as a shock to many, on the eve of World War I. Everything was supposed to be so wonderful! It seemed that the good times would keep rolling, that the numerous problems could be solved through compromise, and that the world economy would continue growing rapidly—with the benefits, naturally, accruing above all to the wealthy countries. In those days, not much attention was paid to the fate of other, less developed regions that were, in relative terms, far smaller than today. In those days, few politicians or other public personages even pretended to care, as their counterparts do today, about the fate of those regions.

The hard times—world wars, dictatorships, the Depression, extreme protectionism, and the closing down of the free exchange of ideas, people, and goods—did not last long. The present phase of permanent globalization followed. According to some authors, it began immediately after the end of World War II, during the initial far-reaching opening up and integration of the most highly developed capitalist economies, and the inclusion in their orbit of the Japanese and German economies as they repaired the wartime devastation. Soon afterward, in the 1960s, the economies of the independent countries emerging from the shadow of colonialism, though not all of them, joined on new principles. The so-called Third World opted in some cases for a noncapitalist path to development, forging not only political and military, but also economic links with the socialist bloc.

The very term *Third World* suggested aptly that there were more than one of these "worlds." The first one was that of advanced capitalism, and the second was that of real socialism. More and more people lived in the second world, not only because of high natural growth, but also because of the fact that the number of economies with a socialist orientation was growing. This led to sharper rivalry between the "first world" and the "second world," not only for hearts and minds, but also for control of the Third World. The Cold War rumbled on, further polarizing the world and its economy instead of integrating them. There was even a time in the mid-1970s when it seemed to some that the world was changing according to their model. The Soviet rulers and their secret services believed that *"mir shol po nashom puti"*—"the world was going our way"—as they fought their silent war in the Third World, just as the West was doing.[10] The world, however, refused to be divided permanently into two blocs and began coalescing again into a single mass. As we know, the "end of history" was even announced, prematurely. That event, however, is a long, long way off, because history will end only with the end of human civilization. That will surely not occur in the present millennium.

The socialist economies were hardly open to liberal contacts with the first world. Often they were closed. Today the term *anti-import manufacturing* sounds archaic, but once upon a time it was supposed to be the engine driving the growth of this part of the world. The world was clearly divided—more sharply in the two generations after the war than in the preceding two centuries. How could anyone speak of globalization in such a situation? Yet many authors did so, especially in the West.[11] With their own particular kind of bias, and at times with downright arrogance, they identified "the world" exclusively with their own part of it—as if the area between the Elbe and the western shore of the Pacific didn't count, or belonged to some other world. (Today, similarly, many people continue to identify Europe, in economic and cultural terms, with the western part of the continent.)

Therefore, by definition, whatever it was that occurred in the capitalist part of the world in the decades after the World War II in terms of liberalization, openness, deregulation, cooperation, or integration, it was not globalization. A vast part of the world and of humanity did not participate in those processes, no matter how far-ranging the implications for the future. The third phase of permanent globalization could only truly begin when the Third World and, even more important, the formerly socialist "Second World" joined the mainstream of the development process. Both of these "worlds" immediately came to be known as "emerging" markets, because that was how they were perceived from the vantage point of the highly developed capitalist market that had emerged long before. This phase began at the turn of the 1980s and the 1990s. From that time onward, we have had to do with true globalization, which resumed after an interruption lasting three generations— the so-called abbreviated twentieth century, from 1914 to 1989. The degree of exclusion from the dormant globalization that was about to awaken with such great impetus was different in different regions of the world.

The processes associated with the increasingly complete emancipation of the former colonies, and even more so with the tempestuous and vigorous transformation in the postsocialist countries,[12] came on top of other weighty processes that gave the third, contemporary phase of permanent globalization its special character. Some of these traits also featured in the earlier phases, whereas others are new. The ongoing scientific-technological revolution, with all its economic consequences, plays a prominent role. We could even call this the globalization of the era of the great digital revolution. We can point out six essential, fundamental characteristics of the present phase of globalization:

1. World trade is growing nearly twice as fast as world output.
2. Global capital transfers are consistently increasing at an even faster rate.
3. The streams of migrating people are growing and escaping from the control of nation-states.
4. New technology is spreading exceptionally quickly, changing the way we do business and creating new types of interdependence on a worldwide scale.
5. The postsocialist systemic transfer has picked up speed, bringing as many as 1.8 billion people from thirty-five countries into the unrestricted world economy.
6. Multidirectional cultural changes, involving the interpenetration of a wide range of values, are under way.

The last of these points involves both positive and negative changes. There is no way to reach a consensus, because what one person regards as progress that adds value, another will view at the same time with disapproval. This can be seen especially in countries with a strong, traditional cultural distinctness (e.g., in the Arab world). Although far-reaching internationalization or an American model of consumption shocks some, the erection of shopping centers on the model of southern California or Florida delights others. Some even believe that the shortest road to American-style success lies not through imitating American productivity and work ethics, but through borrowing the American lifestyle, especially by the local elites. When branches of American universities appear, as they have in Bahrain or Qatar, such people are impressed. When there is an explosion of fast-food restaurants—not necessarily. Yet Kuwait is possibly the only place in the world where you can see a Ferrari in a McDonald's parking lot. Would you ever see that in America?

Globalization is far advanced, but we shouldn't get carried away. Many things that were once impossible have become possible, but let's not lose perspective. A relatively common mannerism in economics writing—not only in the press—is the uncritical citing of catchy but oversimplified viewpoints that use too many mental shortcuts. Fashion also plays a role here. Quite a few people quote Lester Thurow, who jumped the gun when he said that "for the first time in human history, anything can be made anywhere and sold everywhere."[13] This could only be said by someone who hasn't been to very many places—or rather, someone who has been here and there but certainly not everywhere. At what point would it be true to assert that everything can be made everywhere? When geography was reduced to history? This supposition would be true when a company could

- Sell where it gets the highest price, without limitation.
- Raise capital where it's abundant.
- Buy raw materials where doing so pays best.
- Set up production where it's most efficient.

It's a shame that things aren't like this. It's true that an "American" computer can be "made" (or rather, assembled) in Malaysia, some "Japanese" Toyota models are assembled in Turkey, and Skype can offer Internet services from Estonia. But the fact is that the computers could still not be built in the Middle East, Toyotas cannot roll off production lines in central Africa, and Skype could not operate out of Kyrgyzstan. This means that there are technologies so advanced that geography still plays a great role, and there is a good deal of differentiation of various regions of the world in regard to their productive potential: advanced technology, institutional maturity, and a qualified labor force.

What is more, the contemporary economy is a matter increasingly of services and less and less of manufacturing physical goods. It will never be possible to create and sell services "everywhere," especially the traditional ones that, in the great majority, are inseparable from where they are made. By nature, they must usually be made where the customers are; the supply is where the demand is. The Internet and the digital revolution make it possible to transfer certain services—especially information, some kinds of education and entertainment, and financial services—but this does not hold true for having your car washed or your hair cut, or eating supper in a good restaurant. You can't perform surgery on somebody or babysit over the Internet. These services and their consumers must be together, in the same place, at the same time. Those who want to do so can watch porn on the Internet, but they can't have sex there. The world has managed to reduce itself to what seems to be a single point in virtual space, but only there. Elsewhere, it has sometimes proved possible to reduce distances and radically shrink the space in which sales and purchase transactions occur. Yet as long as there is distance, there will be transport costs, and this means that geography remains.

We therefore still have a long way to go before "everything" can be produced "everywhere," but we are closer than at any time in the past. This is an expression of the degree of advancement of globalization in the economic dimension. One might say, "The smaller the role of geography in the economic processes of accumulation, manufacturing, distribution, and consumption, the more advanced the process of globalization, and vice versa."

It is also worth pointing out the spontaneity of globalization. Up to this point, spontaneity has been part of its nature and its great engine; from here on in, it could wither and collapse under its own weight without the required regulation on a global scale. If globalization is to be understood as the spread of the functional principles of the liberalized market over almost the entire global economy, then it can be reduced in essence to the ubiquitous reign of capitalism. From this point of view, those who simply identify globalization with the great triumph of world capitalism are right, at least in the present phase of the development of civilization, because it has turned out to be impossible to make the world fit the socialist or communist models, despite the fact that many not only dreamed of this but above all did a great deal to make it so. However, the international socialist system collapsed radically at the end of the twentieth century, and the market economies that emerged from it have been channeled into the world mainstream in three radically different ways.

It so happens that the integration of the postsocialist economies with the rest of the world is taking place at that historical epoch in the evolution of capitalism when the neoliberal version is in the ascendant. The significance of the spontaneous forces of the market has absolute priority, whereas the role played by the state and its active policy is minimized. As a result, the postsocialist economies, and other countries with medium or low levels of development and weak capitalist institutions that are opening up to the outside world, are undergoing transformation in a centrifuge driven by neoliberal principles. This dominance is fairly universal and, in reference to international economic relations, it is crushing.

The balance of power between spontaneous forces and those resulting from the actions of the state has varied over history, even when the role of the state on a national scale has been immeasurably more prominent than at present—not only in the Scandinavian and Western European social democracies, but also in the United States, Great Britain, and Australia. In the course of globalization, the spontaneous forces have played the decisive role. Nobody invented globalization, and nobody set it up. Nobody wrote a script for this performance and nobody is directing it, although many actors pass across the stage. It is therefore more of a happening than a drama in three acts with a shotgun appearing in the first act that will inevitably be fired in the third. It is clear that the actors in globalization—the nation-states and their governments, multinational corporations, global investors, international intergovernmental and nongovernmental organizations, world media conglomerates, and criminal organizations—have been trying for some time to garner as much for themselves as possible. Some are doing better than others; there are winners and losers in every game.

The fundamental questions looming over humanity concern the outcome of this game. Can it be played in such a way that, even if not everyone can win—and they can't, which goes to the very essence of the capitalism that is now global—then at least there will be more and more winners and fewer and fewer losers? That's possible, but by no means certain. Too many things would have to happen at the same time, but they're not happening. That's either because the overly powerful interests of certain players—particularly the largest nation-states and the mightiest global corporations—don't permit them to happen, or because there isn't sufficient understanding of the process that's unfolding. Both of these obstacles are daunting, and they must be overcome in different ways. In the former case, it will be necessary to expose the real group interests and organize forces that can effectively counterbalance their influence. In the latter case, it's necessary to keep fighting to win hearts and minds, and to explain to the international public in a comprehensible way what the present stage of globalization is about—what makes it irreversible in the foreseeable future, and why it's necessary to organize that international public or, in simpler terms, humanity, in a new way.

Globalization is triumphing, but this does not in any way mean that its proponents should rest easy. To protect the process from self-induced dangers, the good sides of globalization should be maximized while the bad sides are minimized and, where possible, eliminated. There is no shortage of either good or bad sides to globalization. Many point out how the process energizes the economy, raises wages, and multiplies trade. However, the statistical proofs that they call upon usually illustrate the accomplishments of national economies or countries as a whole, in the form of aggregate or averaged data. This isn't worth much; it obscures many divisions. It's necessary to see the poor in the United States and the nouveaux riches in Russia, the misery in Bulgaria and the obscene consumption levels of the elite in Nigeria, the breathtaking Chinese boom and the half century of stagnation in the Democratic Republic of the Congo, the ease of Internet access around the North American Great Lakes and the physical near-impossibility of it in the region of the African Great Lakes.

Yet people in both the poor countries and the prosperous ones complain about globalization without seeing any of these things. This applies to the merchandise market and to the labor market, and thus to the chances of finding a job and the wages paid. In poor countries, they accuse the rich countries of not permitting genuinely free access for competitive products from countries with cheap labor, and of depriving them in this way of a chance for work and income. In the affluent countries, in turn, they dislike the poor countries for the fact that the increasing demand for labor is transferred to where the workforce is qualified but cheaper—in other words, to the poor countries. Is it really true that, in the open conditions of globalization, the less-developed economies take jobs away from the more-developed ones? Are North America and Western Europe therefore right to blame the so-called emerging markets—especially in South America and East Asia, although the ones in Eastern Europe aren't overlooked either—for sucking some of the demand out of their labor markets?

To a degree this is true, yet, at the same time, the very processes that make up globalization—the free exchange of goods and capital and the flow of knowledge and technology—contribute to a higher overall level of productivity in the wealthy countries. As a result, real wages and the standard of living are relatively higher there. We are therefore dealing with two simultaneous processes, one of which causes a fall in the share of wages in incomes, and the other of which leads to a growth in the absolute level of income. The derivative of this is that workers who find jobs receive a smaller slice of a bigger pie, as a result of which they come out slightly ahead. In concrete terms, real wages in the eighteen richest countries have grown an average of 0.24 percent faster each year over the last two decades, thanks to the impact of these processes.[14] Over the entire twenty years, this adds up to an additional growth of 4.9 percent. This isn't much in the light of the high-sounding declarations about the beneficial effects of globalization. Nor is it at all strange that the result is dissatisfaction, growing frustration, and protests. However, it is not globalization that should be held mainly responsible for this state of affairs.

It is a fact that the share of wages in income has declined significantly in prosperous countries over the last quarter of a century. The largest decline has been in Japan, at about ten percentage points between 1980 and 2004, whereas the comparable fall in the United States and the United Kingdom has been about three to four percentage points. We are talking here about the share of wages for hired labor in terms of value added. This has been caused, as is always the case, by a combination of factors, one of which is the globalization of the labor market. The other factors include, above all, technological advances, which in many cases push people out of jobs and transfer part of the newly created value added to the inventors of and investors in such progress. Institutional changes unfavorable to workers are another factor. The latter are what the International Monetary Fund euphemistically refers to as "policies toward the labor market," which, it would seem, happen to minimize its own negative role.

In line with neoliberal preferences and values, the implementation of change consists mostly of what is called increasing the elasticity of labor markets, which comes down in basic terms to weakening the bargaining position of employees versus capital. It is therefore hardly surprising that such a structural policy shifts income from wages to profits. This is the fundamental reason for the fall in the share of income going to labor, and the corresponding rise in the share going to capital. This process is completely natural and conforms to the principles of a capitalist economy; globalization helps it along. At present, this shift is no longer occurring on a local or national, but rather on a transnational and global scale. This in turn makes it harder to control on the national level. However, it is not globalization in itself that is responsible for this shift in the income structure that is so unfavorable to labor, but rather the pressure of capital maximizing its functional goal—in other words, profits. In conditions of world capitalism formed according to neoliberal prescriptions, capital is looking after itself decidedly better than labor unions or the state, which stands, at least in terms of its declarations, on the side of employees and their rights.

Since globalization is supposed to survive the successive challenges that history throws at us, it must move up to a fundamentally new standard of functionality. Some authors, including Joseph E. Stiglitz, known for his earlier sharp criticism of the shortcomings of globalization,[15] have suggested a range of organizational and institutional moves that, in their opinion, could make it work better. This is a typical normative approach, in which they offer advice on how things should be, while some apparently forget why they are the way they are.

Globalization must become less spontaneous and chaotic, and more coordinated and guided. The continuation of globalization in its feral variant will only exacerbate the already enormous inequalities in material status—income and wealth—between regions, countries, professional groups, and individuals. These inequalities are violating the boundaries of social and economic tolerance. As a result, the breadth of the so-called margin of social exclusion is beginning to bite into economic effectiveness. I say "so-called" because it has already stopped being a margin or, from a different point of view, a pathology. It has become a gigantic structural trait in which many people have been relegated to the periphery of socioeconomic life and excluded from any possibility of benefiting from its fruits.

Once a certain threshold is crossed—and we are getting closer and closer to it—the potential for rebellion and a new revolution can only grow, and this, in turn, could send the world back into the uncharted wilderness. This might sound attractive to travelers but not to humanity. The mounting wave of migration, international terrorism, and the shunning by more countries, especially in Latin America, of the American neoliberal way—these are only some of the symptoms of the rising frustration and what may be an impending explosion. Yielding to the inertia of the present course of globalization will make such an explosion inevitable. The only alternative is the reinstitutionalization of globalization. The system of the world capitalist market must be embraced within a framework of regulation and guided in the interests of the development of the world's economy and society. A way must be found to control the particular interests of the big global players, because up to this point they have been getting out of control.

Two negative global processes highlight the necessity for the regulation and coordination of policy on a worldwide scale: global warming and international terrorism. This is where the spontaneity of globalization stands out clearly. If not for this spontaneity and the accompanying regulatory deficit, these plagues of the contemporary world would never have been able to spread on such a scale. Private interests, the greed of untrammeled capital, and the spreading ethos of consumption, without paying sufficient attention to the negative effects of the expansion of certain kinds of manufacturing and consumption, have already caused the contamination and degradation of the environment on a scale that will be difficult to reverse. The weakening of the state under the dictates of the neoliberals and the deregulation of trade in specific sectors, including weapons, have led to the privatization of armed conflicts and regional wars. World terrorism is one more effect of the madness of privatization. If we're to privatize everything, then we'll also privatize the fight for various "just causes" in the name of which terrorists are all too ready to kill others and themselves.

By now we know that no one—not the most powerful countries such as the United States, nor even groups of such countries like the G-7 or the European Union—is capable of single-handedly overcoming global warming, international terrorism, or any of the other global maladies that bedevil us. These are battlefronts that call for teamwork, coordinated policies, and joint organizations. They require the formulation of new rules of the game and economic action on a worldwide scale, and this means new institutions. Spontaneity is great for the local market in tomatoes, but not for the global market in everything. The lack of regulation under the seductive slogan of "economic freedom" means, in fact, concern for the particular interests of the few at the cost of the many, and it has led humanity rather far in terms of economic growth, but the point is that it is possible to go still farther and to accomplish more at a lower cost.

Therefore, in accordance with the principles of economic rationality, we need to act, and on a global scale. Not only in terms of this century and the next one, when some of us will still be alive, but in the long term, the future of globalization will depend on mankind's ability to reorganize and truly take its fate into its own hands. There is no point in leaving things to any other hands, especially the invisible hand. There are too many areas where that invisible hand cannot be seen, because it isn't there. It is present in other fields, but even there it does not act the way it should—it creates more problems than it solves. The key to the future is progress in rationalizing globalization, and this is going to require a new institutionalization of the world economy with all its interdependence. If we manage to implement this in the current century—for it is a project on the scale of centuries—then we will succeed in rescuing globalization from self-destruction.

Globalization is an epochal process. Its historical nature means that it had a beginning, that it is ongoing, and that it should end at some point. Therefore it must lead from one place to another. It is a long road originating in various socioeconomic formations—European and Asian feudalism, the pre-Columbian empires of South America, and the primitive communities scattered around the world. It began in a world divided by geographical, technical, and political barriers that were insurmountable at the time. From there it has arrived at the global cities and villages we share. Half of humanity is urban now, and half rural. Masses of people wander here and there. Interdependence binds us together more strongly than ever before. Perhaps it is therefore better to speak not of a global village or city, but of a global dwelling.

However, although we may know more or less where we come from, it is not entirely clear where we are going. We would all like to be moving toward a better future. Yet this is more of a profession of faith, a particular sort of religiosity, than a scientific assertion or knowledge. The future will be better for some, worse for others, and for many it is unknown. Humanity faces new questions and challenges, some of them posed by globalization. It would be naïve and conceited for our generation to state that this is the last of the great civilizational processes. There will be others. A new green revolution will change the face of the earth once again, when people truly reflect on the fact that our sole chance of survival is to change our way of life to one based on environmental equilibrium, and to shift to development that is truly self-sustaining. In historical terms, we are already in the antechamber of that revolution.

Globalization is thus an open-ended process, but not an unending one. Above all, it is ongoing. It is in its nature to be flexible. It need not necessarily be globalization in the neoliberal style. It need not serve primarily American interests, or the interests of the most powerful corporations and finance companies. At this moment we simply do not know what lies in the distant future or what lies beyond the horizon, despite the fact that the horizon has been expanding as a result of the constant broadening of our perspective and the deepening of our knowledge. All we can say today is that globalization has led to a dynamic market economy, with all its cultural, social, and political traits, that is nevertheless entangled in the countless internal contradictions of world capitalism or, to put it differently, in interdependence on a global scale. It is a living, pulsating organism. Much more will still happen—just as so much has happened over the preceding half century. The colonial system fell, socialism collapsed, and the great scientific-technological revolution of the era of space flight, the computer, the Internet, and biotechnology began. What could happen next?

Globalization remains necessary as an emerging category in economics and the social and political sciences, and interfering in the process would neither interrupt nor reverse it. At the most, it could reshuffle the costs and benefits by reshaping the movements of the flows and resources that determine the structure and dynamics of socioeconomic growth. All of this would be important, but it would be only quantitative change, not qualitative. Qualitative change would require a thorough reevaluation and coordinated action by all of humanity on a historically unprecedented scale. Turning away from globalization as a category of development would be a contradiction of its essence, involving either a return to the status quo ante or a new leap into the future.

In the first case, despite the fact that it seems to us now that globalization is as unstoppable as an avalanche, the amplitude of its impact should not be overestimated. Various winds have blown through history, and there is no guarantee that their direction will not shift once again. If we take a good look around, near and far, we see no end of backwardness, provincialism, xenophobia, isolationism, nationalism, racism, protectionist nostalgia, overgrown bureaucracy, and conservative state interventionism. Once again: All it would take is the coincidence of certain phenomena and tendencies in economics, culture, and politics for the course of history to swerve away from the heretofore dominant megatrend of globalization, just as happened in 1913, when global capitalism failed right down the line.[16] A hundred years ago, the way that the globalization of the day was thriving seemed unstoppable; within a few years, it was suddenly reduced to rubble for decades. It was a fortunate thing that it managed to pull itself together again in subsequent decades.

In the second case, a leap forward, there would have to be a qualitative change to a new, mature worldwide community and global economy at a higher level of civilization—leaving aside what could come of an encounter with extraterrestrials, an eventuality that remains, at present, in the realm of fantasy (yet this too will come to pass, for it would be the height of cosmic arrogance to attribute to ourselves a monopoly on intelligent life in the universe). Back to earth, however—what could constitute such a leap into the future? It would take a global state and a world community. This time, it would not be organized on the principle of conquest, domination, and the subjugation by force of one people by another. That has already happened, during the empires of shorter or longer duration that conquered a smaller world—those of Alexander the Great (356–323 BCE), the Roman Empire, Genghis Khan,[17] or the Spanish Empire in the time of Phillip II (1527–1598), on which the sun may indeed never have set, but which fell short of controlling the entire world, just as was the case with the later British empire. The founders of the "Thousand-Year Reich" had superpower dreams, but it was the good fortune of humanity that the Reich, with all its dire consequences, lasted only a dozen years. Nor can the possibility be excluded that Mao Zedong believed that communism organized according to his ideas could take over the world. This is what serious specialists on the subject tell us.[18] Today, more than four decades after Mao incited the infamous Cultural Revolution, we should add that the rise of an essentially capitalist China into a global power is hardly what Chairman Mao had in mind.

This time, humanity—still loosely connected and integrated despite the existing interdependence—would have to reorganize itself from a world comity into a world polity. The global economy would have to be integrated totally. On that double basis—as if on two solid pillars—the edifice of a world quasi-state would have to be built to organize the functioning of all of humanity, on both the economic and cultural levels, *pro publico bono totus mundi*. This seems a fantasy. Humanity is still incapable of such a coordinated, rational effort on a global scale. It's way over our heads.

We can admire the impressive achievements of economic liberalization in setting free enormous reserves of human energy and ingenuity. We can get excited over the record-shattering pace of technical progress and the spread of new technologies. We might even toy with the mirage of a return to direct, Athenian-style democracy at the interface of technology, learning, and society, except that there would be a slight difference—it would be indirect, by way of the Internet and wireless connectivity, but at least it would be in real time. So it was long ago, when the assembly (*apella*) of adult men (exclusively citizens) in the square at Sparta served as the highest authority in the state. The Spartans called themselves *homoioi*, or equal, despite the fact of blatant discrimination against women. Yet Spartan women had far more freedom than those from other regions, including Athens.

Capital and the political class would never permit any such thing to happen. They will use arguments like the insufficiency of knowledge, information, maturity, and responsibility among the electorate. The chosen representatives of the people, but not the people themselves, know how things should be. At best, there may be a few more referenda than now—but only enough so that our representatives can continue to rule over us.

Once, 100 or 200 years ago, and in our part of the world only twenty years ago, 10 percent of society decided 100 percent of the issues. Today 100 percent of society decides 10 percent of the issues, because most of the other 90 percent is controlled by the market and the forces that govern it. In real terms, many of the matters so important to the great majority of the people are decided without consulting the people, and without the people even knowing about them or perceiving their existence. These decisions need not necessarily follow the real interests of the people. Yet it's all "democratic." There is still a long road to travel before we arrive at full, rather than merely nominal democracy. A twenty-first-century principle of *divide et impera*—divide and conquer—will prevail. Sometimes it will cause so much discontent that governing will not be easy.

We should not allow ourselves to get carried away with technical and economic "science fiction," or "nonscientific fiction," if you prefer, at least from today's perspective: the vision of a friendly fantasy, a harmonious and functional superstate, and an integrated world community well served by technology and a subjugated natural environment that never withers.

It's interesting that when artists—filmmakers, writers, and painters—fantasize about the distant future (aside from the extraterrestrial aspect), they are more likely to imagine the Planet of the Apes, a depopulated and ravaged earth, natural disasters and other Armageddons, but never an earthly idyll. That's not what lies in store for us.

A dramatic leap into the future, involving the jettisoning of globalization's present-day baggage of pain and pathology while preserving the positive aspects, would require the fulfillment of several conditions. In particular, there would be a need for an appropriate global coordinating mechanism. I am not talking about some kind of world quasi-government, because that is neither necessary nor feasible. The trick would be to create a mechanism capable of formulating common goals for humanity and of constructing political instruments for achieving them. Instead of worldwide conflicts, there should be a worldwide—and democratic—dialogue. Instead of institutionalized chaos, there would have to be a new, worldwide institutional order. Instead of frequently unhealthy competition or even conflict, there would have to be work on creative political cooperation and coordination on a global scale—if not at once at the full level of integration that characterizes the United States of America, then at least along the lines of the successfully functioning European Union.

Everything would have to be done with an eye to the supply of an appropriate quantity of global public goods of the appropriate quality. The term *goods* is somewhat misleading here, because it might be associated with material goods. In this case, however, we are talking mostly about services, which are predominantly nonmaterial. Classical public services are supplied by the state and paid for by the state within the framework of the public finance system (through central or local governments). One characteristic of such goods is that, once they have been produced, access to them is usually unlimited. These are what we refer to as pure public goods, and examples of them are national security, the justice system, diplomacy, or administration. The entire populace benefits from these services, and additional users can be added without eliminating any of the previous users, and without incurring any costs for the supply of these goods and services.

If all children benefited from free-of-charge vaccinations against smallpox, or if a benevolent state provided them free of charge with a spoonful of cod-liver oil once a week, that would also be a public good, even though it functioned differently from the protective hand of the state administration or masterful diplomacy. The case with many municipal services is similar, even at the level of the free collection of residential garbage or access to what, for this very reason, are known as "the public roads." A lighthouse at the entrance to a port is nothing more nor less than a public service. It shines for everyone, whether they have paid or not. At present, GPS and other analogous global navigation systems play a similar role. Users pay directly for the technical equipment needed to receive the signals, but not for the public service in the form of the emission of the signal. The same is true of radio or free-to-air television (except in cases where there is a license fee). The situation is similar today with increasingly broad access to the Internet. Soon it will be universal and free of charge, and will become a purely public service.

The economic essence of public services inheres in the following considerations:

- If these are supplied services, then in principle no one should be denied access to them, as, for instance, in the case of broadcast radio.
- The amount of any given person's consumption does not limit consumption by others, as in the case of pedestrians who enjoy the benefits of street lighting without appropriating these benefits to themselves and depriving others of access to them.
- Adding new users does not increase the cost of supplying the service, as in the case of people turning on the television at a given time in order to hear the weather report for the following day without thereby increasing the cost of preparing the weather forecast.

- For these same reasons, excluding someone from the benefits of public services does not lower the cost of providing them, as, for example, forbidding someone to attend parliamentary debates does not lower the operating costs of the parliament.
- Public services are financed from public appropriations, and thus from so-called social consumption funds, meaning that, although they may be consumed individually, they are paid for in an organized way from the public coffers.

In this field, globalization introduces many new factors and makes things more complicated. Types of activity are already appearing in which the smooth functioning of the global economy—and the world community—requires the provision of global public services. This implies the necessity of numerous organizational and institutional changes, including changes to methods of financing and distribution. On the one hand, this is more difficult than it is on the national scale, because there is no world system for collecting funds and allocating them for competitive public use. On the other hand, it is an urgent matter because many problems are outgrowing control at the national level and require action on a global scale. This applies, in particular, to the protection of the human environment; security; a functioning infrastructure that makes the relatively fluid and free movement of information, people, and goods possible; an effective and skillful administrative approach to collective problems on a worldwide scale; and perhaps the guarantee of minimal existential security or even social welfare. On the present wave of globalization—perhaps because of the high degree of spontaneity—no entity has arisen that would be capable of providing these services in a satisfactory way by organizing the supply, financing them, and distributing them all over the world.

It is true that, all of this notwithstanding, much has been accomplished in certain areas, even before the study, classification, and description of the issue in the literature under the heading of global public services. This was possible because the intersection and interaction of various initiatives and proposals finally forced the most powerful players to adopt a partnership approach and negotiate a practical compromise. Later, reality forced the weaker participants in the exchange to sign on. This is how the foundations or fragments of a global system arose. We do not think about it today, but this is the way that the functioning of the postal service was institutionalized in a historical process, sometimes even to the point that a letter from Nicaragua to Sri Lanka takes less time than one from the Wola district of Warsaw to the suburb of Ursynów. Numerous communication routes have come into existence. Although people drive on the left in some countries and on the right in others, there are no longer any countries where they drive in whichever way they choose, because the rules of the road have been established on a global scale. This is not completely true of the calendar, but even those who opt for their own older traditions can still find their way around the Gregorian calendar, which loses only a single day every 3,000 years. Many more examples could be found, but the point is that there are conventions and organizations for all these things— first locally, then internationally, and finally on a planetary scale.

It sometimes happens that a worldwide organization, which also renders a global public service, arises out of a grass-roots initiative, as did the Red Cross back in 1863. Such organizations can have the most varied motivations, including gallant, disinterested concern for the security of humanity. This is how the Svalbard Global Seed Vault came into existence. Starting out as an initiative by scientists, it became a mission by a specially established foundation (the Global Crop Diversity Fund) and is now an organization supported by the UN Food and Agriculture Organization (FAO). The storage facility is located in arctic Spitsbergen, in a shaft hidden deep in the earth but also high enough to remain above sea level even in case of a radical rise due to global warming. The seeds of tens of thousands of the plants on which human existence depends are gathered and stored there in case of an apocalypse or some lesser natural catastrophe. A global public service is precisely what this one-of-a-kind shelter provides. At the base of the project lies the assumption that it should be public, and not commercial or tied to any particular interests. This shelter is a splendid example of wise institutionalization, and of policy implemented and coordinated on a global scale.

There are also cases in which an earlier understanding and a subsequent tradition go to make up a global institution. Leaving aside the English-speaking countries, who have broken ranks with the rest of the world (and this is hardly an isolated instance), almost everyone knows what a meter, a kilogram, a liter, a hectare, or a degree Celsius are, and can use these measures in mutual contacts. They can also reach some understanding with the Anglo-Saxons by converting their measures to the time-honored foot, pound, gallon, acre, and degree Fahrenheit.

They can produce, transport, sell, use, and make measurements. In other words—and this is the cornerstone of commerce—they can compare, all over the world. Almost—because there are still places like Malawi or Gambia where they sell tomatoes by the pile—five in the first level, three on top of them, and one more at the very top. On the totally local market, of course, we can measure things by the distance "from here to that fence." When we wish to set sail on the broader market, the measures are known and acknowledged.

Nevertheless, some universal measurements are lacking. There is still no single world money. In this regard, we even lag behind the situation at the peak of the previous phase of globalization, at the turn of the nineteenth and twentieth centuries. In those days, there were far fewer national currencies, and the gold standard went a long way to playing the role of world money. Now, if for no other reason than the disintegration of the former Soviet Union and Yugoslavia, which have given us twenty varieties of legal tender where there were previously two, there are more currencies than there were two decades ago. This is despite the creation of several common currency zones using the same money. The earliest was the African franc, the CFA.[19] It originated in 1945. Countries signed on at various points in the following years, and some subsequently withdrew. Next up was the Eastern Caribbean Dollar, the EC\$,[20] dating from 1965. The newest common currency, the euro,[21] went into circulation in 1999. A common world currency, which might, for example, be called the "global," would make an excellent contribution to increasing the effectiveness of the world economy by lowering transaction costs and eliminating once and for all the danger of currency crises with all their consequences, both financial and in the real economy.

Although a world currency might be some way down the road, the world has already begun shrinking in this regard. If you stand on the opposite side of the Pacific from Balboa on the beach on the east shore of tiny Wallis Island between Fiji and Samoa, you will always be looking at yesterday, because the International Date Line is quite close. The date changes, but not the rate of exchange between the local currency and those of distant countries. If you are clutching 1,000 of the local francs in your hand, you will always have exactly as much as you would have if you were standing on the far side of the globe, on a Black Sea beach in Bulgaria, with 16 levs and 39 stotinkis in your pocket. That is because economic fate has yoked together these two places that apparently have nothing in common, thanks to the fact that both of their currencies are anchored in the same place. That place is Frankfurt, the seat of the European Central Bank, which issues the euro. There, both that 1,000 and that 16.39, respectively, are worth exactly 8.38 euro.

It is worth noting at this point the original interdependence that resulted from such a complex of histories. Although they followed completely different courses, they are now intersecting in surprising ways at the crest of the processes connected with globalization. Hardly anyone in Bamako, the capital of Mali, is aware that their currency, the CFA, is rigidly connected to the Estonian kroon (EKK). No one in Tallinn, conversely, knows about their currency's unchanging relation with the CFA that is used in the former Portuguese colony of Guinea Bissau. The exchange rate of the Pacific franc (CFP) that circulates in New Caledonia, French Polynesia, and the federated islands of Wallis and Futuna varies in relation to all the noneurozone European currencies exactly the same as that of the Lithuanian lita or the Bosnian mark. These countries and territories, for all practical purposes, have a common currency, and their exchange rates fluctuate in lockstep against the dollar, the yen, and the ruble.

After such different historical fates—colonization and postcolonial connections with the French metropolis and the franc, or a Soviet heritage, the rejection of the ruble, and a postsocialist transformation oriented toward complete integration with the European Union—the CFA countries and the postsocialist countries that have pegged their currency to the euro are de facto members of the same currency zone. As strange as it may sound, the currencies of Togo or of Niger, one of the poorest countries in the world, are today closer to the euro than the Polish zloty or the Hungarian forint, the currencies of two countries that have been leaders in market-oriented reform for many years.

Someday perhaps the world will move more boldly in the direction of a single universal currency. A starting point would be the fixing of the exchange rates of the U.S. dollar, the euro, and the yen, although today that would not be enough, because China, Russia, and India can hardly be overlooked. The euro may be in circulation on islands in Polynesia and the U.S. dollar, in the Caribbean. That is impressive, but it changes nothing on the scale of the world economy. As long as these two key currencies—the dollar and the euro—are not integrated and do not have a fixed exchange rate with the yen, the yuan, the ruble, and the rupee, we are still a long way from a world currency. Somewhere off on their own we have the pound sterling and the Swiss franc, which are not even in a hurry to join the eurozone, let alone any kind of global currency. Nor can we overlook other currencies, which are as much a source of pride in their countries as the national football (soccer) team. Those countries can't imagine themselves without their currencies. However, were the largest economies to move toward a common currency—which is highly unlikely, unfortunately, for at least another half century—many other countries would rush to join them. There's room for a lot of football teams, including national ones, but the fewer currencies, the better.

Of course, this is not a matter of a simple yes-or-no choice. There are serious arguments for maintaining multiple currencies. This situation could have certain advantages, but we must know how to take advantage of them and to avoid mixing the ends of economic policy (prosperity) with the means (a stable currency). National currencies can make it easier to alleviate economic breakdowns (crises) that result from growing productivity differentiation between the countries. At such a point, devaluation—a one-time lowering (weakening) of the exchange rate—offers at least a temporary respite in the form of greater competitiveness for the national economy. The procedure prevents the country's products from becoming excessively expensive in foreign markets—and overly expensive products will soon vanish from any market. If a country's products are priced out of foreign markets, then output and employment will fall. Without a multiplicity of currencies, there is no way to use devaluation to counter the lack of competitiveness. However, this certainly does not mean that it was a bad thing for the United States to introduce a single currency, the dollar, or that China would be served by replacing the yuan with a range of regional currencies. With one currency and a large, differentiated territory in terms of productivity and the competitiveness of companies—which is the way things are inside the large national economies—a country must use other methods that may sometimes be more painful in local terms than devaluation (such as running a high level of unemployment or suffering a wave of bankruptcies in a given season).

There was a day in March 2000 when the exchange rate of the dollar to the euro was at parity—one to one. On that same day, Professor Robert A. Mundell, who had just won a Nobel Prize in economics, was scheduled to give a guest lecture at the Kozminski University in Warsaw. Mundell had received that great scientific distinction above all for research connected with optimal currency zones, the theoretical concept that underlay the practical process of establishing the eurozone.[22] Mundell is known universally as the godfather of the euro. During his lecture, he argued in favor of a single world currency. As a first step, he proposed a fixed, permanent exchange rate between the two main currencies as a way of turning them, in effect, into a single currency. In addition, it would be necessary for the yen to assume the role of a cent, since the exchange rate was approximately 100 yen to the dollar or euro.[23] On that very day, as it turned out, the rate of the Polish zloty to both the dollar and the euro was precisely 0.25. I joked that we could immediately adopt such a system, offering our zloty as a "quarter." To mark the occasion, I even gave Mundell a one-zloty coin. Things turned out differently. We have all been left with a dysfunctional world currency system that drives up the cost of the functioning of the world economy, slows down its relative rate of growth, and will inflict on us more than one future crisis. Mundell's arguments still stand. He also has the zloty I gave him, which appreciated over 70 percent during the subsequent seven years, rising in value by $0.18.

Let us imagine for a moment that things had turned out in such a way in 2000 that the fledgling euro had been permanently pegged to the dollar and the yen and that the zloty had also been added to the fixed-rate configuration. Many other countries, from Latin America through Africa to Central Asia, would have climbed on board. Who would have benefited? Intermediaries on the currency exchange market would have suffered enormous losses, because most of their services would no longer have been needed. The speculators (usually referred to as investors) who prey exclusively on exchange rate fluctuations would be eliminated from the core world capital market, because there would be far less to fluctuate. Also eliminated would be speculation on the direction and intensity of changes in the expectation of economic entities as to currency fluctuations, just as there is no such speculation today between Germany and France, as there was when the mark and the franc were still around. Decisions about saving and investment in the real world, rather than in the realm of speculation, would be made in conditions of significantly lower risk. This would contribute to making these decisions more accurate. There would be fewer misguided investments, operational decisions would be more effective, and companies would be better managed.

In the sphere of the real, the American economy would be forced to undertake the structural reforms and adjustment processes that have been put off so long. The United States continues to live beyond its means, saving little and financing the lion's share of its growth with the savings of others, running up de facto debts—to far too great an extent. This is, unfortunately, made possible by the use of a unique mechanism for financing the gigantic double—budget and trade—deficit: the rampant printing of dollars as the world's reserve currency, which others, at least so far, have been more than willing to accumulate. About 65 percent of the world's currency reserves continues to be held in dollars (with about 25 percent in euros and the remaining 10 percent in sterling, Swiss francs, yen, and South Korean won). The American deficit has been financed (again, so far), paradoxically, by poorer countries that run a structural trade surplus with the United States, especially Middle Eastern oil exporters and China. The tension resulting from the accumulation of these inequalities over the years has reached the boundaries of economic danger. There have been opportunities to relieve this tension partially, but that would have meant slower growth in the American economy over recent years, and faster growth in output and consumption in the European Union. In our hypothetical case, the pegging of the euro and the dollar would mean more countries, probably even the United Kingdom, coming into the eurozone. The French president, Nicolas Sarkozy, would have no reason to formulate such opinions as, "We did not create the euro in order to be unable to produce a single airplane in Europe. That's absurd." It was no absurdity to create the euro. It was a triumph of common sense and a sign of a capacity for long-range action over and above national particularism. The absurdity was to permit the transatlantic exchange rates to be shaped under the delusive sway of neoliberal ideology.

The slowing of the rate of growth in the United States would come above all at the cost of those who have enriched themselves the most on the wave of globalization over the last quarter century. Neoliberal propaganda notwithstanding, this is a fairly narrow slice of the American public, because the real wages of the overwhelming majority of the population have not grown at all since 1981, whereas profits—especially those from speculation—have risen spectacularly. Because of the reduction in transaction costs and the reduction in financial risk, the entire world economy would grow more rapidly in our hypothetical case. The dollar would be stronger than it is, but the U.S. economy would be weaker. The euro would be weaker, but the eurozone economy would be stronger. There would be less inequality of incomes and wealth both within these countries and between them. In sum and *per saldo*, the effect of the redistribution effected against this backdrop would lead to higher growth in world output than at present, and its fruits would be distributed somewhat less unequally. In short: it would be more efficient, and more just.

As for Poland, this hypothetical case would have ruled out the monstrous appreciation of the zloty from 2001 to 2007, which has undercut the competitiveness of the products of the domestic economy. Cheap imports—which generate jobs for people, profits for investors, and taxes for governments in other parts of the world economy—have crowded Polish companies out of the marketplace. At the same time, the unprofitability of exports has led to the elimination of many companies that would have coped perfectly well given a more favorable exchange rate for the zloty. Consent for such a state of affairs or forthright support for it from the independent central bank (independent of the government, that is) has led not to the export of goods, but to the export of labor as people seek work abroad. It has also maintained the disequilibrium in the balance of trade and allowed foreign debt to mushroom once again to a dangerous level. There could have been much more output and consumption, much more value created, and a standard of living on a tangibly higher level. World players outside the country have scooped up the overwhelming portion of the fruits of the growth in domestic productivity. This fundamentally mistaken policy is proof of a complete lack of ability to profit from globalization in the interest of the national economy. Nevertheless, the media and the pseudo-experts, not to speak of the neoliberal wing of the political scene, present it as something praiseworthy.

How is all this possible? If things could be better, why aren't they? Why wasn't the correct path, leading not to the exacerbation of inequality and tension, chosen? Why are decision-making posts held by people who are unable, or unwilling, to make the right decisions that would optimize long-range strategies of balanced development? Sticking to realities now, rather than to our hypothetical scenario, why wasn't the zloty pegged to the euro first, before switching over to the euro in 2007, as was done in Slovakia?

Things turned out the way they did for reasons that we understand perfectly well by now. It wasn't so much out of a lack of scientific understanding of the essentials, but above all because of the dominant position of short-term thinking and the taking of decisions out of a concern for special national, class, and group interests. Nor is it possible to fail to note the role of stupidity and ideological rancor. All those who know and understand may be unsuited for politics and decision making, whereas those who yearn for and push themselves into office may not understand things or be unable to take the right decisions. The decisive factors, however, are special interests and the lack of a political mechanism for the optimal solution of the contradictions between those interests on a national, regional, and global scale. There is a high price for all of this, and only part of the bill has been presented. The rest will follow shortly. It's a shame that those who will have to pay the price are unable to position themselves in global interactions so as to be able to bill others more often.

In outlining a hypothetical, better scenario of the last seven years, which would therefore have been seven fatter years, it is necessary to stress the need for a longer temporal perspective for drawing up macroeconomic accounts on a global scale, as well as the requirement for carrying out difficult structural reforms that would cut into the profit margins of multinational corporations and at least partially eliminate such powerful financial speculators as some of the investment banks and hedge funds. In other words, reform would reach into the pockets of the wealthiest, rather than the poorest, as usually happens. This entire change through redistribution would reconfigure the network of larger and smaller beneficiaries and winners and losers in international economic competition. This would take a political consensus, but conflicts of interest make it impossible to achieve such a consensus. So the game continues according to the old rules. Instead of curbing its excessive consumption, the policies of the United States favor a weak dollar (and therefore exchange rates must remain floating), as a way of enhancing the competitiveness of U.S. goods at the cost of driving goods made in the European Union (and not only there) out of the world market. As a result, output rises more quickly (so far, again) and unemployment is lower on the western shore of the Atlantic, whereas economic dynamism is weaker and, as a result, unemployment is higher on the eastern shore. This is how steps failed to be taken to limit the worsening of some problems in the world economy, even though those steps were perfectly feasible.

On the other hand, the international community has managed to solve many other complex problems on a worldwide scale, including logistical ones. Aviation is a striking example. No matter how bad the situation in the Horn of Africa is, some airlines fly there. No matter how isolated the communist regime in Mongolia once was, foreign airliners flew overhead. No matter how much saber rattling there was in the tense relations between the United Kingdom and Iran in 2007, the scheduled British Airways flight landed at Imam Khomeini International Airport every night, and took off again.

At present, we are witnessing the normalization of the development of the Internet on a global scale. Furthermore, although this may not be totally spontaneous, it is usually happening without government participation. It is backed by intelligent entrepreneurship, the consensus of professionals, and the consent of billions of users to their decisions about norms and protocols, even when they apply to such conveniences as Google or Yahoo. The net relies on organization and institutionalization, and there must always be someone doing the organizing and institutionalizing. So it was with all standardization, whether the early choice of the definitive format for recording television images or the present principles for the distribution of digital music. The current unification at the highest technical level and the accompanying legal disputes over the commercial functioning of organizations like Napster and iTunes will end up the same way as the earlier competition among video recording systems—except that we are now living in a single world that is uniting through the Internet. This is what makes it different from the dilemma that once faced people trying to decide whether to stick to their cubits, quarts, and morgs, or to give in to the foreigners and accept their meters, liters, and hectares.

The interchange of goods and services forces compromises that lead over time to the internal uniformity of techniques and regulations, which is why now, before every takeoff, we must listen for the umpteenth time to the same briefing about fastening our seat belts and how to put on the oxygen masks in case they should be needed. These briefings are given in different languages, but the contents are identical even if the cabin crew wear short skirts in some places and black head scarves elsewhere. Once we have landed safely, the electric current, the plugs, and the computer hookups might not be the same everywhere, but it's easy to use the required converters and connectors to resolve the differences. This book can be written at any number of places scattered around the world, thanks to the compatibility of information and communication systems. This is another result of globalization.

In all these cases, the common interest and the need for contact have been so powerful that terminological, technical, organizational, cultural, and political differences had to be overcome. Nevertheless, the contemporary world and its economy are so complicated, as a result of the interconnected network of interdependence, that many problems, including some with fundamental, existential significance for the fate of humanity, will not solve themselves. Dealing with them effectively now is going to take a collective effort and collective wisdom on a global scale, above and beyond the persistent boundaries of culture and politics. This, in turn, will require the adroit coordination of the policies of countries and groups of countries, and of the strategies of companies and multinational corporations. It is also necessary to bring other global players into the game, especially nonprofit organizations that are nongovernmental and not corrupted by big money. Finally, it will be necessary to fight unceasingly against the fourth sector. The first three sectors are private business, the state, and nongovernmental organizations. The fourth sector is the mushrooming, pathological sector of organized crime and terrorism. It is better organized all the time, and it takes many forms—including a bloodless, digital form.

Against this complex background, it is utopian to see globalization as a contemporary horn of plenty, yet this is the way its apologists want to see it:[24] as a world order no longer dominated by rivalry, but rather by peaceful cooperation and the fair distribution of its ever more abundant fruits. The mirage of inclusive globalization features in almost every multivariant scenario for the future. This results from two different approaches.

In the first case, which is praiseworthy, it is the mirage of wishful thinking accentuating the need to seize the opportunity to create a future that is better to every degree possible. Some determinists talk about the necessity, or, as the idealists have it, the inevitability of this way. Connections could be made here with the communist utopia of a splendid classless world where goods are allotted according to need, or to the idealistic papal vision of a "civilization of love."

In the second case, which is blameworthy, the utopia of participatory globalization is cynically created within the framework of the neoliberal policy trend and the subservient social sciences. Although some of the proponents of this school of thought believe in it—they believe what they certainly cannot know, and are incapable of proving—others treat it cynically, as an instrument in their game. That is, they lie, because they know that the concept they are propounding is not a real option, yet they keep pushing it in order to realize their vision of the world, and above all of their own interests.

Considering the tremendous diversity of the world and the economic circumstances of its inhabitants, as well as the gigantic conflicts of interest that tug at the global economy, it hardly seems appropriate to keep drawing up utopias, even if there are people who inflate the benefits of such intellectual exercises in actively shaping the future. This might be acceptable in literature, for writers who prefer to inspire us with visions verging on the paradisiacal rather than terrifying us with cataclysms. In his dialogue *The Republic*, written around 360 BCE, Plato dangled the idealistic vision of an ancient Mediterranean city-state with philosopher-rulers guided by the ideas of the truth, the good, and the beautiful in a vision of a harmonious society of unanimous consent. Half a millennium ago, Thomas More wrote his *Utopia* in England, in 1516—at the very time when, halfway around a world that was already known to be spherical, the Spanish conquistadors tracing the route of Balboa were boarding their ships on the beaches of Panama to set sail, in the name of their supposedly superior values, for the land of the Incas, where they would destroy a great civilization.

We should know, after all, that "utopia" can mean "good place," but it can also mean "nonexistent place." Nor can utopias avoid politics, even if things work out best when those politics are realistic and pragmatic. Thus, even if the dreamed-of world may strike some as theoretically possible and technologically achievable, it is unfortunately unreal and unattainable in practical political terms. Nevertheless, we can and should continue to aspire to utopia, just as we should keep trying to reach the horizon, because this is what the most profound essence of progress will depend on during the generations to come.

The sense of economic progress resides in the fact that, always and everywhere, it makes sense.

CHAPTER FIVE

The World As It Is

How People Are Coping in
Various Corners of a Changing World

It is not possible to get to a perfect world,
yet it is worth it to keep moving there.

WHAT, THEN, does this wonderful world of ours look like? The definition of "horse" in an old Polish dictionary was: "Everyone can see what it's like." This is the point of view of ordinary mortals to whom words don't come easily. Yet the same approach may also serve others. Albrecht Dürer (1471–1528), probably the most outstanding figure of the German Renaissance, was a master at drawing what he saw. (He drew an immortal rhinoceros, which served to illustrate zoology lessons until 1939, without ever having seen one.) The German artists knew everything about how to paint and had technical backgrounds. After traveling to Venice five centuries ago, Dürer remarked that the Italian masters knew why they painted. They had a theory.[1] Four centuries later, Pablo Picasso (1881–1973) followed their example. He said that he didn't paint what he saw, but rather what he knew. Yet everyone knows different things. That is the way it is, at least in art, which has the right to present the world it wants to present.

What is the situation in science? Science has an obligation not only to represent, but also to reflect and interpret the world. It must reflect the world objectively, and not literally, as in a mirror. Even the best mirror, let alone a crooked one, shows us an image that, although it may not be distorted, is reversed. For instance, left and right are reversed—something that seems increasingly frequent in recent years. Science must interpret things accurately, rather than erroneously or tendentiously, because in such cases knowledge goes out the window.

It is no mean feat to see things as they are. To have a theory, to know why things are as they are, is a great deal more. What, then, is this world like? There is little chance of encompassing its totality, but we can point out the sore points—not in an impressionistic way, as in art, but in a systematic way befitting science. However, even this is a bit like painting: We don't describe what we see so much as we describe what we know. Or rather, we describe how we see things, and the theory that stands behind our personal perception. There's no point describing what everyone can see for themselves.

We live in a time of great transformation. In the European part of the world, the word *transformation* is usually used in the context of a complex, qualitative, dynamic change in the system. This is the way I use it in my works on the systemic passage from socialism to capitalism, or, from a slightly different point of view, from a planned to a market economy. However, if we look at the world in the broadest, planetary dimension, we perceive that we are living in the epoch of a great transformation of economies, politics, and culture, as well as the discipline of economics.

Time is leaving unmistakable marks on the contemporary world. Strangely enough, these marks seem to correspond to the passing decades. The 1950s were the time of the Western European economic miracle and the fall of Stalinism. The 1960s, in turn, brought the spectacular fall of colonialism and the intensification of anti-imperialist moods. The 1970s were marked by the explosion of consumerism and the expansion of worldwide socialism, which seemed to be spreading its wings when, in fact, it was about to fold them forever. The next decade saw the peak of the Cold War and increasingly obvious Western dominance. Then came the 1990s, dominated by the postsocialist transformation and the emergence of a "new economy" of universal computerization and Internet connectivity. The current decade is a period of globalization and international terrorism. The coming decade will be stamped by the rising power of China, and not only in demographic and economic terms. The 2030s will also be a special time, and it cannot be ruled out that a great new world crisis will throw cold water on the drive for unlimited economic expansion and enforce an equilibrium in the flows of demand and supply that are now flooding the globalized economy in an uncontrolled way. The 2040s should bear fruit in the construction of a new, sensible, global institutional order that will make relatively harmonious development possible. What will the signs of the times be in the 2050s?

The contemporary world has many different dimensions, and characterizing them is very complicated. We can identify the basic characteristics as, on the one hand, differentiation, and on the other, interdependence. We might first consider differentiation, because it has far from trivial implications for the future—and the future is more interesting to us than the past, about which we already know a few things.

Differentiation can best be seen when we compare the affluence of people and societies. Or, more precisely, when we compare the wealth of some with the misery of others. Humankind's production (GDP, or rather GWP, that is, Gross World Product) is about $67 trillion by purchasing power parity (PPP). Because there are almost 6.7 billion of us it is easier than ever before to calculate that this comes out to $10,000 per person per year. We should add at once that we are talking here about income, and thus about a flow in time. In international comparisons, these income flows are usually considered in yearly intervals, although this can sometimes be misleading.

In 2006, Ireland's per capita GDP of $44,500 outstripped that of the United States, at $44,000. Several years earlier, Ireland overtook the United Kingdom (where the 2006 figure, according to the same source, was $31,800) in an event that was celebrated more enthusiastically than a victory in football (soccer) would have been. Yet all it takes is to fly to Dublin from London or New York to see which city is richer. Standard of living, after all, is a function not only of current income flow, but of accumulated consumption stocks. Somebody may already be earning more but still live in an older, poorer property; drive a worse car; and be worse dressed. This is why statistics about incomes (and their differentiation) must be read the right way, without drawing conclusions that are too far-reaching. In Equatorial Guinea, the per capita GDP in 2007 amounted to no less than $55,000, placing the country second in the world. This is three times as high as in Argentina or Hungary, but the standard of living in those two countries is three times higher than that in tropical Equatorial Guinea. However, when the proportion of these income flows holds steady for decades and generations, then the resources of the country with the consistently higher income must exceed those of countries with lower incomes. When comparing incomes—and especially GDP—it is therefore better to do so over a longer time span, both retrospectively and into the future.

Average incomes reflect the enormous gaps between countries. If we place the countries at the extremes under the microscope, then the proportion between the per capita GDP in the richest country (Luxembourg, $71,400) and the poorest (Somalia, below $500) is 120:1. If we compare the average income of the wealthiest 1 percent of the citizens of the United States (3 million people with an annual income of $700,000) with the average income of the poorest 1 percent of the population of the Democratic Republic of Congo (650,000 people with an average income of about $140), then the proportion is 5,000:1—as much in four days in the United States as in a whole lifetime, a whole existence in the Congo, taking into account the life expectancy there of fifty-seven years. This gigantic differentiation is a product of history. Remember: five centuries ago, the living standards in America and in Africa were equally miserable. Today the average income in the United States is twenty times higher than that in Africa.

However, the increasing differentiation of living standards between East Asia and sub-Saharan Africa is the work of a mere two generations. In the former region (including China, obviously), per capita GDP has jumped by an impressive factor of 34 since 1960 and enhanced the quality of life of whole nations, whereas in the latter, it has risen by a miserable 25 percent, which might as well be 0, given the time span. Less than fifty years ago, South Korea and Taiwan were as poor as Kenya and Ghana were, and still are. The present per capita GDP in the first two of those countries is $25,000 and $30,000, respectively; in the second pair, it is $1,200 and $2,700, respectively. In 1960, all four countries were at the very bottom in economic terms. The comparison looks similar between Cameroon, which is still extremely poor, and the impressively developing Malaysia. For four straight decades, Malaysia has maintained a rate of growth that has seen the level of output double every ten years and has yielded a current per capita GDP of $5,800 at the market exchange rate and $13,700 according to PPP. The level from which Cameroon started in 1960 was similar ($500 in Cameroon vs. $770 in Malaysia at market rates). Today it is not much higher, at about $920 at market rates and $2,400 according to PPP. Even worse, the

Cameroonian income has declined in actual terms over the last twenty years. There are more such countries, especially in Africa.

These examples show two sides of the same coin: stagnation and development. Because some are stuck in place or crawling while others spurt forward, the growing differentiation of the level of incomes is hardly surprising. Nor should the increasing differentiation between various countries be regarded as something bad, because it results in many cases from rapid development earned through thrift and enterprise, and thanks to wise policies and effective strategies. We can only regret that things have not worked out for others, and consider why.

International trade plays a special role in energizing development. By using its products to reach beyond its borders, a country increases its scale of manufacturing. This not only boosts turnover, but also lowers unit costs. By the same token, there is an increase in profits, which can be used to finance new productive capacity. New people get jobs, they pay taxes, and the state has more for its outlays. The machine starts rolling. Those who are capable of exporting are also capable of developing. This explains a great deal of the economic success of Southeast Asia over the last three decades. This is also the reason for the lack of development in other regions—Africa, Central Asia, and parts of Latin America at present—and erosion of the economic basis of the socialist planned economies in the past.

Much has changed in this world in the last few decades. The group of countries defined in the nomenclature of the International Monetary Fund as "other emerging markets and developing countries"—that is, the whole world outside of the highly developed countries of the Organization for Economic Cooperation and Development (OECD), along with the already "emerged" Hong Kong, South Korea, Singapore, and Taiwan—accounts for one third of the turnover in international trade. A decade ago that figure was only half of the present value, at 17.3 percent of turnover. The share belonging to the wealthiest countries, including the United States, has fallen from 13 percent in 1996 to less than 10 percent at present. With trade expansion as the engine driving their economies forward, the share belonging to the emerging markets and developing countries jumped from 39.2 percent in 1996 to 48 percent in 2006. The year 2008 was a historic one: The poor countries caught up with the rich ones—at present only in terms of GDP (by PPP), but not in terms of per capita. Nevertheless, it is a new world.

Once again, we are speaking about averages, which can conceal unprecedented, spectacular successes, but also pathetic failures—recessions, depressions, and stagnation, a veritable vale of tears. When we look back over the last several decades, most of the cases of chronic stagnation seem explicable in terms of four factors that bar the door to economic progress. First come war and armed conflict: almost three fourths of the people living in poverty reside in countries that have been or still are embroiled in war, including the Democratic Republic of the Congo, Palestine, Cambodia, and Guatemala. Second, more than one fourth of the cases of stagnation and misery can be explained by an inability to benefit from natural resources (Nigeria, Sudan, Liberia, or Bolivia). Third, some countries fail to break vicious circles of helplessness related to especially disadvantageous geopolitical locations, inaccessible geography, or bad neighbors (Chad, Niger, Armenia, and Nepal). The fourth and final factor, which afflicts more countries than all the other woes taken together, is misrule and macroeconomic mismanagement. Please fill in the blanks, one from each continent:

_____

_____

_____

_____

_____

When these plagues overlap, we find ourselves looking at not only stagnation, but even downright regression.

Misfortunes come not only in threes but, at times, in swarms. As if there were not enough causes of poverty and misery, natural disasters in common with a frail infrastructure and the lack of the appropriate material and financial resources lead to far greater destruction in poor countries than in rich ones. An earthquake of the same magnitude in Japan and in Pakistan will wreak quite different effects in terms of casualties and damage. A flood in the Czech Republic and a flood in Bangladesh are different cataclysms, even if the physical scale is comparable. A drought in California and a drought in Baja California are not the same drought. When natural disasters are serious enough, they can cause havoc in the affected areas of developed countries. Small countries can be devastated, with their levels of output set back. When they return to the status quo ante years later, their average growth equals a stagnant zero. In 1992, Hurricane Andrew cost the United States 0.5 percent of its GDP. In 1998, Hurricane Gilbert cost Jamaica 28 percent. This single storm left the rate of growth for the twelve years from 1990 to 2001 at −0.5 percent.

The differentiation of incomes, with all its consequences, takes on various forms. It can be felt within countries, regions, and cities. In Rio de Janeiro, the street that runs between the favela of Rocinha and the affluent Gávea is like the boundary between two different realities. The fact that incomes are seventeen times higher and unemployment only one ninth as high in Gávea has much to do with its greater life expectancy, which is thirteen years longer than in the adjacent slum. Barely less shocking disproportions can be found in the world's wealthiest metropolises—in Melbourne, Hong Kong, Johannesburg, Rome, and Chicago. In the poorer countries, however, in view of the generally lower level of development, these disproportions are often literally deadly to the people at the bottom of the social ladder.

The Gini coefficient is a universally applied measure of income inequality. It can also be used to measure disparities of wealth (assets). It is named for the Italian demographer and statistician Corrido Gini, who developed it in 1912. The Gini coefficient is expressed in percentages from 0 (perfect equality) to 1 (perfect inequality), and an associated measure known as the Gini index is the coefficient multiplied by 100, so that we encounter both forms, giving the figure for Poland, for example, as either 0.341 or 34.1.

An explanation of the method of calculating and interpreting the Gini coefficient relies on what is known as the Lorenz curve, which represents the cumulative distribution function of the dispersal of incomes, showing them in graphic form for each percentile of households as a percent of the total income. A perfectly equal distribution results in a straight line rising at a 45-degree angle from the horizontal axis. This is egalitarianism, when each receives exactly the same amount—each percentile of the population receives 1 percent of the total. This is complete leveling. On the other hand, if the distribution were ideally unequal, then the Lorenz curve would be contiguous with the horizontal and vertical axes. This would mean that one person gets everything and all the rest get nothing.

Reality inevitably lies between these two extremes. This means that the Lorenz curve always has a concave shape in relation to the 45-degree line. Together, the line and the curve have a bow shape, with a taut bowstring and a bent handle. The more bent it is, the greater the area lying between the Lorenz curve and the 45-degree ideal line; the Gini coefficient is the difference between that area and the whole area of the triangle marked off by the ideal line. The Gini coefficient, in theoretical terms, must therefore be somewhere between 0 (total leveling) and 1 (total inequality). In reality, it is located in a relatively large band between about 0.2 and about 0.7.

I have no desire to make things more complicated, but only to explain them; nevertheless, it would be unthinkable to omit a couple of salient methodological reservations here. This is partly because the Gini coefficient is often juggled in a variety of ways, sometimes inadvertently and at other times out of political considerations, depending on whether someone is trying to prove that things are getting better, or getting worse. There is a particularly broad margin for interpretive manipulation, as opposed to the much "harder" data of the inflation or unemployment rates.

The first remark has to do with a significant time delay. The indexes sometimes illustrate the situation from several years earlier, sometimes more than ten years earlier. This must be borne in mind, despite the fact that short-term changes are normally small. The question is: "Are these normal times?" Certainly not in the countries of the postsocialist transformation, where there have been structural alterations of the distribution of income. While the difference between the 1992 and the 2007 Gini coefficients for Sweden or Belgium are minimal, for Kazakhstan or Serbia they are dramatic.

The second remark has to do with the categories of income covered by the Gini coefficient. The figure given earlier for Poland is based on estimates of household income derived from the random surveys of household budgets that the Main Statistical Office carries out periodically. There is a later index that refers to inequalities of wages and salaries, and amounts to 0.345. The difference is minimal, but a meticulous observer might use it to conclude that the situation is getting worse (or better, depending on the kind of differentiation he or she prefers).

The third remark is this: The Gini coefficient tells us a great deal about income disparities, but nothing about wealth inequality. For simplicity's sake, we can assume that the latter is a long-term function of the former, or more precisely, of the part of it that is saved. Theoretically, this would be so—if not for the fact that there are other receipts that income statistics miss. This is why, even in countries with a relatively egalitarian distribution of income, there can be large concentrations of wealth (or assets) in the hands of a small part of the population. In Sweden, for instance, the Gini coefficient is only 0.25 (data from 2000), yet it is estimated that the wealthiest 5 percent of the population controls no less than 77 percent of the wealth. It says something about Sweden that we know this at all, because there are no comparable statistics for most countries. Perhaps it's better not to know.

The fourth remark involves the question of the quality of the data. The minimal difference between calculating the Gini coefficient on the basis of income or wages and salaries might suggest that the data are imprecise. This is because the category of "income" includes several other important components (including capital gains and dividends, disability and pension payments, earnings from activities not registered in the official GDP figures, and transfers from abroad). This accounts for the difference when the coefficient is calculated on one or the other of these bases.

The fifth remark concerns the source of the estimates. The results are usually identical or nearly identical, because they are based on the same data, which usually come from national statistics or use the trusted calculations of such international organizations as the United Nations or the World Bank. However, there are discrepancies that are difficult to explain without detailed analysis. For instance, in the case of Armenia, the U.N. estimate is 0.338, whereas the CIA World Factbook estimate is 0.413. The fact that the first is for 2003 and the second for 2004 explains nothing, because there can have been few important changes in such a short time.

The sixth remark is obvious, but worth making. The Gini coefficient has to do with the proportion of expenditures or incomes. In the case of incomes, it can either refer to those that are in monetary form or take into account the value of goods and services obtained in kind (such as free medicine, health care, or education). In this way, it overlooks other important aspects not only of consumption, but also of access to important services.

Because we want to survey the world, it would be a good idea to leave aside statistics illustrating the distribution of income within countries. However, it would be a mistake to do so too soon, because this differentiation is also an essential part of the global panorama. The Gini coefficient shows great diversity by region, ranging from 0.25 in Europe and 0.33 in South Asia to 0.57 in Latin America and no less than 0.7 in sub-Saharan Africa. Naturally, these frameworks contain a great deal of variation by country. We can illustrate this by turning to just three groups of countries.

First, with the lowest relative level of inequality, we have affluent countries with a socially advanced market economy and an activist state, along with some postsocialist countries. The ten most egalitarian societies in the world, according to U.N. data, are Azerbaijan (with a Gini coefficient of 0.19), Denmark (0.247), Japan (0.249), Sweden (0.25), the Czech Republic (0.254), Norway and Slovakia (0.258), Uzbekistan (0.268), Finland (0.269), and Ukraine (0.281). Not far behind come Germany (0.283) and the majority of the European postsocialist countries.

The second group, at the opposite end of the spectrum, consists of very poor countries. Some of them are at the very nadir globally. Most are African, although three are in Latin America and one in the Caribbean. Two of the highest Gini coefficients in the world are found in Namibia (0.743) and neighboring Botswana (0.63), where white elites own lucrative farms and diamond mines that account for 25 percent of world output, whereas the majority inhabits the sands of the Kalahari. It is worth noting that, after oil-rich Equatorial Guinea and South Africa, Namibia and Botswana have the third and fourth highest per capita GDPs on the continent, at $7,600 and $13,300, respectively. Lesotho (0.632) has a slightly higher Gini coefficient than Botswana. Other countries in this group include Sierra Leone (0.629), the Central African Republic (0.613), Swaziland (0.609), Bolivia (0.601), Haiti (0.592), Colombia (0.586), and Paraguay (0.578).

The third group includes the remaining five countries from the prosperous G-7 club and seven countries that could be referred to as the Alter-G-7, which have a special political and economic position in the world economy because of their resource, demographic, and military potential. Thus, the Gini coefficient in the United States is 0.408, whereas it is 0.36 in Italy and the United Kingdom, and 0.327 in France and Canada. It is 0.567 in Brazil, 0.447 in China, 0.437 in Nigeria, 0.399 in Russia, 0.325 in India, 0.343 in Indonesia, and 0.306 in Pakistan.

Another way of observing the proportions in income distribution is to measure the ratio of the average income of specific segments of the population, ranked by income from highest to lowest. For instance, one can divide the average income of the highest-earning 1 percent of the population by that of the lowest 1 percent, or the income of the more affluent half of the population by that of the poorer half. Two indicators are most frequently applied in comparative statistics: decile ratios (dividing the average income of the upper 10 percent of earners in the population by that of the lowest 10 percent) or quintile ratios (the top fifth divided by the lower fifth).

Each of us belongs to a decile group in our country, in the world, in our place of employment, and in the place where we live. Few people, however, know where they stand, because they never think about it. It's worth taking the time to do so. As I mentioned earlier, the per capita GDP for the entire world in 2007 was about $10,000. We can see how we stand in relation to that figure, while bearing in mind that it is not a measure of monetary income, but of the fraction of the GDP that falls to each of us. The difficulties of aggregating the data make things more complicated when we calculate the income for specific percentile groups.

How do the decile ratios look in different places around the globe? Is a map drawn on this basis analogous to one drawn according to Gini coefficients? Yes, it is similar. There is less disproportion in Europe and Asia, and more in Africa and Latin America. Only Ethiopia breaks into the list of the twenty countries with the lowest decile ratios, with all the rest coming from Europe or Asia. Ethiopia's ratio is 6.5 (the highest-earning tenth of the population garners 25.5 percent of all income, whereas the poorest tenth accounts for only 3.9 percent). This intriguing exception results from the otherwise inglorious heritage of the quasi-socialist Derg military junta, which enforced a policy of radical egalitarianism from 1974 to 1987.

Unfortunately, most other African countries fall at the opposite extreme. Interestingly enough, Latin American countries fare worse when decile ratios are used instead of the Gini coefficient. No fewer than thirteen of them feature on the list of the twenty countries with the highest decile ratios. The ten countries with the highest disproportions of income are Bolivia (157.3), Namibia (129), Lesotho (96.6), Botswana (80.9), Paraguay (75.7), the Central African Republic (68.1), Haiti (68.1), Colombia (67.0), Brazil (57.3), and El Salvador (55.4).

Egalitarian tendencies appear in the same group of postsocialist and advanced-social-market economies as with the Gini coefficient, but also in Bangladesh (6.8) and Pakistan (6.6). Ten countries have decile ratios at or below 6: Norway (6.0), Slovenia (5.9), Ukraine (5.9), Albania (5.9), Finland (5.7), Hungary (5.6), Bosnia and Herzegovina (5.5), the Czech Republic (5.2), Japan (4.5), and Azerbaijan (3.3). The strikingly even dispersion in highly developed Japan results from cultural conditions and long-term state policy that saw balanced distribution as an important instrument for maintaining high economic growth. The case of Azerbaijan is also astounding and must be explained in terms of its unique blend of systemic holdovers, its cultural makeup, and its natural conditions. This post-Soviet republic with a transformed post-socialist economy is also a Muslim country endowed by nature with rich petroleum resources.

Let's think about what these extreme cases mean. In Azerbaijan, the upper 10 percent receives 18 percent of the income and the lower 10 percent receives 5.4 percent; in Bolivia, the top 10 percent takes in 47.2 percent of the income, whereas the same percentage at the bottom of the social and economic ladder earns a mere 0.4 percent of the country's income. Someone might say that these extremes refer to small, unrepresentative groups of the population—that the most impoverished 10 percent of Bolivians amounts to only 910,000 people. The trouble is that, on a global scale, these hundreds of thousands become hundreds of millions. No fewer than 1.3 billion people live on less than a dollar a day, and this is an unsustainable state of affairs.

Surveys carried out on a regular basis by Latinobarometro, a Chilean organization specializing in public opinion research, show clearly that society's patience is stretched thin. In South America as a whole, people are far more worried about unemployment and poverty than about terrorism. Recently, 71 percent of respondents felt that their countries were governed for the benefit of a small group of powerful interests, rather than for the good of the people as a whole. It is more the result of income inequality than of low absolute level of income that many Latin American countries have voted in democratic elections for left-wing parties and leaders, including Evo Morales as president of the extremely unequal Bolivia. Some are surprised that it has taken so long for this to occur, and others that it has not yet happened in more countries.

Leaving aside the ethical and political aspects of such monstrous inequality, there can be no doubt that it is detrimental to economic growth. Poverty does not cause such a patently unjust distribution of income; rather, it is the unjust distribution of income that causes poverty. There is no single, universal threshold of inequality above which the rate of growth slows down (or conversely, below which it speeds up)—this also depends on the historical and cultural context. There are cases where exceeding a Gini coefficient of around 0.35 begins taking the wind out of the sails, and others where this only occurs at 0.45. There is no hard-and-fast dividing line. The important thing is the impact of inequality on social cohesion, because this is what reinforces or hampers developmental tendencies. This is one of the reasons cohesion is such an imperative in E.U. development strategy, and rightly so.

———————

We can now look at income inequality on a world scale, and not only within specific countries. Enormous methodological problems occur here. We shall confine ourselves to the most crucial ones. There are two basic methods of analyzing inequality. In the first, we compare the average incomes of individual countries with those of other countries, using this as the basis for the Gini coefficient. In the second, we treat the entire world population as a single group, and calculate its coefficient— as befits the inhabitants of a single world economy rather than an agglomeration of many national economies. The results, clearly, are different. What is more, there are times when they diverge. This is why it is possible to arrive at seemingly contradictory indications that the inequality of incomes in the world is both rising and falling.

We shall explain this clearly and fully. Let us assume that the world is not divided into some 200, but rather into two countries: the South and the North. Each has a population of two people; the global population is four. Let's compare their incomes, which stand at 3 units and 7 units, respectively, for the two people in the South, and 4 and 6 in the North. What is the degree of international inequality? If we use the first method, we calculate the average income in each of the two countries. In both cases, the GDP is 10, which means that the average per capita income is 5 in both. There is no difference between incomes in this world, but rather absolute equality of the two countries. The Gini coefficient for the world is 0. However, we do have inequality within each of the two countries. In South, the ratio of the 50 percent of the population with the highest incomes to that with the lowest is 2.33 (7 to 3). In North, it is only 1.5 (6 to 4). Now let us look at the Gini coefficient for the global population, with its GDP of 20, broken down as follows: 3, 4, 6, and 7. When we calculate the Gini coefficient, it comes out to 0.175. Thus, there is no equality. Income in this world is unequal. And so, which of these two outcomes is true? Both of them are—just as in the case of data from the real world.

Now let us assume that income dispersion changes in the two countries, moving toward greater inequality in both cases. In South, the incomes are now 1 and 9, and in North they are 2 and 8. If we compare the two countries on the basis of average incomes, we see that they amount to 5 in both cases, and therefore that nothing has changed in the world. Income is divided the way it was before—and yet, when we consider the world population as a whole, with incomes broken down as 1, 2, 8, and 9, the Gini coefficient jumps to 0.375. The world distribution inequalities of the preceding period have become radically worse. So which result is true? Both of them are.

When looking at statistics, then, it is necessary to know not only how to use them, but also what we are looking at. It's necessary to have a theory.

The Gini coefficient calculated for the world through the country-to-country comparison of average incomes of individual countries (based on available data for 156 countries, covering 96 percent of the global population), was 0.549 in 2000 and 0.5453 in 2001. Calculated the second way, taking into account the differentiation of incomes within countries—and not only between them—the Gini was 0.619 in 2005 (based on comparative data available for 126 countries that account for 93 percent of humanity).

This last indicator can be compared with historical calculations made at ten-year intervals. In 1980, 1990, and 2000, the Gini coefficient was 0.667, 0.650, and 0.627, respectively. The figure for 2005 thus confirms the hypothesis of a decrease in income inequality over the last quarter century. Furthermore, short-term data from the beginning of the current decade suggest that inequality is continuing to decrease. This supports the hypothesis that global inequality of income distribution results more from income differences within individual countries than it does from differences between countries.[2]

In an obvious way, the differences yielded by these two approaches must be far greater when more percentile groups are compared. This is why, in such cases, we do not compare national averages, but rather the distribution within countries, including their extremes. The upper decile contains the 10 percent of the world's population with the highest incomes, and the lower decile contains the poorest 10 percent. It is hardly surprising that the decile ratio computed in this way is no less than 61.4, whereas the estimate on a country-to-country basis is only

34.3. We should add that, if you want to compare a given country to the world as a whole, you must use the first, higher ratio. This means that the inequality of the distribution of income on a planetary scale is closer to the figure for sub-Saharan Africa than to that for Europe.

When we use the method of country-to-country comparison, we see that, in 2005, the richer half of the world had an income 4.97 times higher than the poorer half—as if, in our neighborhood, the five most affluent families had average incomes 4.97 times as high as the average for the five poorest families. If we look at this same situation in a cross-border view, discarding the country-to-country perspective, the ratio is 8.63 (as if the average income of the twenty most prosperous people in our neighborhood were 8.63 times as high as the average income of our twenty poorest neighbors).

In the case of the quintile ratio, the figures are 16.39 country-to-country and 29.95 across borders (as if the average income of the two most affluent families in our neighborhood were 16.39 times that of the average for the two poorest families, whereas the average income of the eight highest-earning people was no less than 29.95 times as much as that of the eight poorest individuals). As one might suppose, the difference for the richest and poorest 1 percent is even more glaring. The most prosperous 1 percent of earthlings have an income 60.6 times the income of the poorest 1 percent when we compare the national averages for specific income groups, but this figure jumps to 443 when we analyze all humanity as a whole.

Behind these dry indexes there are real people and their fates. In sixty-one of the planet's 222 countries and territories, life expectancy is below sixty-five years. That is retirement age in the developed countries, and those who reach it will live about twenty more years, on average. In the fifteen-and-above age group, 23 percent of women (760 million) and 18 percent of men (600 million) cannot read or write. In Niger, outside the capital city, 93 percent of women are illiterate. In Cambodia, four fifths of the population has no access to running water. In Uganda, only 5 percent have electricity. This is a vale of tears, indeed.

In recent years, the differentiation of material and living conditions has moved onto a completely new plane, as highlighted by the so-called digital divide. This is the gap between countries, regions, or social groups in terms of their computer hardware and software, and their access to the Internet. The digital divide is enormous and, interestingly, corresponds in certain respects to patterns of income inequality. In 2006, more than a billion people used the Internet. This is a great civilizational advance if we remember that, fifteen years earlier, hardly anyone was on line. However, although more than 70 percent of the people in North America have Internet access, the same is true of only 11 percent of the people in Asia, and fewer than 4 percent of those in Africa.

The influential World Economic Forum, famous for its wintertime gatherings of businessmen, politicians, scholars, and opinion makers in Davos, compiles a Networked Readiness Index (NRI) that estimates the potential for economies and societies to take advantage of information technology and telecommunications as a way of boosting competitiveness and development. The NRI has three components that add up to a maximum of six points:

- The infrastructural and legal environment in a given country or region (state, province, district, canton, township, commune, etc.).
- The readiness of actors (individuals, households, companies, organizations, local and national governments) to use information and telecommunications technology.
- The extent to which these actors make use of the available technology.

The Nordic and English-speaking countries lead the list. The top ten consists of Denmark (5.71 points), Sweden (5.66), Singapore (5.60), Finland (5.59), Switzerland (5.58), The Netherlands (5.54), the United States (5.54), Iceland (5.50), the United Kingdom (5.45), and Norway (5.42). Poland is in fifty-eighth place (3.69), just behind Jordan (3.74) and ahead of China (3.68). The most advanced country from the post-socialist transformation, Estonia (5.02), is in twentieth place, whereas the least advanced, Albania (2.87), is 107th.

The stragglers at the very end of the list are mostly from Africa, with single countries from Asia and South America thrown in. Cameroon (2.74) is 113th, followed by Paraguay (2.69), Mozambique (2.64), Lesotho (2.61), Zimbabwe (2.60), Bangladesh (2.55), Ethiopia (2.55), Angola (2.42), Burundi (2.40), and Chad (2.16).

What does such a low NRI mean? I have been in most of these countries and know that you can find an Internet cafe almost wherever there are telephone lines and a few hours of electricity a day. You can read and send e-mail, but that's about it. Working conditions in offices and at universities make it impossible to use the Internet in any satisfactory way because of the unreliable equipment, slow connections, and limited bandwidth. A notebook in Bujumbura on the shores of Lake Tanganyika, if you happen to have one there, is not the same as a notebook on the shores of Lake Michigan. Internet coverage is sparse, few computers are connected, but there are computers. The libraries lack standard textbooks, but you can try to go online. There are no paved sidewalks, but there are wireless telephones. There's nothing to eat, but there's something to watch. This is a developmental phenomenon; when rich countries were at this low level, there were no computers because they hadn't been invented yet. Even in countries at an average level of development today, the NRI a few years ago was lower than it is in Chad today. Distances in the realm of GDP are measured in centuries, but in the categories of the NRI, they are measured in years. This has implications for development.

Numberless politicians, experts, analysts, and journalists keep lamenting the fact that one fifth of humanity subsists on less than the symbolic dollar a day, the conventional threshold of abject misery. Half the inhabitants of the so-called developing countries, 2.6 billion people, live on less than $2 a day, which is treated as the threshold of poverty. The World Bank and the U.N. development agencies have been bombarding us with data and analyses on this subject for more than a decade. In 2004, the bank made a big deal out of the fact that, for the first time in all the years that it had been applying this simplified, media-friendly measurement, the number of people below the dollar-a-day level fell below a billion, to 986 million. That is only 18.4 percent of the inhabitants of the developing countries.

The political leaders of rich countries, the international economic and financial organizations, and the allied development economists all strained to suggest that this was a result of their aid and of the fact that their advice was being listened to. Yet this is hardly the case. They should have addressed all their gratitude to China and the unconventional path it is following. It is China, by refusing to heed neoliberal counsel, that has created the facts that made such a favorable impression on the World Bank and the International Monetary Fund, and the experts in New York and Geneva. During the fifteen years from 1990 to 2004, the number of poor people barely making ends meet on less than $30 a month (according to purchasing power) in China fell from 374 million to 128 million—that is, from 33 percent of the population to

9.9 percent. This figure continues to fall. By way of contrast, this percentage diminished only minimally in sub-Saharan Africa, from 45.7 to 41.1 percent of the population, and in absolute terms, it grew from 240 to 298 million. In 1990, there were one and a half times as many people living in abject poverty in China as in sub-Saharan Africa; in 2008, there were only a third as many.

Complaints about how hard it is to live on less than a dollar a day are mostly heard at conferences in luxury hotels and resorts, from people who travel business class, all expenses paid. Or they drop from the lips of various advisors and experts from governments, regional development banks, and international economic and financial organizations. They wear themselves out flying from Western metropolises to the capitals of poor countries, where they stay as a rule in luxury hotels, with hardship expense accounts of $100 or $200 per diem, collecting fees of $500 or $1,000 a day.

Expertise costs, but a lot of this money goes down the drain, or into the sand. There is wringing of hands at political summits, in the air-conditioned offices of the bureaucrats, and at more-or-less scholarly seminars. We read about it in the newspapers and watch televised commentaries accompanied by disturbing images, as we sit in our easy chairs, wearing our slippers. Yet hardly anyone is really upset. Not only among the audience, but also among the talking heads and the columnists who write about life on less than a dollar a day, there are few who have ever experienced such a life. What does life on such a budget look like?

It depends on where, but it's not much of a life. It's one thing in the crowded slums of Latin American, Asian, or African urban Molochs, where everything is clamorous, filthy, stuffy, and often perilous, and another thing in the countryside, where season follows season in the effort to make ends meet in the wide-open spaces. Slumdwellers spend most of their time there, although some manage to go into town and earn a pittance at an occasional job. In the villages or in the bush, people sometimes manage to hunt or catch something, but not as much as they used to. There are seldom schools or any kind of medical personnel. There is no running water and there are no sewers. Nor is there electricity or any of the things it powers. Many go hungry and many are sick, more commonly in the slums than in the countryside. Existence depends to a large degree on the weather and the caprices of nature, especially in the villages, where these factors often determine survival to a greater degree than money does. There's hardly any money, because backward agricultural countries do their essential business within the natural barter economy.

The world is getting more crowded, especially in its poorest regions. A hundred years ago, 70 percent of people lived in the poor countries. That was slightly more than 1.2 million people. Today a similar number of people live in extreme poverty, and 80 percent of humanity, or 5.3 billion people, live in poor countries. The majority live in villages, although the number of urban and rural dwellers in the world is now even. People live worst in the overcrowded, filthy cities, without the necessary infrastructure, with enormous rates of unemployment and crime, and in a poisoned environment. Most of the young people want to escape, to emigrate. They know better than anyone that it is impossible to live there in the long term. Few can hold out. Over time, they will have to get out or die.

Those who do not die remain alive in various ways. Those various ways range from misery and poverty through a middle-class existence and relative affluence, all the way to wealth and great riches. At one extreme, existence on the boundary of life; at the other, a life of total satiation. Every day, unfortunately, people die of hunger and malnutrition by the tens of thousands. Every day, as well, people wonder how to squander or invest their money. Unfortunately, there are far more of the former than of the latter. While some, the few, live from project to project, from deal to deal, from one great political event to the next social gala, others, a great many, live from morning to night. Others still, also a great many, live from one paycheck or harvest to the next.

The area of Niger is twice as great as that of Texas or four times as great as that of Poland. It lies partly in the Sahara and partly in the Sahel, on the boundary between the desert sands and the somewhat more productive land to the south. Thirteen million people live there. The poorest 10 percent has an average annual income estimated at 10,700 units of the local currency, the CFA. This is about $22 per person at the official exchange rate, or $76 at PPP.

Among the more than a million people at this income level are the eight members of Sani Barre's family. Their entire annual income, the outcome of statistical analysis and their own hard work, is equal to $600 in terms of purchasing power, which is a concept that no one here understands, and why should they? Here it simply means 86,000 CFA or about 235 CFA per day for the whole household. They seldom see money, however, because the village has a predominantly natural economy. Nevertheless, the relationship between goods and money has been flourishing recently. The waves of globalization have even been reaching here, in the form of needs originating far away. There is a need for their labor, because it yields products that are in demand elsewhere.

Sani is thirty-five and his wife Fatimata is thirty-four. She has given birth to seven children, but one died at birth and another before turning five. They also have Fatimata's sick mother to look after. She is fifty and has trouble getting around. She doesn't have much longer, because no one has very long here. She is the only one in the family who can read a little, but there is nothing to read. None of them can write. However, they can draw, especially the children. They can even draw a rhino, which no one here has ever seen.

There might seem to be an excess of children, but this is not true. It's better that way, because there will always be someone to look after the parents in their old age, just as Fatimata is caring for her mother now. Old age is just around the corner.

They live in Okedede village in the Aïr Mountains, a lovely basalt mountain range and plateau covering an area as large as Switzerland. On the horizon is the endless Sahara. A stone wall, resting on sand, surrounds their homestead, and offers at least a hint of protection against the frequent high winds that blow sand into people's eyes. The Polish proverb about the wind always blowing into poor people's faces could have been coined here.

In one corner of the yard is a little flock of eight chickens, and in the opposite corner are three goats, under a roof on sticks. A nondescript dog, thin but cheerful, plays among the pack of children. Unlike people, dogs can always be cheerful, even when the poverty grinds them down their whole lives long. The one-room dwelling stands at the back of the yard, to the right. The walls are stone, with a mixture of desert vegetation and sun-cracked clay stuffed into the cracks. The roof is made of fiber-cement board, but there are houses nearby thatched with branches dragged here from the savannah.

The house is almost unfurnished aside from a beat-up plastic cabinet, a scratched mirror, and some hooks on which a couple of pots and some clothing hang. Modern conveniences, as they say elsewhere, are completely absent, unless we count the hammock, and an oil lamp that smokes terribly. On the wall is a yellowed Air France calendar, from the year 2000. It shows the Eiffel Tower. If you stacked up all the houses from the three nearest villages, they wouldn't reach to the top of it. In the yard there are two beds, made of boards, covered with blankets older than anyone in the family, but without mattresses. The fireplace is outdoors, in front of the house. In the fourth corner of the yard, there is nothing. Holding her second-youngest child, who tries in vain to suckle at her sagging breast, Fatimata can go over to the wall there and chat with a neighbor woman returning from the desert with a bundle of dry sticks on her back.

Half the people in the village are younger than fifteen. No one is over sixty. Aside from the homesteads, there is nothing here except for a small, attractive mosque, renovated and painted a pale spring-green color, with a graceful minaret. It is only slightly larger than the village houses. A dozen or more kilometers away is a larger mosque, with a Koranic school attached. That is a big thing: as the children copy out verses from the Koran on their tablets, they learn to write. They learn in Arabic, but also pick up Hausa, which is more important than French here, along the way. With Hausa you can make yourself understood at every marketplace. The mosque and the school were built with financial aid from Saudi Arabia.

And then there's the shop. What this means is that one of the houses has a window facing the road. It is hung with every imaginable kind of merchandise, and stays open from dawn until night. There are matches and candles, canned beans and tins of sardines, peanuts and bundles of dried hot peppers. There are always tea and sugar. There is some kind of colorful sweet drink in clear plastic containers. There is Coca-Cola, too. Everything is at room temperature. We are in the mountains, so the temperature is only 85 degrees Fahrenheit. There really isn't much merchandise here, but 8 kilometers away, at the Thursday market— tomorrow—they'll have everything. Tomatoes and peas, chicken and goat meat, material and towels, plastic buckets and tin teapots, sweet mangos and figs, oil and soap, crayons and notebooks. They also have Chinese flashlights.

We get up at dawn, with the chickens. A couple of village roosters begin crowing when the sky is still dark. Everyone who has the strength to do so gets up. No one dawdles, because days are short all year long at this latitude, never more than two hours longer than the nights. You have to fight to survive. It's a slow struggle. Everybody goes their own way, without emotion. The chickens wander wherever they please. So do the goats, but it's a good idea to shoo them to a place where they can find something to pluck at. The Sahel is no alpine meadow. These goats make life possible; they take care of themselves and eat almost anything. They give milk, and when they can't do that any more, they make it possible to have a little meat once a week for half the year. The goats are a matter for the children, that is, for those old enough to have stopped clinging to their mother's only skirt. They don't go to school, so there's a lot of time, right up to dusk. At night, you sleep. You sleep a long time because the evenings are short without lighting, and, besides, you're tired. Why wouldn't you be?

At dawn, there is no breakfast, but the children get a piece of hard-tack each, and a tomato to share. Fatimata wraps her youngest daughter, Leilat, in a scarf (imported from China) and slings her across her back. Leilat looks very frail. Fatimata places a wine-skin sewn from goat leather (a local product) on her head, along with a plastic cup (manufactured domestically), and heads out to get water. The well is not close at hand. What that means is that, this year, it is 3 kilometers each way, because the nearer ones are dry. Other women are also on their way, making everything chatty, colorful, merry, and lively. There they go. They'll be back in two hours. It'll be after eight then, but it won't be oppressively hot yet. That is when the women and the children will eat their meager morning fare.

Other women go to the fields. They're not very big, more like garden plots. Stones still need to be cleared away here and there. That's a good thing, because the stones come in handy for reinforcing the low walls and the houses, but only the heavy ones, and they have to be carried because there aren't enough wheelbarrows to go around.

The fields are like fields everywhere. There are both women and men there. Sani grows onions. Others grow carrots, or a few tomatoes, but most of all there is millet. There is nothing more. Life without millet is impossible. And onions! They said they needed onions. They even came in motor vehicles and gave instructions on how to plant and weed them. There aren't many weeds here, because few things grow at all. The onions, red onions, the best ones in the world, grow. They keep nothing for themselves. It's all for export. They always take a few onions to the market, but those go for export, too. Every so often a couple of men show up with mules. Some of them, the rich ones, even have camels. They take the onions away in sacks. They take them down to the road, to the pickups. From there big trucks take them farther. In the village, no one knows that "farther" refers to the capital, Niamey, and that airplanes take them from there to France, or even farther. That's how good the onions are. Yet no one here knows where they go. They know that it's beyond the desert, but the desert has no end. Or they've even heard that it's beyond the equally great water, but how is it even possible for water to be great?

As long as there isn't a drought or floods from violent rainstorms, things are okay. It's better in the dry season and worse in the rainy season. Then there's less work and more time, and what is there to do? When it pours down rain, there's not even anywhere to go, because the house is crowded when everyone's inside. The worst thing is when the locusts attack, as they did last year. They eat everything. Just like goats, except a goat won't eat a person, because you can drive a goat away. Not the locusts.

Yet perhaps the worst thing of all is when the local wars and border conflicts come here. At such times, more people die than are born. It's a nightmare. It's a good thing that the borders are distant. Here all borders are dangerous. The worst ones are with Mali and Algeria, but the ones with Benin and Libya are almost as bad. Niger can't agree with any of its neighbors except Cameroon about where the border is. It was the French and the English who drew those lines on the map.

All the work in the fields is handwork. There are no farm machines, although there is irrigation equipment, but it doesn't work because there's no money to buy diesel fuel. You have to use a hoe. The rainwater fills up the holes, and you pump it out by hand. It's unfit for drinking, but just right for watering plants. It's pumped into wooden troughs, and from there ingenious chutes carry it to the left and right, among the rows of crops, just like 1,000 years ago.

Fatimata comes to the fields at eleven. There is a twenty-four-hour supply of drinking water at home. It's enough for everyone, because they don't need much. Nobody bathes very often here. You have to wash sparingly. Fatimata has given her children and mother their first meal and now brings her husband his portion. The plastic bowl contains a kind of African pap made of millet soaked in water mixed with goat milk. This is the African equivalent of corn flakes. There's added sugar, because it's healthy that way, and you need a source of energy. It's easy to eat if you don't eat anything else. You get used to it.

Sani remains in the field with his onions until late afternoon. Fatimata returns home. It will soon be two o'clock. The sun is beating down. It's necessary to sit in the shade, but there isn't much of it. Fortunately, an acacia tree growing near the road casts a bit of shadow into the yard at this time of the day. Fatimata sits there with one of her friends to have a lunch that consists of a few peanuts and some tea with sugar.

It is time to clean up the yard. With the goats and the chickens, there will always be dirt. She keeps it clean, really clean, with no litter. There's not much to do in the room, except to sweep and tidy up, and help her mother. There's no toilet here, but people must do what is necessary. Others run to spots far away from the village, but old people don't have the strength. They need help—either to lead them outside, or to clean up.

The children, along with the goats and the dog, are in other yards. They're all over the place. The older ones are in the field, because there's work to do. The middle children spend hours walking around near the village, gathering branches blown on the wind so that they will have something to cook the evening meal with. It's always worth checking the window, that is, the shop. They might have new merchandise. Sometimes they do. There are hairpins, lighters, mirrors, and plastic containers. It doesn't look as if anyone is buying anything, but the shop stays in business.

It's getting chilly, because it's late. It's getting dark. On his way back from the field, Sani stops at the mosque for a moment, squats down, and bows his head to the ground, facing east, toward Mecca. It's his fourth prayer today. He prays for Leilat, for his family, for his village, for the Aïr Mountains, for everyone. The day after tomorrow is Friday, so there will be more people here. It is a holy day. Once again, he will be able to pray for everyone.

The village is buzzing. The farmers have returned from the fields. The goats are home, too. It's not clear who led whom, but perhaps it was the children leading the goats, because the goats are full and the children are hungry. They dropped in during the day for their pap, and now it's time for more pap—couscous. It's made from millet, served with carrots and cooked in a pot over the fireplace. To give it some flavor, a little paprika has been added, just enough. Sometimes Fatimata manages to add an egg, but not today. Tomorrow is market day, so she'll need to sell a couple of eggs. A few CFA will come in handy. She'll be able to buy batteries for the Chinese flashlight, which hasn't been working for a couple of days now. And she'll need more for sugar, peas, and perhaps some second-hand clothes for the children.

It's evening. People are meeting up, chattering, and joking. After all, there's so much to tell about! They sit on the sand near the fire. No one drinks alcohol, and few smoke. However, all the grownups drink strong, sweet tea in tiny glass cups. The men talk business; they talk onions. What's making the merchants with the mules so stubborn that they don't want to pay more? You can see the men's eyes sparkling when they say that the merchants with the mules will be ready to haggle when they learn about the other buyers, the ones with camels.

If there's no demand, they can't sell any more, or at a higher price. The demand for local goods—natural resources and human skill—must stimulate supply. Isn't that how it works? They won't come, not the ones with the mules and not the ones with the camels, unless there are enough onions. So the supply of local goods and services must stimulate demand. Isn't that how it works?

Well, if they had a little more money, then they'd have to decide: a cart, or a wheelbarrow?

The evening doesn't last long, because it's dark and they need to be thrifty with their wood. There's so little of it here. It's time to sleep, on the beds outside the house or on the ground. Inside are only the old lady, sleeping in the hammock, and two of the children on the earthen floor. When the last of the fire stops glowing, you can see the myriad stars sparkling in the sky. Only here, in the Sahel, can you have stars like this on less than a dollar a day. This must be total darkness, not only in our village, but within a radius of dozens of kilometers, and total silence. That's what it is.

Another day has passed, and passed fortunately. There's no drought. Swarms of locusts are not flying their way. Unfortunately, there are few such days. All of them are times of hard work, of the struggle for survival, of the lack of any prospect beyond simple reproduction. Children are the only new thing that comes along. There are also bad days, when people cannot cope. You can keep going around and around within the same horizon, but you can't live on nothing. There are many days full of troubles and misfortunes, of not enough to eat and no strength, of sickness. But the most important thing is that no one fell sick today, and no one died. Leilat will die on Sunday.

The Barre family created and consumed a gross income of $1.60 that day. They even managed to save a bit, in the form of two chicken eggs for the Chinese batteries. For their hearty hospitality—for the African pap, the couscous, a mat in the courtyard, for watching the camel, for the fires of home, a guest from a far country left them 10,000 CFA. For him, that is not quite 60 Polish zloty, or about $20, but for them it is as much as their income for today and the rest of the month. It's enough for them to buy a new lamp and a three-month supply of oil.

They manage from day to day, from market to market, from one visit by the merchants with mules to the next, from rainy season to dry and back again. They spend a lot. Their marginal propensity to consume is equal to 100 percent, and their marginal propensity to save is equal to zero. They accumulate nothing, invest nothing, and eat up everything. If you do not invest, you stagnate.

Before them are more days like this. This is as good as it gets. In Niger, they live an average of no fewer than forty-four years.

So how does one live with a per capita income of more than $2,000 a day? We are not talking about billionaires, but about millions and millions of people. Taken together, they expend $2 or $3 billion a day. They have big problems, because it's impossible to keep spending at that rate, which means that they have to save. Because those savings quickly turn into big money, they have to invest. That's always stressful. Yet no matter how much you spend, you've always got more. Is this the source of the old proverb about how you can't buy happiness?

Switzerland is a small country. Its mountainous area is a little less than twice that of New Jersey, or a mere 13 percent of the area of Poland. Its population is 7.5 million, with an average income of $35,000. Among them are 750,000 people with an annual income at the level of 160,000 Swiss francs (CHF), or about $133,000. That works out to 440 CHF, or $365, a day. Within this category is a subgroup of about 50,000 people with an income of over 850,000 CHF, or $733,000 annually. This is more than 2,400 CHF per day—about $2,000. There are also a few thousand people with an income on the order of 8.5 million CHF, or $7.3 million, which means 24,000 CHF, or $20,000, per twenty-four-hour period, because at this level, you're making money around the clock.

Franz Lendenbaum and his family live in a sixteen-room house with lovely grounds in the exclusive Seefeld district of Zurich. Franz is forty-six, and his wife, Ruth, is forty-two. Their two children attend the most elite of private secondary schools. They have several domestics. The English governess, a native of Oxford, looks after the two daughters' English accents and drives them to school. The French cook comes from Provence. The driver, in keeping with the fact that they own a Maybach, is from Germany. The gardener is local, and the two bodyguards come from Italy. They are Sicilians.

Franz gets up at six. After swimming a hundred laps in his pool, he has breakfast: muesli with skim milk—a kind of European pap, without sugar, because it's healthy that way—and toast. At the table, he joins an intelligent conversation with Ruth, a successful oculist at a private clinic, and the children. How are things in school? "Cool," they say in English. They both like asking their teachers hard questions. What's up at the clinic? There are lots of patients. They all want to see what's going on in the world around them.

It's time to go to work. In the car, he listens to the morning news on Schweizer Radio and skims the *Neue Zürcher Zeitung*. That's enough newspaper time for the day, because too much clutters up the mind. He occasionally looks at a magazine at home. He's in his office by a quarter to eight. It's supercontemporary and elegant, with a stunning view. After briefing his secretary, he briefs his personal assistant. Both women are Swiss from head to toe. There are many technical details to cover, and all of them are important. The meetings begin at nine. For the first one, he has called in the market analysts, department heads, and the financial director. Business is great. Franz is president and majority shareholder in a company that uses high, or, more precisely, the very highest technology to produce and service custom-made equipment for enriching uranium. The company is unrivalled, in global terms, in processing uranium from the deposits in Niger. It also offers sophisticated consulting services, which often makes it necessary to fly to various places. He flies not only to Washington, Moscow, Paris, Vienna, and London, but also to Beijing, and even to the Middle East and Africa. Most frequently of all, he flies to Niamey in Niger.

There are times when he even manages to stay on for the weekend, as he will do a few days from now. He will rent a helicopter from a French company and make at least a short hop into the sublime Aïr Mountains, so different from the Alps he sees every day. A helicopter for two days, a hotel in Agadez, a jeep, a guide, camels with their tenders, and so on comes to a total of 4,500 CHF, a pittance for so much pleasure. There's the atmosphere in Agadez, where Jack Nicholson dies in a little hotel in Antonioni's *The Passenger*. They wanted to know why he was interested in who was selling arms to the Tuareg rebels, which wasn't any of his business.

Franz has a Ph.D. in nuclear physics from the prestigious Zurich Polytechnic. Ruth holds an M.D. from the university in Basel. She earns about half a million Swiss francs a year, but that's her business. She has to buy herself a new car every few years, and her current one is a Jaguar XJ. That's pocket change. Zurich ranks at the top of every survey taken among the business elite on the best places to live. It's also the most expensive, at least in terms of women's apparel, jewelry, and cosmetics. Beverley Hills is cheaper. Even in Zurich, however, you have to go shopping—not because it's cheap, but because it's a good way to run into friends. In a single day, an elegant woman like Ruth can spend several thousand francs on clothes and perfume. Fortunately, she doesn't do it every day.

Phone calls, e-mails, and videoconferences with partners take up the rest of the morning. In this business, the bigger or more important matters are settled face to face. You have to travel, and you have to receive visitors. Today there are three of them. They come from another country and are very important. If there's demand for the company's goods and services, then there must be a supply. Isn't that how it is? Or could it be that the wonderful supply means that there's never a shortage of demand? Isn't that how it is?

Time for lunch: Today Franz joins a friend from the Polytechnic who keeps an eye on what's happening in the field and kindly shares his knowledge. He's also a physicist, but a theorist. He's wasting his talents in academia, so he likes to keep in touch with practical matters and show off in the business world. They have lunch in the Haus zum Rüden. All the waiters are native-born Swiss. This is a place where even someone from Liechtenstein would be considered a Gastarbeiter. It's a light lunch. The best choice is a French dish of foie gras served with incredibly tasty rings of red onion. Where does that onion come from? The chef says that it's shipped in fresh from France, and that the French import it from Niger. It's the best in the world.

Lunch is on Franz's expense account, which means, because he owns the company, that he's paying. The wine was almost as expensive as the onion, and the bill, together with the tip, comes to 200 CHF. Back where the delicious onion comes from, that would be the equivalent of 81,000 CFA. Here, one onion, sliced and presented on a plate, costs as much as what Sani gets for ten sackfuls. Those who buy the sacks from him turn a tidy profit, and those who import them to Europe realize a 300 percent annual return on their capital. It's like the East India

Company in the seventeenth century. After all, "trade, not aid" is the basis of development, isn't it?

The lunch costs the equivalent of the Barre family's yearly income. At the moment, Franz has no idea that the Barres even exist. If he did, then what? Switzerland was also a poor country once, and it pulled itself up by its own bootstraps, just as Franz worked hard for his own company, and for his own money, and it all comes down to partnership, honesty, reciprocity, and liberality. He pays his taxes. Out of these taxes, Switzerland assigns $1.7 billion, no less than 0.43 percent of its GDP, for foreign aid. Some of that aid takes the form of the services his company delivers to the governments of some developing countries in the field of the peaceful uses of nuclear technology.

After lunch comes a meeting with a representative of a consortium of banks financing a discreet operation. This is not a business that craves publicity. You have to get along with the media, but it's better if they don't know too much. Franz prefers to steer clear, because rash commentaries cause more trouble than they're worth. Nevertheless, some media need to be cultivated, and questions are being raised this afternoon about a country that someone has recently placed on the wrong axis.

After another series of professional exchanges with staff about complex technological issues, it's time to head home. After a few last exchanges of private gossip on the computer, he leaves, stopping along the way to pick up a 2,300 CHF suit from Zegna and to look in at the Maserati dealer, because it's time to decide: Maserati or Lamborghini?

The dog, always ebullient, meets his master at the threshold. It's a Doberman. Dogs are always cheerful, even when they're rich. How are the children doing at school?

Supper is at home. It's Wednesday, the traditional day for a visitor. This time it's a friend of Ruth's from Berlin—nothing formal, but you have to take care of guests and show them a good time.

Supper is served in a spacious salon overlooking the Zürichsee. A concert Bechstein stands in one corner, just in case one of the daughters decided to become the next Martha Argerich, although the girls have other ideas. On the wall hangs an original Warhol, and there's some Tiffany glass in view. In the opposite corner are Bang & Olufsen speakers, and Vangelis's *The City* is playing. The drinks table to the right holds the best brands. There is Armagnac, and Dalmore single malt. To the left is a suite of Nicoletti chairs, a sofa, and a table on which *The*

National Geographic, *The New Yorker*, *The American Scientist*, *The Economist*, Le Carré's *The Mission Song*, and Hawking's *A Brief History of Time* may be discerned.

Franz sits late in the evening at the computer, alone in his study and with his thoughts, until midnight. He is mostly thinking about the company, the competition, political aspects, risk, finances, technological advances, and his staff. He has little time for himself or for his family.

One more glance at the markets—the Osaka exchange is opening just as New York closes. As to what's happening in Zurich, everyone knows without making any special effort. What he does not plow back into his own firm, he invests on the exchange. "At market," he says. He doesn't do so personally; he has his people. He only keeps an eye on things, simply out of curiosity. Never, as a matter of principle, does he invest in companies in his own field. Then he'd have to pray for others to prosper—for the competition's profits to rise! Let others pray for that. He prays for himself, his family, his company, for Zurich, and for Switzerland. Soon the holy day will come, and when all of them pray together for themselves, it will be just as if they were praying for everyone.

Who could add up what he spends daily? Yet if you add up all the fixed and one-time outlays, it comes to something in the neighborhood of 10,000 CHF. That is, more than $2,000 per person. It's a day like any other. In the course of it, the Lendenbaums created a gross income on the order of $20,000. Here, however, people calculate things in the long term, strategically, whole years at a time.

They spend little, because their marginal propensity to consume is a mere 40 percent, which leaves a 60 percent marginal propensity to save. They accumulate a lot, invest a lot, and eat up little of it. Those who invest develop.

Before us are more days like this. This is as good as it gets. In Switzerland, they live an average of only eighty-one years.

So it is that some—a multitude of them—live in extreme poverty, which does not mean that they will automatically and always be unhappy. Others float along in abundance—a few of them—which does not mean that they are always happy. One important thing in all of this is the fact that there has been a fundamental rise in income levels over the last few decades, although it is a shame that this does not apply to everyone. The most numerous are all of those in the variegated middle ranges. They are varied, because being in the middle is also a relative concept. It means one thing in Niger, and another in Switzerland—and yet another in Poland, with its middling level of development.

What also counts is the fact that, on the scale of the entire human race, the inequalities are less than they were a quarter of a century ago, and the average life expectancy is twenty years longer than what it was half a century ago. When I was born, the statistics allotted me, as a citizen of the world, a mere forty-six years, just like in Niger. I have managed to outlive that figure and am perfectly willing to keep going even longer. Those born today have a prospect of remaining alive for sixty-six years. They will still be around, on average, in 2076. Some, including many of those being born at present in Switzerland, will live to see the twenty-second century.

––––––––––

All these reflections prompt a somewhat broader, more thorough look at the world community. Gross product is a universal measure, the most frequently applied because it is highly useful and relatively simple to calculate. Economics loves to simplify things. Statistics loves to average them. Both love to make various assumptions to facilitate their calculations. As the old joke has it, statistics are a little bit like a swimsuit: what they reveal is interesting, but what they conceal is crucial.

As a measure of the level of development of national economies, GDP has many drawbacks. It informs us about only a part of the effects of macroeconomic activity, and furthermore overlooks some of the accompanying costs. Although they are sometimes referred to as "externalities," they can in fact be of critical importance. That is why, along with the dispersion of per capita GDP, we must also reckon with other information that is important for socioeconomic development and the quality of life. A statistical-analytical tool that serves this purpose is the Human Development Index, the HDI.[3] It takes three factors into account:

- State of health.
- Knowledge.
- Standard of living.

These are not easy to measure. Therefore, as usual, we will accept these assumptions and make them a little bit simpler. The assumption when assessing state of health is that the healthier people are, the longer they live.

Knowledge is determined from the perspective of education and the ability to read and write. The measurement is weighted. One third is derived from the combined gross enrolment rate, calculated as the sum of children and young people enrolled in primary, secondary, and tertiary education divided by the total number of people of school age, and the other two thirds from the literacy rate for adults (age fifteen and above).

Standard of living is treated as a function of the level of output and consumption. Its measure is the natural logarithm of gross domestic product per capita, in dollars, by PPP.

The index is arrived at by adding up these three measures, which in turn are calculated in detail on the basis of mathematical formulas that relativize the actual distance separating the population of a given country from a hypothetical state of "full development." This state is an arbitrary ideal in which

- Average life expectancy at birth is eighty-five years.
- The gross enrolment rate for children and young people is 100 percent and there is no adult illiteracy.
- The per capita GDP is $40,000 (by purchasing power parity).

In an ideal country, the aggregate index would be 1, and this would be made up of three dimensions, each of which would equal 0.333—or 0.(3). In a country at the human and societal nadir, the index would be only a few percent—after all, someone always lives a certain amount of years, and someone always has income of some sort, no matter how negligible. Theoretically, there is no requirement that anyone be enrolled in school, and everyone could be illiterate. In practical terms, however, there are no such instances in the world, as long as we divide it up into countries. In regions, localities, and families, unfortunately, such cases do exist. There are local communities with a Human Development Index of 1, but there are also enclaves of extreme poverty with an index of 0.1. The estimated index for the lower quintile of the population of Burkina Faso (the average for the 20 percent with the lowest HDI) is 0.140.

Is it possible to live below the very bottom? Yes. The method of estimating HDI applied by the United Nations Development Program

(UNDP) uses a model with a minimum income of $100 by PPP. I have seen many places where it is even less. In Mali, on the border with Togo, the HDI is only a few percent. The same is true in the Mozambique-Malawi borderlands. The HDI for the Barre family in the village of Okedede, Niger, is 0.061, unless they manage to live longer than average. In that case, however, someone will have to live for a shorter time. Averages are just as merciless as they are misleading.

The HDI for the Lendenbaum family is 0.978, if we assume that all four of its members will live out the average Swiss lifespan of 81 years. In view of their comfortable existence, they could easily pass four more years in peace and achieve the august age of 85. In that case, their HDI would reach the maximum. Here it's 1.000, and there it's 0.061. *C'est la vie!*

State of health, as measured by life expectancy, makes up one third of the HDI. If more people die younger, the HDI decreases automatically. Wars aside, people die younger where they give birth to large numbers of children whom they cannot feed and where many people are sick. Once again, things are worst in Africa, although there are other places where they are not good. The World Health Organization (WHO) cooperates with national administrations to monitor the state of threats to health and takes preventive or direct action in critical situations. During only three years, from September 2003 to September 2006, it identified 685 large-scale threats to health around the world. No fewer than 288 of them were in Africa, with seventy-eight in Europe and only forty-one in both Americas. Southeast Asia (eighty-one) and the Middle East (eighty-nine) were only slightly worse than Europe.

It is one of the paradoxes of civilization that things keep getting worse. So it seems when we look at the situation not from the perspective of centuries (because people no longer drop like flies, as they did during the great epidemics of the past), but rather from the perspective of the current generation. The WHO warns that things are worse than they've ever been, because new diseases are emerging at the unprecedented rate of one per year, on average. They emerge but they don't go away. Since the 1970s, thirty-nine new diseases have appeared.

In its report cautioning the world against the risks of epidemics, the WHO comes straight out and says[4] that it would be the height of naïveté to assume that there will be no new diseases with the lethal potential of HIV-AIDS or SARS. It has to happen sooner or later. A flu pandemic could attack more than 1.5 million people; that is, one human being in four.

In a situation where 2.1 billion passengers travel by air each year, viruses and other disease carriers spread very easily, quickly, and far. This is something else that makes today's world different from the past. Not only progress and technological advances, but also sickness and death propagate rapidly. The figure for air travel means that, on average, everyone on earth flies once every three years. However, it is frequent fliers who make up the total. I am one of them. I sometimes fly more than a hundred times a year, and so I am listed a hundred times among the 2.1 billion. Most people have still never seen an airplane up close, and a great many have never even seen one from a distance. Yet the infections that circulate around the world twenty-four hours a day with the frequent fliers are easily visible, and those airplanes have been known to land with something completely novel on board, like bird flu or the Ebola virus. We need to learn words like *Marburg* or *Nipah*; these are not new makes of cars but deadly viruses, about which we will hear more.

Unfortunately, old demons sometimes awake to claim new victims. Cholera is making a comeback, and yellow fever is on the offensive. In the five years from 2002 to 2006, the WHO listed more than 1,100 epidemics, including cholera and polio, that were eliminated in the Western Hemisphere, apparently once and for all, in the second half of the twentieth century. Infections caused by the meningococcus virus (*Neisseria meningitidis*) are spreading. The mycobacteria responsible for tuberculosis are growing more resistant to the antibiotics taken by carriers. Tuberculosis felled many people in the prime of life in Europe in the nineteenth and twentieth centuries, and now it is once again becoming endemic in some regions, especially in Africa. It claims almost 2 million lives per year, with ten times as many in the advanced stages of the disease.

People fall ill and die, lives are ruined and shortened, and the statistical indexes fall, either directly, as in the case of the HDI, or indirectly, as in the case of GDP. Diseases and the fight against them involve costs. When SARS flared up in 2003, the countries of Asia—China, for the most part—lost $30 billion. Prosperous countries and those as large as China can cope with such blows; similar epidemics are devastating in poorer countries. They unleash pandemonium there, affecting the quality of life at its roots and diminishing the potential GDP as a consequence.

On top of all this, we have—how could it be otherwise?—special interests and politics. The best way to see what the world is like is to travel, but you have to be incredibly cautious in the places where deadly diseases are rampant. This makes things difficult, but not impossible. It's worth taking the risk, because travel is educational. It's also necessary to read, and to read a lot. This reading should include not only professional reports from the United Nations or the WHO, and theoretical treatises in subjects ranging from economics and geopolitics to psychology and medicine, but also good books of fiction. For instance, John le Carré's *The Constant Gardener* is a fictional depiction of the ruthlessness, brutality, cynicism, and greed of major pharmaceutical companies that turn enormous profits by manufacturing drugs. Attempting to improve medications so as to boost their profits, they test them on the inhabitants of Kibera, a giant slum in Nairobi. To see how people live (and die) there, watching the film adaptation of the novel is not enough. You have to see for yourself. Life is hard, and death comes easily. Life is cheap, because medicine is expensive.

Is this fiction? Where there's smoke, there's fire, goes the saying. We could also say that, in the case of a writer of le Carré's class, there is no fiction without facts. The slums, the drug, and the company may all be different, but the problem is the same. The struggle for mass access to cheap medication that alleviates the suffering of HIV-AIDS is still going on between the poor and their advocates, especially in Africa, where this misfortune is more widespread than anywhere else in the world, and the powerful multinational pharmaceutical firms and their advocates, who can be found in the governments of countries where their factories are located, and even in certain international "aid" organizations, not excluding the WHO.

The poor countries do not have the means to pay the producers for vaccines that cost a lot to produce, especially at the testing stage before they can go into production. It takes fifteen or twenty years for these drugs to appear on the market at accessible prices. As a result, 3 million people, half of them children, die year in and year out from diseases that can be prevented through vaccination. They do not die because the vaccines do not exist, but rather because they are so expensive—and also because a very large profit margin is built into those prices. The pharmaceutical industry is one of the most lucrative in the world.

Indonesia refused to supply the WHO with samples of the H5N1 virus that caused the infectious and highly dangerous avian flu, because the country feared that the samples would be turned over to drug companies working to develop an effective vaccine that Indonesia would later have to buy at high prices. Not until the summer of 2007 did China turn over the first such sample. This is a sick state of affairs, in both political and economic terms. It illustrates the magnitude of the problems, not only medical and pharmacological, that we confront. A complex solution can only be achieved if national, transnational, and global political actors commit themselves to conciliation at the interface of business and the health services. In the contemporary world, there is an increasing need for the global coordination of treatment and prevention policies in the face of the epidemiological threat.

The ranking of the HDI of 175 countries (including the Palestinian Authority and Hong Kong) has been headed for years by Norway at 0.965. The world average is 0.741. Differences are minimal among the twenty top countries, which include all the world's richest states. In all of them, the HDI is 0.936 or above. Countries with a social market economy do especially well. The ten countries that come next after Norway are Iceland (0.960), Australia (0.957), Ireland (0.957), Sweden (0.951), Canada (0.950), Japan (0.949), the United States (0.948), Switzerland (0.947), The Netherlands (0.947), and Finland (0.947).

The small postsocialist country of Slovenia (0.910) comes in at twenty-seventh, between South Korea (0.912) and Portugal (0.904). This is the only case in which one of the new E.U. member countries outstrips one of the old ones. The Czech Republic is only slightly behind Cyprus, and Hungary is close to overtaking Malta. Other postsocialist transformation countries also show excellent results. All of them occupy much higher places in the HDI table than on the GDP list. This is a consequence of the positive heritage of the socialist system, which completely eliminated illiteracy, introduced universal primary schooling and greatly expanded the reach of secondary and tertiary education, and offered universal health care that led to a leap in life expectancy. The high growth rates under the old system also played a role. The average HDI for the twenty-eight postsocialist countries of East Central Europe and the former Soviet Union is 0.802, as compared with 0.923 for the OECD countries with their far wealthier levels of output. (The OECD does include five postsocialist countries—the Czech Republic, Hungary, Poland, Slovakia, and Slovenia—but they lower the OECD output average to only an inconsiderable degree.)

Cuba is a particularly spectacular case. Its per capita GDP of about $4,000 leaves it in 123rd place in the world, but its HDI of 0.826 places it in the leading group, in fiftieth position. This reflects a concern for education and health care, and the human condition in general, that stems from socialist values and is qualitatively different and far higher than in other countries with a comparable income level. It is interesting to note that the two countries next to Cuba on the per capita GDP list, Syria and Indonesia, lag far behind on the HDI list, in 107th and 108th places, respectively (with HDI scores of 0.716 and 0.711).

This shows the importance to economic development strategy and the quality of life of investment in social capital, education, science, culture, mass sport, and health care. Above all, it highlights the significance of the systems of values that guide countries. This is trivial and may sound like the kind of moralizing that should be avoided, but the facts confirm the thesis, and the scientific truth should be proclaimed—especially because trivial lies are sometimes held up as revelations. After all, it is not simply a matter of being mistaken when people deny, in spite of the facts, that social policies expressed in fiscal transfers to help the less privileged result in higher levels of development.

The fact is that holding the scale of income inequality within certain limits, and the accompanying budgetary redistribution—above all through the progressive taxation of relatively high incomes, with the receipts financing public investment in human and social capital—yields rapid, tangible results. This applies to both the wealthy countries of Scandinavia and the postsocialist countries, with their medium levels of development. Even in poorer, less-developed countries, a more socially balanced distribution of incomes enhances social capital and the level of satisfaction that the people feel in regard to their work and their lives.

Ten countries from sub-Saharan Africa occupy the bottom ten rungs on the Human Development Index ladder: Mozambique (0.390), Burundi (0.384), Ethiopia (0.371), Chad (0.368), the Central African Republic (0.353), Guinea Bissau (0.349), Burkina Faso (0.342), Mali (0.338), Sierra Leone (0.335), and, at the very bottom, Niger (0.311). The situation is even worse in terms of living standards and the quality of human capital than they are in terms of GDP. These countries are worse off than the poorest countries of Asia, Latin America, and the Caribbean. In the group of thirty-one countries with the lowest HDI, only two, Haiti and Yemen, are non-African. *Afrique Paradis?*

At this lower end of the scale, just as at the top, changing the distribution of the national income may not of itself lead to an immediate rise in the GDP, but it can improve the human condition somewhat. So as not to refer again to Cuba—I don't want to upset anyone—we can look at Samoa, the cleanest country in the world (El Salvador is the dirtiest). At an even lower level of income ($2,100 GDP per capita, 168th place in the world), bearing in mind what we have already said about not identifying GDP with the level of social development, it is nevertheless possible to attain a higher level of social satisfaction and have better human capital. Samoa's HDI is 0.778, ranking seventy-fifth in the world. Better human capital is not only the goal of development, but also a condition for it. Other cases demonstrate that the converse is also true. Angola has a per capita GDP of $4,400, which is 10 percent higher than that of Cuba and more than twice as high as that of Samoa, but Angola's HDI, at 0.439, is little more than half as high as Cuba's.

All of this depends on values and preferences, on the dominant conception of economic development, and in the direction of outside influences. As always, as well, it depends on war and peace. Even a small investment in human capital, financed by an outright grant from abroad, can change things. Ten dollars will equip an entire family in a Mozambique village with mosquito netting, and this means saving people from the dire consequences of malaria. Ten thousand dollars will build a new school for a whole village in Burundi—a breakthrough equivalent to the introduction of public education in Central European villages after the war. Ten million dollars would overhaul the harbor infrastructure in Guinea Bissau, and this would be a spur to production, trade, and tourism. A few less deaths, a few dozen less illiterates, or thousands of new jobs all add up to a better life, which is reflected in a few more points on the HDI graph. Values and policy are decisive; they unleash motivation, and this determines, in turn, what people do and don't feel like doing.

The human capital indicator contains far more information than gross domestic product, but it does not take income inequality into account. There are certain correlations between income distribution and access to education and health care. A comparison of the HDI and the Gini coefficient will provide a more complete picture. We can then see that it is possible for both of these indexes to be at a relatively high level in the same country. This is both bad news and good news. For instance, the very high Gini coefficient in South Africa and Namibia is bad news, but the good news is that the HDI is relatively high in both of these countries, at 0.653 and 0.626, respectively. On the other hand, Azerbaijan, which has an exceptionally low Gini coefficient, also has an HDI of only 0.736, one of the lowest of any postsocialist country. Good news and bad news, opposite in implications, comes in from southern Africa and Central Asia.

As always, the world looks different, depending on whether we take national borders into account. Our examination of income distribution shows the contrast between nation-by-nation results as opposed to those that consider humanity as an aggregate. Just as with GDP, we can calculate HDI by taking either national averages or the averages for different groups without considering national borders. The results are very interesting.

If we placed the two HDI values for the upper and lower quintiles of the Nicaraguan population on the existing world list of countries, we would find that they were eighty-seven places apart. For the Republic of South Africa, the corresponding difference would be no fewer than 101 places. The HDI of the upper quintile of the Indonesian population is equal to that of the Czech Republic (0.885), whereas the lower quintile from Indonesia is tied with Cambodia (0.583). The upper quintiles of Americans or Finns would reign as unchallenged leaders of the world list, at values very close to 1.000, whereas the lower quintile of Americans would hold only fiftieth place in the world, tied with Cuba. This means that every fifth American lives at the same level as the overall average in Cuba, a country that has been subject to boycotts and discrimination for fifty years.

Let's look at the upper quintile of poverty-stricken Bolivia, with its per capita GDP of $3,100. This quintile has an HDI equal to the overall figure for Poland, where the per capita GDP is $14,200. The lower quintile from Poland, in turn, has an HDI equivalent to the overall average for Pakistan, where the per capita GDP is $2,600. The HDI for the 20 percent of Bolivians with the highest incomes in their country and the HDI for the 20 percent of Poles with the lowest incomes in theirs would be separated on the world country-by-country list by ninety-seven places, with Poland in thirty-seventh place and Pakistan in 134th.

To see the world from the perspective of the distribution of the human capital index, we would have to color in yet another map. It would be easy this time. All we need are crayons in the colors employed for streetlights: green for the countries with a high HDI of 0.8 or more (developed countries), yellow for the medium countries between 0.501 and 0.799 (developing countries), and red for the countries with the lowest HDI of 0.5 or less (least-developed countries). The map does not look like a patchwork. Europe, North America, Japan, Australia, and Oceania are green, as are Argentina and Chile (tied with Poland for thirty-seventh place on the world list at 0.862) in the southern cone of Latin America, the Emirates at the corner of the Arabian Peninsula, and Malaysia and South Korea in Asia. All the rest of Asia and South America are yellow, as are the Arab countries of North Africa, and South Africa and Namibia in the southern part of the continent. All the rest of Africa is red. The average HDI for the green countries is 0.923, that of the yellow countries is 0.710, and that of the red countries is 0.427.

Which world is best? The one with a somewhat smaller GDP and a somewhat higher HDI or the world where only the absolute level of the per capita GDP counts? We must bear in mind, of course, that one third of the HDI is a function of GDP—but only one third. There is no simple answer. The best thing to do would be to ask people what they want. Even if we knew their answers, we would have to be cautious about drawing conclusions. We know that people give different answers to the same questions, depending on whether they treat them in terms of value or in terms of strategy. Cultural conditioning aside, if we asked an Indonesian whether he would like to move to Cuba, where the HDI is higher with a similar per capita GDP, we might expect him to treat this as a question about values and to say yes. However, if we said, "Let's go," we would hardly be surprised if his reply was, "You go. I'm staying here." There would be many reasons for this, and one of them is the fact that even the broader perspective of the HDI fails to take several important things into account.

An interpretation that is elastic, if not overstretched, might assert that the Human Development Index implicitly contains information about the state of democracy. Some sociologists and political scientists, along with more than a few economists, feel that there is a strong positive correlation between the level of economic development and the advancement of democracy. In other words, we could expect to find more advanced democracy in countries with higher per capita GDP, and vice versa. Given a few additional assumptions and simplifications, this is indeed the case in general, especially in the long term. In the real world, however, we also find countries with relatively high levels of income and low degrees of democracy (Belarus, Iran), as well as less-developed economies where there is a relatively advanced democracy (Benin, Surinam).

It would be good to fit democracy into the formula for calculating the HDI, but this is unlikely. I once brought this up when talking to Amartya Sen, the 1998 Nobel Prize winner in economics. While remarking on the limited information provided by traditional measurements of development, and criticizing the drawbacks of the Gini coefficient, Sen proposed a broader approach. He helped create the HDI, which only went into use in 1990, and deserves having that index named for him, although this has not happened so far. Gini was luckier. Sen attaches enormous importance to the significance of democracy in development. One of his recent books is titled *Development as Freedom*.[5] Nevertheless, there are at least two reasons this idea will never become canonical.

On the one hand, this is a far more complicated matter than the impact of education or life expectancy on output. How can a free press or an independent judiciary be factored in with the value of crops or industrial articles? On the other hand, the HDI is quasi-official information; an international organization, the UNDP, compiles it. It would therefore be regarded as politically incorrect to point out, officially, the places that are more democratic, or less so. Nongovernmental organizations (NGOs), on the other hand, do so enthusiastically, even when there are reasons to doubt the transparency and impartiality of their rankings. A great deal of attention is paid to judgments passed by the Heritage Foundation and Freedom House, an organization located in Washington because the U.S. government funds it—as is also the case with some other NGOs.

Every year, Freedom House compiles a long list of countries assessed by their degree of freedom and democracy. It uses groups of observers and experts to monitor the political scene, representative bodies, freedom of speech and elections, and media and judicial independence. The results of these rankings evoke a great deal of criticism, because they are based to a large degree on the subjective assessments of respondents and the generalizations of experts who are sometimes tendentious because they have their own political sympathies. Countries are graded on a scale from 1 to 7. The range between 1 and 2.5 is "free," that from 3 to 5.5 is "partly free," and 6 to 7 is "not free."

Of the 193 countries on the list, ninety were acknowledged as democratic.[6] This is not bad at all and is qualitatively better than the situation a quarter of a century ago. Sixty-one countries earn the optimal score of 1, and another twenty-nine have scores of 2.5 or better. These include

- All the countries of the European Union (and Andorra, Liechtenstein, Monaco, and San Marino, located inside the E.U.), Croatia, and Serbia.
- All the members of the OECD except Turkey.
- A dense assortment of fifteen island-nations from the Caribbean and all three oceans (with the largest number of them from the Pacific), which might be explained in part by a special mix of cultural and natural conditions (strong tribal or local communities with traditions of direct democracy and an imperative to make a collective effort to overcome the forces of nature), as well as by external political pressure (with respect for democratic institutions made a condition for aid).
- Aside from OECD member Mexico, such South and Central American countries as Argentina, Belize, Brazil, Chile, Guyana, Costa Rica, Panama, El Salvador, Surinam, and Uruguay.
- Benin, Botswana, Ghana, Lesotho, Mali, Namibia, South Africa, and Senegal from Africa.
- Aside from OECD members Japan and South Korea, India, Indonesia, Israel, Mongolia, and Taiwan (here accorded the status of a state) from Asia.

The second group, the "partly free" countries, includes fifty-eight states, ranging from wealthy Singapore to poor Haiti. The list ends with forty-five countries that, in the opinion of Freedom House, are "not free." The worst score, 7, is assigned to Saudi Arabia, Burma, Cuba, Libya, North Korea, Sudan, Syria, and Turkmenistan. Freedom House also places China and Russia in this group.

Authoritarian Saudi Arabia (seven points) has a per capita GDP of $13,600 by PPP. In fully democratic Tuvalu (one point), the corresponding figure is $1,600. No fewer than twelve of the poorest societies on earth, with per capita GDPs of less than $4,000, are listed as democratic. Ten of them are tiny island-states. This is amazing, both in terms of the success in maintaining democracy in the face of such misery and in terms of the fact that the level of development is so low in spite of democracy. To gain some insight into this conundrum, we must look in more detail at the feedback mechanisms at work here, because this is not merely a simple cause-and-effect relation. The whole issue must also be placed in the proper context of other circumstances that help determine the outcome.

The most important fact is that the world is getting better as the years go by. This is certainly true in terms of political and democratic freedom. All its shortcomings notwithstanding, the Freedom House analysis captures these improvements. In 1995, there were seventy-six countries listed as free; by 2000 the figure had risen by ten. By 2005, there were thirteen more free countries, and another four were added in 2007, bringing the total to ninety-three. This is almost half the countries in the world, although only a quarter of the people live there. There's a long way to go.

Some general comments suggest themselves. Democracy is a little bit like health: as the saying goes, you don't miss it until it's gone. For affluent societies, democracy is so obvious that it seems to be something they received from nature, and not through history. When we have a lot of it, we are surprised to see that others have so little. Those who have little are less surprised by this, because they have no idea what they're missing.

In rich countries, democracy has been a given from one generation to the next. Only when it is restricted, as has happened, for instance, on the pretext of the struggle against terrorism, do they stop and think about how much there is to lose. Where democracy arrived only recently, it is also treated as something normal, and people only wonder why they had to wait so long for it. Where there is no democracy, people don't spend much time thinking about matters that they regard as falling within the purview of the intellectual and political elites. Many people in poor countries have no appreciation of democracy because they have never known it. They don't know it because they don't have it. This is a reason to be cautious about exporting democracy, just as it was once worthwhile being cautious about exporting revolution. It might not work out.

Democratization must be a gradual, bottom-up process, and not something precipitously imposed from above. Democracy in poor countries does not depend on giving out t-shirts in return for voting correctly in free elections monitored by delegates from wealthy countries. This formula has turned out to be ineffectual. The most important thing is the compatibility of processes of political democratization and economic liberalization achieved through pragmatic rather than doctrinaire methods. These two fundamental processes of the contemporary world, and especially the poorer, "emerging" part of it, must be compatible. If they do not result in economic growth, then poor people will lose their appetite for the authentic freedom represented by democratization. Freedom is choice, and that choice must extend to far more than the choice of names on the ballot.

Another frequently cited source is the Heritage Foundation, also based in Washington—where else? Like Freedom House, it has a distinctly neoliberal bent. Aside from private interests, nothing is so corrosive of objectivity as ideology. The Heritage Foundation intentionally promotes free enterprise, a limited role for government, personal freedom, and what is known as traditional American values.

The problem with this is that many countries have their own traditional values, which can be different from the American ones and, in many cases, are. People in China and India have values with deeper cultural roots than the American ones, and they are also interested in exporting their values. This can be seen wherever you find Chinese restaurants and Indian shops around the world. Russia has no complexes because it has a sense of the deep roots of its own traditional values. Few of these Russian values are suitable for export, but for the sake of balance, Russia itself has no great inclination to import values. The centuries-old traditions of the peoples who live in the Andes are different from the younger traditions, born of the American melting pot, of the people who live in the Rockies. Even on the pampas of Patagonia, there are traditional values different from those found on the prairies of what was once the North American Wild West.

In its ranking of what it calls economic freedoms, Heritage House uses ten criteria. They concern the regulation of areas that are essential to the functioning and competitiveness of the economy and that have a profound influence on economic growth. These ten "freedoms" relate to

1. Property rights.
2. Business freedom.
3. Trade freedom.
4. Fiscal freedom.
5. Government size.

6. Monetary freedom.
7. Investment freedom.
8. Financial freedom.
9. Freedom from corruption.
10. Labor freedom.

Points from 1 to 100 are awarded in each of these categories and then compiled into an overall "index of economic freedom." Despite all its shortcomings, this index provides valuable information. What does it show?

In the first place, it shows that the countries with the greatest economic freedom are also the richest countries. All the top ten countries on the Heritage Foundation list are among the twenty countries with the highest per capita GDP (excluding several mini-states and territories). These countries and the scores awarded to them in the "economic beauty pageant" are, in order, Hong Kong (89.3), Singapore (85.7), Australia (85.7), the United States (82.0), New Zealand (81.6), the United Kingdom (81.6), Ireland (81.3), Luxembourg (79.3), Switzerland (79.1), and Canada (78.7). In these league standings, Singapore scored highest for liberal labor regulations (99.3) and lowest for financial sector regulation (50.0). Interestingly, the fraternal spirits over at Freedom House gave Singapore a mediocre score of 4.5 for democratic freedom (or the lack of it), relegating that country to a position on the list near those of Nepal and Uganda.

Second, when deliberating about economic freedom and the way national economies differ in this regard, we must keep reminding ourselves that the Heritage Foundation results represent the average of ten different parameters. Identical scores do not mean that the countries are the same. Great Britain and one of the Commonwealth countries, New Zealand, both score 81.6, but the internal differences between them include such areas as freedom from corruption (scores of 96 and 76, respectively), and investment freedom (90 and 70).

Third, countries that impose political restrictions or bureaucratic controls on the freedom to do business end up at the very bottom of this ladder. The ten cellar-dwellers are Guinea-Bissau (45.7), Angola (43.5), Iran (43.1), the Democratic Republic of the Congo (43, despite the adjective in its name), Turkmenistan (42.5), Burma (40.1), Zimbabwe (35.8), Libya (34.5), Cuba (29.7), and North Korea (3.0), which is always a category unto itself in such rankings. It is also worth noting that the ten countries coming just ahead of these pageant washouts include a further three postsocialist countries: Belarus, Laos, and Vietnam.[7]

Fourth, the countries characterized by a medium level of economic activity—with per capita GDPs on the order of $10,000 to $20,000—are predominantly clustered among midtable positions in these lists, although their rankings for freedom are more widely scattered than the values of their total output.

In some cases, it is difficult to avoid the impression that the assessments of certain concrete countries are distorted. This happens for various reasons, although only rarely do the distortions appear to result from purely formal considerations, unless we assume that ordinary methodological sloppiness accounts for some of the scores.

A total of 157 countries are ranked. How are we to explain Italy's appearance in sixty-seventh place, with a score of 63.4, between Uganda and Nicaragua, and trailing Oman (63.9), Belize (63.7), and Kuwait (63.7)? Somebody might not like the Italians, but to this degree? Is economic freedom in France equal to that in Jamaica, because both countries score 66.1? Why is Poland, at 58.8 points, in ninety-fourtth place, just behind Senegal and Saudi Arabia, and just ahead of Pakistan and the Cape Verde? How credible is it to place China and Russia, on equal scores of 54, in 126th and 127th place, behind Lesotho and ahead of Yemen? Why is Ukraine, at 53.5, just ahead of Niger (53.3)? Vietnam, a country that has shown rapid economic development over the last thirty years, receives 50.0 points, almost the same as the economically stagnant Central African Republic (50.3). Then there's Iran, eight places from the bottom—another country that somebody doesn't like.

It's worth retaining some sense of balance and seriousness. All rankings by a plethora of organizations, associations, and forums, including the World Economic Forum in Davos, should be treated with the appropriate distance and skepticism, even if they arise out of political and ideological goodwill. It is worth knowing what, aside from an incontrovertible desire to discover the truth, lies behind the results. What ideals, values, and interests prompted someone to commission the estimate and someone else to carry it out? Having the results publicized is no great feat, because this is the sort of thing the media eats up, the kind of story they love to cover.

On the one hand, rankings like this should not be ignored; instead, they should be subjected to critical analysis. They shape public opinion, influence the expectations of economic entities, and prompt nervous politicians and bureaucrats to set real economic processes in motion. On the other hand, however, it is essential not to be terrorized by these lists and the media coverage of them. Interest groups use rankings to manipulate policy and shape public opinion. It is no paradox at all that lobbyists sometimes use rankings about democracy to push agendas that are not necessarily democratic.

What are the general conclusions? For the moment, three, all of them the result of carefully studying several maps of the world that are color-coded to illustrate ongoing changes in time and space. It is amazing how many maps of the world there are beyond the physical, political, climatic, and geological ones they showed us in school (assuming, of course, that we had a school to go to).

The first conclusion is that the level of development attained, measured in per capita GDP, shows a strong positive correlation, through a feedback mechanism rather than a cause-and-effect relation, with advances in economic liberalization and political liberty. There are exceptions.

The second is that the rate of the growth of output and, even more clearly, improvements in the development of human capital, do not exhibit such a clear-cut correlation. The situation is different because other important, and sometimes far more important, factors help determine improvements in these two parameters, GDP and HDI. There are exceptions.

The third is that differences and inequalities in the distribution of income and property are not a function of the level of development, but rather of the choice of dominant values over the long term, the socio-economic policy choices made on the basis of these values, and the systemic regulations that serve the execution of these policy choices. There are exceptions.

The exceptions prove the rule.

Here is a general assertion: You shouldn't allow yourself to be seduced by stereotypes, consensual truths, or the conventional wisdom. For instance: There's no economic development without democracy. Just compare China and Mexico. Or: You can't have economic freedom without political freedom, or political freedom without economic freedom. Just compare Argentina and Mexico. Or: You can't be rich without natural resources, but when you have those resources, then you are rich. Just compare Germany and Nigeria. Or: A more equitable distribution of income damps economic growth, and a more unequal distribution encourages it. Just compare Japan and Colombia.

Things are far more complicated than the opinions that result from the human love of convenience. On an intellectual level, these opinions come down to mental shortcuts and simplification. They're misleading. At times, they're tendentious, or result from the misinterpretation of the facts or from trying to shoehorn reality into a theory that serves particular interests. This is harmful. It's hard to say whether such opinions are more common in economic disputation or in polemics over the environment. The disparity in expert opinions on these matters is so vast that they leave politicians and the media little room for maneuver. All the more so because there is no shortage of people who deliberately mislead the public. They're not wrong—they're lying. There's no shortage of examples.

Take, for instance, the spectacular behavior of two neoliberal think tanks, the Cato Institute and the American Enterprise Institute, after the 2001 publication of the book *The Skeptical Environmentalist*,[8] which tendentiously questioned the risks of resource depletion and pollution. This played into the hands of certain interest groups, mainly from the energy sectors and the associated political spheres. Scientists from these two think tanks were deployed into the fray, and the zealous media did the rest. Some in the media were hired, and the rest followed an irresponsible herd instinct.

If there had been scientists around at the time when the dinosaurs were going extinct, and they had been able to come to some ultimate conclusion about the cause of the catastrophe, and if there had also been media around to cover the story, then whatever slant the media took would surely have prevailed. There would have been many conclusions floating around, and if one of them had been the correct conclusion, it would not have had a chance to come to the surface. If there had still been some chance to save the dinosaurs, it would have been lost— not because of insufficient knowledge or the frailty of scientific reasoning, but because of the excess of politics and the power of the media. What does that have to do with the real world today? Nothing more than the fact that right now, authentic scientific controversy notwithstanding, there is political grandstanding and a media circus on the state of the natural environment, while species are irreversibly dying out and nonrenewable resources are being squandered.

As for the state of the natural environment, can't everyone see what it's like? Hardly—and that's what makes the situation complicated. Things in the economic sphere, all things considered, are getting better; in regard to the ecosphere, the environment, and natural resources, however, more things are changing for the worse. This dissonance will have increasingly serious consequences for the functioning and development of the world economy, and for the way people feel about things.

A comprehensive census of the dolphin habitat concluded in 2007. In the Yangtze River, zoologists were unable to find even a single one of the freshwater dolphins known there as *baiji*. Ten years earlier, they managed to find thirteen dolphins there. They are gone forever.

Several score freshwater dolphins of a slightly different variety still live in the picturesque Si Phan Don wetlands on the Mekong River in Laos. The locals call them *pakha*. After an unforgettable close encounter with them, I asked an expert from the most famous bank in the world whether he had ever seen these beautiful animals. He, in turn, asked me if they looked any different from the dolphins in the sea. If not, then what's the problem? Obviously, the first disappearance from our planet of a large mammalian species in decades is not upsetting to some people. Earlier, around 1950, the thylacine ("Tasmanian tiger" or "wolf," a marsupial closely related to the kangaroo but with a canine appearance) disappeared forever. There are two and a half times as many people now as there were then, and we're still alive. Let's not get carried away.

Unfortunately, those who warn that humanity's natural environment is deteriorating at an alarming rate are not getting carried away. Comparing the present day with the distant epochs known from fossils and excavations, we see that living organisms, flora and fauna, are disappearing from 100 to 1.000 times as fast as they were then. Plant and animal species are becoming extinct as a result of the aggressive exploitation of the earth's organic and nonorganic resources. The living world is poorer than it has ever been, even as there are more of us—the beings who think, although not always rationally—than ever.

The United Nations sponsored a comparative study of the condition and exploitation of the natural environment on an unprecedented scale, the Millennium Ecosystem Assessment (MA).[9] It concluded that the last fifty years have seen the greatest disturbances to the ecosystem in history. More than half of the world plant biomass has been transformed (on the order of 20 to 50 percent) to adapt it to human use. The most rapid changes are occurring in the tropical and subtropical forests, which are shrinking. About 35 percent of the mangroves have disappeared. Anyone who wants to see a mangrove should hurry to the few remaining places where they grow, such as southern Senegal or the Florida Everglades. About 20 percent of the coral reefs are gone. Anyone who wants to dive among these fairytale surroundings should hurry to the few remaining places where they can be found, such as the Maldives or the Great Barrier Reef.

A third of all amphibians, a fifth of all mammals, and an eighth of all birds are in danger of extinction. Since the start of industrial-scale fishing, it is estimated that 90 percent of large predatory fish have vanished from the oceans. These are vertebrates, but other types of animals are also dwindling.

Wild animals are being thinned out on a catastrophic scale even in places where the layman might think they are safe. About 100,000 tigers roamed India a century ago. Now barely 1,500 are left. As recently as 2002, a census counted 3,642 of these beautiful animals. Kenya has lost more than a third of its wild animals in the last twenty years, and the figures for South Africa are similar. Anyone who wants to experience a safari where the animals still outnumber the tourists should hurry to Etosha and Ngorongoro, because things are looking bleak in Masai Mara and Kruger National Park.

How will it feel to see the last plant on earth? How will it feel to stand before the last couple of animals in a country? It'll feel terrible. As if we were about to lose a part of ourselves.

On the banks of the Zambezi, on the Zambian side, I encountered the two last black rhinoceroses in that country. They were even more beautiful than the reproductions of the Dürer engraving that they showed in schools for centuries. Not long before, there had been five of them. Poachers killed one of them, because there is a great demand in distant countries for a potion made from the horn of this majestic animal. A second was sucked into the nearby cataracts just before Victoria Falls, and drowned. The third died of natural causes. If the fate of the world depended on this pair, like our Adam and Eve, then we wouldn't be here. Fortunately, it doesn't, and fortunately the world is bigger than this paradise. Black rhinoceroses live in other countries in the region, and so the species, despite being under serious threat, should survive.

More than 10,000 miles to the west, amidst the peaceable waters of the Pacific and just at the equator, lies the Galapagos archipelago. Lonesome George, a turtle aged about ninety, lives here. He got his name from the fact that he is the sole, and therefore the last, representative of a subspecies found on Pinta Island in 1971. All efforts to induce him to flirt with females from closely related varieties have failed. When George dies, his subspecies will be no more. When Charles Darwin arrived in the Galapagos in 1831, he was greeted by about a quarter of a million turtles of the *Geochelone nigra* species, which was then divided into fifteen subspecies. Now there are no more than 15,000 of them in eleven subspecies, of which soon there will be only ten.

Several thousand miles further south lies the most isolated of all inhabited places on earth. The 1994 film *Rapa Nui* (the place that later colonizers christened Easter Island is called *rapanui* in the local language) depicts horrifying scenes from several hundred years ago. Literally the last tree on the island is being cut down. This is what really did happen, before the arrival of Europeans, and specifically the Dutch, who did not arrive until 1722. The trees that can be seen today, mostly eucalyptus, were planted recently. While wandering among the eerie *moai* statues, carved out of volcanic rock by a lost civilization, it takes a leap of the imagination to see this mysterious corner of the earth overgrown with palms and ferns. The inhabitants destroyed their own natural environment by subjecting it to greater stresses than nature could bear. Nature took swift revenge, depriving them of the biological conditions for existence.

Sailing west across the Pacific Ocean and almost the entire sweep of the Indian Ocean, we land in Mauritius. Here too we could exclaim: *Que pacífico!* Here, not in the movies, but in real life, grows the last tree in the world, and that means in the universe. In the little town of Curepipe in the center of the island, surrounded by a low wall, stands a 10-meter-high *Hyophorbe amaricaulis* palm. This species is as close to extinction as a species can be. It is about fifty years old and has only a few years left. It will die. It cannot reproduce, because its male and female flowers bloom at different times. Attempts at grafting and cloning have failed. Even if the tree sprouts and begins to grow, it will die if it is transplanted. This is extinction.

The Khmer civilization left behind one of the most splendid architectonic heritages in human history, if not the most splendid of all:

Angkor. Flourishing from the ninth to the fourteenth centuries on a scale unmatched at the time, the Khmer culture produced temples in various styles. The ruins are still dazzling. They erected at least seventy-four of these temples in an area of 3,000 square kilometers. Almost forty of them remain, to varying degrees. Some, unfortunately, are in ruins, but others, including, fortunately, the most splendid edifice in the world, Angkor Wat, are in decent shape. There was nothing like this either in antiquity or in preindustrial Europe, nor in China or Japan, nor in Arabia or among the Aztecs. Precisely here, about 1,000 years ago, cultural and environmental conditions converged to produce such glory. At the apogee, half a million people lived here, on fertile soil with a well-organized irrigation system. At some point, it became evident that this was more people than the land could support. The over-population, excessive exploitation of the farmland, soil erosion, and deforestation did their work. Pressure on the neighboring forces devastated the environment. Tree-cutting severed the roots of the civilization, which fell faster than it had arisen. A great community of half a million people disappeared. The climate was such that the jungle survived and is now encroaching on the temples, making them look even more otherworldly. All that remains of that people is their temples, and for whole centuries even they were forgotten.

The incomparable Tikal, the city at the center of the Maya culture in what is now Guatemala, covered an area a twentieth, or even a thirtieth the size of Angkor. It flourished on the opposite side of the world at almost the same time. Its downfall came earlier, but also resulted from ecological disaster. The beautiful pyramids, the monuments, and the sculptures remain, but the people lost out.

Three places on the globe so widely spaced that a geographer could not have placed them better were the sites of three great civilizations, and three great disasters with the same cause: the violation of the equilibrium between humans and their natural environment.

Environmental devastation brought down those civilizations. What about our own, with far more people and far fewer natural resources? Will we make the same mistakes? No, but it is possible that we will make far worse ones. As spectacular and dramatic as they were, those were local catastrophes, affecting only small patches of the earth and a relatively small proportion of its inhabitants. The present risk is not that we will upset the equilibrium, because we have already done so. The risk now is that we will lose control entirely.

The emission of harmful gases increases the dimensions of the threat. They contaminate the air and cause increases in the atmospheric temperature. Even worse, this is happening at an increasing tempo. Among the twelve warmest years since 1850, no fewer than eleven fell between 1995 and 2006. One promising note is that, if not in North America, then at least in the European Union (thanks to efforts by Germany, the United Kingdom, The Netherlands, and Finland), the emission of greenhouse gases may be starting to fall. Emissions fell by 0.7 percent in 2005 in comparison to the previous year, and this trend continued in the following years. Now the idea is to maintain the trend for a decade in this part of the world without making things worse elsewhere. This would be a positive step, for once.

A study prepared by the American National Academy of Sciences finds that, whereas these emissions grew an average of 1.1 percent per year in the 1990s, this rate rose to more than 3 percent in the first five years of the following decade. This is worse, the report emphasizes, than even the most pessimistic earlier forecasts by the U.N. Intergovernmental Panel on Climate Change (IPCC), which was the winner, jointly with Al Gore, of the 2007 Nobel Peace Prize. This body was convened especially to prepare an independent, authoritative review of the state of the climate and the way it is evolving, in order to foster a less politicized discussion of the subject.

Here, however, we can see immediately how easy it is to manipulate data. As soon as the findings were published, some voices proclaimed that the situation was improving because emissions were growing more slowly than world economic output, which was indeed increasing in real terms by an average of about 3.8 percent per year at the time. Others characterized the situation as deteriorating because, once world economic growth was adjusted to take account of population growth, it turned out to be less than the rise in emissions. The world per capita average annual GDP growth in those same five years was slightly above 2 percent. Under this interpretation, the world was not only using more energy, but also polluting more as it did so. Because the great majority of people have no way of analyzing this kind of information, let alone comparing and interpreting it, they must rely on what they read, see, and hear, allowing the opinion-manipulators to lead them. When there is much information on a given topic, there are many images of the world.

The devastation of nature is continuing. This also applies to the nonliving world, through the extraction and processing of minerals, including those that are burned to generate energy. The big problem is that this is not only a byproduct of human economic activity, but also, to an increasing degree, a barrier to further development. Those incapable of thinking in categories on the scale of the whole planet, or who are not worried by the way our reserves are dwindling, should have a look around their own place in this world. Where there were once meadows, there are now housing developments. Where people fished, there is sewage. Where mushrooms grew even without rain, nothing grows now. Where forests stood, weeds flourish.

The view from Central Europe and the view from South America are different, yet reflect similarly depressing underlying realities. While some complain that they can no longer spend their vacations in the countryside the way they used to, others have nowhere to raise crops. Soil erosion, deforestation, desertification, and poisoned rivers and lakes mean not only the loss of places where people once spent their weekends or vacations, but also the possible loss of the basis for existence. Natural disasters take a much higher toll on such devastated lands. As a result, as if they did not already have enough troubles, it is poor people, and especially in poor countries, who suffer indiscriminately. Even in the big cities in the prosperous world, the quality of life is felt to be declining. Stress and illnesses make people feel worse, but they also reduce their capacity for work, and this has long-term consequences. A feedback mechanism exists between the natural world and human destiny. The ecosystem benefits people, but overexploitation weakens the system. People living in agricultural regions are particularly dependent on nature. The degradation of their biosphere quickly results in the degradation of these people.

There are many unknowns and controversies, although certain trends stand out unmistakably. The climatic map of the earth must be redrawn. The maximum summer extent of the arctic ice cap is diminishing by about 7 percent each decade. The west winds have grown stronger over the past half-century. For seventy years droughts have been becoming more severe and have been lasting longer. Heavy rains and the floods they cause are more prevalent. Northern Europe and both Americas are becoming more humid, whereas the Mediterranean and southern Africa are getting drier.

Is this the beginning of the end, the real end of all history? Not yet, and not only because the news is not unrelievedly bad, but also because mankind is taking some important action.

As for good news, it must always be weighed in the context of the bad news, especially if it is offsetting or compensatory. Bad news and good news have different impacts. Someone may be cheered by the apparently minor detail that a family of hedgehogs has appeared in their backyard in the suburbs of Warsaw. They are happy not only because the animal is cute, but above all because it is intelligent enough to choose to live only in unpolluted surroundings. On the far side of the planet, someone else is happy to come across a different prickly creature in the tropical forest of Papua New Guinea. Traces of a species of spiny anteater once regarded as extinct have been found there.

Someone else is even more cheered by the news that an expedition in the spring of 2007 examined a single square kilometer of jungle and discovered six previously unknown animal species living there. Perhaps one species of bat, one rat, and two shrews, even though they are mammals, do not make up for the Yangtze River dolphin, yet identifying them is still an event, and two new frog species were also found there.

A comment is necessary: the changes in the world are multidirectional and differ in time and space. The dolphin is lost in China, but four small mammals and two frogs are found in the Congo. They were already there, of course, but we were unaware of them. A new kind of ratlike marsupial was identified a year earlier in the forests of Borneo, but some of the joy is offset by the irreversible loss of the larger, doglike marsupial in Tasmania.

The scale of the good news can sometimes be large, or even staggering. It is big news that from 5,000 to 11,000 magnificent clouded leopards are living in the inaccessible forests of Borneo. That is a large number of leopards, and there are 3,000 to 7,000 more on Sumatra. As if to offset the melancholy news about the disappearance of the river dolphin, sensational news arrived during the fall of 2007 that tigers from a south Chinese species previously regarded as extinct had been seen in Shaanxi province for the first time since 1964. Their numbers in the early 1950s were estimated at 4,000.

There is also news so astounding that it forces us to reflect again on whether the situation is as bad as commentators say (because that is how they see it), or whether it might not be a little less worse, if only we had more information. It was shocking, in the positive sense, to learn from a professional organization, the Wildlife Conservation Society (WCS), that 1.3 million antelopes, gazelles, elephants, and other large animals had been "found" in places where no one expected to find them. These are not new species, but old acquaintances, such as 800,000 graceful, white-eared, medium-sized kob antelopes. This is not Jurassic Park, but it's more than frogs or mice. We're talking about antelopes and elephants. The 2007 WCS announcement indicated that the discovery resulted from the first aerial survey in twenty-five years of the southern Sudanese borderlands, which had been closed because of local warfare. The area had been closed to outsiders, but not to the warring local tribes or—and this was the point of the announcement—to the enormous herds of animals. Every cloud has a silver lining, they say, although it is scant comfort that the animals roaming the endless savannahs of the Serengeti had survived thanks to a war. People were busy reducing their own population, and not that of the animals.

Other good news can sometimes be attributed to human wisdom, and especially to the fact that development policies take the ecological balance into account. In recent years, since President Luiz Inácio Lula da Silva was elected in 2002, the rate of destruction of the Amazon rain forests in Brazil has fallen by 25 percent. This shows that, in difficult conditions and in poor as well as rich countries, unfavorable trends can be slowed and even, with more effort and better international coordination of ecological policy, reversed. Our future in this regard will be challenging and interesting. The challenging things are never boring.

———————

The second basic characteristic of the contemporary world, in addition to many-layered differentiation, is the interdependence of events and processes. This is shown in many ways. It can be seen in the case of the natural environment, the state and evolution of which are in a feedback relation with the economy. Events occur as they do in relation to the environment because many things happen at the same time, both within the environment itself and at the interface with human economic activity.

Interdependence in the global economy is particularly visible in the sphere of international finance, in connection with trade and the flow of capital. The world is leaning sharply away from the vertical in this regard, which makes it hard to move around. What, then, is the state of trade and financial (im)balance, and what opportunities and threats result? Indeed, opportunities and threats, because a state of imbalance is a serious threat to some, whereas for others it is an excellent way of making big money and offers opportunities for the future. This is one of the main reasons the imbalance exists.

People who profit from the imbalance have an interest in maintaining it. As is often the case, those who benefit most are the same ones who orate loudly about the alleged necessity of eliminating it. Let us try to imagine the minister of finance of an indebted country who stumbles on a way of promptly and radically eliminating the budget deficit. Financing that deficit and the accompanying public debt are excellent prey for speculative capital, and so the speculators would use any pretext to get rid of that minister (there is never a lack of such pretexts either in democracies or in autocracies) before he managed to eliminate the source of their lucrative business. Trading in debt is something that they depend upon.

An asymmetrical image of the world is emerging. While some countries roll up enormous current account surpluses, others suffer from deficits. It must be emphasized that this is true of both prosperous countries and the economically less advanced ones. Current account surpluses are a simple accumulative function of a positive balance of foreign trade. Their core is a surplus of income from exports over expenditures on imports. With deficits it's the other way around. However, apart from exchanges of goods with foreign nations, other factors count, including various forms of financial transfers, such as interest on deposits and credits, dividends, profits, monetary transfers, transfers resulting from foreign trade, and the balance of capital transfers.

The aggregate financial balance includes all transactions, by both the government and private sectors. A current account deficit basically equals a capital account surplus, and vice versa; that is, a current account surplus is equal to a capital account deficit. In the mathematical sense, they have the same value, but with the opposite plus or minus sign. They add up to the balance of payments. On one side of the equation, we have the value of exports, income and current transfers from abroad, plus the inflow of foreign capital. On the other side, we have the value of imports, foreign payments and the outflow of capital abroad. The two sides are balanced by changes in foreign exchange reserves. On the other hand, the net value of foreign assets and debits, the so-called net international investment position (NIIP), is a result of the balance of payments situation. This means that if a country has a current account surplus (a deficit in the capital account), then it is a net exporter of capital, and that this capital is a source of financing for other countries. Things are the other way around when a country has a current account deficit (a capital account surplus), because it is then a net exporter of capital, and thus is financed by other countries.

Foreign exchange reserves can grow or fall in either case, because they are also determined by other factors, especially changes in the exchange and interest rates. This is highly dependent on the situation in the debt market, where government paper (government securities and treasury bonds) are traded. If the central bank keeps the interest rate at a relatively higher level than in other countries with similar inflation rates, then such a monetary policy will attract foreign speculative capital with the prospect of quick, easy profits. In order to buy another country's debts, foreign investors first buy that country's currency. Because the demand for the currency is growing, its price rises. The currency becomes stronger, even though the economy may become weaker. Foreign means of payment have come onto the market, and the central bank now purchases them and places them in the reserves that it administers. There is now more money in the treasury for expenditures, and the paper provides income for the foreign investors. The treasury, at the taxpayers' cost, pays the interest to the foreign investors. The government (and the public) thus have more debt, whereas the central bank has larger reserves.

We should add at once that foreign exchange reserves held by one country, whether justified or not, are an exceptionally easy and rich source of income for banks and investment funds in other countries, and that they serve to finance the budget deficits of wealthy countries. These reserves are not held in cash in the vaults of the central banks (except for the gold reserve, which plays a marginal role these days), but in low-interest, very safe bonds issued by other countries (e.g., in American, German, or Japanese bonds), or in the form of deposits in prestigious Western banks.

It is not at all out of the ordinary for the same bank—the very same one—to take on deposit with one hand the reserves of a given country, amounting, let us say, to $1 billion, on which it pays 3 percent annual interest, while with the other hand purchasing that same country's bonds, on which the country, in turn, pays 5 percent per year. Yes—the bank uses the reserves to buy the bonds. Yes—without going to any particular trouble, it earns $20 million a year in clear profit. Yes—that money is paid by the citizens of that country in the form of the taxes levied on them. When reserves and debt are each on the order of $50 billion, the financiers say that the net debt is zero, but the profits of foreign financial intermediaries (as well as the compensation for their local proponents) are far from zero. They walk away with billions of dollars. Taxes, in the local currency, will rise by that amount.

It is above all because of these considerations that central banks treat the administration of their foreign exchange reserves as a ceremony shrouded in secrecy, even as governments slave over the flows of budget receipts with the door wide open, under the fire of public criticism and the supervision of democratically elected parliaments. When international financiers and their mouthpieces in the media agitate for what they call the independence of the central banks, this factor is just as important as the rational arguments about avoiding political pressure to print more money, which raises inflation.

Present-day central banks make far more mistakes administering the foreign exchange reserves under their control than in managing the money supply. This explains why there is so much chatter about issues of minor importance, including the manipulation of interest rates by fractions of a percent. Interest rate changes are too important to ignore, but we should not exaggerate their importance. This chatter drowns out the less frequent calls for the rationalization of foreign-exchange-reserve policy, which should serve the public interest and advance social-economic development. Institutional solutions to the management of foreign exchange reserves would make fundamental reform necessary.

Usually, a country that runs a trade deficit (trade surplus) will also run a current account deficit (surplus). However, there is nothing to stop a country from simultaneously having a trade deficit and a current account surplus, or vice versa. For many years, Britain imported far more than it exported and therefore had a trade deficit, while making up for this with a surplus of transfers resulting from a plethora of foreign operations, including above all income from investment portfolios (in securities) and direct investment (in real capital). The situation is the opposite in the Czech Republic, which has a trade surplus of $2.9 billion but a current account deficit of $5.3 billion, or 4.1 percent of GDP.

Some poor countries import far more than they can sell abroad; nevertheless, they have so many citizens working abroad that the money they send back home (remittances) helps to maintain the overall balance. This is the case in Moldova, where export earnings are equal to a mere 45.7 percent of GDP, payments for imports are worth 93.3 percent of GDP (2006), and remittances from people working abroad stand at a record-breaking 30 percent of GDP. Nevertheless, the country has a 12 percent current account deficit. This gap is closed by grants (direct donations of foreign aid), direct foreign investment, and financing from the International Monetary Fund and the World Bank.

In itself, then, a negative trade balance is neither good nor bad. The same is true of a current account deficit. It all depends on how it is financed, because there are various ways of covering it. The most risky is to finance the deficit with short-term speculative capital. Every day, millions of befuddled people hear and read about the investors who control this speculative capital and how they supposedly improve things by supporting equilibrium and development in their countries and economies. They may indeed occasionally be of some help, but they can plainly cause harm as well.

The best way to finance these deficits is through direct investment from abroad. This makes the deficit less risky, and it can be a positive sign, because it indicates that foreign investors have confidence in the economy. These investors only believe in a country if they have good reasons for doing so. This tells others that they can have positive expectations about the future and improves the business climate. The new productive and service capacity financed by direct investment is usually characterized by high technology and good management. This in turn contributes to economic growth, often through the expansion of production for export, which is stimulated in a particularly effective way by foreign investment. For these reasons the contemporary world features heated competition between countries and regions desirous of absorbing the greatest possible dose of this type of foreign capital—it makes it possible to invest without saving, and everyone likes that.

Another good thing about direct investment is the fact that its physical effects, in the form of new plants, construction companies, hotels, and shopping centers, cannot flee. The owners are somewhere out there in the wide world, but the production and service capacity are right here, with all the consequences of that fact, including job creation and income for the budget. Even if the investors decide to withdraw their capital, they must sell to others the buildings, machines, and infrastructure that are its real form. They can take their money out of the country, which is also true of the money in investment portfolios, except that with investment portfolios, nothing except money is involved. However, they cannot take away a steel mill, because that involves more than money.

The investors may escape, but the real property remains behind for the long-term, which cannot be said of short-term speculative capital.

In some countries, deficits can threaten financial stability and economic growth. In others, the surpluses can be absurd in terms of economic rationality. This is not the case with super-rich Norway and its surplus on the order of 14.4 percent of GDP, not only because it is due to the high cost of the petroleum that the country exports, but also because of the way the Norwegians use it. They put most of the accumulated surplus in a special national fund for the sake of future generations, when the oil deposits will have been exhausted. The same cannot be said of the 16.1 percent surplus in Switzerland, which clearly does not know how to invest this money sensibly in its own economy, as is shown by the fact that its 2007 per capita GDP by PPP, at $35,000, lagged well behind Norway's $48,000. Similarly, The Netherlands runs a 7.7 percent surplus. Singapore has a gigantic, structurally inbuilt surplus equal to 25.6 percent of GDP, while also managing to run a public debt equal to 100 percent of GDP.

Many Middle Eastern oil-exporting countries have irrational surpluses, especially Saudi Arabia, where the surplus, which amounts to 25.8 percent, should be regarded as a result of the current business climate in the sense that it will last only as long as the price of oil remains favorable to this monoculture state. Despite their general lack of development, these countries do not know what to do with their capital. As a result, they "invest." Recently, a Saudi prince who was formerly his country's ambassador to the United States had trouble finding a buyer for his $135-million Colorado residence, which was one of his earlier investments. (The appearance of this residence can be seen in the 1972 Francis Ford Copolla blockbuster "The Godfather," starring the late Marlon Brando.)

Zimbabwe, with its population of 12 million, has foreign exchange reserves of a similar order. In Saudi Arabia that is the share of GDP that goes to 10,000 of the prince's countrymen, or to a single one of them over the course of 10,000 years. More than 30 percent of adult Saudi Arabian women are illiterate. How many children could be taught to read and write for $135 million? Some of the nearby countries act more reasonably. Qatar and the United Arab Emirates are attempting to diversify the structure of their economies and are investing part of their reserves into funds similar to the Norwegian one, with an eye to future generations.

Russia, with a current account surplus equal to 6.8 percent of its GDP, is another country that has unwarranted reserves. On the one hand, it has much ground to make up in development, which requires significant investment in up-to-date technology and in social capital. On the other hand, Russia is senselessly holding on to $400 billion worth of excessive, unproductive reserves, some of which it holds in a special stabilization fund in case oil prices fall. Prudence alone cannot justify such a level of reserves. Only recently, during President Putin's second term and under the Medvedev presidency, did a relatively modest proportion of this sum go to developmental purposes. Wisely, the country also paid off a significant part of its external debt, including much that had not yet come due.

There are no prizes for guessing that these moves drew heavy criticism from domestic and foreign neoliberals, who said that the deficits should be maintained and that countries can be indebted at the same time that they amass foreign exchange reserves. After all, that's good for business. The trick is to avoid going so far that the unbalanced country loses its equilibrium entirely and topples over. That's bad for business. Russia was engaged in practices that were good for business when Yeltsin was president, up to the point when the roof fell in during the financial crisis of the summer of 1998. Russia has been engaging in practices that are bad for business under Putin, since it began to improve its financial policy through budgetary discipline and coordination on the part of the government, aided by the monetary policies of the central bank.

China presents greater interpretive difficulties. Its gigantic foreign exchange reserves are significantly more than $1 trillion, not counting the approximately $140 billion in Hong Kong, $11 billion in Macao, and $270 billion in Taiwan, which should also be counted in the long term. China continues to have a very high trade surplus and a current account surplus on the order of 10 percent of GDP. Every year, a broad stream of more and more billions flows into the foreign exchange reserves of $1.4 trillion, as much as those of Japan and the eurozone combined. In 2008, China held one quarter of the world's foreign exchange reserves, or 30 percent when those of Hong Kong, Macao, and Taiwan were added. The question is: Why? Is this rational?

Taking advantage of the unprecedented expansion of its own economy and the problematic imbalances elsewhere, China is playing in a league of its own, and it is playing for the highest stakes. When the time comes, these reserves will be used for world economic domination, combined with the creation of strong structural beachheads for further expansion in the countries that are now the wealthiest, beginning with the United States. In short, China, which already puts a tremendous amount of money into its own economy, will invest an enormous part of this surplus outside its own borders. It will not do so in as frivolous a way as the spendthrift Middle Eastern "investors," although the time will come when wealthy Chinese own luxury residences in the United States and elsewhere. Furthermore, the Chinese currency, the yuan, will become one of the world's main reserve currencies. It is not too early to start preparing for this now. Before long, not only will China be investing its reserves in other countries, but other countries will be keeping part of their reserves in China.

In most cases, these countries are not yet tottering so far from the vertical, although the situation varies. A deficit on the level of 2 to 3 percent of GDP can be enough to pose dangers to the equilibrium of an economy and the fluidity of the process of macroeconomic reproduction. So it is in debt-burdened Italy at −2.3 percent or in Colombia, with its internal conflicts, at −3.2. Yet it is also possible to develop more or less unperturbedly with a deficit on the order of 5 to 10 percent, as shown by Australia at −5.4 percent or Spain at −8.8. However, a deficit of 5.2 percent is regarded as too high in Hungary. The same is true of the 8.4 percent deficit in Greece, because the level of public debt stands at 105 percent of GDP at a time when the Maastricht criteria allow for a maximum of 60 percent. The situation becomes perilous if some unanticipated negative factor, like the catastrophic wave of forest fires in Greece in 2007, is added to this instability.

In the face of such significant deviations by individual countries, the general economic situation in the eurozone is very well balanced. Budget deficits (calculated as the sum of the deficits of all the countries in the zone) amount to only 0.7 percent of aggregate GDP, and there is a minimal current account surplus of 0.1 percent. This is worth remembering when comparing the economic situation on the two sides of the Atlantic.

Accumulating reserves at an excessive level is expensive for society and the economy. Poland's reserves (about $55 billion) are three times higher than those of Spain, a country with a comparable population and rate of inflation (about 2.5 percent). However, Spain imports about two and a half times as much as Poland (265 and 100 billion euro, respectively). According to classical economics, this would justify a higher level of foreign exchange reserves for Spain. Poland's foreign exchange reserves are equal to those of Austria, Belgium, Finland, Spain, and Portugal combined.

Foreign exchange reserves are the least effective way of investing a capital surplus. This is worth knowing and remembering. It is least effective for the state and society, who own the reserves, but it is extremely profitable for the financial intermediaries who trade them. All attempts at constructive criticism of this irrational policy elicit ripostes about the sanctity of the "independence of the central bank" and an aggressive campaign by neoliberal politicians and the media they manipulate, which in turn manipulate public opinion. This is where economics, and particularly the branch of economics known as international finance, turns extremely political.

Nowhere is it so evident as in international trade and finance that the only truly closed economy is that of the world as a whole. Every model of global growth and every model of the world economy must take this into account. A surplus in one place automatically means a deficit somewhere else. A shortfall in one country is a windfall in another. One country's debts are another country's credit. If someone has too much, then someone else will have too little. On the scale of the globe as a whole, there is no deficit and there is no surplus, and things will remain that way until we begin making interplanetary loans, which is not likely to happen during the current generation.

It is true that the *CIA World Fact Book*,[10] a highly useful source of information, says that the world is $44.6 trillion in debt (close to the value of world gross product at exchange-rate parity, $46.8 trillion). Even the CIA gets things wrong sometimes. The world is not indebted by this amount, which is rather simply the sum of all the world's national debt, and this is equal to the aggregate credit of all the world's countries. Or if we choose to follow the CIA's way of thinking, then the world owes this money to itself. Although it may seem that we are breaking even, there is a large problem lurking here. No matter how integrated the world has become, it is far from one big happy family where everybody keeps all their money in the same joint account—and more than one family has split over such issues.

The indebtedness of the contemporary world toward future generations is an important issue. A part of the assets being consumed at the
moment, both real and financial, will burden future generations. This
problem is far from trivial not only in the poorest countries, but also
among the most heavily indebted wealthy countries. The greatest paradox is that it is the poor who extend credit to the rich. Sometimes
they not only extend credit, but also, through foreign exchange mechanisms, actually subsidize them. Bangladesh or Brazil do not hold their
foreign exchange reserves in the currencies of Egypt or Nigeria. Like
many other countries, they deposit these reserves in the wealthiest
countries, because the banks there are the strongest and, let's come
right out and say it, the most reliable. The government securities of the
wealthy countries are the most solid, aren't they? Yes, they are—at least
for the moment.

Basically, there are no debt-free countries in the world. Everybody
owes money to somebody, and first of all to their own societies who
support years of debt to cover budget deficits and the cost of serving
them. Countries also borrow from domestic and foreign banks. The
network of the flow of capital with its intersecting streams of money,
securities, debt, assets, liabilities, credit, and debt is extremely complicated. Superimposing it on a map of the world would result in a tangle
that would be almost indecipherable and that would bear little resemblance to our other maps.

The clearest part would be the tiny points scattered across all the
oceans. Aside from Liechtenstein, which has no debt at all, the twenty
least-indebted countries are all miniscule island-states, more because
no one wants to lend to them than because they don't want to borrow.
These countries are all so small that it makes more sense simply to give
them money than to lend it to them and then worry about how to get it
back. It doesn't cost much to grant subsidies to such places, and it pays
off politically. The largest member of this group is Malta, with a population of 402,000 and a debt of about $190 million. The smallest is
Palau, in the Pacific, with 21,000 islanders and a debt of zero. These are
just points on the map.

The big splotches are elsewhere. On a black-and-white map, this is
where the dark grays and blacks would predominate. The richest countries would be darkest in color. In absolute terms, the leader is the United
States, with a debt of more than $10 trillion. This is almost one fourth of

the world's combined national debt. The next four countries on the list all belong to the G-7 rich list: Great Britain, with $8.3 trillion in debt; Germany, with $3.9 trillion; France, with $3.5 trillion; and Italy, with $2 trillion. The other two members of the G-7, Japan and Canada, are not far behind, with $1.5 trillion and $700 billion. They rank eighth and twelfth on the debt list, respectively. Rounding out the top ten debtor countries are The Netherlands, in sixth place, with debts of $1.9 trillion; Spain, in seventh place, with $1.6 trillion; and Ireland, in ninth place, with $1.4 trillion.

China and Russia also carry considerable debt, at $306 billion and $287 billion, respectively. In the case of China, the country's foreign exchange reserves dwarf its debt. Latin American countries with large debts include Mexico ($178 billion), Brazil ($177 billion), Argentina ($109 billion). Turkey's debt is $194 billion and Indonesia's is $130 billion. All these debts represent significant problems. The largest debts in Africa in absolute terms accrue to resource-rich South Africa ($56 trillion) and Sudan ($30 trillion). Poland has the twenty-eighth largest external debt in the world, at almost $150 billion. It ranks between Brazil and India, which has debts of $135 trillion.

These sums should be relativized. Usually, this stock, for debt is a stock, is compared with exports or with that most general of all yardsticks, GDP. For comparative purposes, it is calculated per capita. Generalized in this way, the data contain more information and are used to assess the condition and prospects of different national economies. We can then see that Poland, with a per capita debt of $3,860, is more indebted than Russia, with a per capita debt of $2,030. However, if we express debt as a percentage of GDP, then the two countries are much closer together at 43.6 and 39.1 percent, respectively. If we express debt as a percentage of exports, then the figures are 133 and 90 percent. Russia does better because it sells so much expensive oil and gas to other countries, including Poland. For all these calculations, we use the market currency exchange rate, because these are the rates at which debt is accrued and repaid.

The indebtedness of the United States is enormous, but the country's foreign assets are even greater. Households and the federal government are the most in debt, but the private sector also carries a gigantic burden. The aggregate external debt (not counting the foreign exchange reserve) of the world's greatest military, political, and economic power amounts to 76 percent of its GDP. This is $33,330 per capita, a little more than two thirds of the $47,300 in Germany but sixteen times the Russian per capita debt. The American debt is 1,016 percent of the country's annual exports. This might seem shocking to some, but such are the facts: Whereas Russia exports about a third more each year than its total external debt, the United States exports only a tenth of its external debt. If both countries stopped importing, Russia could pay off its debt to the rest of the world in about ten months; it would take the United States ten years. It is no wonder that American investment and commercial banks, private companies, and the government itself show such concern about the condition and solvency of their overseas debtors. Any problems they have with meeting their payments are a major problem within the United States, and for the United States. There is a lot to keep an eye on.

Thoroughgoing adjustments in Latin America; the elimination of the direct consequences of the financial crises in Southeast Asia, Russia, and Turkey in the 1990s; the consolidation of economic growth in the European postsocialist countries (including the reduction of the Polish debt by half); and the writing off of most of the debts of the world's poorest countries have made it possible to defuse the threat of an imminent world debt crisis. Although not a matter of crucial importance to the world financial system, it was an unprecedented humanitarian act to remove the debt burdens of the least-developed countries. These debts could never have been repaid, but it took ten years of persistent public pressure before the G-7 (along with other creditor countries) and the World Bank agreed to the write-off in 2006.

There are forty-three Heavily Indebted Poor Countries (HIPC), of which thirty-three are from Africa, five from Asia, and five from South and Central America: Afghanistan, Angola, Benin, Bolivia, Burkina Faso, Burma, Burundi, Cameroon, Central African Republic, Chad, Congo (Brazzaville), Congo (Democratic Republic), Ethiopia, Gambia, Ghana, Guinea, Guinea Bissau, Guyana, Haiti, Honduras, Ivory Coast, Kenya, Laos, Liberia, Madagascar, Malawi, Mali, Mauritania, Mozambique, Nicaragua, Niger, Rwanda, Sao Tome and Principe, Senegal, Sierra Leone, Somalia, Sudan, Tanzania, Togo, Uganda, Vietnam, Yemen, and Zambia. Thirty-five countries have so far received full or partial debt relief. Many were spending more on servicing their debt than they were capable of appropriating for education and health care. The program gives them a chance to begin emerging from structural stagnation.

However, the problem will return, perhaps more dangerously, if economically weaker countries like Indonesia, Brazil, Poland, Egypt, or Turkey find themselves unable to sustain a sufficiently high, export-driven rate of growth. The situation is not one of structural equilibrium, nor it is not one of teetering on the brink. Unfortunately, it is closer to the latter than to the former.

This background makes the direction of capital flows around the world all the more interesting. It should be stressed that not only a layperson, but even a perfectly qualified expert will be unable to make any a priori statements on this subject with certainty. The amateur might even do better than the expert. New and surprising circumstances, some of them one-time or short-term events, keep springing up. Once the dust has settled, the experts, and above all the bank analysts, can tell us exactly what happened. When they make prognoses, however, they do so in as vague a way as possible, just as weather forecasters try to avoid coming right out and telling us whether it is going to rain or not.

There are enormous transfers from developing to wealthy countries, especially the ones that use government securities to finance their budget deficits, and repayments from poor countries to rich creditors and organizations like the International Monetary Fund and the World Bank. Over the four years from 2003 to 2006, the poor countries paid back a total of $185 billion more than they received. They must repay their debts, plus interest. However, the increasingly important flow of private capital more than offsets these payments. During those same four years, the inflow of private capital was $1.9 trillion. The surplus rose from $169 billion in 2002 to $647 billion in 2006. That is the difference between what private financiers from developed countries invested in the rest of the world and what they took out of the rest of the world. This external boost provides substantial support for homegrown savings and capital as the key to financing development. The majority of this external capital takes the form of direct investment by multinational companies. Next in importance are purchases of government securities (debt financing), and finally investment in capital markets, including stock exchanges.

The greatest capital flows are between the richest countries, mostly in the form of direct investment and company mergers and takeovers. This does not increase the amount of capital in the short term, but it does allocate it better by sending it where it will earn higher profits for shareholders. This is why the amount of capital increases in the long term. In 2006 alone, the members of the OECD made direct investments of $1.1 trillion outside their own countries, a rise of 29 percent over the previous year. Over the ten years from 1997 to 2006, the total was more than $8 trillion, with American investments accounting for $1.6 trillion. Interestingly, Belgium and Luxembourg combined to come second at $1.2 trillion—not because the citizens of those countries had so much spare capital to invest, but because these countries are hospitable to various holding companies founded to carry out special investment operations, often on a one-time basis. Next came the United Kingdom with direct foreign investment of just over $1 trillion, and France, at $0.9 trillion.

Neoclassical orthodoxy holds that excess savings from developed countries should be transferred to and invested in developing countries, but the opposite can be true. The most radical exception to the "rule" is the case of China and the United States. Through its large trade and current accounts surplus, China extends credit to the far wealthier American economy, which in turn is mired in a deep, structural double deficit—trade and budget.

The heart of the matter is that China, like several other countries in Southeast Asia, deliberately holds down the exchange rate of its currency. This encourages exports, the engine of growth in output, employment, and government revenue. The exchange rate is lowered when one unit of foreign currency, for instance a dollar, buys more units of the domestic currency. When the domestic currency is low, it is more profitable to place domestic products on the world market (including the wealthiest and still the largest part of that market, the United States). For every dollar obtained through export, you get more domestic currency than would be the case if that local currency were stronger; that is, if it had a higher exchange rate. A stronger domestic currency, as in Poland, for instance, is less conducive to economic growth.

When the income from exports is not fully utilized, a capital surplus is created. A state-run, largely centralized system invests this surplus in securities issued abroad to finance deficits, especially those of wealthy countries. Such capital may also be used, as is increasingly the case, for direct investment in other countries. This is possible because poorer countries have an excess of savings (above the already high level of investment), due to the fact that their own financial markets and instruments are underdeveloped. They must therefore "push" their capital surpluses into other parts of the world economy, and they prefer to push them into rich countries with trade and budget deficits.

The very high level of domestic saving in the countries of Southeast Asia is, to a large degree, a function of the fact that they have no guarantee that they will be able to borrow capital if times are hard in the future. This makes it necessary to save now. Because there is "nothing to invest in" domestically, they invest abroad. Leaving aside direct investment in new productive and service capacity, it is easier in China, Malaysia, South Korea, Singapore, or Taiwan—as well as in the oil-exporting countries, including Russia—to place capital in "hard" assets, such as new skyscrapers or other kinds of real estate, than in domestic securities that may be more or less sophisticated. There may not be enough of these local securities to go around, or they may not inspire sufficient trust. There is a safe outlet abroad, where deposits are protected better than they are domestically.

If this is the basis of world disequilibrium, then it will not be corrected swiftly. This is not only because it will take a long time to liquidate the double deficit in the United States and to limit the budget deficits in some other highly developed countries, like France and Italy. It is also because the financial systems in the countries with capital surpluses take longer to reach maturity than the real economies. Many of these countries are already at the same technological and economic level as the wealthy countries, even while their financial systems lag behind. We think nothing of buying iPods or plasma TVs manufactured in Korea or Taiwan, but when it comes to derivatives or stocks, we buy American or British. The fact that fistfights sometimes still break out in the parliaments of the former countries but are only historical curiosities commented on by tourist guides in the latter might also have something to do with it.

The country's unique position in the world economy offers advantages to the United States. The financial flow gushing in from abroad raises the market price of American assets while also making it possible to keep interest rates relatively low. Interest rates are the price of capital, and capital is so abundant that there is no demand to raise the rates. These two factors make it easier to fund domestic expenditures. In external terms, American foreign assets are greater than the debt, and the income from those assets is greater than the cost of servicing the debt.

A weak dollar, encouraged by discreet U.S. policy, is great business for the country. Here is how the mechanism works. The revenue that foreigners earn by investing in the United States is denominated in dollars, whereas the income from U.S. direct investment and shares in foreign markets and the payments on credits to other countries is denominated in foreign currencies. The fall in the exchange rate of the dollar in recent years means that the value of U.S. foreign assets increases in dollar terms. By the same token, the net debt owed to foreigners (gross debt minus foreign assets) decreases in dollar terms. Through the end of 2005, as a result, the income earned by America from its foreign assets was higher than the money America paid out to the owners of foreign assets in America.

Here is an example. Wall Street portfolio investors bought $1 billion worth of Polish government bonds at a time when the exchange rate was 4 zloty to the dollar. For transaction purposes, they exchanged that $1 billion for zloty because they had to make the purchase with Polish currency, and that $1 billion eventually made its way into the Polish Central Bank, the National Bank of Poland (NBP). The $1 billion became part of the Polish foreign exchange reserve, and was still worth 4 billion zloty. The NBP bought U.S. securities with the money. Let us assume that both the Polish and the American bonds paid 5 percent per year, although in reality the Polish bonds paid more. The dollar then proceeded to weaken, and the zloty strengthened. The Americans still have their 4 billion zloty overseas, except that the rate of exchange is now 2.5 zloty to the dollar. This means that the American-owned Polish bonds are now worth $1.6 billion, plus interest. Poland still owns its $1 billion dollars in American bonds, plus interest, except that back home in Poland, they are now worth only 2.5 billion zloty. The NBP has therefore lost 1.5 billion zloty of the taxpayers' money. When the dividends are paid, each country enters the outlay and income in its balance of payments. For the American side, this is an annual outlay of $50 million, and it is also annual income of $50 million for the Polish side, except that it is now worth only 125 million zloty at the current rate of exchange. At the same time, the Americans receive 200 million zloty in interest on their $1 billion investment in the Polish bonds, and that interest payment is worth $80 million at the current exchange rate, which is the sum that appears on the income side of their balance of payments. As a result of the shift in the exchange rate, the

Americans have cleared an extra $30 million—no less than 3 percent of their original investment—because this is the difference between what they paid and what they received. And it is all thanks to the movement in the exchange rate—the weakening of the dollar and the strengthening of the zloty—which has been profitable for the Americans and costly to Poland. Completely aside from the interest, by lending Polish currency to Poland (the Polish money was made available to them), the Americans have made a 60 percent return. They started with $1 billion, and now they hold bonds worth $1.6 billion. Poland has lost 37.5%, having started with 4 billion zloty, and being left with 2.5 billion. Many billions of dollars are at play in similar transactions all over the world.

This is only a simple example, but it is based to a large degree on reality. It shows how easy it can be to use the intelligent control of the rate of exchange to influence the current account balance and shape a favorable balance of payments in the interest of taxpayers and the national economy. It should be added that a fall in the currency exchange rate leads to a growth in revenue, counted in the domestic currency, for goods exported abroad. The United States obtains $100 for selling goods worth 250 zloty in Poland; earlier, when the dollar was stronger, that same 250 zloty obtained for a smaller quantity of exports was worth only $62.50, or 37.5 percent less. The weaker dollar has a positive effect on the growth in exports and, consequently, on domestic output, employment, and budgetary revenues in the United States. The opposite is also true. A fall in the value of the dollar (and the corresponding rise in the value of the zloty) improves the business climate in the United States, while hampering the expansion of the Polish economy. The weaker dollar enhances the American balance of payments, and the stronger zloty impacts negatively on the Polish balance. A weak dollar is good news for American workers, consumers, and taxpayers. A strong zloty is bad news for Polish workers, consumers, and taxpayers.

Aside from cheaper foreign vacations, the only benefit from a strong zloty is the lower cost in the domestic currency of servicing the foreign debt, because we pay only 2.50 zloty for each of the dollars needed to make payments on the principal and interest, along with the fact that imported goods are relatively cheaper. They cost less in the appreciating domestic currency. Imports worth $100 now cost 250 zloty (with the exchange rate at 2.5 zloty to the dollar), and not 400 zloty as they did at the earlier rate of 4 zloty to the dollar. Inflation is relatively lower with a strong zloty—relatively, that is, in comparison to the hypothetical situation in which the zloty remained weak, although in fact other factors pushed up prices and caused inflation. The converse is also true. In a country with a currency that is depreciating (not "devalued"—devaluation is a one-time change in the official exchange rate), imported goods are more expensive, because it takes more of the local money to buy merchandise imported for the same amount of foreign currency. In America, 100 zloty worth of imports now costs $40.00 with an exchange rate of 2.5 zloty to the dollar, rather than the $25.00 that it cost when the exchange rate was 4 zloty to the dollar. Inflation in the United States is relatively higher, and foreign vacations are more expensive for Americans. This, rather than fear of terrorists, explains why they have become a less common sight around the world in recent years.

What can be done in such a situation? There are many such cases. Precisely because these cases occur so frequently and mean so much, the United States has a deliberate but discreet policy of weakening the dollar. The fact that it gives the opposite advice to other countries is part of the policy. The American maxim "Do as I say, not as I do" is applied with iron consistency. The amazing thing is that so many fall into line. Not everyone does, however.

How can countries defend themselves? Theoretically, the best thing would be to have neither a deficit nor a debt, and thus to avoid exposure to the speculative debt game. However, as we know, only Liechtenstein and Palau have no debt. For various reasons, all other countries have decided to run debts. The most sensible solution is to lower the magnitude of the external debt while simultaneously reducing foreign exchange reserves. This is what China, India, Russia, and Brazil are doing, at least in part. It requires the coordination of government and central bank policy. Despite the evident rationality of this, many countries find it impossible in the face of the autonomy of their central banks.

In Poland recently, state foreign debt has slightly exceeded the level of the foreign exchange reserves. In 2006, it was $58.9 billion, and in the following year it rose to $60 billion, which is about 40 percent of the overall debt, with the rest owed by the private sector and the populace. At the beginning of 2008, the value of the reserves, 145 billion zloty, was slightly higher than that of the debt, 142 billion zloty ($61.3

billion).[11] It would be possible to take half of the reserves and use it to pay off half of the debt, without any harm to the country's financial security, and with the benefit of relieving the budget and the taxpayers of part of the cost of servicing the public debt. With the average interest on the foreign debt at about 5.3 percent, and the interest on the reserves at 3.2 percent, this would result in net savings on the order of 1.6 billion zloty (2.1 percent, or the difference in interest rates on a reduction of about $30 billion, converted to dollars at the market rate). This much more money on balance would be available to the state budget. On the one hand, the government would receive less from the profits of the central bank, which would fall due to the reduction in the reserves. The government receives about 95 percent of these profits. On the other hand, foreign interest payments would be far lower as a result of the reduction in the debt. The saving of 1.6 billion zloty represents the difference between these two figures. It would be a clear gain.

It would also be possible for the countries that have external debts to curb the speculative movements of capital that exert pressure for strengthening the currency. Special fiscal instruments that impede speculative transactions could be used. James Tobin, 1981 Nobel Prize winner, proposed something of the sort as long ago as the 1970s. He suggested introducing a universal transaction tax of 0.1 to 0.25 percent, known as the "Tobin tax," on all international currency exchange operations. Such a small transaction tax would be completely sufficient to dampen speculation, which involves many small currency transactions made with great frequency. For speculation to continue to pay, each exchange operation would have to yield a higher return than the amount of the tax. If such an instrument, at 0.25 percent, had been imposed in Poland when the exchange rate was about 4.3 zloty per euro (a far more beneficial rate for the economy and the public than the strong zloty), it would not have made sense to speculate on fluctuations of less than 0.01075 zloty. When billions are traded on tiny fluctuations of even less than this, millions are made. It is worth knowing how things happen, who benefits, and who pays.

Although Chile applied a similar instrument with success for a time in the 1990s, there was silence over Tobin's proposal for a quarter of a century. Then the Southeast Asia crisis brought it back to the front burner in 1997. When I was lecturing at Yale the following year, I discussed the issue with Tobin. He had no illusions about the fact that the introduction of such a logical instrument was being blocked not by substantive arguments, but rather by the private interests of Wall Street, financiers, and their supporters and hired guns around the world. The literature on the subject reflects those discussions and certain active steps in economic policy.[12]

Some countries have succeeded in using an active exchange-rate policy to make rampant speculation impossible. The attitude of the NBP rules out such a policy in Poland at present. Yet such steps are all the more necessary because other factors encourage excessive currency appreciation beyond the use of differing interest rates to attract short-term capital. In Poland, as well as in the other new member states of the European Union, the degree to which the basic interest rate exceeds that set by the European Central Bank has been decreasing. Hence, this factor plays a relatively smaller role. On the other hand, capital continues to flow in from outside because of, first, estimated rates of return on investment (profit) and, second, the diminishing risk assessment. However, it is currency appreciation that makes these profits truly attractive. Appreciation is thus both a result and a cause of the inflow of capital. This is another reason for the central bank to become actively involved in shaping the exchange rate of the country's currency, steering the exchange mechanisms, and intervening with all available means to prevent fluctuations. Failing to do so costs taxpayers money, slows growth rates in the long run, and represents a fundamental error in monetary policy.

Other countries use a so-called currency board and make the exchange rate completely rigid by pegging their domestic currency to some foreign currency. Hong Kong is pegged to the U.S. dollar; Estonia, Lithuania, and Bulgaria, to the euro; and several territories, to the pound sterling. Other countries use less radical methods, including administrative measures and central bank intervention. China, India, Russia, more than a dozen African and Caribbean countries, and some in the Middle East maintain a stable nominal exchange rate. Because of inflation, a stable nominal exchange rate leads to real depreciation, and this in turn increases the country's export competitiveness. There is a double benefit: Foreign speculative capital is prevented from profiting at the expense of the country's taxpayers, and domestic companies and employees in the export sector do better.

The great financial and economic crisis hanging over the United States will be restorative of health in the long view. However, the crisis need not occur as soon as some skeptics predict. This is a case where deep disequilibrium may yet endure for a while. However, it cannot go on for too long, because everything must come to an end. One of the things that must surely end is the paradoxical extension of credit to the wealthy by the poor. Medium-range International Monetary Fund forecasts insist that the enormous disequilibrium in current accounts will persist if changes in real exchange rates do not occur. They are talking about the yuan and the yen. The continuation of the present state of affairs will lead to the accumulation of horrendously high assets by China and Japan and to unmanageable liabilities on the American side. This would lead to a sharp rise in American foreign obligations from about 26 percent to 51 percent of U.S. GDP in 2011.

This forecast raises the question of how much longer foreign investors will continue to regard American investments as safe. They have surely already stopped being safe. The United States may now be in the same situation that so many poorer countries have been led into by the debt trap in the past. To draw in the foreign capital necessary to finance its double deficit, the United States will have to make investments in the American market more attractive. That is costly, because the way to do it is to raise interest rates. Even in the United States, doing this cannot be put off forever. Action must be taken now. It is too late to withdraw American assets from overseas, because they are more lucrative outside the country than inside it. The time has come for a radical belt-tightening. America must now apply to itself the therapy it has been urging on others for years.

It would be better for all concerned to speed up the onset of the American financial crisis, and the world crisis. No other, more creative or sensible way out of such a deep state of disequilibrium is in prospect. It must involve deep budget cuts (particularly in the U.S. military budget) and higher taxes. Ecological taxes would be best because they would offer a chance of killing two birds with one stone. Economic growth must be slowed down, and it will even be necessary to limit the absolute level of income. This in turn will mean limiting consumption, especially by the best-situated groups. There does not seem to be any prospect of firm adjustments being made before the fact, that is, before the crisis hits. Therefore, we should help to bring it on, in order to compel the necessary changes after the fact.

This is not good news, but it is the truth. There is no autonomous mechanism at work in the world economy to restore financial equilibrium. Intervention is required, and no longer on a national scale, but rather on a global scale. Vigilance has been lulled to sleep, because it has turned out over the last dozen or so years that it is possible to maintain much greater disequilibrium in current accounts than was previously believed. This has been put to both good and bad uses. New financial instruments have appeared. All of this makes it possible not only to manage risk, which is always present in the capital and financial markets, but also to provoke even greater risk. The trick is to avoid going too far.

How, then, is the situation of planet Earth changing? What is the economic condition of humankind? Is the global economy changing for the better or for the worse? The world is changing into a different world. Everyone can see what the world is like. Yet everyone sees something different. That is what makes it worthwhile to make the effort to understand it better and find out what it is really like.

———————

We each have the kind of world that we are capable of understanding.

CHAPTER SIX

The Withering of Neoliberalism and Its Tattered Legacy

Why a Harmful Concept Rose to Temporary Ascendancy in Half the World and What to Do About It

Even in good times, worthless ideas bear worthless fruit.

THE WORLD would look far better, and would be more developed and far less unequal, and above all would have far better prospects for the future if not for the powerful wave of neoliberalism that has swept through the last generation. How was it ever possible for an economic and political concept that serves so few at the cost of so many to attain such status and such bargaining power?

There is a great deal of confusion in economics because, despite the fundamental progress in the discipline over the last few decades, there is still confusion and error with regard to concepts, phenomena, and processes. Sometimes interchangeable terminology is used to denote the same categories, or the same term is used to define varying phenomena and processes. Terminological rigor is essential to argumentation and clarity of views. Sometimes the complexity and dissimilarity of concepts make it difficult to achieve this.

What is this "social market economy" that many authors refer to? Or what is "neoliberalism," which some authors erroneously identify with "classical (or neoclassical) mainstream economics"? When such an identification takes place, it is impossible to agree with the view that neoclassical economics has passed the test of veracity and correctness because economic policy based on its theoretical assumptions has been proven in practice over the course of history, and especially during the last few decades.[1] If we take the methodologically and scientifically correct view that neoclassical economics must be distinguished from the deviation known as neoliberalism, then it becomes clear that neoliberal economic theory has not worked in practice because following its dictates has not led to balanced, long-term financially, socially, and ecologically balanced growth and economic development. Therefore, it is a false theory.

Almost everywhere, high inflation characterized the 1970s, especially the period after the great price shock of 1973–1974, and the 1980s. Today it is hard to believe that there was a time, especially around the middle of that twenty-year period, when inflation in the most highly developed countries, measured by the yearly rate of growth in the price of consumer goods, was in double figures. In the worst year, 1980, inflation reached 18 percent in Great Britain and 13.5 percent in the United States. Inflation raged in less-developed countries, especially in Latin America. At the same time, other demand constraints accumulated to bring about a relative stifling of economic growth. This put an end to the postwar boom that had lasted for a quarter of a century and ushered in the phase of "stagflation"[2] in developed capitalism—high inflation combined with high and increasing unemployment and a low and falling output rate. In extreme cases we faced recession and stagnant output. This is why it was called stagflation. Another term, *slumpflation*, denoted simultaneous inflation and a fall in the absolute level of output—in other words, recession.

The socialist countries took shelter from stagflation behind a cordon of price control mechanisms but nevertheless began to feel increasing supply shortcomings. The shock from outside was exacerbated by systemic frailty, especially the lack of strong mechanisms for capital allocation and the permanent difficulties, due to soft budget constraints, of balancing the demand and supply. In other words, the system functioned in such a way that the money supply was more adjusted to the demand for money than vice versa—in capitalism, the demand for money must adjust to the money supply, because of the systemic hard budget constraints. Then, after the price shock of 1973–1974, which the socialist countries only apparently managed to avoid, began the process of the slow dissolution of the centrally planned economy, despite the adoption of market-oriented reforms here and there. This dissolution occurred, above all, because of the lack of capacity for competitive technological progress and the insufficient openness of these economies to the flow of ideas, people, and goods. Administrative price-control mechanisms did not so much restrain inflation as postpone and suppress it.

Open inflation, manifesting itself in price increases that nevertheless had the effect of clearing the market, devastated the capitalist market economies. At the same time, suppressed inflation, making itself felt in structural supply shortages, eroded the socialist planned economies. On the basis of his observations of this phenomenon, János Kornai created a whole refined theory of the economics of shortage.[3] He argued that shortage is an underlying category that cannot be eliminated from centrally planned economies based on state ownership of the means of production and the bureaucratic control of economic processes. During the debate at the time about the directions and methods of market-oriented reforms and the limitation of inequality in the economy, I coined the concept of "shortageflation."[4] It entered the economic literature but did not achieve popularity matching that of the comparable "stagflation."

The shortageflation syndrome highlights the fundamental contrasts in the alternatives that the socialist and capitalist economies suddenly found themselves facing. In the former, our dilemma was whether to choose higher open (price) inflation and lower shortages (a symptom of suppressed inflation) or lower price inflation and higher shortages. On the other hand, the capitalist economy found itself, at least for a brief period, facing the alternative described by the so-called Phillips curve: higher inflation with lower unemployment or lower inflation with higher unemployment.[5] Thirty years after his theoretical treatment of these issues, Edmund S. Phelps[6] won the 2006 Nobel Prize in economics. Before this could happen, the economic thinking that arose in the 1970s and 1980s had to achieve political dominance, and it did so. Unfortunately, it was distorted in its practical application in economic theory and exploited in ways that did not necessarily coincide with the intentions of its authors. Such things happen, especially when politics intrudes on economics.

Working people and investors (who themselves work very hard) felt the effects of inflation more and more acutely. In the long run, no one, not even politicians, likes inflation. It lowers general economic effectiveness by eroding the motivation for work and distorting the information, so useful to producers and investors, that is encoded in prices. Inflation was already so powerful that it rendered largely ineffective the Keynesian prescriptions for manipulating aggregate demand as a way of stimulating the business climate. Although the inflation was mostly caused by supply factors (increasing production costs, especially of raw materials), an additional injection of demand, often financed by budget deficits, would only stimulate the inflation more and induce an upward price spiral. This was not permissible, and so the search for another path began. Waiting with suggestions were supply-side economics and monetarism, which became as fashionable as Keynesianism had been for a third of the twentieth century, from the American New Deal to the 1970s.

The new school of thought treated inflation as a purely monetary phenomenon. It called for a restrictive monetary policy and the lowering of demand by cuts in public spending. It picked up adherents and supporters, and quickly found political sponsors. The Conservatives, led by Margaret Thatcher, came to power in Britain in 1979. Soon afterward, the Republicans won the White House with Ronald Reagan. Aside from catchy but delusory slogans like Thatcher's TINA, or "There Is No Alternative," the rhetoric and arguments appealed to everyone who wished to see a return of stability and reasonably sensible growth. This was the wish not only of the capital, finance, and business spheres, but also, at least for a time, of labor. By the time labor learned what was really at stake, the unions had already been effectively pacified and were bargaining from a position of weakness, as if there really were no alternative.

Of course, there is always an alternative. It was not the Chinese option, because no one was yet talking about a Chinese economic "miracle." Nor was it the option of a Soviet and Eastern European economic miracle, because things were steadily deteriorating there. Neither of these was anywhere close to being a realistic alternative for market capitalism in the highly developed countries. The situation was different in the developing world, where socialism and capitalism were fighting for dominance as the Cold War went on. The West spurned both of these socialist options and, unfortunately, had little time as well for the Western European and especially Scandinavian social market economy.

For reasons of culture and its own structural crisis, the Japanese model had no chance for domination—the Japanese "miracle" was slowly drawing to an end. Aggressive neoliberalism, growing out of the soil of stagflation and the crisis of Keynesianism, gained the upper hand. Its influence around the world grew and grew, even in the less-developed countries where, after the collapse of real socialism, the neoliberal indoctrination became increasingly insistent.

The neoliberal trend in economics proclaimed the unconditional supremacy of the free market and private enterprise over the state and social policy, and soon led to neoliberal policies that limited the role of the state in the economy. Theory and practice reinforced each other, especially in the English-speaking world, first in the United States and the United Kingdom, later in New Zealand and Australia, and at times in Canada and Ireland. Both Margaret Thatcher and Ronald Reagan were big successes. They managed to turn what had previously been one of several ideological and intellectual trends into the political mainstream. As David Harvey aptly notes, "the alliance of forces they helped consolidate and the majorities they led became a legacy that a subsequent generation of political leaders found hard to dislodge. Perhaps the greatest testimony to their success lies in the fact that both Clinton and Blair found themselves in a situation where their room for maneuver was so limited that they could not help but sustain the process of restoration of class power against their own better instincts."[7]

Neoliberalism began by facing a challenge, and then received a gift. The challenge was a structural crisis in the Latin American economy, and the gift was the collapse of the socialist system.

South and Central America were in a downward spiral of deficits and inflation, stagnation and recession, and growing public debt, especially external debt, with all the accompanying social pain and political destabilization. Few in the rich countries lost any sleep over the social pain, but the political risk, and especially the danger of being unable to collect their debts, was a different matter. The political risk was not that Latin American countries would choose socialism, an option of dwindling attractiveness until the fall of the Soviet Union left it completely discredited, but rather that undemocratic regimes would come to power. They might refuse to pay the debt, claiming that their countries had suffered at the hands of the banks and the wealthy countries in the past. The experience of Salvador Allende's socialist government in Chile had been discouraging and unsettling enough. Democratically elected in

1970, Allende was brutally overthrown three years later by Pinochet's CIA-backed military junta. Governments need not necessarily embark on thorough, rapid privatization; they could also start nationalizing. This challenge could not be left unanswered, and no one would benefit from a replication of the Chilean variant. The world had changed. The "Washington Consensus" had been born.

In fact, not even in Washington was there any consensus, in the true meaning of the word, in the final years of the Reagan presidency and the first years of George H. W. Bush's term, beginning in 1989. Reaganomics, denoting the economic policies begun in 1981, had become popular in many circles both inside and outside the establishment, but disputes and arguments were still going on. Nevertheless, there was fairly wide agreement among influential economists and politicians about the remedies that should be applied to make sure that the Latin American economies generated enough of a surplus to make their debt payments. Economic growth was needed, but also the appropriate division of the spoils. Companies and capital from the creditor countries should also have better access to the markets in the debtor countries. These countries were increasingly dependent in economic terms. They first needed to "emerge," so that their markets could be better penetrated. This is the origin of another term that has had a grand career in the last decade or two: "emerging markets."

There is already a copious literature on the so-called Washington Consensus. It has as many critics as enthusiasts,[8] although the latter have been dwindling away lately. Despite the intentions of those who coined the term,[9] it has also become one of the leading examples of mumbo-jumbo in this period, because of both its interpretive elasticity and the way it has been abused by being stretched to describe situations that often have little in common. The fact remains that, with a large dose of monetarist influence, a powerfully promoted and fairly universally accepted concept of economic policy grew out of neoliberal economic theory at the turn of the 1980s and 1990s. It entailed rapid, thorough privatization; the liberalization of prices, trade, and capital transfers; and an austere financial policy covering both the government budget and the monetary activity of the central bank. Its basic weakness lay in failing to pay enough attention to the institutional and social aspects of economic growth, as well as in ignoring the cultural conditioning of development.

This conception was widely influential and quickly achieved a dominant position in the analyses and programs of key departments of the

American administration, as well as in the opinion-shaping research centers, consulting firms, and media in Washington and the international financial institutions located there, such as the Inter-American Development Bank, the World Bank, and the International Monetary Fund, which are under de facto American control. As a result, criteria and policies were formulated that the American government and the international organizations suggested to, or even forced upon, countries that were dependent on them or that were applying for aid. In extreme cases, there were even whispers that the wealthiest countries, and especially the United States, had deliberately entangled poorer countries in debt, in order to bring them under control and manipulate their economies in a self-serving manner.[10] Such claims should not be rejected out of hand as nonsense, because there are some persuasive arguments behind them. At present, they cannot be proven. The judgment of history may be another matter.

It was the intersection of a Latin American debt crisis that the region could not solve on its own with the evolving neoliberal school of thought that resulted in the Washington Consensus. As a visiting expert at the International Monetary Fund in the early 1990s, I had a chance to see at first hand how that way of thinking gained ascendancy and how it influenced a completely different part of the world. For it was just then that Washington received a present. The socialist system collapsed and the Soviet Union fell. The ideas and practice of central economic planning and a dominant state-owned sector were completely discredited everywhere, with the possible exception of Cuba and North Korea. However, the thing that took everyone by surprise was the number of applicants for advice and money who turned up, with the exception of China, which "failed to collapse." This is something that has long-term consequences for the entire world economy.

The postsocialist countries appeared. At first there were a handful of them, then a dozen, and finally more than thirty. The West had nothing ready for them, aside from its own experience with a highly developed market economy, not exactly suited to the occasion, and the Washington Consensus, which had been prepared for completely different circumstances. Yet the need to do something was the chance of a lifetime for the neoliberals. How could they pass it up? Now neoliberalism, including its Washington Consensus variant, could hold sway over an enormous portion of the world. The chance did not go begging. The 1990s were the apogee of neoliberalism.

Its teachings fell on very fertile ground in the postsocialist countries of East Central Europe, more fertile even than the Latin American countries, with their strong ties to the United States. For a time, the neoliberal teachings were even dominant in some Asian transformation economies. Until the end of socialism, these had been bastions of orthodoxy, with almost none of the reform tendencies familiar elsewhere. So it was in Laos and Mongolia. Washington "assigned" these two countries to Australia and New Zealand, respectively. However, the real clash did not take place in the Mekong valley or the Mongolian steppes. The final, decisive battle of the Cold War occurred in Poland.

An additional surprise for the West was the great opportunity opening up in the form of markets that had previously seemed as remote as the steppes or that had been completely invisible behind the Iron Curtain. Their accessibility for the rich countries' goods and capital, both direct investment and short-term speculative portfolio investment, depended on how quickly and how widely they could be opened up for penetration. With its ideology, rhetoric, and incentives, neoliberalism was perfectly suited for the task.

The United States and the United Kingdom were particularly active. Once again, many things were happening at the same time. Both of these countries had significant amounts of loose capital, and they were looking for advantageous investment opportunities abroad. Japan had entered its off-putting crisis, China was still more closed than open, Africa was completely unattractive, and Latin America had just gone broke. Here was new territory that only needed help in "emerging" and opening up. It wasn't "Open Sesame," but it was a stone's throw away.

In terms of politics, it is no mystery that further undermining the Soviet Union advanced the strategic interests and global hegemonic ambitions of the United States. Britain was a faithful and far from disinterested ally. Now there was a chance not merely to undermine Reagan's "evil empire," but to bring the Soviets crashing down.

It is worth noting that, given the right conditions, the USSR could have lasted longer. Its collapse came as a complete surprise. There are many conceivable scenarios. When I asked Francis Fukuyama if a different outcome had been possible, he answered that yes, of course it had been. He speculated that things could have been different if one of the conservative leaders, Yuri Andropov (who died in 1984) or Konstantin Chernenko (1985), had lived longer. I found this interesting, because my own speculations tended in the opposite direction, that the USSR could have survived if Mikhail Gorbachev had come to power sooner, perhaps a decade sooner. In the late 1990s, I asked Gorbachev himself, a great statesman to whom the world owes an enormous debt, if he thought that the USSR would have lasted longer if Boris Yeltsin had taken over the leadership of the party and the country from Gorbachev at the very beginning of the 1990s. Without a moment's hesitation, he answered in the affirmative. Perhaps it would have turned out that way. In the end, one of the reasons that the USSR disintegrated was that the only way to take power in Russia was to break up the Union. Yeltsin was determined from the start to rule; only later did he begin wondering about how to do so.

Other significant countries entered the game only half-heartedly or not at all, for various reasons. Distant Japan was in the clutches of its own crisis, and in any case regarded Southeast Asia rather than East Central Europe as its primary target for economic penetration. Germany, close at hand, was busy with its own incredibly costly reunification process, which it wanted to bring to a conclusion as quickly as possible. The Scandinavian social democracies had a smaller combined population than that of Poland, so what could they offer in economic terms? Furthermore, the World Bank and the International Monetary Fund were in Washington and Wall Street in New York, not Copenhagen or Stockholm. Finland itself was suffering from the fall of the USSR, with which it had maintained a range of profitable subsidized commercial arrangements. France and Italy also had their own problems. Italy's were mostly internal, whereas France had more urgent and important issues to settle in its former African colonies. So it was that the United States and the United Kingdom called the shots, and these were the countries where neoliberalism was in its glory. It was entirely natural to offer neoliberalism as a solution to the cascading problems in East Central Europe. The supply was available. It is easier to supply soft advice than hard money.

There was demand, too. The demand came first from Poland, where many things were indeed happening at the same time. Along with Hungary, Poland was best prepared for the introduction of a full-fledged market economy, above all as a result of the earlier systemic reforms introduced under the umbrella of martial law in the early 1980s, and even more so in the so-called second stage of economic reform at the end of that decade. Socialism had fallen, and there was an urgent need for something to replace it. It was clear that the Soviet Union, already in its own death throes and absorbed by its own problems, would not intervene. The Germans also had far too many of their own problems to worry about introducing the theory and practice of the social market economy to their eastern neighbors. In Poland, the labor union utopia promised by Solidarity had stirred strong antistatist sentiment. There was no shortage of politicians eager to seize on the foreign neoliberal model and make it their own. They even supplied it with a naïve, folksy slogan: "shock therapy." The laboratory was ready.

This peculiar demand for a neoliberal policy that minimized the role of the state and advanced narrow group interests at the cost of the public as a whole defied all macroeconomic rationality. It also flew in the face of everything that had been agreed on at the Round Table talks in 1989 and, even more important, of the hopes of a decided majority of the public. This was all the more true after November 9, 1989, the day when, inevitably, the Berlin Wall at last came down.

The original economic program immediately underwent radicalization. The slogans took wing: Now or Never! Everything's Possible! TINA! That was the autumn of a sharp turn. In his inaugural speech in September, the prime minister had sketched a social-democratic program of building a social market economy (as was reflected even later in the constitution, in a purely pro forma way). Suddenly, things swung toward neoliberalism of a quite extremist variety. This happened under pressure from foreign advisers, mostly brought in from the United States and Britain. These were not people of great intellectual quality; they simply played an instrumental role in advancing the interests of the groups they served, consciously or not. It goes without saying that they were financed in various ways by a wide range of sources in their home countries.

It is baffling that the first postsocialist prime minister, Tadeusz Mazowiecki, is unable even now, all these years later, to perceive that radical shift in policy. When I asked him about it in the summer of 2007, he said that he did not think there had been any turning point. He thought it was simply a matter of preparing a legislative package embodying needed structural reforms. He felt that the only thing that had happened was to hasten the abandonment of the Round Table settlement. He contended that he had announced his intention to do so when he was nominated in August to form the government. According to him, that moment had been the turning point, a shift from an agreement to share power to a complete takeover. He said that the new political priorities led to the reassessment. The Solidarity position at the Round Table, a mixed state-private economy, was replaced by the option for a capitalist economy—except that it was supposed to be a social market economy. I think that is what Prime Minister Mazowiecki wanted. Others, plainly, did not.

I was a member of an advisory body known as the Economics Council of the Council of Ministers, headed from 1989 to 1991 by Professor Witold Trzeciakowski. I took part in many professional discussions there, although few people outside the government paid much attention to us. I also directed the Research Institute of Finances, which issued commentaries and alternative policy proposals. Most of the time they were ignored. Others made the proposals that were adopted. The interesting thing is that even the experts from the International Monetary Fund, who were already quite active and enjoyed the backing of the United States and the other G-7 countries, tried to tone down what they regarded as an overly radical liberalization and stabilization program. They failed.

Doctrinaire attitudes gained the upper hand. Some advisers, so it seemed, were eager to experiment on the organism of a living economy. It was a unique chance, and in this regard it really was a matter of now or never. All known methods of privatization were tried out, and a few completely new ones as well. Almost every possible exchange-rate mechanism underwent testing. Different variants of trade liberalization were assessed and tweaked to make them more radical or more moderate. Policy based on the Warsaw version of the Washington Consensus was one big experiment, and it yielded masses of material for the further study of neoliberal economic thinking, and even more pain for Polish society.

As poorly as the off-the-scale naïve neoliberalism fit postsocialist reality, the imported idea known as shock therapy gained acceptance. Leszek Balcerowicz, the deputy prime minister of the day, who was also the minister of finance and who coordinated government economic policy, gave it his seal of approval, even though he would previously have denied professing any such options. The government was not fully informed about the possible consequences of this policy and accepted it under the pressure of time and specious arguments. In reality, the idea came down to a multitude of needless shocks (such as the excessive devaluation of the zloty or the imposition of backbreaking new interest rates on preexisting commercial credits) and a meager dose of therapy.

On the one hand, economic liberalization was incorrectly presented as identical to the shift to a market economy. On the other hand, many of the fiscal and monetary parameters of the stabilization policy were fixed inaccurately, and this led to badly missing, or overshooting the targets. The institutional dimension of the construction of a market economy was underestimated. The social aspects were dismissed as unimportant.

The fact that some measures were correct, such as the ongoing radical liberalization of prices or the introduction of domestic currency convertibility, did not change the fact that we were dealing with a compound mistake: The program was ill conceived and poorly executed.[11] Everything indicates that, regardless of warnings, the government was not fully aware of what it was getting itself into. It placed excessive trust in a narrow group of people who prepared the crucial packet of changes, and as a result it fell under the spell of irrationally optimistic forecasts. It remained easy for the leaders, the government economists and their advisers, and the obedient part of the media to persuade people that there was "no alternative," and to mislead them by promising results that enlightened economists immediately questioned as not feasible.[12] The domestic political atmosphere and the external pressures combined in such a way that economic nonsense, from the point of view of the interests of the national economy and the public, came across as an economic policy program that was actually being carried out.

"Shock therapy" is garden variety mumbo jumbo. The constant proximity of the words *shock* and *therapy* makes it seem as if the first must inevitably lead to the second. It would have made just as much sense to talk about "shock failure" and "gradual therapy." A combination of circumstances made Poland exceptionally receptive to this mumbo jumbo, with all the negative consequences that many social-occupational groups and regions of the country feel to this day, twenty years after the failure of the enterprise.

This is how it was possible to carry out the neoliberal experiment in a postsocialist economy for the first time, and to do so in the largest such economy in the region and the one that had paved the way for the transformation in other countries. Several years later, as a result of important changes in development policy and systemic changes, the economy did in fact enter a period of rapid growth. At that point, out of understandable psychological and political motives, there was an attempt to claim this success as the positive result of the neoliberal experiment, occurring somewhat later than had been expected. In fact, that relative economic success, particularly visible in the years 1994–1997, when the per capita GDP increased in real terms by 28 percent and Poland became a member of the Organization for Economic Cooperation and Development (OECD), was achieved in spite of, rather than because of, "shock therapy." Anyone who contends otherwise and who attributes the later success to the earlier actions, and particularly those of the period from late 1989 to 1991, is guilty of the logical fallacy of post hoc, ergo propter hoc. So-called shock therapy ended in failure. The attempt to introduce it did indeed solve some problems, but it needlessly caused others. In sum, not only were the costs of the exercise far higher than predicted and its results far scantier than promised, but the costs were much greater than they need have been and the benefits far smaller. Is there any better proof of the pointlessness and irrationality of the whole venture?

From mid-1989 until mid-1992 we had "shock failure," as a result of which the per capita GDP fell by almost 20 percent. Next came a phase of "gradual therapy." Later still, the erroneous policies of the period from 1998 to 2001 brought the rate of growth down from 7 percent to zero. Had it not been for these neoliberal excesses, exacerbated in the latter episode by their complete incompatibility with right-wing populism, the Polish per capita GDP today could be not 70 percent but 170 percent higher than it was in 1989. All it would have taken was the more thorough and less revolutionary introduction of systemic changes, the refusal to exaggerate the stabilization policy in the early 1990s, and instead of cooling down the economy at the end of the 1990s, the continuation of the effective policy that combined structural reforms with socioeconomic development in the mid-1990s.

In the days leading up to the parliamentary election in September 1997, the leader of the neoliberal party with the lovely name Freedom Union, or UW, proclaimed a brief manifesto calling for the doubling of the GDP within ten years. Together with their right-wing populist coalition partner, Solidarity Electoral Action, or AWS, Freedom Union won the election. The party and its leaders may well have been subjectively convinced that what they were saying was possible. Given certain conditions, it could have been. They may even have thought that their economic knowledge and political acumen would help make it so. Unfortunately, they were wrong. Probably, in any case, what they were really concerned about was the short-term propaganda effect on the voters. This leaves us with a harsh alternative: Either they were wrong or they were deliberately misleading people. This is made all the more evident by the fact that the manifesto in question was preceded by a period during which the GDP had grown faster than at any time in the previous twenty-five years. From 1994 to 1997, it grew by an annual average of 6.4 percent on a per capita basis. Neoliberal economists criticized this as too low a growth rate. In 1997, the growth was 6.8 percent, and the annual rate in the last quarter before the elections was 7.5 percent.[13]

For income to double in ten years it must grow at an average annual rate of 7.2 percent. Arithmetic does the rest, through the magic of compound interest. Maintaining the growth rate achieved through the effective policy of the previous few years would have done the trick. It was possible. It would not have required anything more than admitting that the economic theory and strategy of the political and academic adversaries of neoliberalism were correct, and should be continued. Sound policy must rest on correct theory. Theoretical mistakes produce practical errors, although they are sometimes good business. Unfortunately, for extraneous reasons like political preferences and ideological entanglements, the actions that would have served the public interest were not taken. All it required was admitting being wrong, and acknowledging that someone else was right. In politics, that is a great deal, and usually it is too much.

Instead, politicians followed the destructive political logic, which makes no economic sense, that the first priority is change, even if it makes things worse. And it did. They cooled down the economy, with all the economic and social consequences. Excessive financial restraint and the abandonment of industrial and commercial policy brought the rate of growth as low as 0.2 percent in the last quarter of 2001. The average rate from 1998 to 2001 was not 7.2 percent, as they had implied, but a mere 3.5 percent. The amount of realistically possible GDP growth that did not happen in that time span, the missed opportunity, was 17 percent, which is a great deal to lose in four short years.

This had an automatic impact on the lives of people, because unemployment mushroomed despite the ebullient forecasts trumpeted in the media. It didn't have to be this way. Unemployment could have continued falling, just as it had fallen by more than a million between 1994 and 1997. The propaganda organs of naïve Polish neoliberalism proclaimed that "if we do not create three to four million new jobs over the next few years as a way of 'utilizing' the demographic boom and eliminating hidden rural unemployment, then this bomb will detonate, and it could ruin what has been achieved so far in the Polish transformation." Economic nonchalance led, in fact, to a rise in joblessness from the level of 1.8 million that had been achieved under non-neoliberal policy to a sobering 3.2 million at the end of 2001, as a result of that neoliberal binge.

Many factors were favorable during this period. More pro-market changes came into effect, private enterprise continued to flourish, and external conditions were only slightly worse than during the previous years. Nevertheless, so much of what the neoliberal politicians promised turned out to be so wrong that the insistent question returned: Were their declarations mistaken, or were they lying in order to mislead the public? This is not only an intellectual dilemma, but also an ethical one, especially when the outcome has such negative economic consequences for almost the whole country. Almost, because a small minority came out ahead, and some did very well. For the rest, the lost years are gone forever, and many people lost hope along with their jobs.

Even with such consequences at stake, the dilemma of "Were they wrong or were they lying?" is seldom brought to public attention or resolved. There are reasons for this. A massive, well-financed propaganda machine exists solely to prove that black is white, or vice versa, as the situation requires. Its job is to obscure responsibility for the mistakes or lies and to blur the fact that the special interests are being served even while proclaiming a desire to serve the public interest. It is worth keeping this in mind, because it has happened before and will happen again.

Public discussions, even those of an ostensibly academic nature, often come down to stonewalling. People say things that are the exact opposite of what they said not long before, and they refuse to discuss those previous statements. What else can they do when their main goal is to avoid admitting that they have been wrong? If they were wrong in the past, the last thing they want to do is to admit that they could be wrong in the present. And so, once the damage has been done, they talk about the importance of institutional and cultural factors in development, and the importance of effective public policy, when not so long before the only thing they wanted to discuss was their determination not to "play politics." The assertion that neoliberal policy is an effective way to make up for shortfalls in development is a blatant contradiction of a mass of facts, visible to the naked eye, showing that no one ever made up for shortfalls in development through neoliberalism.

Even worse is twisting the facts and stressing the importance of mechanisms that in fact the neoliberals never even used. They try to convince themselves and others that their policies included aspects that they never implemented, like investing in human capital or encouraging business to be more competitive. They contradict the arguments that they made in the past. Perhaps this is a subconscious compensation for the fact that they can never come out and say that their opponents were right. Or perhaps it is simply a way of trying to get out of the corner that they painted themselves into with their false doctrines. At the same time, they try to link every positive development, and there is always something positive happening, to causes over which they had no control or even tried to block.

Between 1989 and 2008, the Polish GDP grew at an average annual rate of 3.0 percent. If it had grown at an annual rate of 5.5 percent, then the GDP at the end of that period would have been 270 percent of what it was at the beginning. Some countries, which are better at benefiting from globalization, have indeed grown at 5.5 percent a year. During the years of the Strategy for Poland, from 1994 to 1997, growth was almost a full percentage point higher than the target of 5.5 percent. After the start of the Program for the Improvement of the Finances of Poland in mid-2002, during the lead-up to European Union integration, it was a little bit less than a point lower. Thus, for more or less half of the transformation period, when economic policy did not cave in to neoliberal dictates, the growth rate was entirely respectable.

The missed growth, which didn't happen even though it could have, with all its economic and social consequences, illustrates the price that Poland and its population as a whole paid for the adherence to the naïve, homegrown variety of neoliberalism. Part of the loss resulted in additional income for our partners in other parts of the globalized economy. Many of them took advantage of this to eliminate competing Polish companies from the market, which meant that many jobs moved elsewhere. This state of affairs is reflected in a structural trade deficit and in the fact that profits from both manufacturing and speculation are transferred out of Poland instead of being invested there. Other potential profits ended up never being created at all.

It should also be added that neoliberalism guided the monetary policy of the National Bank of Poland throughout the transformation period, even when the government was following a sensible policy of reform and development, trying to construct the institutions of a market economy while maintaining social cohesion and introducing microeconomic policies that encouraged entrepreneurship. Unfortunately, the central bank either did not want to or could not support these policies. It allowed itself to be swayed more by the international financial markets than by domestic development requirements. Neoliberalism is canonical for the global finance markets, because nothing is better for their interests than that doctrine and the policies that result from it.

The Polish experiment at the intermittently unsuccessful combining of transformation with development policy was a serious failure for neoliberalism in the new, wide-open spaces of the postsocialist economies. It is therefore not surprising that the neoliberals refuse to face up to this debacle. They will carry this refusal to their graves, but life is short, the failures are piling up, and the apologists for neoliberalism are becoming scarce.

This is because the doctrine is failing elsewhere, in both rich countries and poor ones. As for the rich countries, the best example is the very cradle of neoliberalism, the United States. At least seven aspects of this state of affairs need to be considered:

1. Financing economic growth and its consequences for the level of public debt and financial disequilibrium.
2. The choice between working time and income levels.
3. The growing inequality of income and wealth.
4. Scenarios for alternative, non-neoliberal development histories.
5. The loss of world political leadership.
6. The growth of anti-American sentiment around the world.
7. The rising level of frustration within the United States.

To take the first point: American expansion is the result, to a large degree, of the country's special position as the issuer of the dollar, the world's basic reserve currency. This is changing slowly. The fiscal and trade positions are changing rapidly, and for the worse, to the point where there is a danger of a complete upset. The American current account deficit of about $800 billion is twice as large as the combined deficits of the next twenty countries on the list. The European Union lives within its means on its current income. The United States, with its so-called double deficit of close to 10 percent of GDP per year, lives largely on credit. As is known, loans must be repaid at some point. This means that the time frame of the analysis must be stretched, not only thirty years into the past, to a point where output was growing faster in the United States than in Western Europe, but also thirty years into the future, when we can expect that output will be growing faster in Europe.

Second, the proponents of neoliberalism like to contrast the United States with somewhat less-developed countries, including those in the European Union, which is said to lag twenty years behind America. This difference is based on a straightforward comparison of the level of per capita GDP, which shows that the level in Europe, about $30,000 by purchasing power parity (PPP), is the same as it was in America twenty years ago. Now the U.S. figure is almost 50 percent higher, at close to $45,000. This is true, but it applies to only the single category of income levels and the rate at which they change. However, there is more to the picture, including the differences in values and preferences that determine how the effects of the growth in productivity are allocated. Americans prefer a growth in income, whereas Europeans prefer more free time.

The truth is that American output has grown rapidly in recent years not because the system is more liberal (which, the neoliberals claim, makes it more effective). Economic effectiveness and productivity have been increasing at a similar rate on both sides of the Atlantic.[14] Output has grown more rapidly in America because there has been hardly any reduction in work time there. In European countries, and not only the members of the European Union, a large part of the gain in productivity has gone to reducing work time, because that is what the people want. True liberalism rests on authentic free choice, not only for capital, but also for people, and for people above all. If the society prefers slightly lower increases in income while reducing the time spent earning it, which means having more time for the consumption of that income, then the choice is theirs.

The OECD estimates that the average annual number of hours worked by each employed American has fallen by 5.3 percent, from about 1,900 to 1,800, since 1970. In Germany, with its preference for a social market economy, hours worked have fallen by 26.5 percent in the same period, from about 1,960 to 1,440. The figures in France are similar. For British workers, the reduction has been 13.4 percent (from 1,940 to 1,680), and for Italians it has been 15 percent (from 1,870 to 1,590). In other words, if German or French workers had followed the American model and plowed almost all their productivity increases into their incomes, and thus into the GDP, then they would have a present-day income comparable to that of Americans. They made their choice and opted for free time instead. They work shorter hours in a shorter workweek, take longer vacations, and retire younger. Their free time is good free time, which means time to enjoy life outside of work, as opposed to the bad kind of free time, which comes when you don't have a job.

Third, it is a glaring fact that the beneficiaries of economic growth in the United States are a relatively small group. This is because economic policies fashioned along the lines recommended by the neoliberal school, dictating a limited role for the state in income distribution and social intervention, make it easier for a narrow, privileged group to capture the lion's share of the benefits of rising output. This group includes the upper and upper-middle classes. For a large part of the population, real incomes have not risen at all in the last several decades and have even declined in absolute terms. The minimum wage was left unchanged for a decade, despite the significant rises in overall prosperity, until the Democrats forced a raise of a scant $0.70, to $5.85 an hour, in 2007. As a result, the minimal monthly U.S. wage of about $1,400 is equal in nominal terms to the average wage in Poland and in real terms it is far lower than that in Poland, where the per capita GDP is only a third of that in America. (The average nominal pay in Poland is about 3,200 zloty, or about $1,020, which works out to around $1,670 at a PPP rate of 1.64.)

In other words, many citizens of the richest country in the world earn less now, in real terms, than in the 1970s and 1980s. This is not because they are less productive. They are, in fact, more productive as a result of being better qualified and of technical and organizational progress. However, they earn less because income distribution mechanisms have been created that deprive them of the chance to take advantage of economic growth. This is thanks to the so-called flexibility of the labor market, which is something that the neoliberals would also like to see in the European Union and the emerging markets. The fact that it is plainly unjust worries few. However, excessive inequality has a negative impact on economic growth,[15] and this should worry many. The effects are already visible in the United States. Economic growth would be higher if not for the enormous, increasing differentiation of income and assets. This is one reason that the average rates of growth in the United States and the European Union for 2007–2008 were almost identical and are estimated at between 2.2 and 2.3 percent.

The share of income received by the most affluent 1 percent of Americans doubled between 1980 and 2004, from 8 to 16 percent of the income of the whole population. The income of the highest-earning one-thousandth has tripled, from 2 to 7 percent. The highest-earning one ten-thousandth—a group of about 14,000 taxpayers—has seen its income quadruple, from 0.64 to 2.87 percent of the total. In other words, one ten-thousandth of the population receives one fortieth of the national income. Nor is it strange that the largest numbers of persons with liquid assets of more than $1 million (that is, excluding property and real estate) are found in the United States. Merill Lynch estimates that there are a total of 8.7 million of these people in the world, with aggregate liquid assets amounting to $33.3 trillion, and that 2.9 million of them are Americans. Europe has a total population twice as high as that of the United States but only 2.8 million of these very wealthy individuals. There are 2.4 million Asians in this category.

In the United States 36 million people also live in poverty, according to statistics from the U.S. Census Bureau. This is more than the population of Canada. Despite the rapid growth at an annual rate of more than 3 percent between 2002 and 2006, the poor were increasing by about a 1.5 million per year. They now make up 13 percent of the population. Among African Americans, the figure is 25 percent. In other words, one in eight Americans lives in poverty, and one in four African Americans.

In 2004, the average American family in the lower decile earned $15,600, and the current figure is not much higher. This represents a fall of 12 percent since 1969. This is not, as some neoliberals contend, because "they don't want to work." Over the same forty years, the percentage of poor families with at least one member in full-time employment has risen from 12 percent to 30 percent.

The Gini coefficient has been rising steadily in the United States since around 1980, reflecting the increasing income differentials. When Ronald Reagan won the presidency, it was "only" 0.403. A decade later it was 0.428. By 2000 it was 0.462, and in 2005 it was at a historical high of 0.469, similar to the figures in the Philippines or Madagascar.

An American neoconservative or a European neoliberal might say: "So? That's the natural order of things. That's what the market wants, and the market rules and rewards the factors of production—capital and labor—in an equivalent way according to their deserts." This is demonstrably false. The economic and political instruments, including the tax and electoral systems, are constructed in such a way that the major part of the impressive American growth takes place at the cost of those who are driven into poverty. Wealth is created as a result not only of innovation and productivity, which merit all possible praise, but also of greed and redistribution. What is worse, it leads to the piling up of what is called structural inequality, which cannot be reduced without modifying the very foundations of the system. That would mean state intervention in the way the distribution takes place according to the logic of the free market—which would be a complete repudiation of neoliberal doctrine.

Where does the truth lie? What are the reasons? No one should need convincing that the escape from stagnation into civilizational development depends to an overwhelming degree on the quality of human capital and that this increases as society attains higher educational levels. This, in turn, is easy to accomplish when students are more intelligent. Every teacher and professor knows this, as do increasing numbers of students. We could leave things to nature and the invisible hand. But we could also take a more serious approach. After years of debates, psychologists have concluded that intelligence depends in more or less equal measure on genetics and environment. The appropriate government policy can therefore manipulate factors that are partially responsible for the intellectual development of the young in a way that raises their intelligence quotient. To do so the government itself must be intelligent and able to assign the appropriate public expenditure to the educational-cultural sphere, having first taxed those who are capable of being taxed.

It is worth comparing the experience of the social market economies of the Nordic countries from Finland through Scandinavia to Iceland with that of the English-speaking countries. The difference in terms of social mobility through education can be seen at a glance. A research group[16] has ranked countries on a scale where 1 denotes the complete lack of mobility and 0 means ideal mobility. A score of 1 means that the income of children is exactly the same as that of their parents, and a score of 0 means that there is no correlation between the incomes of parents and children. The coefficient in the Nordic countries is 0.2. In Great Britain it is 0.36, and in the United States it is 0.54. This means that the income level of each new generation is far more dependent on that of the previous generation in the United States and Britain than in the Nordic countries. In the former two countries, only half the children (in effect, the boys) born into poverty in the late 1950s managed to pull themselves out of it by the time they were in their forties, whereas 75 percent of those born poor in the Nordic countries managed to do so. Countries with social market economies and the corresponding public policies have somewhat higher taxes, but they have also managed to break the connection between the incomes of parents and children. With its fundamentalist market economy and neoconservative social policies, the United States has failed at this. Things are not quite as discouraging in the United Kingdom. Another myth is shattered—the myth of "opportunity" in a land of profound structural inequality.

All these things have happened in the United States despite the growth in employment and productivity, and despite the failure to reduce working hours. It has happened thanks to a flexible labor market and cuts in social transfers. "Triumphant" neoliberalism has things to be proud of, but it also has things to be ashamed of.

Fourth, as for the real economic dynamism in recent years, the facts are known. The per capita GDP in the United States has risen at an average of 2 percent annually since 1980. However, we do not know what the alternative history could have been, "If only. . . ." What would things have been like if, instead of neoliberalism, the United States had been dominated by neoinstitutionalism, a new institutional economics, and if the idea of the social market economy had taken root instead of aggressive, unrestrained capitalism? Would it have been *Amérique Paradis*? This was not a real option, because essential factors were missing. Nevertheless, GDP growth in such a scenario would not have been lower and would probably have been significantly higher than in real life. Americans would have more free time to satisfy their needs for consumption and personal cultural development. The differentiation of incomes and property would be significantly less, as would the scale of social exclusion. There would certainly be less anti-American sentiment around the world. This would make it easier for the United States to maintain its leading economic and political position, and to play a greater and more constructive role in the badly needed new institutionalization of globalization.

Fifth, even if anyone still believes that neoliberalism has contributed to the absolute and relative improvement of the economic position of the United States, which slid below one fifth of world output in 2008, it is easy to see that, in terms of politics, the country is quickly losing its position of leadership. Clinging to the neoliberal model is only making matters worse. This comes out in numerous ways. Even with its slower rate of growth, the European Union, which never embraced neoliberalism, is in a relatively stronger position today. The common European currency, the euro, has gained considerable strength against the dollar. China is only a few steps away from equaling the American share of world GDP. Americans and their advice are less and less welcome in many regions of the world. Their influence in international organizations has waned.

Sixth, anti-American sentiment is rising on the wave of rampant neoliberalism in its expansionist variety that tries to impose the American model on other countries and presses them to adopt economic policies that ignore their local values and cultures. This is especially true in countries that have suffered neoliberal confusion of their own and are unable to come up with an effective and convincing development model. This is why such feelings are milder in, for instance, China or Scandinavia, and more pronounced in the Middle East, North Africa, or Latin America. Anti-American feeling has risen markedly in Muslim countries over the last few years, but to varying degrees. Between 2001–2002 and 2005–2006, "unfavorable views" rose from 64 to 79 percent in the friendly country of Saudi Arabia, where the undemocratic regime exercises full control over the press. They rose from 33 to 62 percent in NATO ally Turkey and from 41 to 49 percent in politically amicable and relatively stable Morocco. Intriguingly, the only Islamic country to buck this trend was in a country belonging to George W. Bush's "Axis of Evil," Iran, where the antipathy declined from 63 to 52 percent.[17]

It is worth noting here how easily public opinion in the "free world" is manipulated by politicians and the media, which arbitrarily portray other countries, such as Iran, as "evil." Unfortunately, this is true even of such serious and influential publications as *The Economist*, which ran an article on July 19, 2007, entitled "The Riddle of Iran." It began: "'The Iranian regime is basically a messianic apocalyptic cult.' So says Binyamin Netanyahu. If he is right, the world is teetering on the edge of a terrifying crisis."[18] Things are little better on the public opinion front in Latin America, where 64 percent of Argentineans, 57 percent of Brazilians, 53 percent of Mexicans, and 51 percent of Chileans have a "basically negative" opinion of the neighbor to the north.[19]

Seventh, there is growing discontent within the United States over the existing state of affairs, and increasingly sharp criticism of the economic and political, domestic and foreign, and local and global excesses of American neoconservatism. In the opinion of some influential commentators, this powerful and long-splendid country has arrived at a risky crossroads.[20] This would never have occurred if not for the excessively prolonged one-sidedness of the policies dictated by the waning but still influential ideology of neoconservatism.

The United States, the other English-speaking countries, and the most advanced parts of Europe are not the only rich countries on the planet. There is also Japan, where neoliberalism never spread its wings, either during the boom that carried the country into the forefront of the world's economy by the 1970s and 1980s, or during the subsequent grappling with great structural problems and stagnation. In both of these phases, Japan was deaf to neoliberal advice. It went its own way, with strong state involvement in economic development and social solidarity that was genuine rather than merely declarative. Cultural conditions had great significance in the development process: strong family traditions, an attachment to small business, employment stability (the famous *shūshin koyô*), and a sense of loyalty between employees and employers that was unthinkable elsewhere.

When it became clear around 1990 that the latest "economic miracle" was drawing to a close, Japan was subjected to increased external suggestions and pressure, urging it to choose the neoliberal road out of the crisis. The Japanese responded skeptically and continued along their own path. They felt that, because neoliberalism hadn't worked anywhere else, it wasn't likely to pass the test in a country that combined the traditional and the contemporary in a unique way. Recent economic reforms had increased the scope of entrepreneurial freedom and made the economy more free in general, but not in the neoliberal way. Japan proved that up-to-date capitalism can flourish in good times and bad by taking account of national particularities and values, even while shunning the neoliberal prescription. With a labor market less flexible than the American one, Japan quickly began thriving again while keeping its companies highly competitive. Nothing better illustrates this than the way Toyota overtook General Motors as the world's largest carmaker. World travelers and suburban commuters alike are more likely to climb behind the wheel of a Land Cruiser than a Jeep.

The Japanese economy has been keeping pace with the American from 2006 to 2008, with annual GDP growth of about 2.3 percent.

In poor countries, the situation varies. They are in a tricky predicament, because the Soviet style has ceased to be a realistic option, if it ever was. As for capitalism, these countries can see for themselves that the neoliberal drive to repudiate Keynesianism and interventionism looks increasingly shopworn. It has failed in developed countries, developing countries, and those that would love to develop. The evidence abounds in both the postsocialist and Latin American economies, where the Washington Consensus, tailor-made for that continent, has proved to be an uncomfortable fit. After some temporary positive effects, indebtedness began rising again without being matched by any significant or durable acceleration of growth. The only clear plus was controlling inflation, something that could in any case have been achieved through less painful and less socially costly alternative structural reforms, or by following unorthodox economic policies. This is what Malaysia managed to do as it successfully pursued a boldly antiliberal line.

Latin America noted all of this, although not immediately. Only after 2000 did more and more Latin Americans renounce the neoliberal experiments and begin searching for other ways to pull themselves out of stagnation and speed up development. Many turned explicitly to the left in their economic and social policies, upsetting and irritating the Big Brother to the north. This was understandable, because it was supposed to turn out otherwise. Here were democratic regimes, with democratically elected parliaments and presidents, coming out right down the street and talking about Latin socialism. The most active was President Hugo Chavez of Venezuela, but the heads of such states as Ecuador, Bolivia, and Nicaragua joined in. Argentina distanced itself from Washington's prompting, consensus or no. Then Brazil, Uruguay, and Chile climbed on the bandwagon. This is an important political challenge that neoliberalism is incapable of dealing with. It's too late. Neoliberals demanded that others play by their rules and adapt to globalization and the emergent new economic order, but they themselves could not adapt to a changing environment. As we know from the sad story about the dinosaurs, those who cannot adapt, perish.

The heaviest blow to neoliberalism came from a completely unexpected direction. Chairman Mao had indeed threatened that China would overtake the British economy. No one outside China took him seriously, and it is doubtful whether anyone in the Forbidden City did either. It was as if the Congo were to announce today that it would soon overtake France. The per capita GDP in China stands at only 75 percent of the world average today, but the population is so large that the country is now second only to the United States in absolute terms. Mao's prediction came true in 2006, when the Chinese GDP surged 7 percent ahead of the United Kingdom at market exchange rates, by $2.51 trillion to $2.34 trillion. Using the more informative PPP measure, the Chinese GDP of $10 trillion is more than five times as great as the $1.9 trillion GDP of Britain.[21]

China will become the largest economy in the world in about twenty years at the current exchange rate, and by 2011 at the PPP rate. In that same year, the GDP of China will also exceed that of the six non-American members of the G-7, the group of the richest capitalist countries (France, Japan, Canada, Germany, the United Kingdom, and Italy). The only thing that could prevent this is World War III, which is not going to happen, or a radical swerve by China in the direction of neoliberal policies in the style of the Russia of the 1990s, or of Poland at the beginning of the shock-therapy period or the time of the unnecessary "cooling-off" at the end of the 1990s. That is even more unlikely than World War III.

From the point of view of economic development, China made the correct choice three times in a row. None of the other postsocialist or currently emerging countries got it so right.

First, in 1977, when Deng Xiaoping decided to make a strategic departure from orthodox communism and to reform the socialist economy in a pro-market direction.

Second, in 1989, when the country made the incredibly difficult choice, involving the tragic events at Tiananmen Square, to suppress the democratic forces trying to undermine the centralized state and the one-party system while intensifying the economic changes that were under way.

Third, after years of campaigning and successful reforms, when China committed itself to a full-fledged market economy by joining the World Trade Organization (WTO) in 2001.

Despite persistent urging, China never chose the neoliberal road. The country never took these counselors seriously, because the Chinese political reformers and economists knew their own system and culture better than anyone else. They were also more resistant to intellectual corruption than many people in other parts of the world.

China followed the Chinese road, which turned out to be the right choice for development. It has several specific traits, but the most interesting for us is the way it enabled the country to escape from a double bind: on the one hand, the complex heritage of socialism and central planning, which created as many problems as it solved, and, on the other, the syndrome, typical of Third World countries, of low development. China had one foot in the socialist world and the other in the Third World. No country in either of these worlds could match China's determination to move into the First World, but on its own terms. China defied both its own previous communist orthodoxy and the alien orthodoxy of neoliberalism.

Nevertheless, increasing numbers of economists and social scientists have recently begun making convoluted arguments purporting to interpret the Chinese transformation as a kind of neoliberalism, as if coordinated market reforms and macroeconomic development strategies guided and supported by the state could have anything in common with that philosophy. The conscious, deliberate, controlled use by the state of market institutions as tools of socioeconomic reform have nothing to do with the chimera of neoliberalism. The active role of the state in Chinese economic policy is the very opposite of neoliberalism, and analysts who say otherwise are grasping at straws.

The Chinese example has quickly spilled over into neighboring countries that have also decided first to renounce central planning and then to embrace the market. The small Indochinese economies of Cambodia and Laos notwithstanding, the important case here is the success story in Vietnam, with its population of almost 90 million. Despite often unfavorable external circumstances, it has been growing at an annual rate of 7.8 percent and doubling its GDP every ten years. Today that GDP is four times what it was when the country opted for market reforms. This has been accomplished under state guidance and control, with the inspiration of the Chinese achievements and Russian thinking from the Gorbachev era. The Polish lesson has been learned too. The Vietnamese reforms began in 1986, and they use the slogan *doi moi*, which means "reconstruction."

These are the characteristics of the Chinese path:

- It is different from the course followed by the Soviet Union, which made one mistake after another when globalization was picking up steam, and where Gorbachev's reform efforts, universally known as "glasnost" and "perestroika," were too little, too late.
- It is qualitatively different from that of the East-Central European countries, some of which, like Yugoslavia, Poland, and Hungary, had already begun early efforts at market reform and limited openness to the outside world, whereas others, like Albania, Bulgaria, and Romania, were unreformed until 1989, when all these countries, sooner or later, were sucked into the neoliberal centrifuge for longer or shorter periods.
- It is different from the unsuccessful Latin American efforts at following the Washington Consensus, which failed to produce the expected rapid growth and, perversely, led to the revival of socialist ideas with a face that was neither Russian nor Chinese, but rather South American.
- It is different from the disastrous African road. Per capita GDP in sub-Saharan Africa did not increase at all in the 1990s, whereas it soared by more than 176 percent in China. China paid the high price of authoritarian population policy, with limits of one child per family in cities and two in the countryside. This held population growth to an average of 0.9 percent from 1990 to 2007, whereas it was 2.5 percent in sub-Saharan Africa. Given free choice, Chinese women would also have had more children—perhaps not seven, as in the poorest African countries, Niger and Mali, where women give birth to 7.46 and 7.42 children, respectively. Chinese women could have had almost as many children, in which case one in four of them would not have lived to the age of five.[22] The majority of those who survived would have lived in grinding poverty.

Avoiding neoliberalism is the cause for Chinese success, but the cost of success has been high. The country has paid for economic progress with the lack of democracy, or more precisely with such hobbled progress towards democracy that, during the 30 years of progress, it has lagged far behind the economic changes. Still, China is qualitatively more democratic than it was in 1977, not to mention 1957 when it dreamed of overtaking Britain with a combination of communes and direct economic coercion. Unfortunately, Chinese democracy also differs qualitatively not only from the norms accepted in the West, but also from those that prevail in increasing numbers of emerging market democracies.

I have had a couple of occasions to talk with Henry Kissinger, who, as befits an American statesman and intellectual, is a strong proponent of enlightened political and economic liberalism. Yet he unreservedly agrees with the view that, if China had opted for thorough political liberalization in 1989, for democracy on the Western-European or post-Soviet, then it would never have achieved its unprecedented economic growth. Later, I had a chance to talk with Wen Jibao, the premier of China, whose views—and this should surprise no one—are similar to Kissinger's. If China had gone down the road of postcommunist neo-liberalism, things would have been even worse there than they were in Russia, which lost about 60 percent of its national income from 1992 as a result of bumbling experimentation. After all, the Chinese baggage of the Maoist deviation and the cultural revolution was more of a burden to market reforms and rapid socioeconomic development than the in-heritance of the collapse of Soviet socialism in Russia, Ukraine, and the other members of the Commonwealth of Independent States.

Here is a sidelight. In the 1960s, Soviet Leader Nikita Khrushchev was also making promises—namely, that the USSR would overtake the United States in economic terms by 2000. It took Russia until 2007 to return to its own 1989 level of output. In 1989, the output of China was equal to that of the Soviet Union. Afterward, Chinese gross national income increased by a factor of 6.2. Russia's current GDP stands at 14 percent of America's, and only 17.2 percent of China's.

China has enjoyed great success in adopting good options from others while rejecting bad ones. It has taken the good things from liberalism—and most of liberalism is good—by opting for economic freedom. Yet, by retaining the most important social elements of the old system, it has avoided throwing the baby out with the bathwater. This is unfortunately impossible in regard to full employment, but it is possible for investment in human capital, infrastructure development, and the building of institutions that make it possible to combine state social policy with a more competitive market economy.

China has done better than almost anyone else at blending systemic change (transformation) and development policies. Pragmatically, without sacrificing the one on the altar of the other and without being dogmatic, official rhetoric notwithstanding, it has created and made use of the synergy of these two processes that are decisive for the success of great changes. The Chinese reforms did not miss the globalization train in its current phase. This populous country has managed globalization for the benefit of the national economy, Chinese companies, and citizenry. It has maximized its own gains by being open to the inevitable risks of taking part in the world economic game and being ready to bear the associated costs. It has positioned itself well in regard to the need in the rest of the world for Chinese resources, especially human capital, and the output that these people produce. It has made excellent use of the savings of others, directing them to needed direct investment as a medium of technological progress, while also accumulating mighty financial reserves. Instead of uncritically accepting the domination of its lucrative domestic retail market by foreign capital, it has applied policies that encourage investment in manufacturing. It will soon be using its accumulated reserves to begin buying up segments of the retail and financial sectors in the wealthiest countries, including the United States. We will have not only branches of Western banks in China, but also branches of Chinese banks in the West. The best running shoes will not be American ones made in China, but Chinese ones made in America. China has put aside over a trillion dollars for such opportunities—not for a rainy day. The rain falls on those who submit to the naïveté of neoliberalism, and not on those who have a sensible development strategy—and who think in terms of, for instance, forty years, rather than four.

Yet again: Events occur as they do because many things happen at the same time:

First, globalization. The Chinese didn't invent it, but they knew exactly how to adjust to it and take advantage of it.

Second, market reform. They did it thoroughly and gradually, without unneeded shocks but with a healthy dose of therapy.

Third, a long-term development strategy. They had a long-term strategy instead of believing in the magic power of a liberalized market and of keeping the state out of it.

Fourth, an enlightened if undemocratic political regime. Their government was characterized by something like enlightened absolutism, except that this time it was built on a cultural base that included Confucianism, Taoism, and the positive heritage of socialism with its respect for the collective and its collective responsibility.

Fifth, they mobilized, coordinated, and guided vast numbers of people. Everything is multiplied by 1.3 billion.

The Chinese are lucky, not because there are so many of them, but because they're in the right place at the right time. The time is globalization and the place is Asia, or, more precisely, the Middle Kingdom—more middle than ever before. They're lucky to live in a country where the development processes are controlled to an increasing degree by objective economic processes. Their government is wise enough to put its trust in reliable theoretical assumptions that are often little-known elsewhere, because a hundred times more economics books are translated into Chinese than from Chinese. These policies define the broadest institutional and social frameworks for human activity and for individual and collective enterprise. The market, which is increasingly solid, fills this framework with substance, telling them how and what to produce, which services to offer and to whom, and what to invest in, and where.

This time around, the Chinese experiment is not only great, but also successful. In the seventeenth century, as we know, China grew into even more of a world economic power. Now it's happening again, and the reasons for this are as seemingly trivial as the rejection of the neoliberal recipe that gained the upper hand elsewhere, to the detriment of the economies and societies that got entangled in it. China will get to democracy in its own time, but the market comes first. Only when an appropriate level of economic advancement has been achieved will the one support the other. This will happen sooner rather than later, not under the influence of external pressure, but because the time comes when things ripen.

China is the most spectacular example, but we cannot forget about India, which has been developing rapidly since the 1990s, at an annual rate of 6.4 percent. Following its own Indian path, the country has also resisted the pressure from the adherents of the Washington Consensus, who nevertheless insist that the Indian acceleration results from the application of the neoliberal formula. In fact, that acceleration began much earlier, before India began liberalizing trade, and with forceful government stimulation of the development processes. Here, too, resisting the neoliberal siren song was the key to success. Although India remains a poor country, its gross GDP is already $4.3 trillion, which is more than twice that of Britain. India's output is the second largest in Asia, behind China but ahead of Japan.

About two fifths of the present growth in world output can be marked up to the great expansion of China and India. In other words, when the GDP of the entire world grew by about $3.3 trillion in 2008, more than $1.3 trillion of this growth came from China and India. Some people, at least, may note with satisfaction that neither of these countries denies that they have drawn inspiration from Poland in certain areas, both positive (what to do and how to do it) and negative (what to avoid doing and why). For my part, I have tried through numerous publications, including some in Chinese, dozens of visits, and direct consultation, to offer as much effective advice as possible. Especially in the case of China, the development strategy deserves the greatest acknowledgment. It is amazing, especially in comparison with other countries, to see how astutely formulated and timely the questions asked by politicians responsible for economic matters are. It is also amazing to see that, unlike other political luminaries, they are capable of listening and drawing the right conclusions.

Today China and India are the two countries that are changing the face of the world. Statistically speaking, their mushrooming share of world output is having a powerful impact on the averages. Their combined share of world GDP in 2008 was 20 percent, more or less as much as that of the United States or the European Union. Their population mass influences the statistics. The combined 2.5 billion Chinese and Indians constitute almost 37 percent of the world population. As a result, all data coming out of these countries immediately affect the averages. Yet these countries are changing the face of the world in other ways beyond the statistics. Their presence, in terms of people, goods, restaurants, and recently, capital, can be seen almost everywhere in the world, no matter how remote. Above all, they are a model, and a guide.

There is also a third vast country, Russia, which has a particular kind of experience of neoliberalism. It was a disastrous experience. Not as a result of the Soviet legacy, but more as a result of the erroneous policies of the 1990s, production fell by a total of about 60 percent during that decade. This is astounding in peacetime conditions. Amazingly, however, the advocates of neoliberalism in both the East and the West hail it as an achievement. There is a plain psychological explanation: The many economists, analysts, advisers, and politicians who played a role in that era want desperately to save face. There are two more reasons for trying to place things in context.

First, neoliberalism is an ideology and an economic program with a definite agenda. Beneath the lovely slogans about freedom, democracy, and enterprise, it is an instrument not only for enforcing effectiveness, but also for redistributing income for the benefit of the elite, at the cost of the general population. Second, neoliberalism is a tool for plunder on a gigantic scale. The depletion of the national wealth on a scale like that in Russia is a rare event in history. No reasonable person, of course, will insinuate that neoliberalism in its essence is an instrument of plunder and theft. However, the weakness of economic institutions makes such things possible. This is why it happened in Russia, and why it could not happen in China.

For some people, the neoliberal policy in Russia was great business. Zbigniew Brzezinski, the influential political scientist who was President Jimmy Carter's adviser, admits as much. Placing the key words in quotation marks, he notes that a swarm of Western "consultants," most of them Americans, often conspired in "privatization" with Russian "reformers" and made themselves rich, especially through privatization of energy assets.[23] I know that warnings to this effect reached the very top of the political establishment in Washington but were ignored. This "larcenous" privatization, the role that American partners played in it, and the tolerance shown by the American authorities have all been described in analytical and specialist studies, and elsewhere. However, the cacophony of neoliberal propaganda and the pressure from the interest groups that benefited drowned out these warnings.[24] High-ranking American officials, right up to the White House, sounded the alarm about the disastrous consequences of pathological Russian-American neoliberalism. Fritz M. Earmath, a former senior CIA officer, told me at a Jamestown Foundation conference in Washington in the summer of 1999 that one such urgent report came back with a one-word annotation by the vice president: "Bullshit." Zbigniew Brzezinski was also present at this conference and criticized the discreet sympathies between some elements of the American establishment and corrupt Russian politicians.

Why did dubious excesses take place on such an enormous scale in Russia, but not, for example, in Poland? The fact that structural reform policy was much better carried out there, especially in the mid-1990s, had something to do with it. Mainly, however, it was because Russia contained far more resources to pillage and control, and still does. The neoliberal trend combined with the general disarray made things all the easier. The one-of-a-kind Russian-American "public-private partnership" was in its element. Earmath wrote to me in the fall of 1999 that, "The fortunes to be made and moved out of Russia were so huge that they, like gravitation attraction of mass bodies, attracted powerful Western stakeholders. Perhaps Poland benefited not only from better initial conditions and policy, but by not being so rich in plunderable resources." He had no doubts either then or now—how could he?—that the truth about the Russian transformation was known to those in the United States with a need to know. He stated that "the whole top echelon of our administration pretty much knew the true picture in Russia all along. They have to have known that, at least after late 1997, the GKO (Russian short-term securities) market was being used by Russian officials and all speculators as a means of plundering the Russian budget and the IMF money. What do you think Talbott, Summers, Lipton, Chubais, and Berezovsky chatted about when they got together in July 1998?"

There can be no doubt that we were dealing not so much with neoliberal obtuseness as with simple criminality. This, it should be added, was superorganized crime. Earmath concluded:

I have come to understand another dimension of this, which is more crime than folly. From various very credible Russian sources it is now clear that the short-term government debt (GKOs) that was soaking up so much public money in 1997–98 became, not a grotesquely irresponsible and risky means of bringing money into the budget, but a means by which government officials, Central Bank bonzes, and speculators (Russian and Western) plundered the state budget . . . deliberately. And the clear purpose of the last IMF tranche in summer 1998 was to keep the bubble up for a last round of profiteering and a well-timed collapse for the benefit of insiders, Russian and Western. This is so widely understood in Russia now that they are bored with the topic. The really interesting question is what USG and IMF leaders knew and thought about what was going on, especially when Chubais came to Washington in July to arrange the last tranche with Summers, Lipton, and Talbott. There are only two possibilities: Either they were ignorant of activities that involved dozens of knowing players, and hundreds of speculators and this was, hence, a hugely expensive blunder of intelligence and policy; or they wittingly bought into the scheme for some reasons of greed or pressure. I am convinced this picture is true.

So am I.

Earmath added:

> You could have a considerable voice when the discussion turns to the question of future policy. . . . Maybe wait and see if any debate is provoked and reconsider this . . . But, by all means, write a fresh piece, and offer alternatives to the IMF. Maybe we could provoke Congressional hearings on this topic. . . . The most important thing: It is vital that you and others who can do so get into this debate to educate the politicians about what did and did not work in the most successful transition so far, Poland. . . . Call it chance, call it Allah's mysterious ways: It is our job to take advantage. . . . People must be reminded over and over again about the real Polish story, as well as the folly of the IMF in Russia.[25]

When I was working on this book eight years later, I asked Earmath for permission to use excerpts from our correspondence. He consented without hesitation, because he is more convinced than ever that he was right. He added: "American political and business interests got involved with Russian corruption and plundering from the beginning. It has continued to this day." Nevertheless, Russia repudiated the naïve neoliberal line that it followed through most of the 1990s, and enjoyed seven fat years from 2001 to 2007. People laughed when President Vladimir Putin announced that GDP would double within a decade, but it started coming true. Yet isn't this more a matter of the high price of Russia's key exports, oil and gas, than of structural reform? Well, that only shows that the country is capable of taking advantage of opportunities and circumstances—both those that turn out to be favorable regardless of policy choices and those that the right policies can bring about. Even if those policies have been insufficiently reformist and did not squeeze all the possible benefits out of an oil boom that turned out to be impermanent, they are nevertheless fundamentally different and qualitatively superior policies.

In the current decade, Russia is trying in its own way to combine its policies for systemic change with policies for development, while refraining from letting go of its national wealth and natural resources too quickly, or too cheaply. The country wants to profit as much as possible from hitting the ground running in the international economic arena while coming out ahead on globalization, rather than allowing others to take advantage of it. It is refusing to allow itself to be turned into another "emerging market," which would mean forfeiting its economic sovereignty and submitting to pressure from supranational capital. It's hardly surprising to hear the arrogant question, "Who lost Russia?" still being asked in the West. People started asking this question when it became clear that Russia was going its own way, that the country with the largest land area and the richest natural resources in the world was not going to allow itself to be sucked into the neoliberal whirlpool. The fact is that some companies lost what had looked like a good chance of gaining access to vast natural resources at bargain-basement prices. No one lost Russia, however, because no one ever had Russia. It is Russia that is slowly finding its way among the post-Soviet and postsocialist realities, in the reality of globalization and the game for its own future place in the world. That place will be increasingly important.

As a side note, it is embarrassing to see neoliberal publications of the stature of *The Financial Times* or *The Economist* advocate the sanctioning of lawbreaking under the cloak of a concern for democracy. They admit over and over again that one oligarch or another is no saint and that some of the things done during the Russian privatization of the 1990s cry out for punishment. Yet, at the same time, they call for leaving the present state of those oligarchs' holdings untouched in exchange for the payment of a quasi-fiscal "windfall profits tax." As much as this might be justified for small businesses moving out of the shadow area and into the official, registered, and taxed economy, it amounts in the case of the oligarchs to tolerance for economic crimes. Of course, this would safeguard the interests of companies with a "pro-Western orientation." Companies should have a pro-profit orientation and not worry about points on the compass. Unfortunately, there are those who are always willing to treat democracy not as a value in itself, but as an instrument useful for protecting private interests. Or are "pro-Western" energy companies automatically associated with "freedom" and "democracy," and all others with "authoritarian tendencies"?

Taxes are paid on legitimately earned income and profits from capital with honest origins. Taxes may also occasionally be applied to assets when their value increases radically as a result of beneficial circumstances that have nothing to do with their owners. The British government did precisely this in regard to certain energy companies in the recent past. Yet this is not the right way to treat wealth arising in large part from fraudulent transfers that cheat a country and its citizens. Taxes are not a way of settling the accounts for crime, but rather a means of redistribution in the name of economic and social equality. Prosecutors and judges, not tax collectors and the revenue service, deal with criminals. Illegal deals in the style of some of the Russian oligarchs in whose defense *The Economist*[26] has amazingly spoken out would earn sentences of ninety years in the United States, not nine, and no one would accuse the judges of being politically motivated.

Things are worst when the abnormal becomes the norm. Yet what is normal, and what is abnormal, and who has the right to decide this? History? Certainly, but we have no time to wait for history's verdict, because some matters must be settled here and now, and not in the distant future, when the controversy has died down. Controversy springs from emotion and from cold calculation, from differences of values and from intractable conflicts of interest. Much controversy derives simply from radically different interpretations of what is happening.

This is the conclusion that Peter Mandelson, then European Commissioner for Trade, arrived at fifteen years after the fall of the Soviet Union. Following a visit to Moscow, he realized that the Russian skepticism about the introduction of Western-style democracy and free markets was based to a large extent on the negative experiences of the systemic transformation. What looked normal in the West did not necessarily look that way in Russia, and vice versa. Above all, Russians assess the facts in cold, concrete terms, "in view," as the BBC reported, "of the unhappiness caused by economic liberalization and privatization during the 1990s."[27] This is indeed true of a considerable part of the Russian public and political elite, and also of the many economists who, in their unsparing criticism, certainly did not treat the misguided choices made during the 1990s as something normal. Forced democratization and free markets *à la Russe* were a far cry from what the West regards as normal democracy and a normal market.

The missionaries and warriors of the neoliberal ideology continue to regard the Russian economy as nonmarket and the country as undemocratic. They are less picky in regard to China, which has learned to deal with them. They act like sixteenth-century Spanish conquistadors who wondered whether the natives they encountered were people with souls, or whether it would be better to chop off their heads than to go to the trouble of trying to convert them. However, as the old Polish folk saying goes, "He who laughs last laughs best."

We do not know who will have the last laugh, since history is ongoing and the roles will reverse many times more, but it will surely not be the neoliberals, neither the orthodox ones from the West nor the naïve ones from the East who think that following the ideology is the best way to turn themselves into the West. They don't have much to laugh about when it is not some Beijing or Moscow party organ, or even an English-language newspaper from New Delhi, but rather the CIA that writes in an online report that "global output rose by 5 percent in 2006, largely thanks to growth in China (10.5), India (8.5), and Russia (6.6)"[28] These three great countries do not follow the Washington Consensus because they did not cave in to pressure from special interest groups and the associated neoliberal ideology. The population of these three growing economies is 40 percent of the world's total, and their share of world output is almost one fourth. These are three dynamic societies with ever-greater human capital, and the first person to stand on Mars will come from one of them. He who laughs last will last best.

Furthermore, the eminent Chinese economist from the University of Beijing, Justin Yifu Lin, who for many years was a member of the Academic Council of the TIGER think tank, of which I am the director,[29] became vice president for development and chief economist of the World Bank. One swallow does not make a spring and we should be under no illusion that his appointment will change things much, but it represents at least a chance that the neoliberal orthodoxy will no longer be so dominant and that a more balanced approach to development will take its place.

We might therefore expect that more and more of the economies emerging from neocolonialism, statism, socialism, or isolationism will search for recipes of their own. They will carry out this quest somewhere between the unprecedented Chinese success and the antiliberal Latin American approach, between the positive example of India and the not particularly encouraging experiences of a Mexico that has remained under the powerful influence of Washingtonian neoconservatism, between the accomplishments of Scandinavian social democracy and the positive experiences of some East-European countries. In turn, the relatively more advanced countries will look again to Japan as it returns to an active role on the global scene, and to the encouraging achievements of the Nordic social market economies.

Remaining within the realm of pragmatism and rationalism, there is undoubtedly a great deal to be learned by borrowing from neoliberal ideology and practice the things that are sensible—and the majority of what is there makes a great deal of sense. The trick is to get to the nub of the rational elements and to discard those that foster stagnation, that cause imbalance and dissension, and that encourage mistakes by falsifying information. The things that enrich some at the cost of impoverishing others and that slow the general progress of civilization should be excluded. Even if the announced demise of neoliberalism turns out to be premature, it is hardly too early to sketch out the rough draft of the obituary.

What we need is economic freedom and a strong state. This strength is expressed through functionality and public and economic utility. Where the state is institutionally weak, as in many African countries, or where it has been weakened by doctrinaire and short-sighted politics, as in some of the postsocialist European countries, the economic results are far worse than they need be. An African giant like Nigeria is a good example of this, as is Zimbabwe, which was prospering until not long ago. The Russia of the 1990s under Boris Yeltsin was such a country, and Ukraine still is. In these and other countries, insufficiency of the state has become more of a barrier to catching up to the more developed parts of the world than insufficiency of the market. This is one more proof of how the market needs the state.

Regulation is needed whenever an invention (like dynamite), a product (like the airplane), or an idea (like freedom) becomes a threat to the interests of others. This always raises the question, "If not the state, then who?" Neoliberalism, especially in its naïve varieties, offers no answer. The state must be efficient and strong through its institutions, which are crucial to the construction and development of a full-blown market economy. The state is irreplaceable in terms of reflecting social preferences and formulating development goals. It is vital to forging the social consensus that a market economy requires. It is a positive factor in the formation of knowledge. However, it also represents a constant temptation to overtax the earnings of those who are entrepreneurial and creative. Budgetary redistribution does not always foster development; sometimes it is an occasion for wasting public money. Finally, state bureaucracy can interfere in market mechanisms.

As long as the state, as an institution, interferes in market mechanisms—which, from our point of view, means forever, or at least as long as there are people alive to engage in business—then the question of the "size" of the state will be controversial, for the simple reason that the state means redistribution. Through its fiscal system, the state takes in part of the income at the point of origin (which nobody likes) and transfers it where its expenditure is called for (and there is never enough of it). There's the rub: Called for? Desirable? Needed? Or perhaps not needed at all? The differences on this point will never be resolved. At the most, the debates can become more or less incendiary. This is because the state distribution of the national income increased almost unabated throughout the twentieth century, and in some countries, including very wealthy ones, it exceeded 50 percent of GDP. So how "big" should the state, that is, government, be?

Perhaps the neoliberals are right when they say that the smaller, the better. Not really. This is an inherently false assertion, not so much out of ideological considerations, as because it is an answer to the wrong question. In speaking about the "size" of the state and the scope of its interference in economic activity, and especially in the distribution of income, a distinction needs to be drawn between the functions of the state, on the one hand, and the strength and efficiency of its institutions, on the other.

Today certain state functions require limitation because others need strengthening. The former include, for instance, research and development, which are successfully performed to a large degree by the profit-oriented commercial sector. The latter include environmental protection, where the for-profit sector has shown itself to be incapable of coping. In the wealthiest economies, the state can allocate relatively fewer resources to health care, because increasingly affluent households cover many of these costs through private insurance. At the same time, international terrorism is forcing the state to play a larger role in ensuring the security of its citizens. Changes in these fields are multidirectional and of varying intensity. We need "less" state in some places, and, at the same time, "more" state in others.

Calling for "a small state" or "less government," as much as calling for "more government," is a sign of being out of touch with social and political reality. Both positions miss the point. The state is not supposed to be "big" or "small," but rather "efficient." Political slogans in Poland promising a "cheap state" are similarly naïve. The job of the state is to supply the population with the public goods, at the requisite level of quality, needed to function and develop. That costs money, just like a good car. It's amazing how many people are willing to shell out money for a good car but allow themselves to be misled by doctrinaire slogans telling them that they can have good government on the cheap. Quality comes at a price. There are "small," "cheap" governments in Papua New Guinea or in Somalia, but there's no development there.

When the functions of the state are overgrown, as is still the case in some postsocialist transformation countries or in ill-regulated social market economies, it's bad for competitiveness and long-term development capacity. There are certainly some good points about the neoliberal view of government, including the unceasing pressure to limit bureaucracy and the wasting of public funds, which can never be eliminated entirely. The main thing is to come out strongly against corruption, but then again, everybody's against corruption.

Neoliberals exert pressure through the governments of the most powerful countries, which in turn make their treatment of less-advanced countries dependent on the seriousness and efficacy of their efforts to curb corruption. International government organizations like the World Bank and the regional development banks are serious about their anticorruption crusades. Big corporations are generous in funding global nongovernmental organizations like Freedom House that hold "ugly contests" to stigmatize the most corrupt countries. It is worth noting that the least-corrupt countries at the top of the "clean government" lists are invariably those with relatively "big governments."

There is constant chatter in the media, sometimes general and at other times specific, about this problem. It's a good thing when this concerted pressure helps prevent the kind of corruption that distorts the allocation of capital and thus lowers overall economic effectiveness, which worries big capital more than the moral aspects. From an ethical point of view alone, corruption is of course worthy of condemnation. However, neoliberalism fights corruption for purely pragmatic reasons, two of which are most important.

First, corruption leads to protectionism. It causes it and exacerbates it. Businesses corrupt the authorities in order to win protection from competition, privileged positions, and toleration for the distortion of information about the market. In other words, the corruptors "purchase" a service in the form of a protectionist shelter. Protectionism is the prime enemy of liberalism of all types, including neoliberalism. This is not a matter of ethics, but of business.

Second, the fight against corruption enables capital to penetrate state organizations. Such campaigns allow oversight of governments and their departments by monitoring the regulatory process, legislation, and political strategies. The situation is the opposite of what it used to be. Once upon a time, governments and their agencies worked together to gather information about the structure and organization of capital. They could decipher its intentions and dealings in order to protect the public interest and prevent the strong from lording it over the weak. Today big business gathers information about the government to ensure that corporate interests take precedence over the public interest. It is easier for domestic and multinational businesses to inspect the budgetary process than for government to look into the books of domestic corporations, not to mention multinational ones. Information gathering by business is presented in public discussions and the media as an expression of concern for the public good, whereas information gathering by government comes across as bureaucratic meddling in private enterprise. The institutional balance has been upset, and this is always detrimental to development, even as it supports the private interests of capital.

We should add that the most socially effective and developed economies are by no means those with "small government," that is, with budgets accounting for a relatively low proportion of GDP. The leaders are the Nordic countries, where budgetary redistribution, the flow from tax revenue to public expenditure, accounts for as much as half of GDP. This is more than in any of the postsocialist economies.

All the commotion about the superiority of "small" or "cheap" government over "big" or "expensive" government is easy to decipher. The richest "small government" states in the world include Australia, Japan, Switzerland, and the United States, where the state takes in a mere 30 percent of GDP to cover its expenditures. "Big government" can be found in The Netherlands, Italy, and the Nordic countries, where the state redistributes about 50 percent. In regard to a whole range of important measures—long-term output growth, income levels, educational levels, infant mortality, life expectancy, unemployment, and inflation—the results are practically equal in both of these groups of countries and economic systems.

So what is really at issue? There is a single, glaring difference. Inequality of income is far greater in the "small government" states than in the ones with "big government." Although the ratio of the average income of the top one quarter of the population to the bottom one quarter in the latter countries is about 5:1, in the former group it is as much as 8.3:1.[30] This ratio has held steady in observations of generational cohorts in the 1970s, the 1980s, and the first half of the 1990s. In subsequent years, it has grown even greater, and not only because of the increased stratification in the United States. Here is incontrovertible proof that greater social justice—or, if you have ideological reservations about this formulation, less income inequality—is perfectly compatible with high economic efficiency. Another myth of neoliberalism comes crashing down.

The problem is not that the state as a fundamental institution is wanted by some and not wanted by others. Everyone needs the state, just as they need a roof over their head. All, however, want the kind of state in which they feel comfortable. A business owner's idea of comfort is not necessarily the same as a union organizer's. Investors and the professional management elite who run things for them have different preferences from their employees, who themselves are a varied lot. But they all feel that the state stands in their way, or at least casts a shadow over their lives. If it is not shouting straight at them, they hear its echo. Yet if you take a good look at the strategies of various lobbyists and listen closely to what they say, you realize how much they need the state. In many cases, especially in emerging markets, business interests are more effective in their calls for state aid than all the white- and blue-collar employees put together. This might not be the way that the press and TV show things, but a keen political observer realizes what's going on.

The broader or narrower scope of state functions notwithstanding ("big" government or "small"), what really counts is the strength and vitality of public institutions. It's easy to say that you can never have too many good institutions, but that's not true. Everything is good in the right proportion. This also applies to the rules for the market and structural frameworks in economics, over which the state, itself a megainstitution, stands guard.

No country has perfect institutions. They are always worth improving, and improvement is always possible. The spectacular superscandals in the United States featuring supercompanies like Enron showed that stockholder interests are not always protected in the home of free enterprise the way the textbooks say they are. Many institutions in China are still weak, especially in such fields as guaranteeing the transparency of real estate deals. In Brazil, the institutions responsible for education and the distribution of agricultural land are getting stronger. In Poland, local governments are functioning better than they once did. In Russia, the shadow economy is being reined in.

Nevertheless, institutions in postsocialist countries still leave a good deal to be desired. The old ones have been destroyed or are dwindling away, and the new ones are still shaping up, especially where countries have joined the European Union, with its developed market institutions. The postsocialist countries offer particularly striking examples of how naïve struggles against the state can go wrong. When they undercut the government, whether out of ideological or group-interest motives, they reduce overall competitiveness and harm the public interest. This is both a short-term and a strategic loss, because a weak state means worse growth prospects for the economy as a whole. The key issue is not increasing or cutting back on the scope of state functions, but rather making sure that the state institutions function better.

Furthermore, questions about the proper size of the government must be posed within a historical context. What seems big today might not have seemed so in the past, or might not seem so in the future. The optimal size of government is different in peacetime and wartime. A given size might be good when a boom generation is in the prime of life and fending for itself, but not when it is at school or swelling the ranks of retirees.

The role of the state must be correlated with its functions. Some functions, like defense or diplomacy, are irreducible. Others, like culture and research, are optional and depend on values and the degree of authentic social cohesion. Over time, this all evolves and changes in directions that sometimes conflict. Government, then, is necessary for an efficient economy and dynamic, balanced growth, but it must be in harmony with the market. The unending search for exactly what this harmony should look like is one of the reasons that we have economics as a science, and politics (unfortunately, at times) as practice.

The market, in turn, consists not only of dynamics and balance, but also of chaos and the unpredictable. The market must correct and control the excesses of government, and vice versa. The very idea that anyone could even think about something as naïve as a strong economy combined with a weak government in the early twenty-first century, and not in the era of nineteenth-century *laissez-faire*, is staggering, especially in the wake of a historical period so abounding in crises, conflicts, wars, crashes, and bankruptcies. So we find ourselves asking once again: Is this a difference of opinion, or a conflict of interest? Few ideas are as silly as the one saying that the state should not interfere in the economy—except perhaps the idea that the state should stick its nose into every detail, the way it did in Poland from 1950 to 1955, when the Six-Year Plan set not only the number of tons of steel to be produced and ships to be launched, but also the amount of pickles that were supposed to go on the "market"—as if they feared that there wouldn't be anything to munch on between shots of vodka.

States, along with their global and transnational agreements both permanent and ad hoc, are indispensable actors in politics of all kinds, including national and regional politics and wherever private enterprise and the unpredictability of the market are insufficient to get people working, to invest in human capital, and to create the cultural basis for business activity. There are places in the world, after all, that lack the kind of bourgeois private sponsors who ordered paintings from Rembrandt in Amsterdam, or the contemporary American foundations that keep the art galleries running. It's not a matter of a lack of talent. Some of the poorest countries in the world, like Mali or Burkina Faso, make better films than some of the wealthiest, like Norway or Switzerland. This is one more proof that not everything is decided by money alone, or talent alone. There is no lack of either in Norway and Switzerland. What about demand? People go to the movies far more often in rich countries than in poor ones. Most of the people in Mali and Burkina Faso have never seen a film, not even on TV, because there is a lack of both TV sets and electricity in much of the Sahel. What is the decisive factor then? Politics. If the market has an invisible hand, then politics has a visible head.

It is worth noting that specific coincidences decide such matters, because many things happen at the same time. Government policy by itself is not enough. The talent must come from somewhere, and it is more likely to amount to something if it can be noticed young enough to be educated and trained. As luck would have it in the case of Mali and Burkina Faso, both the metropolitan power, France, and the Soviet Union, with which these countries flirted during their experiments with African socialism, educated some of the best African talents in their excellent film schools. They educated more Africans than filmmakers from Norway or Switzerland, which did not have the good fortune of being French colonies or belonging to the part of the world that the Soviets believed "was going our way."

It is the combination of the one with the other, of government with the market—that is, of politics with the unpredictable, consciousness with spontaneity, and security with risk—that will continue to change the world. If the blend is the right one, it will be change for the better. Should we pass up the chance because neoliberalism is finished? That would be yet another historic mistake. Unfortunately, the chances of making such a mistake, despite everything we have learned so far, are not negligible. It's something to think about.

The crucial matter here is the coexistence in time and space of globalization and neoliberalism. So far, as we know, globalization has been a mostly spontaneous process, and it continues to be one. Its dynamics are determined by unpredictable factors, and not by politics, let alone strategic planning. As a recipe for economic life, neoliberalism has been ideal for the present, chaotic form of globalization. The less regulation and intervention, the better. Yet the question remains: "Better for whom?" For everyone? Absolutely not. For the majority? This is not the truth even in the richest countries, as we have seen in the case of the United States, let alone the whole world. Is it better for some? Absolutely. It is better for those whose positions and the places they occupy in the world economic game mean that they stand to gain the most.

Big capital is an absolute winner. It has torn free of the supervision of the nation-states and become not so much stateless as state-free. It acknowledges no sovereign. It can choose where it wants to go. It enjoys increasing opportunities to dictate where investments are made and how they are brought to fruition. Governments and publics accept this, because their choices are limited or nonexistent. Capital behaves rationally and optimizes its functional goal, which is to maximize the rate of return on investments. Others behave irrationally because they have insufficient information or, even more so, insufficient power to look after their own interests effectively, be they national, local, or individual.

As a result, globalization as a complex process becomes less rational, or downright irrational. It is also difficult for individual countries to be rational when they are already entangled in the global political and economic game. Some of them, and especially the richest capitalist countries, are so strong that they can allow themselves to do more, and if they play it right, they can gain more. China behaves rationally. Rejecting the philosophy and practice of the Washington Consensus, it has, a few details notwithstanding, charted a course that is almost perfectly adapted to globalization. It is winning in this process because, better than anyone else, it combines liberalization with regulation and microeconomic entrepreneurship with macroeconomic strategy. It integrates these factors rather than setting them against each other, as was done naively by East European neoliberalism in general, and by Russian and Polish neoliberalism in particular.

Especially in the West, where mainstream neoclassical economics still reigns supreme, questions keep being asked about the source of the Chinese success. Yet the answer is very simple. All it takes is to break out of the intellectual corset of neoliberalism to note that the Chinese success is no orphan: It has both parents. Its mother is the market and its father is the state. Only the merging of market dynamism and spontaneity with the strategic actions of the state could yield such excellent results. If matters had been left to the market and the private sector alone, China would not have been able to minimize the costs associated with globalization while maximizing the resulting benefits. In any event, China was able to use the need of the world economy for Chinese goods to energize its own development, on the one hand, while attracting external capital and investment, on the other.

Many economists, including those connected with international organizations that plainly have little or nothing to do with the Chinese success, are cheered by this rational approach. It may run counter to the advice they give, but it looks good, and these economists can claim the credit. Certain organizations and governments have done so. Averaged data define the prism through which the world economy is perceived, and the data coming out of Beijing improve the averages. After all, the Chinese data apply to almost one tenth of the world's imports and (when Hong Kong is included) one seventh of the world's exports, as well as one sixth of the world's output (not counting Hong Kong) and one fifth of the world's population (with Hong Kong making little difference one way or another).

In other words, globalization is relatively less irrational thanks above all to China and its unconventional ideology and policy, which reject neoliberalism. This is a lesson with enormous implications for a great part of the world economy. Whatever the outcome of globalization, each of the interdependent national economies of the less-advanced countries must have its own development strategy. Globalization does not free them of this obligation or deprive them of this opportunity. They only need to know how to take advantage of it and, just as in life, have the desire to do so.

It should be clear to everyone that inclusive globalization, in which the largest possible segment of humanity benefits and wins, is a pipe-dream. The ideal world proclaimed in neoliberal thinking, and especially in its political mission statements, is unreal and unfeasible. This includes the statements authorized by governments, or supplied to them by international economic and financial bodies that, in turn, are more at the service of certain governments than of others. It hardly needs adding that these bodies are at the service of the interests of capital. The fact that they declare an unrelenting war on poverty or a balanced development strategy as their absolutely overriding goal is more a question of "political marketing" than of their real intentions.

We will leave for another occasion the question, for which we are prepared by now in methodological and substantive terms, of who is wrong here and believes naïvely in this pipe dream, and who is deliberately and consciously proclaiming it while treating it instrumentally, in their own interest. We sometimes hear the view that neoliberalism is the last great utopia of the twentieth century. When we take a look at its doctrinaire proponents and irrational apologists, we can see the point. However, the doctrinaire proponents and ideologues, along with their hired guns in the media and politics, act as the servants of certain easily identified interests of narrow groups of beneficiaries. Viewed in this way, neoliberalism is seen not as a utopia, but as an effective method of protecting group interests at the cost of the interests of others. The ideological utopia has thus become a pragmatic strategy. For this to happen and be effective, it must use falsehoods and lies as instruments for manipulating public opinion. We must further admit that, in this regard, it has probably been even more effective than other twentieth-century utopias—so far.

While we wait for this utopia to arrive, life goes on and business is done. Naïve people allow themselves to be led by the nose. They not only believe that things must be the way they are, but even show a tendency at times to take the side of a setup that does them harm. They throw their political support behind the power elites and capital in charge of this setup. I remember witnessing a scene of symbolic import when I was out jogging in Manhattan at dawn. In a nook next to the warm exhalations of a subway vent near a street corner, a homeless man who had just woken up was perusing the market reports in *The Financial Times*. No doubt, he was looking there for a better future. . . .

The political marketing and the media onslaught get the job done. They keep the masses excited over the stock market quotations, as if the eternally fluctuating prices had some significant influence over their lives. This distracts their attention from more important matters, and draws in small-time investors who, en masse, can be useful in the speculative game. People are caught up in the unending wobbling of exchange rates, even when the oscillations are practically imperceptible. Huge numbers of people know, pointlessly, where the Dow Jones average stands and how much it changes each day. A handful of politicians are aware that there are such things as the HDI (Human Development Index) and other indexes of well-being that are worth taking account of in their strategies.

The alliance between neoliberalism and capital, which is almost unrestricted in today's world and wields greater influence than governments, international organizations, or any other potential partners, leads to a race for the bottom. Tax cuts and the weakening of the state under the slogan of "small government" are a part of this. The state is weakened to prevent it from being able to stand up to the power of capital. The cuts extend to social transfers and the safety net for the poor and the socially excluded. Pay is cut in both relative and absolute terms. Limits on regulation weaken the institutions of a healthy free market, rather than strengthening them.

Rhetoric from docile economists, analysts, media commentators, think tanks, and politicians who are doctrinaire or simply corrupt accompanies this process. They talk about a flexible labor market, cost competitiveness, the elimination of superfluous budgetary transfer payments that make people lazy, the simplification of the tax system, and the removal of bureaucratic obstacles.

Capital behaves in a rational way within its own frame of reference, and it must be admitted that it has accomplished a great deal. This is seen most clearly in the postsocialist economies, which are particularly susceptible to neoliberal indoctrination and pressure groups. This is why social market economies—those that guarantee personal entrepreneurial freedom and free-market competition while using the state to watch over the division of the spoils of economic growths and balanced social development—cannot arise during the present phase of globalization in either the postsocialist countries or other "emerging economies." In the postsocialist countries, the particular combination of circumstances in the early 1990s that we have already examined made possible the temporary triumph of neoliberalism with all its faults. In other emerging economies, institutions are generally feeble, public funds are in short supply, and the tug-of-war between neoliberalism and populism has a devastating effect on development potential. A social market economy requires a strong state and a durable political consensus, and these are things that do not exist either in postsocialist countries or in what used to be the Third World, which in fact is the same world it always was even if it now appears on the global stage under different names.

Social market economies can exist today only where the combination of political, cultural, and economic circumstances that they require came about at some point in the past, and became entrenched enough to endure. We should add that the many social and welfare values of a functioning socialist economy, with the accompanying cultural attractiveness, constitute one such condition. Propaganda, or PR, as we call it today, also made an impact. Blunting the socialist or even communist leanings that appeared here and there in the West from the 1940s to the 1960s required the expansion of the "welfare state" and greater concern for the lot of working people, but culture also gained. It is no secret that the explosion of museums and galleries under the Kennedy administration was a reaction to the dynamic cultural scene in the USSR. Many Americans regard the Cold War period as a golden age for the arts and scholarship. The government was less miserly then and spread the money around to make a more flattering impression at a time of rivalry between the superpowers and the two antagonistic systems. Thanks to this, and the forces of inertia and habit, we still have many splendid museums in the United States along with more than 400 professional and about 1,500 amateur symphony orchestras. Some highly developed capitalist countries are still reaping the benefits of ideas borrowed from the ideology, and even the practices, of the now defunct socialist world. The eastern bloc never intended to help shore up social market economies in the West, yet this is what happened. History is full of paradoxes; this is a beneficial one.

Today these vestiges exist in abbreviated form. They have been cut down in scope, even in the richest countries, not only because of the enormous costs resulting from provisions for a society that is growing older, but also because of the pressures of the global market and international capital. Even in those mainstays of the social market economy, Canada and the Nordic countries, the state and its social welfare measures have been weakened, the aggressiveness of the markets has increased, and the margin of social exclusion has broadened. Nevertheless, it is the Nordic countries—Finland, Sweden, Denmark, Norway, and Iceland—that dominate the top of the world rankings, not only in such specific areas as competitiveness, institutional maturity, the quality of human capital, the condition of the environment, public safety, and internet access, but also in the most general measures of economic development levels and living standards. Even there, unfortunately, neoliberalism and the negative aspects of unbridled globalization have had a destructive impact.

The race to the bottom must end someday, but it will not be a happy ending for everyone, and especially not for those who hit bottom. It would be best if the race ended before the dysfunctionality of the state and its institutions becomes unbearable. Almost every crisis, including the one being brought on by the race to the bottom, represents a chance to think things over afresh and make changes. Unfortunately, this will not happen until the crisis hits hard enough. We are incapable of taking the needed rational measures before then, because they would cost too much. Neoliberal delusions have left the beneficiaries of chaotic globalization unable even to grasp the scale of the risks hanging over them, and the degree to which irrationality suffuses the entire world economy.

Greed is a great motivator, except that it usually encourages actions that are irrational from the macroeconomic and social points of view. This is truer of the world economy than of national economies. Greed befuddles people. Although the fact that neoliberalism is falling should be a source of gratification, it is impossible not to worry that it is bequeathing to the world and to us (not all of us, indeed) such a meager legacy.

———————

The folly that apparently wise people can commit and the harm they can do themselves are amazing.

CHAPTER SEVEN

What Development Is and What It Depends On

Where Socioeconomic Development Comes from and How It Can Make Us Happy

The best way to deal with the unimpressive legacy of neoliberalism is to escape into the future.

IT'S NEVER easy to change course in the economy, not so much because we don't know what we should do as because there's a lack of the political will to use this knowledge to make the right changes. Above all, we have to know how to make those changes, and that means answering the question, "What do growth and development mean, and what do they depend on?" This is a daunting task, perhaps more so now than ever before. On the one hand, we know more than we did in the past. On he other, the processes of reproduction, that is, of repeating the current cycle, are much more complicated than in the historical past because of globalization and its consequences in terms of the interdependence of the processes of the accumulation and allocation of capital, and of production and distribution on a supranational scale.

Our knowledge enables us to transfer from the future to the present savings for financing development and demand to spur the market in goods and services that can be manufactured and rendered with our current capacity. No one, however, can carry over from the future to the present the knowledge based on experience, and the theoretical generalizations based on that knowledge. We must therefore rely on the only knowledge at our disposal, which comes from the past, to shape economic processes of the future. However, we must beware of the danger of making the same mistakes over and over, because the future is never like the past. Today's unprecedented dynamism and profound structural changes make this more true than ever. This is another reason to be extremely careful when making suggestions, because there is no reason for the determinants of past socioeconomic growth and development to continue to be true when conditions are changing continuously. There is a need for a deep theoretical understanding of the mechanisms of development in the past, but also for serious, interdisciplinary studies of the future, on the micro-, macro-, and megaeconomic scales.

To know means to want change, because things are not going well. Moving forward and making the progress that most of humanity is calling out for will require change. It will even be impossible to maintain the natural environment, the economy, and society in relative equilibrium without making significant changes. These changes will require economic growth, even if that growth is not as dynamic as the great expansion of recent years, or if it is different in kind.

Thinking of the future in terms of the simple and uncritical extrapolation of past trends, or in the belief that things are bound to continue improving, is dangerous. Trying to shape the future on such a basis is even more dangerous. The rules we know from the past will only partly continue to govern the social processes of production, distribution, and consumption. Similarly, it will be only partially possible for others to catch up with the wealthiest nations. Those who did not seize the chance to enrich themselves during the long-term, rapid growth of the past may not have such favorable opportunities in the future. Developments that run shockingly counter to the conventional wisdom, however, are sure to be abundant in the future.

Clearly, there can be no growth and development without capital. This is just as banal a statement as the assertion that capital alone does not suffice for development. History is littered with regions, countries, and periods where something other than insufficient capital brought production to a standstill. Often it was a lack of common sense. Other things—phenomena and processes—must happen simultaneously to mobilize capital in ways that bring about higher output levels and better living standards. Development is change for the better. Because things can never be better for everyone, they must at least be better for the majority.

Once, when I had influence over major economic policy decisions, I got into an argument with one of the richest people in one of the largest countries undergoing postsocialist transformation. He was trying to convince me not to allocate a billion zloty from the national budget (the money, we could say if we wanted to keep things simple, came from taxes on the profits made by business) to raise pension payments for almost 10 million retirement and disability recipients. This would have amounted to an average of 8.50 zloty per month. The wealthy man argued that it would be preferable to cut the income tax on entrepreneurs, despite the fact that there had already been a series of such cuts, and leave the money in the pockets of those entrepreneurs. He claimed that it would be better for a few wealthier people to invest the money in future production than for the many poor to use it to buy "a couple of extra liters of milk." I responded by asking him if it wouldn't be best of all for growth if the entire sum of a billion zloty were turned over to the single richest investor. He replied that yes, of course it would be. For him, it was obviously better to permit the superrich to multiply their existing fortunes (which would produce clear benefits for others), than to waste it on "one more glass of milk for a retired person who doesn't even work anymore." A whole book could be written on the basis of this dialogue and the logical conclusions to which it leads. However, because we have quite a few other issues to cover, we must limit ourselves to a one-page summary.

In the first place, we must be clear about what the dilemma is. It's not a matter of large numbers of people drinking one more glass of milk a day (although this too is significant) or having a little bit more to cover their expenses. It's a matter of how the two options influence future economic processes, how they create flows of income. We must decide whether this is a matter of dividing up disposable income that has already been created (while also taking account of the growth of the public debt, because in this case there is a real-life budget deficit, and therefore things are even more complicated, which is the result of not so much the distribution of income as the distribution of debt) or of doing something that will increase future income.

Consequently, we have a dilemma relating to the ultimate division of national income for consumption and accumulation. There is a natural dichotomy: What is designated for consumption cannot be designated at the same time for accumulation (investment), and vice versa. Furthermore, because this is consumption by a generation of people of postproductive age, it does not even have a direct impact on worker productivity. It might have an indirect impact, because currently employed people are future retirees, and they might regard current pension increases as a positive signal about the favorable nature of income policy and therefore an inducement to work more productively. They might also note that the level at which their own future pensions begin is raised by increases in the monthly pension that occur before they retire.

The dilemma looks different in the short run and in the long run. In economics, the short run is the period of time during which factors of production (including the related technology) are fixed. They can be utilized to varying degrees. Increasing this degree of utilization immediately leads to an increase in output (and vice versa). These are real-time effects that may be one-time or recurring, but only within the framework of the cyclical fluctuations of the economic climate, which can move in either direction. The scale of growth is limited by the size of the existing reserves, that is, the capacity not used in the previous cycle.

The long run is the economic category in which the factors of production expand as a result of capital accumulation and investment, and the whole process of output growth is set in motion as a result. New factories, often based on the latest technology, produce new products. New firms render additional services. More merchandise of better quality (more valuable) is manufactured. Income thus rises—both the portion of it that finances a growth in current consumption and the part of it set aside and invested, directly or through intermediary financial bodies such as banks and the capital market. As a result, we are dealing with expanded reproduction: More and more is produced from one time period to another.

Clearly, it is not senior citizens receiving an additional 8.50 zloty per month who invest in new productive capacity; rather, it is entrepreneurs who make greater profits. However, it is also clear that this additional billion zloty in income in the hands of consumers will increase the effective demand and thus, from the point of view of business opportunities, increase potential sales. In short: it's good for business. If there is unused productive capacity, then production will rise by this same 1 billion. If there is no excess capacity, then there will be either a corresponding importation of goods from abroad and production will increase there, or—in the least desirable outcome—prices will rise to purge the market of the excess flow of demand. In the latter case, there will be no positive effect in the form of growth in production. Even worse, the increased inflation may slow the rate of economic growth as a result of price deformation.

We could also theoretically assume that the retirement and disability recipients bank their additional 1 billion zloty, which would then reach the capital markets in the form of deposits and credit, and eventually be invested. Leaving aside the structure of the investment, the result would be similar to that of the same amount of money being invested by the smaller group of businessmen. In practical terms, however, in view of the level of real income of the pensioners, we can assume that their modest additional income would be devoted in its entirety to financing growth in consumption, rather than being saved. (The same reasoning can be applied to other social groups, such as teachers or nurses.) This is a matter of what economists refer to as the marginal propensity to consume. If all additional income goes to finance growth in consumption, then that propensity is 100 percent.

If, instead of 10 million people each receiving 100 zloty more per year to consume, 100 entrepreneurs each pay 10 million zloty per year less in taxes and have extra income totaling 1 billion zloty, then they may invest that capital. If they invest all of it, then their marginal propensity to save will be 100 percent. However, we live in a global economy, and the money could be transferred abroad and invested there. Then it would contribute to economic growth in some other part of the world. Alternatively, this 1 billion zloty might be invested neither here nor anywhere else, and used for the consumption of luxury goods. Knowing our own abilities at producing luxury goods, we should assume that they would be imported, increasing sales and current production somewhere else—for instance, in the diamond mines of Yakutia, the BMW assembly lines of Bavaria, the Bombardier business jet plant in Canada, or the shipyards building yachts in Denmark.

There are thus many variations to both the supply and the demand sides of the process of reproduction. Is it additional demand that boosts output? If so, then under what conditions is this true? When are the effects positive, in the form of supply, and when are they negative, in the form of inflation? Only the Scots could create a constant flow of demand for something that does not exist—the Loch Ness Monster. . . . Or could it be that the additional productive capacity that arises as a result of new investment not only increases the potential output, but also automatically increases output itself? Does this lead to an immediate rise in sales? Or does it add to inventory? When higher profits lead to expenditures on consumption rather than to the financing of investment, does this contribute to increased output? Under what conditions? Today, with such advanced globalization, should we look at the potential and real possibilities for increased output in domestic (national) terms, or in world terms? Finally, from the point of view of social cohesion and consumer satisfaction, is it better to give a lot to the few, or a little to the many?

These are only a sample of the responses to this apparently simple dilemma, along with the further questions they raise, because we are dealing with a whole causal chain that produces differing outcomes in differing time frames. If we go deeper into things, we see that setting a desired process in motion—in this case, long-term economic growth, and not merely a one-time demand pull or supply push—requires the convergence of at least several specific economic circumstances. In fact, the necessary circumstances go beyond the purely economic.

A curious (or attentive) reader might ask how I solved the dilemma of "a billion for one or a hundred for many," since something like this did actually take place, and similar situations occur all the time. First, and above all, the expectations of both parties, the mass of consumers and the business elite, were brought down to earth and placed in the context of the actual situation with the budget, because the problem of the national income is constantly tangled up with dilemmas about how to distribute it. Afterward, following a thorough examination of the arrangement and power of the supply and demand factors in real-life growth mechanisms, on the one hand, and considering social reality, on the other, a creative compromise was arrived at. As a result, the larger stream was directed to the market as additional household consumer demand. With greater competitiveness on the domestic market, this created greater utilization of existing productive capacity, thereby yielding a one-time impulse for more output thanks to the rise in the production of consumption goods. The smaller part of the stream through the tax cut reached the investment-goods market, expanding the productive capacity, thus generating longer-term growth. Some portion also doubtless went for increased consumer imports, but this was a small piece.

This example shows us how complicated the processes of output growth are. Socioeconomic development is even more complicated. It also shows us, in this one-page summary, that it is necessary to be very careful with tempting generalizations, because falling for them can lead us into the trap of oversimplification. After all, output growth depends equally (and simultaneously) on supply and demand, the magnitude and structure of capital and social transfers, expenditures by business and the national budget, the nature of consumer and investor expectations, domestic and external demand, and the marginal propensities to consume and save among a variety of social and income groups, as well as many other economic and noneconomic factors that never even appeared in this ostensibly emblematic example.

Both business and the government must take pains to ensure a constant supply of the conditions for production, or the reproduction of capital, including human capital. The basic difference is that business has a shorter temporal perspective and a narrower social horizon than the state. They concentrate on different things, have different financing preferences, and make different financing decisions. For example, business does not pay for children, despite the fact that, were there no children, businesses would sooner or later find themselves with no one to employ and would have to lock their doors. The state pays in various ways and to varying degrees. If the ruling elite is closer to the business circles, then the government will shorten its temporal perspective and narrow its social horizon. When the government is closer to labor, it broadens its social horizon and lengthens its temporal perspective.

When a rise in output is not accompanied by an improvement in living conditions for the public, it is hard to talk about economic development. Certain symptoms of such a model appeared in the late twentieth century in the United States, especially during the ascendancy of the neoliberal recipe for economic growth. This resulted above all in a rise in nonwage income, mostly in the form of profit and various kinds of rents and earnings from ownership or access to capital, whereas income from labor did not increase, despite an improvement in productivity. Some authors refuse to refer to this kind of expanded macroeconomic reproduction as development, but that is going too far. After all, the American economy not only grew, but also developed very rapidly, as reflected in unprecedented scientific and technical progress and structural changes. The fact that a significant part of society did not share in the fruits of that development means that it was flawed, not that it did not occur.

Some say that Russia has also seen growth without development in recent years, because consumption on the part of many income groups has not increased. Although the basic level may be different (lower) and the production structure different (traditional), similar phenomena can be seen in many less developed economies, where it is difficult to speak of socioeconomic development in our sense of the word, despite quantitative growth as reflected in GDP statistics. Although increases in the volume of production and average consumption show up in the statistics, they may not increase for years at a time for the overwhelming majority of the population. Some—the few—manage to break free of underdevelopment and enjoy a living standard that would place them in the middle class in a wealthy country, but others—the many—remain mired in poverty.

Year in and year out, in a centrally planned socialist economy, we saw many of the elements typical of growth without development. People talked back then about the "producing for production" that characterized the doctrinally motivated preference for the expansion of heavy industry. When the growing imbalance on the state-regulated quasi-market in consumer goods forced yet another price reform, there were mordant jokes about how the price of ham may have gone up, but locomotives were cheaper. If this had at least been accompanied by improvement in the quality of passenger services, then we might have been able to talk about development, but this did not always happen. The neglect of reproduction in the agricultural and light-industry sectors even as the manufacture of means of production received priority was one of the main reasons for the relatively low rate of output growth and socioeconomic development in comparison with the potential of the existing capital resources. During the periods when the consumer sphere was regarded as both a legitimate outlet for and an engine of production, labor productivity and overall output rose, and that growth was accompanied by development.

However, the chances for development are missed when growth comes from increased arms production or causes the devastation of the natural environment on a scale that outweighs the quantitative rise in output. It is possible for there to be higher output of widely desired articles that are socially deleterious and lower the quality of life, such as cars that cause paralyzing urban congestion. We need not linger over the question of whether a rise in the production of narcotics, alcohol, or tobacco is a sign of development or the exact opposite.

Changes in the structure of output can sometimes mean development in view of the nature of technological progress and the resulting innovation that may accompany quantitative growth, although it need not necessarily do so. If a new product of the same utilitarian value as the old one is more energy efficient, consumes fewer raw materials, or can be recycled more easily, then we are already justified in talking about a development process: The quantity is the same but the quality is higher. This makes the level of development higher.

The situation becomes even more complicated when we consider social and economic scales that go far beyond the particular place and region where we live. Everyone lives, and therefore consumes, not only in a given country, at a given address, but also in the world. The world, as we know, is very big, and highly varied. We must therefore make generalizations. This means simplifying. It also applies to the theoretical interpretation of the processes of growth in output and consumption, and socioeconomic development. It might seem to an impartial observer that a theoretical model of growth complicates matters, because everyone knows that production rises when people work more (or when the rulers govern better). In fact, even the most recondite, highly complex mathematical model of growth will always simplify matters to some degree.

In the simplest view, economic growth equals an increase in the value of output—the sum of goods manufactured and services rendered—over time. We are talking about growth in the overall level of output, because the production of some specific items is always going up while that of others is going down. In the most sweeping of generalizations, output increases when either the number of people employed increases or the productivity of the employees rises. In the former case, we are looking at growth in output, on the assumption that employment grows over the long term at the same rate as the population, but not at an increase in the value of output per capita. This is growth, but not development. This extensive type of growth does not lead to an improvement in living standards. For that to occur, we need a rise in productivity, which yields intensive growth. No development or civilizational progress can occur without productivity growth, which is why productivity growth is the key to improving the situation.

When trying to answer the question of what growth depends on, we must first find a way to maintain employment at least at the level of population growth. If this happens (and it doesn't in some places and for some countries), then it comes down to growth in labor productivity.

We can also look at this issue from a somewhat different angle—namely, from the perspective of capital utilization. Economic growth requires more capital, particularly growth in the productivity of the capital used. Those who do not invest do not develop. Nor do those who invest badly. However, growth in capital productivity must always manifest itself in growth in labor productivity. This is the heart of the matter. If the rate of output growth and improvement in the standard of living depends on increased labor productivity, on what does long-term growth in labor productivity depend?

Development (we sometimes add the adjective *socioeconomic* to direct our attention to the complex nature of the process) is an upward movement of the entire socioeconomic system. It occurs through quantitative and qualitative changes not only in the sphere of production and distribution, and investment and consumption, but also in reference to

- The application of the techniques and technology of production.
- Methods of management.
- The economic policy used.
- The nature and quality of the institutions, or the rules of the game within which the economy functions.
- Cultural preferences and the values espoused.
- Social relations formed in connection with the course of the processes of reproduction.
- The state of the natural environment.

By its very nature, development is therefore far more complicated than growth. As a result, we have problems not only in measuring it, but even more so in creating it, formulating the optimal development strategy and carrying out policies that promote it. In the case of economic growth, it is universally regarded as justifiable and admissible to reduce its measurement to changes in the value of the gross domestic product or derivatives of it, such as net national product, gross national product, or such even more limited yardsticks as the value of sales to industry or the amount of exports. In relation to the estimation of the level of socioeconomic development and the dynamics of this process, there is no consensus. This has far-reaching theoretical and practical consequences.

The dilemmas of choice remain enormous even if we assume that the category to be maximized is not GDP (and it should not be), but rather social capital measured by an index of the development of human capital, the HDI. Social and political judgments are crucial and can make all the difference. Let us take Poland as an example. This is a country aspiring to the status of highly developed, and it has a chance to satisfy these ambitions within the lifetime of a single generation. This could indeed happen, but not necessarily. It all depends.

Let us also assume that even if development is not limited to the level of output, education, and health as reflected in the HDI, these three categories also indirectly reflect other important aspects. We can therefore treat the HDI, and maximizing the HDI, as the core of development activity. In formulating a long-term strategy for Poland—over a dozen or more years—the public and policymakers thus face the question of what should increase, at what rate, and in what order, because it is impossible to do everything at once. Obviously, there is also the question of how to finance it.

As a starting point, we have an index of the development of human capital of 0.862. This is the outcome on the basis of hard statistical facts, according to the accepted methodology: A per capita GDP by PPP of $13,000 (in 2005; in 2010 it had risen to more than 17,000), an educational enrolment of 86 percent (this is one third of the educational component of the HDI) and a literacy rate of 99 percent (the other two thirds of the component), and an average life expectancy of 74.6 years. The three components are 0.272 for GDP, 0.315 for education, and 0.275 for health. This adds up to Polish HDI of 0.862.

Let us now assume that we wish to climb to the level of development characterized by an HDI of 0.902. That would mean achieving an increase of 0.040 and attaining the standard of living that the citizens of Cyprus and Portugal enjoy today. There are various ways of doing this. We shall examine three hypothetical variants:

- Doubling per capita GDP from $13,000 to 26,000 while retaining the present levels of education and health.
- Increasing GDP by 56 percent to $20,300 (which yields a rise of 0.024 in the HDI, while raising the educational enrolment by

young people from the present 86 to 100 percent—in other words, ensuring that everyone graduates from secondary school), thus raising the HDI by 0.016 while retaining the present level of health.

- A leap forward in public health that increases life expectancy to 81.6 years (thus raising the HDI by 0.040) while stabilizing income and education at the present level.

Which to choose? Someone might say, "Maximize output, because a higher GDP means creating wealth that can be used to improve education and health over time." Someone else says, "Maximize expenditures on schooling and education, because wise, well-educated people will create more GDP over time and then there will also be money for health care." Yet another person suggests, "Health is the absolute priority because, if we're healthy, then labor productivity will rise, the GDP will grow, and over time we'll have money to pay for better education." Obviously, the best thing is to have your cake and eat it too, while losing weight in the process.

There are a great many things to consider. In real social and economic processes, there are never such extreme choices. The options in our examples are unreal because it takes increased funding to improve education (and thus there must be a rise in output), and better education also raises output. It's the same with health. In all these cases, funds must be set aside to pay for improvements, and these improvements lead, in turn, to more funds. The feedback mechanisms are powerful, although the correlations are variable. In the short run, obviously, funds can be shifted from one application to another or budget deficits can be used to finance pro-development public services, but this is not the path to progress in the long run.

Practical solutions are always compromises of a sort. It cannot be otherwise. The range of available compromises--those that are always available, we might add--is large enough to cover the whole chessboard. Taking the middle road, we could propose a strategy of balanced social development that would yield a rise of 0.040 in the HDI over the posited time frame on the basis of the growth of the three factors as follows:

- An increase of 0.013, achieved by increasing the GDP by $8,300 per capita, to $21,300.

- A similar rise from education, by increasing the enrolment rate by twelve basis points to 98 percent.
- A similar rise in health, achieved by raising life expectancy by 2.4 years, to 77.

Choosing such a path has enormous practical consequences in political, legal, economic, financial, and organizational terms. Legislation would be required. A certain taxation and budgetary policy is implied. A wide range of technical, operational decisions would have to be made. Above all, there would be a requirement for a comprehensive approach resting on solid economic theory, on the one hand, and, on the other, social consensus as to the goals of development at a given historical moment. Are these the sorts of things that can be debated in parliament? How many parliamentarians would be capable of grasping the dilemmas—real policy dilemmas, we must stress—in the proper way? That is, could they grasp them not in terms of the next parliamentary elections, because many are capable of this, but in the sense of competing options that must be determined in a sensible way? Socioeconomic development always involves public money, because it is a public matter. The optimal allocation of that money is crucial to development. This is the sort of thing that parliament is supposed to discuss, but how many senators think in complex ways, rather than about their own political interests? How many see as far as the next generation, and not just the next election? They can focus on serious matters, but development deals with a time frame that is longer than the electoral cycle if it is to be balanced in social and ecological, economic, and financial terms.

Reality is more intricate than this economically, socially, and politically complicated example. The way to manage socioeconomic development and even to measure it will remain open questions for a long time. More than that, they will always be open questions. The level of development is what makes an economy "beautiful," but judgments of beauty are elusive. We find something beautiful or not, but have notorious problems when prompted to say exactly why. Should we measure wealth quantitatively and compare it to the measure of poverty? Is longevity the key, or should we try to measure social satisfaction? How should we measure the quality of life, or human happiness? These questions transcend the boundaries of economics, but it is worth pursuing them because every discipline is most interesting at the point where it comes into contact with other ones.

Interestingly, one of the most original contributions to the debate over the essence and goals of development came not from the academics and politicians of the most highly developed countries, but rather from King Jigme Singye Wangchuk, the forward-looking and very young, as he was then, ruler of the beautiful but extremely poor country of Bhutan, which is squeezed between China and India and had a per capita GDP of barely $1,400. In response to criticism from *The Financial Times* over Bhutan's unspectacular growth rate, constrictive traditional social structure, and isolation from the Western world, the king proposed the Gross National Happiness index (GNH).

The GNH is a step forward, although in some ways it is also a step sideways. It emphasizes the significance for a contented society and a satisfying life of not only the level of output, but also cultural traditions (the Buddhist tradition is salient here) and the condition of the natural environment. While classical models of growth focus on the quantitative aspects of economic expansion, the GNH emphasizes the synergy and positive feedback mechanisms of the material and spiritual aspects of development. The concept of GNH thus rests upon four pillars:

- Equitable and sustainable socioeconomic development (in the traditional sense).
- Concern for and protection of cultural values.
- Conservation of the natural environment.
- Good governance and management of the economy and public affairs.

The people of Bhutan are happy, as shown by research at the interface of psychology and economics. The first-ever World Map of Happiness has been developed at the University of Leicester in the United Kingdom. It is based on a rich array of comparative data on not only the level of wealth (income and equity), but also health and access to education. Furthermore, some 80,000 people in 178 countries were surveyed on their subjective feeling of well-being and satisfaction with life. These results were used to compile a composite index of Subjective Well-Being (SWB), which ranks countries on a scale from 100 to 300.[1]

The survey gives the inhabitants of poor Bhutan an SWB of 253, the same as in Ireland, Canada, and Luxembourg, with which it is surprisingly tied for eighth place. Only the most prosperous countries place higher. Switzerland and Denmark are tied for first place, with 273 points, followed by Austria and Iceland (260), and Finland, Sweden, and the Bahamas (257). Bhutan's neighbors, China and India, are in eighty-second and 125th place, respectively, with 210 and 180 points. The United States is in twenty-second place, with 247 points, and Russia is in a distant 167th place, with 143 points. With 197 points, Poland is in ninety-eighth place. The unfortunates bringing up the rear are the Democratic Republic of the Congo, Zimbabwe, and Burundi, with 100 points. Not far above them are the postsocialist countries of Moldova (117) and Ukraine (120). The highest-placed postsocialist countries are Mongolia, in fifty-ninth place, with 223 points, and Kyrgyzstan and Slovenia, tied for sixty-first position with eight other countries (220 points).

In this context, it is puzzling that Bhutan is down in 135th place on the HDI, with a score of 0.538. The difference is that the HDI considers education and health along with GDP, while the GNH is based on the GDP, culture, and the environment. Neither index takes note of income distribution. The time will come when we have a synthetic index that will integrate the human development (HDI), gross national happiness (GNH), and the Gini coefficient.

Doing the sums is no problem; the problem is agreeing how to weight the different factors. That is a complicated affair, as can be seen by attempting on one's own to come up with a formula for aggregating such nonadditive categories as personal income, education, health, longevity, free time (the good kind, outside of work, if you have a job), subjective feelings, including the awareness that others are far wealthier or far poorer, the condition of the natural and cultural environments around us, and the degree of satisfaction or dissatisfaction with the functioning of your government and democratic institutions.

I propose a system with four groupings. The first is output—GDP per capita. The second is the sphere of subjective feelings, connected with one's own health, the degree of satisfaction with the phases of life we have lived so far, a realistic assessment of how many years lie before us, education level, and the quality of community life (government and democracy). The third is the perceived state of the natural environment (its influence on subjective feelings, health, and living and working conditions). The fourth is an assessment of free time and the cultural values that can fill it. The key is the GDP, the material basis of life. I propose to make it worth two fifths of the total. The other three groups count for one fifth each. The four components can add up to a maximum index of 100—a maximum of forty points from GDP and twenty points each from the other three. GDP has reached such levels in our day that I propose $50,000 or more as the level that gives 40 points, and $500 as the lower limit, equal to zero points. I leave it to the political scientists, ecologists, economists, sociologists, anthropologists, lawyers, and doctors, along with the ever-useful interdisciplinary generalists, to assign weights to the subcategories in the other three groups. If they succeed, as they should, we will have the ISI—the Integrated Success Index—and one more map to color in.

Success is not only a better term than *output* or (level of) *development*, but also a better word than *prosperity* or *happiness*. The category of success is understood to be broader than happiness, because it also includes the effect of calculated economic activity and captures the essence of what we are trying to attain in development that is balanced in all its aspects. It is interesting to note that in the Polish language, people do not wish each other "good luck" in a political or business context, but rather "success." This is more than a question of semantics. *Success* sounds more active, whereas *luck* denotes a more passive stance. Active is better. It is clear that development should indicate as much of a balance as possible of the *financial, economic, ecological, social, institutional,* and the *political.* "As much as possible" because perfect balance is impossible and any such expectations would be wishful thinking. Success, like luck, includes cultural and spiritual aspects, and it has to do with state of mind, emotions, and subjective feelings about ourselves. Many of these aspects lie outside the purview of traditional economics, but that's the whole point. Getting outside of conventions and traditions is intellectually productive.

In almost every language, and even more so across languages ranging from Polish through English through the Dzongkha language of Tibet, spoken in Bhutan, the words for happiness, good luck, and success are used in ways that sometimes overlap and allow for a blurring of their respective semantic fields.

If we go back to the intriguing and edifying example of Bhutan, we must note that conditions have improved there since the king took up the issue of happiness. The fact that the Gini coefficient has fallen to

0.365 might have something to do with it. You might say that the poverty is somewhat more fairly distributed. People appreciate this. The economy, from a very low absolute level, is developing, As we climb the Himalayan trails, we reach either hamlets where the Gini coefficient is 0.418 or *geog* administrative districts of several villages where the coefficient is lower than the national average. Qualitatively speaking, the HDI has risen in a generation from a 1984 level of 0.325, which is low even by the standards of the poorest countries, to its present position in the lower range of the world middle class. Such a leap is remarkable on a worldwide scale.

As an aside, how significant is it that both the index of human development and the index of happiness have Eastern roots? An economist from India and another from Pakistan joined Amartya Sen in developing the HDI. The king of Bhutan created the GNH index. They worked under the strong influence of Eastern culture and religions. King Wangchuk was educated at an exclusive English boarding school before being crowned in 1972, when he was only seventeen. The creators of the HDI graduated from and then lectured at the prestigious British universities of Oxford and Cambridge, and the London School of Economics. Their ideas stem from a meeting of the values of East and West. The most interesting ideas arise at the points of contact between not only different academic disciplines, but also different cultures. Multiculturalism has a colossal future.

A deeper statistical analysis reveals that the level of happiness in different countries is linked most strongly with health (with a statistical correlation of 0.62), affluence (0.52), and education (0.53).[2] This might explain why the results of a BBC survey in Britain came as a surprise to traditional-minded economists. No fewer than 81 percent of respondents felt that the government should concentrate more on making people happy than on making them rich. That depends on what kind of government one has, but in general it's a good idea for governments to stay away from trying to make us happy—as if they didn't have anything else to do. However, government should pay attention to how the country fares according to the happiness index and draw the appropriate conclusions. Money by itself can't buy happiness. Health, wisdom, and personal attractiveness count for more—but acquiring all these attributes, as we know, costs money, including public money from the government.

Unfortunately, the GNH index has not yet made much of an impact, although it has provoked some intellectual and academic ferment on an international scale, as reflected by a stream of articles and the occasional conference. The HDI, with all its drawbacks, is used more frequently in international comparisons. Its main drawback is that it simply combines information on output, health, and education, yet even this is a step forward, in the right direction. The HDI does not reflect either income equality or the influence of free time on social well-being, however, and thus distorts, for instance, the actual relationship of well-being on the two sides of the Atlantic.

Things are going relatively well on the northern shores of the Atlantic, where there is much affluence and little poverty. In the countries on the southern shores of the ocean, however, as in many other poor parts of the globe, policy focuses on other issues, especially on the great development deficit in comparison to the wealthy world.

In this context, the United Nations marked the turn of the Millennium by proclaiming the Millennium Development Goals in response to pressure from poor countries, the increasingly influential (as it should be) lobby of economists dealing with development issues, and the increasingly numerous and active nongovernmental organizations. The affluent countries subscribed to the plan. Some (e.g., the Scandinavian and Benelux countries, and Canada) were keen on it, whereas others (e.g., the English-speaking countries, Japan, and Italy) were less so.

The Millennium Development Goals set standards for meeting basic social needs that should be achieved by 2015. These are not only development goals in themselves, but also conditions for continuing development in the future. Basically formulated with an eye to the countries of the poor south, they also, unfortunately, apply to some postsocialist countries affected by a painful transformation recession in the 1990s that markedly worsened living conditions for large parts of their populations.

The Millennium Development Goals have an extensive structure made up of goals, targets, and indicators. The idea was to avoid generalizations along the lines of the necessity to improve living conditions, or the statement that things cannot go on like this (because they can). The goals identify eight areas in which palpable improvements should take place over the course of fifteen years, mainly through ambitious development policy coordinated in part and supported by the joint efforts of the entire world community under the auspices of the United Nations.

These eight main targets are

1. Eradicate extreme poverty and hunger.
2. Achieve universal primary education.
3. Promote gender equality and empower women.
4. Reduce child mortality.
5. Improve maternal health.
6. Combat HIV/AIDS, malaria, and other diseases.
7. Ensure environmental sustainability.
8. Create a global partnership for development.

A system for monitoring changes has been put into operation, with a special U.N. website (http://mdgs.un.org/unsd/mdg/Default.aspx) updated on a running basis. Each of the goals is broken down into more specific tasks. There are eighteen of these targets. Indicators have been designated for each of them to monitor quantitative progress.

For example, the first goal—the elimination of extreme poverty and hunger—depends on meeting two targets:

- Halve, between 1990 and 2015, the proportion of people whose income is less than $1 a day, and
- Halve, between 1990 and 2015, the proportion of people who suffer from hunger.

In turn, progress toward the first of these targets (halving the number of people on less than $1 a day) is to be measured by three indicators:

- Proportion of population below $1 (PPP) per day.
- Poverty gap ratio, a complex statistical measurement of the scale of poverty expressed as a percentage of income equal to the poverty line. This is calculated by multiplying the percentage of people living below the poverty line by the difference between the poverty line and the average income of those living below the poverty line (unfortunately, there is no simpler way to explain this[3]).
- The percentage share of the lowest quintile in the overall consumption by the entire population (and a quintile, we recall, is one fifth of the population).

Progress toward the second target is supposed to be assessed on the basis of two indicators:

- Prevalence of underweight children under five years of age.
- Proportion of population below minimum level of dietary energy consumption.

Two thirds of the time span allocated for achieving the Millennium Development Goals has already elapsed, and results are mixed. All the applicable indicators are updated annually and accessible online.[4] Even a cursory look shows that many of the targets will not be met, and the situation could even worsen in extreme cases. This is due in part to the fact that the targets are unrealistic and rather arbitrary (why, for instance, should the scale of hunger decrease by exactly half?). Even more so, it is due to the lack of an appropriate development strategy. Finally, it must once again be emphasized that the progress being made in China, and recently in India as well, has an enormous positive effect on the averages.

Although the Millennium Development Goals were formulated in 2000, they are defined retrospectively, for a time span beginning in 1990. Comparisons on any meaningful scale can be made only for the first half of the time span, that is, the years from 1990 to 2002. Let us take a look at four of the five indicators listed earlier that apply to the first two Millennium targets, which are certainly the most important. After all, it is a disgrace for all humanity that we are still grappling with poverty and hunger on such a scale when, as of 2008, the average per capita income for the whole world has surpassed $10,000, or that one sixth of the world's people must (must they really?) get by on less than one thirtieth of the average income.

Let us put some extreme examples under the magnifying glass. In terms of halving the number of people who exist on less than $1 a day, the greatest progress has been made in East Asia, where the percentage fell from 33 percent in 1990 to 14.1 percent in 2002. The worst case is in sub-Saharan Africa, where the shockingly high percentage declined almost imperceptibly from 44.6 to 44.0 percent. In postsocialist East Central Europe, the percentage jumped from 0.4 to 1.8 percent, and in the post-Soviet Commonwealth of Independent States, it soared from 0.4 to 2.5 percent. Overall, in what the United Nations defines as developing regions, it fell from 27.9 to 19.4 percent. There is thus a long way to go before it is halved.

As for the poverty gap, it barely budged in sub-Saharan Africa, falling from 19.5 to 18.7 percent. On the other hand, it will perhaps come as no surprise that it dropped sharply in East Asia, from 8.9 to 3.1 percent. In the two groups of postsocialist countries mentioned earlier, it rose from 0.3 to 0.5 percent and from 0.2 to 0.6 percent, respectively.

If we look at the third indicator, the percentage of chronically underweight small children, we see that it has declined from 33 to 28 percent in the overall population of the developing regions. It decreased from 19 to 8 percent in East Asia, but only from 53 to 47 percent in South Asia and from 32 to 30 percent in sub-Saharan Africa.

The fourth indicator is intake of fewer calories than the figure that nutritionists regard as essential. From 1990 until 2002, the overall measurement declined from 20 to 17 percent. In sub-Saharan Africa, where things are worst, undernourishment still affects almost half the population, having declined from 33 to 31 percent. Things improved most in East Asia, where it fell from 16 to 12 percent, and South Asia, where the figures were 18 and 12 percent.

There can be no doubt that it will take a longer temporal horizon than 2015 to meet these and other ambitious development targets. This would even be the case if the Millennium Goals were met, because the idea is not to limit these afflictions, but to eliminate them. The latter, unfortunately, is impossible, even in the long run. However, significant improvement is possible, and on an even larger scale than the targets set in 2000. The higher the rate of economic growth, the greater the chance for success.

The present-day situation in terms of the conditions, mechanisms, and perspectives for both growth and development is becoming more complicated, above all because new barriers to economic growth are being reached. We have often been warned that output growth is coming to an end. This is because it is becoming impossible to feed the growing population masses, which is what the British economist Thomas Malthus (1766–1834) said two centuries ago, when he determined that, whereas population was growing at an almost exponential rate, the production of food could increase at only a linear rate. Another reason is that nonrenewable natural resources are being exhausted, which is something that the reports from the Club of Rome have been warning about urgently since 1970.

The first of these warnings has turned out to be exaggerated, at least over the past 200 years, but the second is taking on increasingly real form. Not even the Malthusian "population law," however, can be rejected totally and uncritically. In the world as a whole, it has not come true because of technical progress in agriculture and the so-called green revolution. Nevertheless, it unfortunately seems to be accurate in the least-developed regions of the world, where the production of food has indeed failed to keep up with population growth. This has resulted in chronic starvation and, ultimately, has limited population growth in those regions.

As for the second warning, the exhaustion of the nonrenewable natural resources essential to the continuation of the processes of reproduction and the present style of life, we are not dealing with any exaggeration. The real-life world is facing an unprecedented resource barrier. All we need to do is to remind ourselves that the extension to the entire world of the North American level of output and consumption, with all its resource hungriness, would require the mobilization of three times the earth's entire stock of resources. Where can we find two additional earths? We won't, and that is why this scenario will never occur. It will never be possible for humankind, even if the population remained at the current level of 6.8 billion, to achieve the output standards of the United States. The future of the world cannot, and will not, look anything like North America or Western Europe. Those economies can serve as a model, a reference point, to which a Chile, a Poland, or a Malaysia can aspire with greater or lesser degrees of success—but not the world as a whole.

Because of the objective resource barrier that is becoming physically palpable to an increasing degree, and despite the technological progress that makes production constantly less resource and energy intensive, there are periodic calls for the slowing of growth or for downright "zero growth." This was the recommendation of the Club of Rome report. More than a generation has passed, world output has once again doubled and then some at the cost of enormous quantities of resources, and the calls for speeding growth continue to drown out those for slowing it down. How can we resolve this paradox? Is the world economy growing too fast or too slow? Are Eastern European ambitions of overtaking the Western European outlet level justified, or merely another illusion? Is it a good thing or a bad thing that Africa has moved off of bottom dead center after so many years of stagnation? Should we cheer for or worry about the mushrooming output from Southeast Asia?

Let's step back for a moment and pose the question differently: Is it possible, or desirable, for output to continue to grow on the same scale and in the same proportions as, for instance, over the last twenty years? The answer is that it is neither possible nor desirable. This statement has far-reaching consequences, all the more so because the rate of output growth over the last two decades is seldom characterized as excessive, and indeed is often treated as insufficient. The fact is that it has been insufficient for the great majority of humankind and continues to be so, and not only in terms of meeting the basic requirements of life. At the same time, it can be seen as excessive in regard to the wealthiest countries. This is not a question of needs. Needs can be even more unsatisfied than they were in the past, when there was less prosperity, as long as consumer appetites grow faster than the real potential for satisfying them. It is a question of the availability of the resources required for the growth in output and consumption.

Today the question of output growth and socioeconomic development must be seen as part of a worldwide configuration. Unfortunately, most theoretical concepts and models, let alone practical development strategies and policies, fail to do so because they are still dominated by thinking in terms of national bailiwicks. There are two common approaches. The first takes as its starting point the open, economically developed and institutionally advanced countries with established capitalistic systems, and the accompanying value systems. The other begins from the least-developed countries, those that are frequently referred to as "developing," even if that development sometimes never occurs. These countries are characterized by poverty, structural insufficiency, and institutional frailty.

This simplified division of the world into two types of countries demonstrates the need to go on searching for answers to what seems to be a single question: How do we increase output and consumption within the framework of a national economy? That is, how do we maximize GDP, which by definition applies to a single, national domestic economy? Because the initial conditions are so different, and sometimes radically different, in these two categories of countries, the recipe cannot be the same for both. The question of how to increase production as rapidly as conditions permit must yield two different answers.

Yet the truth is that this is not the right question. The world is no longer made up, as it once was, of the sum of various competing, more- or less-developed countries or national economies. It is made up of interdependent regions and countries. They are more open and integrated than ever before. The continuing division into national economies cocontiguous with the corresponding states reflects irrational political pressures or our limited statistical abilities more than it reflects economic good sense. On purely logical economic grounds, it is amazing how political and cultural nationalisms undercut the efforts that peoples are making by the sweat of their brow to improve their own lot in life. Multinational corporations have already drawn the right conclusions from this fact in terms of effective ways to increase output. They maximize their aims in a global rather than a national system. Time—a great deal of time—will have to pass before states, societies, and their governments acquire similar skills.

Despite these observations and their consequences for thinking about the future, here and there, from the poorest to the richest countries, we see the temptation to turn back in the direction of protectionism, and to think in nation-state terms above all. Yet the mercantilist option of returning to national boundaries and limiting economic activity to what can be achieved with domestic resources would be pure nonsense. Today the rate of output growth does not depend on possessing natural resources of one's own, but on having access to them. This access, in turn, depends on a range of other political and economic factors, and especially on financial reserves. The situation can reverse, and it will do so farther down the line, when those who have their own natural resources, or at least absolutely guaranteed access to them in other parts of the world, will sleep soundest. Awareness of this fact is growing, and it is already casting a visible shadow on geopolitics. We need only trace the evolution of political and economic relations between China and Africa or Russia and Germany, not to mention the United States and the Middle East.

The resource factor, which played a fundamental role in the historical process of economic growth, will thus return to prominence. The more the supply of resources is limited in relation to demand, the greater its importance will be—not only in terms of market price, but also in terms of the vigilance of those who control them. The wheel of history keeps turning. The significance of natural resources was relatively less in recent centuries, but it will be greater in the coming centuries. This is most obvious in the case of water. Some go so far as to say that the next wars will be fought not over energy sources, but over water. This is already happening on a smaller or larger scale—for instance, in the apparently hopeless situation of Darfur, on the border of Sudan and Chad. The discovery of underground water reserves may offer a way out of even this nightmare.

We will not have to wait centuries to learn whether, instead of killing for gold, *lebensraum*, or energy, we will kill for water. We will feel the mounting pressure of this challenge within the next few decades. However, it is not natural resources but other vital factors that will make the difference in growth rates during this time frame, and human resources will be most important of all.

As far as world output and the determinants of its growth in the interdependent conditions of the contemporary world economy, the most sensible kind of growth—that, is, the most desirable in terms of overall social and economic rationality—is characterized on the one hand by general balance on both the global and regional scale, and on the other by the harmony of all development processes at a rate of output growth that is higher in the poor countries and lower in the rich ones.

The first part of the formula, balance, comes down to the equilibrium of growth in terms of

- The natural environment.
- Saving, investment, and the flow of capital.
- Productive capacity and the need to utilize it.
- The demand for and supply of goods and services.
- The social dimension of the distribution of income and its growth.

The idea is for this growth to be relatively balanced, because complete balance can never be achieved outside of the one place where it is necessary—in economic models. In real life, we should strive for balance to the degree permitted by our knowledge, and even more so by the political conditions under which we operate. And these conditions are such that the former vice president of the United States, Al Gore, can organize a series of concerts from Sydney through Tokyo and Rio de Janeiro to Washington to mark Live Earth, which summons humanity to ecologically balanced growth while the serving president of the United States at that time (to whom Gore lost the 2000 election when more people voted for him than for the winner) adroitly blocks a range of initiatives that aim for such growth.

In the second case, things are just as complicated, or perhaps even more so, despite the fact that they seem far easier in theoretical terms. Political considerations sometimes make it incredibly difficult or downright impossible to accomplish the things that should be easiest according to theory or models. In this case, we are talking about deliberately slowing the average rate of growth in wealthier countries at the same time that we accelerate the growth rate in poorer countries. The only thing needed to accomplish this is to change the present distribution of accumulation on a worldwide scale, and more specifically to shift a part of saving and investment from the richer countries to the poorer—nothing to it! To accomplish this, we must have the appropriate instruments, including fiscal and budgetary ones. The present stage of globalization has not yet produced such instruments, and there should be no illusions (although neoclassical orthodoxy and neoliberalism have such illusions) that the problem will solve itself through the global peregrination of private capital.

More precisely, this is a matter of tweaking the growth indicators in such a way that the economic situation of the decided majority of humankind improves palpably, while the situation of people in the wealthy countries improves only a little. It is worth noting at this point that a 1 percent rise in per capita GDP for the richest countries equals about $400 in absolute terms; in the poorest countries, $400 would amount to a 50 percent rise in income. Alternatively, if the equivalent of one year's rise in the GDP of the United States were shifted to Africa, this would mean an additional $300, or 10 percent, for each resident of that continent. At present, no mechanisms exist for such shifts. However, if the future of the world and the imperative for global social balance are to be taken seriously, then it is necessary to aim for this type of shift in income growth. This is a challenge that extends beyond the present century.

It is also clear that significant inequality exists within the wealthy countries and that it is increasing. The income of the poor people in these countries should therefore grow more quickly than that of the rich. In such a case, we would move along the path of growth while reducing the excessive differentiation of incomes within countries (where it is present), and within the system of the world economy and all of humanity.

If the world were made up of only China and the United States, we could say that this is exactly the path it is following, but only in an international perspective. Over the last generation, the rate of output in China, which is poorer, has been growing distinctly more rapidly than in the wealthier United States. In both countries, at the same time, the income of the richer strata of the populace has been increasing more rapidly than that of the poorer. The first of these processes can only be seen as positive, whereas the other is far more complicated. Leaving aside the issue of "equitable distribution," there are increasingly distinct symptoms of social tension and harbingers of slower growth against the background of the excessive differentiation of income and assets. Above all, however, the problem is that the world is far, far more complicated than this hypothetical system consisting of two countries.

———————

The question therefore arises of the degree to which this kind of model of economic growth and socioeconomic development is possible—a model that offers a chance of the complex, balanced development of the entire world economy, while also providing relations of output growth that reduce the inequality of development levels and realistic access to the dwindling stocks of nonrenewable resources.

In other words, when we ask about the conditions and chances for a sensible model of economic growth, especially in regard to the appropriate rate of growth, we must try to answer two questions simultaneously:

- First, at what rate should world output as a whole grow?
- Second, how should the effects of this growth be distributed across the various regions of the world?

In 2007, overall world output grew by about 5 percent. In terms of value, this is worth almost $3.3 trillion (for the sake of comparison, more or less the combined GDP of Brazil and Russia). Therefore

- Can the earth and the human race go on at this rate in the long run?
- From the point of view of maintaining the capacity of the world economy for long-term development, what is the best way to divide the effects of this growth among regions, countries, and so on?

The answer to these questions is nonconventional. Although output on a world scale has been growing too quickly, at an unsustainable rate, it is growing too slowly in regard to the decided majority, about two thirds of humanity. Therefore, even though this rate must slow in overall terms, it must accelerate for about two thirds of the world's countries. In arithmetic terms, this implies the necessity to slow growth in the wealthy countries. The political consequences of this conclusion are as profound as possible, and we must come to terms with them—the sooner, the better.

The imperative to direct the rate of growth on a differentiated scale in terms of the world and its regions (i.e., the necessity of slowing it down in some places and speeding it up in others) is something new in economic theory and practice, although the question of the source of economic growth and the means of stimulating it have been with us for centuries. The debate on this subject attaches varying degrees of importance to the different factors involved in growth. This results either from the way their significance has changed over the history of development or from differences in interpretation. There is a vast literature on the subject, perhaps the richest of all branches of economics. In simple terms, we already have theories and models of economic growth that place the emphasis on

- Development based on raw materials.
- Strategies for the development of heavy industry.
- Rapid industrialization.
- Import substitution ("anti-import" production).
- Pro-export output expansion.
- Development balanced by branches and sectors (means of production and consumption; industry and agriculture).
- The knowledge-based economy and the information society.

These models of growth apply most of all to the countries that are highly developed today. The time has come to open a new chapter in economic research that attempts to provide answers (i.e., answers that encourage socioeconomic development rather than hamper it) to questions about sensible ways to slow the rate of output growth in those countries. Glimpses and mutations of these theories and models have appeared in less-developed countries at various times. Several decades ago, these countries were advised to pursue development based on their own natural resources, if they had any. At other times, they were counseled to develop heavy industry. More recent times have seen the prevalence of support for the pro-export expansion of output while also maintaining a balance in the development of branches and sectors, especially on the basis of agriculture and light industry.

Some dream of them, but no such models exist; there is, however, a viewpoint and an associated hypothesis that the acceleration of economic growth and the launching of development can be achieved through the greater occupational activation of women. There is something to this. Zealous feminists note that the largest market in the world is not America, but women, and that American women outnumber the entire Japanese market. Cool-headed economists point out the degree to which the levels of economic and sociopolitical activity by women is correlated with the overall level of development. In the world as a whole, women are the sole breadwinners for about 25 percent of families and are the primary sources of support for another 25 percent of all households.

Among labor economists, there is general agreement that women in all countries are paid less than men for the same work. The less developed the country, the greater the difference, and vice versa. Aside from its clearly discriminatory nature, this nonequivalent exchange may indeed enhance the potential for capital accumulation by employed women, but it reduces the purchasing power of households and, in turn, deprives producers of part of the potential demand for their products.

However, if it is not to take place to the detriment of men, the employment of women requires creating appropriate conditions, and above all jobs. This costs money and brings us back to questions about the ways of increasing employment and the sources of the capital to create these new jobs. The argument about the efficacy of increased employment for women in economic growth turns out to be identical to arguments for increasing the overall level of employment. The thing that is worth trying to bring about is gender equality. There is a great deal yet to be done, and the lower the level of development, the more there is to do. That is why the occupational activation of women must be seen mainly as an instrument for bringing about equal rights, not as a means to economic growth. It is a significant issue in its own right.

Psychologists and sociologists have shown that, in regard to many issues, women have a different value system from men. Even without psychologists and sociologists, a look around proves that this is so. People are people, but preferences are not the same. Women, generally speaking, are far more sensitive to social aspects. They pay more attention to workplace safety and conditions, advocate a more equitable distribution of income, show more concern for the interests of the consumers of the goods and services created at their places of employment, and attach greater importance to the observance of ethical norms in business. On a wider scale, in public life outside the company, they notice social equality, their neighborhoods, and their natural environment. They attach more importance to education, and not only for their own children. They are surely more committed to the conditions for family life than all the male hypocrites who squabble so boldly in the political arena over "family values" put together.

Even a cursory comparative analysis shows to a striking degree that, where women are more involved in economic and political life, we are far closer to a social market economy model. Whereas in Sweden women hold (only?) 45 percent of top-level government posts, the figure in the United States is 14 percent. In Saudi Arabia, it is zero. This sheds considerable light on the scale of inequality of income distribution and the distance separating these and other countries from the social market economy model.

To digress: As deputy prime minister and finance minister, I brought a dozen or more women onto the government economic team, including seven in key deputy ministerial posts. Two of them later advanced to cabinet rank in the government, and one became a European Union commissioner. All, of course, were leading professionals, holding doctorates or other academic credentials. However, I mainly followed my conviction that women are better at certain things that are highly valuable in politics. They are more patient and less scheming, more pragmatic and less demagogical. They also have more social sensitivity than men but are less susceptible to populism. Perhaps this is because they are also in charge of their homes and have a better sense of what makes something completely useless. I will leave it to the econometricians to determine the degree to which the work of these women contributed to the success of the structural reforms we successfully introduced, and the growth of the GDP by one third.

What, then, does economic growth depend on? Above all, what will it depend on in the future that we can foresee and imagine? To foresee something and to imagine it are not the same. This is why we must emphasize the evolution of the factors of development. The things that were important 200 years ago were not the same as those that were important half a century ago. Certain things are fundamental at present, but the engines of economic growth will be different in fifty or 100 years. We cannot realistically see that far ahead, but we can and should look for answers within the perspective of the coming generation. What will output growth depend on? Will it be

- Natural resources and riches?
- Abundant cheap labor?
- The correct adjustment of macroeconomic parameters?
- Government economic policy?
- The quality of company management?
- Cultural determinants?
- Foreign aid?
- Geographical location?
- Climate and the prevailing weather?
- Fortunate combinations of circumstances?

Even listing the questions shows that the answers are sought on various levels—in the real sphere and the regulatory sphere, in terms of real and human capital, in natural resources and workforce qualifications, within and beyond national economies, in classical economic factors and noneconomic cultural conditioning, and in natural conditions and placement on the map of the world. Nor is it strange that all these domains are involved to a degree. This is why we have passed through various "schools" and economic theories of growth over the last few centuries. This journey is far from concluded. new interpretations will appear, such as the present conception of the knowledge-based economy as an element of growth and development.

For many years, it has been the natural desire of economists to grasp the essence of the processes they study and to capture this essence in rules and generalizations that can be turned into objective laws. However, the subject under study keeps changing, and this means that the generalizations must change as well. There is no way to remain in one place when the floor, ceiling, and walls are in motion. Economic theory itself is evolving. This is true in spades of theories of economic growth. There have been many of them. Each has contributed something to our considerations, and some remain valuable to a greater or lesser degree, making it easier to interpret what is going on around us, or what could go on.

In its centuries of history, and on the basis of theoretical and empirical studies, economic thought has created many models of growth and development. Economic history, describing the formation of socioeconomic phenomena and processes against their political background over the course of history, is fascinating. No less striking is the history of economic thought, which has described the search for answers to the question of what determines development. Like development itself, this is an unending quest. The study of development is historical. Conditions and models once regarded as explanatory have grown obsolescent, just as the canons revered today will someday be found only in the museums of economic thought.

The models that involve a long-term perspective are especially interesting. By their nature, output growth and development are not short-term processes. There are Keynesian or Neo-Keynesian models that emphasize the importance of the growth of autonomous demand, especially investment demand. There is also the older tradition of classical or neoclassical models. Since the days of Adam Smith, the father of classical economics, it has been accepted that production is a function of three variables: labor, capital, and land. In times when the abundance of land has ended, the last of these variables has been conceived more broadly, as including nonrenewable natural resources, among other things, and it has become far more important than it was in the days when land was thought of mainly as pasture for the sheep, fields for the crops, and properties with coal on them.

The simplest models are the single-variant ones, which present the dependent variable as a function of a single independent variable. These models also tell us the least. The growth in output (or national product) is a function of changes in a single variable regarded as explanatory, usually labor or capital. The growth process is better explained by models involving two or more factors, where it is, for instance, a function of labor and capital, or even more variables, such as technology. Multivariable models can be brought closer to real life, but also made more complicated, by breaking down their factors further. For instance, capital can be categorized as old, recycled, or newly created as a result of saving and accumulation. Labor can be subdivided into various qualitative categories. The number of independent variables in the formula can also be increased.

Models of economic growth can be exogenous or endogenous. It may seem surprising to us today that until quite recently[5] technical progress was regarded, in a great oversimplification, as exogenous and as the result of deliberate human activity. Exogenous models pay particular attention to the role of technological accoutrements to labor and the store of scientific and technical knowledge. Robert E. Lucas, who won the Nobel Prize in economics in 1995, took things one step farther with a simple model in which capital determined output growth, except that it was broken down into real capital and human capital. Lucas added the additional simplistic assumption that the positive effect of technology is a constant, like the labor supply.[6]

Modeling the process of economic growth involves, on the one hand, numerous assumptions and simplifications that make it possible to grasp the cause-and-effect relationships and the more complex feedback mechanisms. On the other hand, it requires great definitional discipline and intellectual precision. It is governed by strict statistical determinants and falsification criteria, so that it can be verified scientifically. As a rule, economic models, including those referring to economic growth and development, take the form of mathematical or econometric formulas.

Estimates of specific parameters in econometric models may seem doubtful because of the probabilistic nature, that is, the randomness, of the phenomena and processes being analyzed. Mathematical models, in turn, may seem overly deterministic. They assume that economic growth is a matter of causes and effects, and therefore that the appearance of phenomena and processes is determined by previously occurring phenomena and processes. This may be true but need not necessarily be so in view of the nonlinear nature of the process of macroeconomic reproduction and the far-from-trivial significance of randomness, and thus of coincidences, including those that the models completely ignore.

Each of these theoretical approaches is a partial answer to the question about the source of economic growth. None of them is complete or exhaustive. This is why, naturally, there are so many different interpretations, and so many misunderstandings. Some are purely intellectual. Others are entangled in political and ideological disputes. This is why the search will continue for a theory that best synthesizes the rational elements of the many theories that already exist.

Almost all the theoretical approaches, regardless of their degree of sophistication, take proper account of the significance of technology in production processes. Technical progress has been the engine of economic progress and growth over the centuries, and will continue to be so. In the long run, economies and civilizations do not move forward without technical progress. This is why we place such emphasis today on the importance of science as a direct productive force, and the fundamental role of knowledge-based technology, including research and development. These are the sources of invention and innovation, which spur technical progress and increases in the quantity and quality of products and services. The countries incapable of creativity on their own resort to imitation, through which they acquire the skills of invention and innovation.

Japan once showed us how much can be achieved in this way, and China is showing us today. The things that worked in Western Europe and North America are now working in East Asia. Will they also work someday in Latin America or the Middle East? This eventuality should not be ruled out in advance, all the more so because, as we recall, leadership has already passed from one region to another. Brazil did not invent passenger jets, but it is now producing them and selling them on the highly competitive world market, something that few people expected a few decades ago. Today it is hard to imagine any African country, except South Africa, accomplishing anything similar. However, there is no telling where the road from imitation to innovation or even invention will lead in the future. Nevertheless, questions arise as to why technical progress has occurred

- In certain places, like China and the Arab countries long ago, and then later in Western Europe and its cultural successors in North America, Australia, New Zealand, and Japan.
- And at certain times—at the turn of the first and second millennia in the Arab and Islamic countries (Persia), and in China during the first 1,400 years of our era.
- And yet has never gotten off the ground in certain parts of the globe, especially Africa.

These questions cannot be answered without referring once again to the principle that processes unfold the way they unfold because many

instances, but there is no need to sign up exclusively to either of the two schools. The trick is to know how to make use of both of them.

At this point, drawing everything that is useful from other theories, we might lay out the viewpoint that is represented everywhere in these pages, which stresses the coincidence of the various circumstances that evoke a given phenomenon, or set a given process in motion. Coincidental circumstances of various types are precisely the things that create the critical mass for these phenomena and processes. The differentiation of these types of conditions and circumstances is of the utmost importance. That is because other theories, in a naturally theoretical way, always simplify and usually concentrate on homogeneous circumstances. As a result, they have a tendency to lose sight of cultural specifics and to ignore a great many unique conditions and one-time factors.

Recently, some authors have been placing particularly strong emphasis on the desirability of moving away from the excessively simplified homogeneity of models of economic growth. Dani Rodrik writes metaphorically of the need to let a thousand models of growth bloom,[2] like flowers in a lush garden. There is a need to search out the most varied methods leading to output growth and improvements in living standards, to combating poverty and enhancing prosperity, and to support these methods. This is a philosophy to which everyone should be able to subscribe.

Our mantra—that things happen the way they happen because many things happen at the same time—can be understood differently, and more fully, after all these considerations. In real economic mechanisms, an outcome is seldom caused by a single causal factor that precedes it. Even if we identify such a factor, it is clear that it acts in concrete surroundings. There are other factors, as well, but we attribute a causal role to only some of them. They could not play such a role if not for the simultaneous existence of other circumstances. It is the combination of them that brings about the movement, and not a single incident.

The difficulty is to define this combination adequately and to identify its constituent parts. It is also necessary to grasp the nature of the combinations that may connect them. "May," because these parts can occur either in mutual combinations or autonomously, independent of each other.

Whenever possible, it is necessary to weigh them up and quantify them. This will require the creation of formalized mathematical models.

There is no doubt that such models can be constructed, defining the variables, estimating their parameters, and weighting them. This will have to be left for some other occasion. I have no doubt that there are scholars who will eagerly take up the task.

———————

Somewhat like new economic history or new institutionalism, coincidence theory comes strongly into contact with other disciplines and uses their analyses and syntheses. The interdisciplinary approach greatly enriches the field of observation, bringing new values to both analysis and synthesis, and to both the descriptive and the normative approaches. True, this may blur the picture for the untutored eye, but it means that those who peer intently will not only see more, but also see more clearly. Without historical analysis, it is impossible to capture the significance of cultural factors for development. Without psychological analysis, it is impossible to say anything sensible about changes in the nature of expectations on the part of economic actors. Without management studies—a young discipline spun off from economics only recently—it is impossible to study the international differentiation in capital and labor productivity. Without venturing into innovative future studies, there is no way to apply economic theory in a creative way to the active shaping of the future.

Comparative economics is an essential methodological component in the coincidence theory of development. It is possible to produce a logical demonstration that there is no *differentia specifica* among economies and firms, phenomena and processes, or categories and institutions, without comparing them to others. Only then, through comparison and contrast, and against this background, can we see how things stand. Those who do not compare do not understand. Comparison is an exceptionally valuable research instrument, because it allows us to pick out the critical elements, the presence of which can determine the existence of a phenomenon or process, from among the whole gamut of conditions for growth and development. In such a methodological perspective, we note with surprising frequency that a practical problem can be solved by placing in motion only a single additional factor that is critical to the entirety of the coincidental circumstances.

This is connected with another essential characteristic of our theory, which is the capacity for orientation in a specific, multidimensional space. These dimensions are concrete historical, geographical, cultural, institutional, political, social, and thematic realities. We may well have stated that a tremendous amount depends on culture, yet culture itself is always located in more than a single dimension. That is why almost every issue must be properly approached, identified, and located at a particular point in this multidimensional space. Then it becomes impossible to fall into the silly notion that, for instance, overcoming inflation requires only the appropriate damping down of the money supply (according to one-dimensional monetary theory, this phenomenon has to do with nothing but money), or that all you have to do to improve the competitiveness of companies is to privatize them as quickly as possible, and the market will do the rest (according to neoclassical orthodoxy, this is sufficient without regard to institutional characteristics).

Finally, there is one more important thing that might not even be worth mentioning, were it not for the fact that other theories muddle it up. In theory, and especially in practice, it is necessary to make a precise distinction between the ends and the means of economic policy. This distinction is easier when speaking about growth and development. When speaking more broadly about economic policy as such, there are cases when means and ends are confused or even identified with each other. One such evident mistake is the neoliberal insistence, without regard for social costs, on balanced budgets (or at least the lowest possible budget deficits) or low inflation as the ends of economic policy, when they are only instruments of that policy. A similar error is the populist treatment of the expansion of certain budgetary transfers as an end in itself, when it is only a means of policy. Uncounted mistakes of this kind have been made throughout history, in various economic systems. It is worth remembering that even classical capitalism treated the maximization of profit as the end, or goal, of production. Yet that microeconomic end did not suffice to ensure harmonious development, which must be the overriding aim of economic policy.

We may observe that applying the rule of distinguishing ends from means is very difficult. Some theories of development even treat this problem as partially unsolvable. Axiologies, or theories of value, differ, and the values, and therefore the ends derived from them, can also differ. This applies as well to the values that guide development policy. If we assume that the end is happiness, then broad-based, balanced socioeconomic development is surely only a means to this end. However, if we take development as the end, or goal, then output growth is without doubt a fundamental method of attaining it. Yet if we take growth as the goal, then increased productivity must be seen, in turn, as a means to the end. Productivity growth must be a goal for state industrial policy or the management of a company operating in a specific market. The trick is to weigh up the interrelations, especially in the short run and the long run, and to strike the appropriate harmony in economic policy and business management. One person's end is another person's means. What looks like a means in one time frame may look like an end in another. A pragmatic solution to the highly complex problems of choice that arise must therefore be not only a function of logic based on the scientific identification of the indicators of development, but also a derivative of social preferences, which cannot be determined without a well-organized public discourse. It is an illusion to believe that centralized authorities can give the right answers to these questions on their own, but no less delusional is the conviction that the ordinary interactions that take place on the market, and the signals coming from there, can provide the answer.

The characteristic approach of the coincidence theory of development is profoundly heterodox. We might say that it is anti-orthodox, since, as opposed to the single-mindedness that dominates orthodox economics, it emphasizes the role of various kinds of growth factors. There are many drawers in the cabinet containing these factors, from natural conditions (climate and resources) through the cultural and institutional, the social and political, and the technical and technological to the strictly financial and economic.

The coincidence theory seeks these conditions in time and space, that is, in different physical and historical locations, because we understand by now that apparently similar factors act differently, or have acted differently, at different places and times. This approach facilitates the search for circumstances similar to those that apply to the economic problem under consideration. We must solve the problem in the here and now, but the inspiration for the solution can be found in the there and then. This is the opposite of the typical neoliberal "one size fits all" approach. No, it doesn't fit, but ours might, as long as we can match the right interpretation or policy to the right problem.

To sum up, the eight main constituent characteristics of the coincidence theory of development are

1. The rejection of dogmatism as an intellectual straitjacket that is overly restrictive of the search for answers to specific questions.

2. Refusal to submit blindly to any ideology or political line, while searching instead for the objective truth without regard to conventional wisdom or consensus.

3. The discouraging of holistic attempts at creating a universalistic theory of economic growth, by focusing on the specific characteristics of phenomena and processes integral to macroeconomic reproduction.

4. An interdisciplinary approach that enriches economic thinking with solutions from other disciplines, especially history, future studies, geography, law, sociology, psychology, management, and network studies.

5. The broad application of comparative methods of economic analysis.

6. Movement through a multidimensional space consisting of specific historical, geographical, cultural, institutional, political, social, and thematic realities.

7. Distinguishing the ends of action from the means.

8. Instrumental elasticity open to a multidirectional search for adequate means fitting a specific situation

The last of these characteristics requires commentary. Above all, we should stress the necessity of the pragmatic approach as an absolutely overriding trait of the coincidence theory of development. This explains the need for an approach that not only is interdisciplinary, as should be clear to everyone by now (which hardly means that it is easy to understand and apply), but also cuts across various theories. As long as the interpretations or remedies proposed by those theories do not contradict each other—for example, by suggesting that the interest rate be raised and cut at the same time and in the same place, or that external trade be both liberalized and brought under protectionist measures— then they should be combined, even if their dogmatic adherents oppose doing so. It is perfectly possible to borrow various elements from supply-side economics and combine them with appropriate elements of demand theory from the Neo-Keynesian school. Note that we were able to do this in Poland while carrying out the Strategy for Poland, but not during the cooling off of the economy in the subsequent years, which was based on monetarist patterns. Others can do this sort of thing even better, if for no other reason than that they have been doing it longer, as in China, Malaysia, Chile, and recently Brazil.

I might add here that when I was looking for a development strategy best suited to the postsocialist Polish realities of the 1990s, I naturally drew sustenance from the universally correct laws of neoclassical and Neo-Keynesian economics—but I was also inspired by practical experiences from places that were quite distant, even if they were close at hand in terms of time. On the one hand, it was very useful to turn to the negative experiences of the attempt to implement the structural reforms and stabilization policies of the Washington Consensus in Latin America. On the other, there was a great deal to learn from the positive experiences of the rapidly growing economies of Southeast Asia, especially about the role of the state in building the institutions of a market economy and steering industrial and trade policy.

Pragmatism, then, is needed on a grand scale—as little ideology and as much pragmatism as possible. I could even be so bold as to define it as "the new pragmatism," because it must rest on a new approach derived from the analytical and theoretical approaches presented here. It is also new in that it takes account in a comprehensive way of the new, changed economic conditions emerging as a result of globalization. The coincidence theory of development, on the one hand, as soon as it is fully worked out, and the approach to specific kinds of development challenges, on the other, will combine to create an excellent leverage point for pragmatic action to solve a variety of problems. The new pragmatism is therefore the discourse that accompanies the theory. Yet it is more than this. It is the essence of a method of development strategy and economic policy.

Another logical consequence of this way of thinking is the need for a new approach to state interventionism. This cannot consist of interference in production processes, but should instead be confined to the intelligent manipulation of the conditions of production, once they have been identified. Therefore, I do not list the new interventionism as a separate characteristic. It cuts across and depends on the eight features listed earlier.

Concern for macroeconomic equilibrium, a relatively balanced budget, low inflation, and a stable currency is no longer enough. Nor is concern for social capital and the state of the infrastructure (including the natural environment) . The state must get involved in the subtle regulation of the activity of economic entities in order to moderate the conflicts that inevitably spring up between them and, best of all, to create institutional frameworks that prevent such conflicts. The new pragmatism therefore requires a new interventionism that has different ends and means from the Keynesian interventionism born after the Great Depression of 1929–1933.

The new pragmatism is no respecter of ideological taboos, nor is it afraid of political incorrectness. When policy was too mindful of such taboos, statism and populism interfered with the justified microeconomic rationalism of privatization. When policy was too respectful of neoliberalism, the ideologically motivated shouting about "small government" led to the removal of some social transfers from the budget, and this had a deleterious effect on the quality of the social capital necessary for balanced development. When policy bows to nationalistic calls for "economic patriotism," the door to antigrowth protectionism is flung open again. The new pragmatism refuses to be caught up in sterile debates about the superiority of one color over another, as long as the cat catches mice. There is no lack of mice to catch, in the form of both large and completely minor problems clamoring for solutions.

These problems are plentiful today. It is easy for economists to quarrel, because there are so many of them. They usually see the greatest number of problems in their own backyards. There is a tendency to underestimate the accomplishments of one's own country and to overestimate the difficulties there, while at the same time overestimating the achievements of others and underestimating their problems. After all, the problems are completely different in Chad and Norway, Canada and Egypt, or Eritrea and Portugal. The barriers to growth are different in Hungary and Georgia, and it's all about one thing in France and something completely different in the United States. When people fail to notice this, they sometimes ship expert advisers off to the wrong countries. If the post office delivered as many letters to the wrong addresses, it would be a scandal.

It is politicians and businesses guided by self-interest rather than theory who send advisers to other countries. Some of these interests straddle the dividing line between organized finance and organized crime. There were Western emissaries in the early 1990s who could not tell Budapest from Bucharest or Latvia from Lithuania, but they knew which side their bread was buttered on. Even today, some of them mix up the Balkans and the Baltic, the Persians and the Arabs, or India and China with Indochina.

To be serious, we should be pragmatic and concretely precise. The only point of piling up the intellectual complications is to be able to strip as many of them away later as possible, leaving a sensible proposal. Coincidence theory cannot be comprehended and interpreted through facile simplifications. We have to keep using different instruments to examine different situations. When we go back for another look at what's apparently the same thing, we sometimes see something different. When we measure again with the same yardstick, we sometimes end up with a different answer. Different subjects, different dimensions, and different answers are preferable to the same old advice.

Highly nationalized Czechoslovakia and highly developed Britain needed completely different approaches to privatization. Privatizing a bank in Bulgaria, where they were 100 percent state owned, was a different proposition from privatization in Peru, with its mixed economy. Both cultural and natural conditions make industrialization dissimilar in Mauritania and Nicaragua.

Running a budget deficit to invest more in technological progress is one thing, and spending the same deficit on importing military hardware is another. You should react differently when a drought leads to lower crop yields that diminish the supply of foodstuffs and cause a blip in the consumer price index, and when an equal rise results from the fact that wages are rising faster than productivity. What works for the sophisticated securities exchanges of highly developed capitalist economies will not work, for institutional reasons, in emerging markets. It's one thing to liberalize access to your domestic markets when your partners on the global scene are doing the same and another when some of them are starting to feel the protectionist itch. Instead of the measures it forced on Indonesia in the late 1990s, the International Monetary Fund should have noted that the budget was balanced, and so it was not government spending that was causing tension in the balance of payments. Sometimes overlooking even a single factor in the blend is enough to make the proposed therapy ineffective. Sometimes the treatment is right but it's the wrong patient. Pragmatists do better at avoiding such slip-ups than doctrinaire practitioners.

The instruments available in economic policy should be used selectively and sparingly. This banal observation extends to the management of economic processes at all levels, but above all at the national level, where decisions affect the economy of the whole country. Yet caution must also be exercised at lower and higher levels. The lower levels are regional and local government, and the higher levels include integrative organizations on the regional transnational level, and increasingly on the level of the world as a whole. An appropriate institutional setup is needed for the world economy. In its global dimension, the new pragmatism requires new institutionalization that is up to the challenges of development. These solutions must meet urgent practical needs, rather than embodying a haphazard selection from the obsolete armory of compromises that the bureaucrats from the old international organizations hammered out in times gone by.

The flexible application of economic instruments to resolve specific problems is all the more important because we have fewer and fewer such instruments at present. Of problems there is no end. The ongoing liberalization of economic relations, the mutual opening of national economies to penetration through increased levels of trade and investment, the decentralization of the state, the explosion of the private sector and the shrinking of the public sector—all of these, by and large, are desirable structural changes. In the long run, they should encourage growth and development, although not to the same degree. Some of them stimulate output growth, but not necessarily (or automatically) development. The quantitative growth in production resulting from these changes can also lead to increases in already high levels of income inequality, or harm the natural environment.

One economist takes heart from the relatively smaller number of instruments at the disposal of economic policy (the government can cause less harm through its ham-fisted intervention), while another worries that there are too few of them (the government could fix more things if only it had the instruments). The pragmatic approach says that the contents of the policy toolbox are not fixed for all time. Some instruments need to be discarded and others invented. The question is not whether there are too many or too few of them, but whether they are right for the job. On the one hand, we have basically repudiated direct state involvement in production processes or price administration. On the other, in order to carry out infrastructure projects or provide certain services (hospitals or prisons), we are increasingly resorting to the new instrument of the public-private partnership. Such partnerships are the best examples of pragmatism, because they help unravel problems without wasting time haggling pointlessly (as still happens in some places) over whether a certain good should be manufactured or a service delivered by the public or the private sector, by government or business. We need to lock some instruments away in the attic, and put others in place on the firing line.

In every case involving barriers to and conditions for economic growth, the pragmatic approach requires the examination of the concrete conditions under which action must be taken. Knowing that the key lies in the appropriate combination of factors making up the whole blend, we should try to furnish whatever elements are missing. Sometimes we are missing a few, but at other times we only need a single one to achieve critical mass.

The circumstances that interest us come together in different ways. As befits a market economy, they usually come together autonomously and spontaneously. If we left them that way, we would be looking at the kind of chaos that is sometimes best for development. However, there are other cases in which chaos turns into confusion that hampers the expansion of the economy by knocking it out of balance or blocking the emergence of circumstances without which the desired chain of causes and effects cannot be set in motion. Then it is necessary to make selective interventions in the construction of a blend that helps to bring about or activate a factor that will not appear on its own.

———————

From a theoretical point of view, there is an optimal system of institutional solutions and macroeconomic policy parameters that I define as "the golden sequence." It depends on an arrangement of growth rates in basic macroeconomic categories so that the conditions for future economic growth are created at the same time that there is a tangible improvement in the degree of satisfaction of social needs. There are eight basic, interconnected categories:

1. Investment.
2. Exports.
3. Gross domestic product.
4. Consumption from personal income (known as individual consumption).
5. Labor productivity.
6. State budgetary revenues.
7. Consumption financed from public funds (known as collective consumption).
8. Budgetary expenditure.

The "golden sequence" is made up of the rates of growth in these categories, arranged in order from the first to the last on the list above. Thus it is investment that grows fastest, followed by exports (and the imports that they finance), all the way down to collective consumption and state expenditures. They all grow over periods of years, but at different rates. Economic macroproportions thus change, but in the case of the "golden sequence" this is subordinated to overarching social interests and in accordance with the imperative for long-term balanced development.

The "golden sequence" indicates an improvement in economic effectiveness, which is expressed through an increase in labor productivity and the standard of living. This in turn is reflected in increased consumption and the financing by the state budget of investment in social capital. It also indicates the creation of structural foundations for future economic growth, and this is expressed in a growth in investment and the penetration of external markets through the expansion of exports. Such an arrangement additionally contributes to an improvement in the operating conditions for enterprises as a result of the limitation of the scope of fiscalism, which is also tied to a reduction in the scale of budgetary redistribution and a more pro-development profile for the structure of public expenditures.

The "golden sequence" is a rare phenomenon in real development processes. Approaching this arrangement of macroeconomic parameters only happens for short periods, especially in boom times, in countries characterized by a large degree of social cohesion and a high level of political culture. Above all, this exists in the Nordic countries. Some of the symptoms can also be seen in other countries attempting to implement a social market economy. A unique case, against this background, is that of Poland, which followed the "golden sequence" for several years during the time of the Strategy for Poland, after significant changes to the macroeconomic parameters and the pro-development institutional transformation of 1994. This was followed by a marked increase in the rate of output growth, and the years 1995–1997 were characterized by dynamic and balanced growth along the "golden sequence" trajectory. Investment (19.3 percent) and exports (17.0 percent) grew faster than GDP (6.8 percent on the average). Individual consumption and labor productivity were slower, at 6.7 and 4.7 percent, respectively. Budgetary revenue (2.6 percent) and collective consumption (2.7 percent) grew at similar rates, and budgetary expenditures (1.2 percent) grew most slowly of all.

The rate of growth of individual consumption is higher than that of labor productivity when new jobs are being created. In such times, the growth in per capita consumption financed by personal income is in part a function of the growth in expenditures resulting from the growth in household income owing to increased employment, when a jobless person finds a way to make some money or a previously unemployed member of the household gets a job. In other circumstances, the principle of a rate of growth of labor productivity higher than that of individual consumption holds true. While employment grew a total of 6.4 percent during the four-year period from 1994 to 1997 inclusively, it grew at an annual average of 2.3 percent from 1995 to 1997. This fully explains why the growth rate in consumption financed by the family from its net disposable income (in both money and kind) was higher than that of labor productivity. In the case of a relatively stable level of employment, things would be the other way around.

Development always requires a sort of catalyst to reach the critical mass necessary to set the desired processes in motion. Despite the claims of simplistic theories, there is no single "magic stone"—a concept more fit for alchemists than economists. If there is any sort of "magic," it lies in the method of thinking about combinations of various factors that are specific to various conditions.

Depending on the specific circumstances, any one of a number of instruments from among the many in our cabinet could turn out to be the one that gives us just the right blend of factors to galvanize the process. This will be different for economies at different stages. Luck might sometimes seem to play a role, but history does not acknowledge luck's part in such important matters. In the end, it comes down to a deliberate choice.

In one case, it might be a change to the nature of an institution that acts as the catalyst in the development process, stimulating or simply unblocking the potential of human, natural, or real resources. On another occasion, it might be macroeconomic policy. Perhaps it is a matter of putting a great amount of effort into forming desirable cultural characteristics, such as entrepreneurship or reduced aversion to risk. Management training can turn out to make the difference, or increased funding for research and development, or government-supported housing. Perhaps the right blend can be reached through cutting tax rates or interest rates. Import tariffs may need to be reduced at the same time that monetary instruments are used to block the depreciation of the national currency. The situation is similar in medicine, where different cases require different treatments—not radically different but not identical either. Many people still do not realize that in economics the diagnoses are far more varied and the therapy is much more complicated.

The new pragmatism has no aversion at all to enlightened interventionism. Once upon a time there was a concept of dividing what was God's from what was Caesar's. This was done for the sake of peace (it could have been done for development too, but those were times of stagnation). The same kind of thinking lies behind today's acceptance that interventionism is inevitable. Render unto the market what is the market's, and what is public render unto—well, that's the question. Render unto whom? Today intervention limited to the national scale is not enough. It's insufficient in the epoch of advanced globalization, because there's also a need to intervene in the functioning of transnational structures and the global players in the economic game.

Despite its checkered past, state interventionism must be applied in the future—precisely because the past was so checkered. There were times when it succeeded. The institution of enlightened interventionism will pass the test if it is used pragmatically rather than ideologically, for economic rather than political reasons. This interventionism must be founded on a sound understanding of the coincidence theory of development. The social mechanism of macroeconomic reproduction can be interfered with only very selectively and very accurately. *Selectively* means choosing only those elements from the blend of circumstances that stimulate development that need intervention so that they can function on their own. *Accurately* means in a very precise way, not blindly, so as to avoid uncontrolled negative side effects. In practice, every one of the instruments at our disposal can produce various results, including undesirable ones. The art of applying national, regional, and global instruments of intervention consists in doing so in a way that brings about the desired phenomena and processes while avoiding the undesired ones. When this is impossible, the undesired effects must at least be kept to a minimum.

The new pragmatism is forward oriented and progressive. Although the past has much to contribute, the basic orientation is toward the future. The question of who could take the lead in the historical development process was once decided by the ability to make the transformation from technological progress driven by sometimes serendipitous discoveries to progress resulting from systematic research on a solid theoretical basis. In the future, which has already begun, it is not those who live in the recent or remote past (some of the postsocialist countries, or the Arab countries, respectively) who will take the lead, but those who are able to shape a present informed by a vision of the future. Having a vision firmly grounded in science is the way to make this possible.

In real social and economic mechanisms, it is the interaction between the past and the future that decides the present. Until now the past has tugged at our heels and defined what goes on around us, but from now on it is a realistic vision of the future that will increasingly define the world we live in. This is already true to a large degree, more in Finland than in Poland and more in North America than in South America, and above all because of cultural considerations.

The heart of the matter is the way that visions and ambitious plans for the future (if we dream of development, our plans should always be ambitious) influence the shape of the institutions being formed, and the policy being carried out right now. Sometimes, this is banal: Interest rates should be based on business expectations about the future, rather than on the extrapolation of past trends. Sometimes it is profound: University-level education should be based on estimated future needs, rather than on even the best traditions.

I remember traveling to Bucharest in 1997 to give a talk on development at a conference organized by the *International Herald Tribune* for international (or "foreign," as they were still called) investors. Emil Constantinescu, the president of Romania, honored the gathering with his presence, and encouraged those present to consider investing in his country for reasons including its highly advantageous location: It lay right at the intersection of the Silk Road and the Amber Trail. Someone might be able to develop this theme into a tourist attraction, and tourism is a great development opportunity for certain regions that have no other basis for competitiveness. Now, however, is the time to build competitiveness by shifting the present into the future, rather than by getting excited about the past. If it were otherwise, then the Middle East would be more attractive to investors than North America.

———————

The fruits borne by the change of paradigm I am proposing—going over from concentrating on causes to concentrating on the coincidence of factors, and building individual development strategies and policies through the intelligent manipulation of coincidence as far as possible—should be material as well as intellectual. The new paradigm opens up new fields for observation and analysis, but, above all, it defines a new approach to economic practice in an epoch of globalization and the growing role of soft factors of development, especially knowledge or, more broadly, culture.

There are some similarities between the economy and technology: You have to invest in things that will pay off later. Sometimes you have to wait. As you wait, you have to keep fighting to prove that you were right. James Watt already had a working steam engine before Adam Smith published the *Wealth of Nations*, but he had to wait a long time to see the start of the industrial revolution that transformed the world. Watt didn't just sit back and wait, because you never accomplish anything that way.

There should be a pro-growth lobby to oppose stagnation and push for development, but interest groups of this kind are still a rarity. The neoliberals and their ideological bedfellows lobby for growth, of course, but only when it is fragmentary growth that benefits narrow groups at the cost of the general public. In countries with an advanced economic culture, strong institutions, and thriving democracies, associations of domestic investors, manufacturers, and financiers sometimes lobby for growth. In most cases, however, they lobby for their own interests even while trying to pass them off as macroeconomic and for the general good. Foreign lobbyists often talk about investment, which is fundamental to growth, but they are always interested in the value of their own holdings rather than the level of output and prosperity in the countries they invest in. The government bureaucracy can never act as a lobby, because what it always wants is to be left in peace, and this means opposing change, which is what development is about.

A lobby is an imperative. It cannot be limited to any single social-occupational group, even enlightened capitalists (who have taken to calling themselves "employers," even in countries with high unemployment, or an employment deficit), although they must be a part of any such lobby. It must be a heterogeneous group, cutting across traditional social structures and hierarchies, and including practitioners and theorists, politicians and academics, economists and lawyers, and more of those who are young and looking toward the future than of those who are older and burdened by the past. By definition, they must be more interested in economic growth and development than the growth of their own wealth. The latter may result from the former, but priorities must be upheld.

A pro-development lobby is worth working toward. The trouble is that its potential members often work on different sides of the wall. The effort that could go into shared conceptions and a concerted push for growth is squandered on political disputes and infighting. The media, which in an ideal world would be a forum for such a lobby, prefer to cover the squabbling. Time is passing, while the economy moves forward too slowly and burning questions go unaddressed.

Understandably, expectations that the coincidence theory of development could be used in a nonideological, nonpolitical way are naive. This could only happen in a future purged of great intellectual discourses (which would be a great loss) and of ideological and political conflicts (which would not be as much of a loss). These things will be around for the foreseeable future, even if we can wish for a future that is more peaceful and less bloody than the past. History teaches that theories are interpreted in various ways, often far removed from the intentions of their creators. Facts matter, but so do the words used to talk about them. Correct ideas deserve to be defended as ardently as mistaken ones are promulgated. None of this will change in the future, because there is no way of eliminating economic and political conflicts. The approach I am advocating might assuage such conflicts and promote international solutions, but it is incapable of eliminating them. That can happen only in a utopia, and we will continue to see fresh versions of utopia, such as the "new economy" based on the Internet, not to mention twenty-first-century Latin American socialism or the versions of a conflict-free world served up by one pope after another. We can pray for such things, but we should not expect them.

It is also clear that, as a method for economically, socially, and ecologically balanced long-term development, the new pragmatism will not be spared ideological and political temptations. More than a few schools of economic thought set out to shape reality in the direction of output growth but ended up being intellectually abused and politically instrumentalized for purposes often the opposite of what their originators intended. The advantage of the new pragmatism is that it is so capacious that it can work for balanced development under a broad diversity of conditions while at the same time resisting attempts to use it in ways we have expressly distanced ourselves from throughout the present work.

Neoliberal fundamentalism and the populist reaction to it could both claim to be rational, practical approaches. This may be so, but theirs is not a general rationalism or a pragmatism that takes into account the conditions in a globalized economy based to an increasing degree on knowledge. Instead, theirs is a group rationality (a Marxist would call it class rationality) for the sake of particular interests. These are characteristics that do not fit into the categories at the foundation of the coincidence theory of development and the new pragmatism.

Clearly, the twenty-first century and those to follow will not bring peace to humanity or spare us ideological and political conflicts. Some old conflicts and problems have faded into the past, although we remember them, whereas others only doze and wait before reawakening and coming back on stage—even such despicable ones as racism and cultural intolerance. Others still are yet to be born.

These conflicts will have no less of an impact on the future than the aspiration toward general rationality that characterizes true science and the progressive part of the world community. We would wish for that future to be as quiet and merry as the countryside once was, but it will not be. We must keep moving on, because we cannot stand still, and can only hope that we do not lose the way.

There are no miracles, but sometimes there are lucky coincidences.

CHAPTER TEN

The Uncertain Future

*What Awaits Us in the Near and Distant Future
and What Say We Have in It*

The greatest of human migrations lies before us—
the voyage into the future.

WE ARE CREATING this world for ourselves, more in its cultural and economic dimensions than in the natural one. The more we know and understand, the more we will be able to create. Almost everyone thinks about the future, often with misgivings and apprehension. People are afraid of what they do not understand.

We have a choice: a future of understanding or a future of misunderstandings. The latter would be, or will be, exceptionally costly for development. What we need to understand, however, is that most of the misunderstandings result not from the "clash of civilizations," but from the clash of ignorances. The clock is running. Tomorrow will be today, and today will be yesterday.

If you listen to what some people in Iran think about the United States and how Americans feel about Iran, it's hard to be an optimist, but it's also hard not to see that a great deal could be achieved through a sensible, substantive dialogue without preconceptions. Yet they're not exactly falling over each other to get started. Leaving aside such extreme cases as Israel and Palestine, where there will not be any sensible conflict resolution without strong and rigorous pressure from outside, the mutual perceptions of the United States and Venezuela or Great Britain and Zimbabwe would make an objective outside observer's hair stand on end. The degree of neighborly misunderstanding between Poland and Belarus or Russia and Georgia is enormous. It's not much better if you listen to what they say about Russia in Washington and New York, or about the United States in Moscow and St. Petersburg. It's all somewhat reminiscent of Japan's relations with the rest of the world on the eve of the Meiji reform era, except that now it's twenty-four hours a day, at the speed of light, and accessible to almost anyone who cares listen in.

Today such syndromes cannot be overcome by sending in the British troops or the American frigates, as was done when China was forced to buy opium or Japan was made to open up to external commercial contacts. It takes intellectual effort and political action on both sides. Just as unrestrained economic expansion helped break down the isolation of the Far East, so economic interaction can accomplish a great deal today, in reference not only to investment and trade, but also to research and education. The best example in recent years is the significant improvement in bilateral relations and mutual understanding between China and the United States, not to mention the encouraging example of the integration of the postsocialist countries into the mainstream of the global economy and world culture. The role of intellectuals and of entrepreneurs, who make direct business contacts without government interference, in creating an atmosphere of mutual understanding, tolerance, and respect should be emphasized.

In searching for answers to questions about the sources and mechanisms of development, we have worried on more than one occasion about the way that practice has been led astray by ignorance, greed, or emotions, even when there was scholarly understanding of the issues. Time has been wasted. More precisely, it has been wasted from the point of view of the interests of the majority and the general population, because there were some people who were making very good money out of the situation and who continue to do so.

At times, however, the fact that something that is "theoretically possible" fails to happen is proof of the superiority of practice over theory. This is true in physics at least. This is why we are still waiting for the end of the world, even though it could theoretically happen right now. If it happened now, it would result not from ignorance, but from the accumulation of immense quantities of knowledge and the success of yet another great human endeavor. At the beginning of 2008, the power was switched on at one of the most complicated devices in history (and also one of the most expensive, since it cost over $8 billion). This machine is relatively more complicated, for us, than the Antikythera Mechanism was for the ancient Greeks. We are talking about the Large Hadron Collider (LHC), the particle accelerator located in a 27-kilometer tunnel outside Geneva, which may help us to answer some questions about the structure of the universe, or universes. The fascinating thing is that the results of these experiments and theoretical studies might even show that the Big Bang never happened and that we will have to rewrite the few things we think we know in our brief chapter on the history of the world.

Some people think that this "Geneva Mechanism," built by the consortium known as CERN (Conseil Européen pour la Recherche Nucléaire), could create a small black hole. Is this merely additional mumbo-jumbo, but from the world of physics? Perhaps so, although even *Scientific American* cautioned about such a possibility in the summer of 1999. It is "theoretically possible"; the probability is close to zero—yet it is still greater than zero. Back then the context was a smaller collider, the RHIC (Relativistic Heavy Ion Collider) at Brookhaven National Laboratory. MIT physicist Frank Wilczek (the grandson of immigrants from Poland) explained that the threat was not really a black hole, but rather something known as strangelets. Some physicists (physicists too have opposing views, although for different reasons than economists) contend that neutron stars could be turned into this hypothetical form of matter. This would mean that something referred to as an ice-nine transition could occur, although there is still no proof. If this occurred on earth, then the entire planet could be converted to strange matter and the world we know would be gone. The administrators at the RHIC convened a special committee of scholars that ruled out such an eventuality and calmed the overexcited media speculation about the danger. Frank Wilczek went on to win the Nobel Prize in 2004, although not for his work on strangelets. He is yet another Nobel Prize laureate who understands things that no one else, or hardly anyone else, understands.

Theoretically possible though it may be, then, the end of the world will not take place, or at least not this year. Numerous new mistakes in economics, business strategy, and public policy are also theoretically possible. What is worse, they are inevitable for reasons with which we are familiar by this point. Nevertheless, we must go on looking for economic theories that are just as accurate as, and more comprehensible than, the intricacies of particle physics, and for practical applications of the factors that encourage progress. Despite the great volume of accumulated knowledge and the wealth of historical experience, the problems keep coming. This is one more paradox of development.

Some believe that there is no point writing about the future if you cannot terrify your readers. This is not so, but it is also wrong to lull people into complacency. The one thing that is certain about the future is that it is uncertain.

The signs are increasing that the world will be unable to escape the spiral into which it has fallen without a crisis and new revolutions. It would be better to escape this spiral through evolution and universal development that is politically, culturally, socially, ecologically, economically, and financially balanced, but it is both too late and too early for that. What kind of crisis will it be? We do not know. When will it happen? We do not know, but it is only a question of time, because there are more and more contradictions, and they are becoming increasingly antagonistic. Overcoming them will take movements on an almost tectonic scale: profound structural changes, the adoption of a new value system, and a different balance of power and allotment of roles on the world stage.

Leo Tolstoy (1828–1910) liked to say that all his troubles came from the fact that his imagination was slightly more vivid than that of other people. He was not the only one to have such a problem. Yet it is a good problem to have, because it is an inspiration for critical thinking. People who have such good problems should not feel bad, and societies and nations should wish for more such problems. The thing to watch out for is a superfluity of really painful problems. The only way to deal with them is to stretch our imaginations about ways to shape our future.

Knowledge about the future and after-the-fact speculation in the alternate-history mode should be of help. Intelligently asking "What if?" can be highly creative. We know how and why certain processes turned out the way they did, and we know that many of them could have ended otherwise. It is a certainty that this will continue to be the case in the future. The future is partially determined, and there is nothing for us to do except wait for it and take advantage of the best parts. Much else, however, depends on our actions. These in turn depend on what we have really learned from the past, both remote and recent. To have any sort of perspective, we must understand history.

It is hard to evaluate hypothetical scenarios for the future because it is hard to compare them, not only because of the enormous differences of subjects, scope, depth, and time frame, but also because of the impossibility of subjecting them to the falsification test. We cannot disprove something that has not happened yet. By the time anything turns out to be true or false, it belongs to the past.

All sorts of analytical and prognostic centers sketch out scenarios for the future, even such serious ones as the CIA and its affiliates. They go so far as to publish such scenarios, which might seem surprising for an intelligence agency—not that we believe they publish all of them. The most intriguing scenarios are surely stamped "Top Secret." Yet even the ones available on the Internet can serve as inspiration.[1] We should add that these published scenarios are intended to influence the future, because they shape expectations that have an impact on the behavior of various entities. The purpose of some forecasts is to prevent things from happening, rather than to encourage them. Other predictions aim at making it so. In the short term, this also applies to the financial analysts in the service of speculative capital, who do their part in manipulating the markets. On the most important issues, the time frame is very long, so that we will have to wait thirty or seventy years for the archives to be opened and the "Top Secret" material declassified. To avoid being shocked, we can try to have somewhat more vivid imaginations than other people.

Nevertheless, we will get things wrong. Only afterward do we learn how well we did, in big matters and small. In 1975, *Business Week* wrote about the coming paperless office. Since that time, paper consumption in the United States has tripled. We were supposed to be flying hypersonically by now, but in fact we are flying as slow, or as fast, as we did in the 1960s, or even slower, since the supersonic service of Concorde flights has been shut down altogether (in addition, the airline meals are worse, which no one could have predicted). In the mid-twentieth century, we were promised electricity so cheap, thanks to nuclear power, that it wouldn't pay to meter it. We were supposed to be living on other planets, to eliminate pollution on earth, and to vanquish poverty and hunger. Now we are only aiming to halve these scourges by 2015. Artificial substances were supposed to solve the problem of resource scarcity. In a depiction of the year 2000 from my schooldays, I learned that there would be moving sidewalks everywhere, but the kids are still trudging up the hill to my old school building today. The science columns in the newspapers promised that robots would cook our dinner and brew our tea. Today many economists, and others as well, are just as enthusiastic about the "new economy." No "new economy" will solve our age-old problems.

These blunders can have serious consequences for planning. To hold them to a minimum, we need to ask as many questions as possible. Sometimes a good question is more informative than a partial answer. Questions, as opposed to answers, don't insist. They hint. They give us a nudge about which direction we should be looking in.

We should be looking all around the horizon. It can be divided into a dozen compass points: the Twelve Great Issues for the Future. These are the things we should keep examining all the time as we try to peer into the future and ask, "What next?" What happens next will depend on things that happen at the same time. Many events will take us by surprise, but much else should be less than totally unexpected, because it depends on conscious human actions. These twelve compass points are

1. The rate and limits of economic growth.
2. The evolution of values and their cultural implications for development processes.
3. The institutionalization of globalization versus the growing chaos and lack of coordination.
4. Regional integration and the way it meshes with globalization.
5. The position and role of nongovernmental organizations.
6. The natural environment and competition over dwindling natural resources.
7. Demographic processes and human migration.
8. Poverty, misery, and social inequality.
9. The knowledge-based economy and society.
10. Scientific and technical progress.
11. The evolution of networks and its economic consequences.
12. Conflicts and security, war and peace.

—————

The first compass point, the issue of the rate and limits of economic growth, could just as well conclude our reflections as open them. If we understand the rate of growth as referring to gross domestic product, then we should be under no illusions that its average rate over the last ten or twenty years cannot be sustained in the long run, over a period of, let us say, fifty or 100 years. As surprising as this may seem to some, the facts are plain—the world must slow down. However, "the world" does not mean everyone, or everywhere, or to the same degree.

The poor countries should speed up the development of their economies in terms of the quantitative growth of output and the accompanying, interrelated structural changes. This is desirable and, as we know well, possible. However, for it to happen, these countries must base their development strategies on the correct theoretical premises, as derived from the coincidence theory of development. They must also define long-term national development strategies, based on the new pragmatism, that mesh with the continuation of globalization. There should be no illusions that they will repeat the success of Europe—first Western, and then Eastern—or North America. At best, they can significantly reduce the development gap with these most highly developed regions of the world.

The postsocialist countries of East Central Europe should set out to maintain a rate of GDP growth twice as fast as that of the richer part of Europe through the coming generation, in the temporal perspective of 2035–2040. They have a realistic chance of doing so. This will completely eliminate the gap in income levels and reduce the gap in living standards in a tangible, visible way. However, it will not happen by itself. Transformation and integration with highly developed countries, and especially the European Union, will be a great help, but the effort will not succeed without the appropriate national development strategies.

Among the post-Soviet republics, the ones endowed with rich reserves of energy resources are in a particularly good situation, on the condition that they prove capable of taking full advantage of favorable combinations of circumstances—the bounty of nature, continuing high energy prices, and the transformation to a market economy. So far, they have not done particularly well, because they have relied too much on the easy pickings that they owe not to wisdom, organization, and hard work, but to the generosity of Mother Earth.

The remaining former Soviet Republics will be in a difficult situation, and the distance separating them from the more developed parts of Europe and Asia will probably increase over the next few decades. Ukraine, of great strategic importance in post–Cold War cooperation and confrontation, finds itself in a special predicament. Its fate depends on whether it manages to become integrated with the European Union over the next decade or two, draws closer to Russia, or splits up. The most favorable variant is integration with the European Union, on the condition that it is not used as an instrument for weakening Russia, but rather as a geopolitical meeting ground for mutually advantageous cooperation. Belarus will soon face the same problems as Ukraine. The whole sweep of the postsocialist countries, however, from Mongolia and Tajikistan to Kosovo and Macedonia, will develop faster than the world average.

Over time, China will slow down. Warnings issued repeatedly since the mid-1990s notwithstanding, that time has not yet come. We may assume that efforts to provoke the disintegration of China, on which the West may be relying, will not succeed. It should also be assumed that the Chinese authorities will continue, as they have for the last thirty years, to combine enlightened policies, aimed at structural reform and the construction of market institutions, with development. If they also decentralize the administration in a systematic, gradual way while slowly making the political system more democratic, the Middle Kingdom may succeed in continuing to develop more rapidly than the average for the rest of the world for another decade or two, although not as rapidly as in recent years. Taiwan may be joined to the motherland in a similar time frame, especially because the differences in levels of development with the southern regions of the mainland will disappear, which will add further to Chinese power.

Africa must speed up. This region in particular must develop faster than the rich countries in order first to keep the chasm from growing, and then to begin narrowing it. All it will take—no small matter!—is for Africa to continue to grow faster than the rest of the world. The continent grew at 5.8 percent per year, as opposed to the world average of 5.0 percent, from 2005 to 2008. These are overall figures, which equate to about 2 percent less per capita in Africa. We should add at once that the essential conditions for progress include a significant limitation of the rate of population increase and a fight to maintain the long-term growth in GDP per capita in the range from 2.5 to 3.5 percent. This is daunting but not impossible.

The rich countries, and above all the United States, must moderate their economic growth. It is doubtful that they would do so voluntarily, and so they will have to be compelled. This will happen either gently and gradually, with growth being curbed as a result of rising prices and increasingly difficult access to certain raw materials, or radically and suddenly, as a result of An Even Grander Crisis. Such a crisis could be set off in various ways. The classical way would involve a chain reaction of negative adaptations of the real sphere to the structurally imbalanced financial sphere. In that case, however, we would be looking not so much at a slowing of the rate of growth as at a deep collapse—no one knows how deep—of the level of output, and a fall in its absolute level, before growth resumes at a slower rate than previously.

To some degree, this moderation of growth must be connected with a deliberate resignation from some part of financial accumulation. Instead of investing capital domestically or in other parts of the global economy as direct or portfolio investment, it should be transferred to the poorest countries in Africa, South and Central Asia, Latin America, and the Caribbean. The sooner the transfer of 0.7 percent of GDP from the rich to the poor stops being a slogan for international bureaucrats and becomes an instrument in a planetary development strategy, the better. It will also be better for the wealthier countries, which will then be under less migratory pressure from the wretched of the earth, because there will be fewer of the wretched.

There is justification for warnings about the enormous risk that aid, in the form of a small fraction of the income of the wealthy countries being transferred to poor countries, could be wasted. Nevertheless, it is an undeniable fact that this aid, no matter how modest, leads to improvements. It is true that the greatest accomplishments in fighting poverty and breaking out of stagnation have been made by the countries of Southeast Asia, which have benefited to a minimum degree from external transfers while making strong progress thanks to trade expansion and their own entrepreneurship. Africa has not done this.[2] The truth is, however, that about one percentage point of the economic growth in the poorest countries during the last generation is attributable to direct foreign aid.[3] Without it, the misery would be worse. If there had been more aid, the present level of output would be higher. What about the fact that there is a need for special institutional and political measures to prevent these aid funds from going astray? We already know this. We must take action, and development economics tells us what action to take. By the same token, we know that aid money should not be assigned to arms imports—another country's exports— or returned through other channels to the "givers."

Therefore maintaining the world growth rate at a real level oscillating around an annual average of about 2 percent for the next several decades would be a great success. It would be an even greater success if we managed to maintain that average with the rate being higher for the poor countries and, as a consequence, lower for the rich countries. Is this possible? It all depends on what happens in the other points of the compass in the horizon that surrounds us.

Let us now look at the second of these compass points, the question of the evolution of values and their cultural implications for development processes. This is an important matter. To date, humanity has produced splendid civilizations. Some were being born while others were on the way out. Sometimes they vanished on their own, in a natural way; at other times they were helped off the stage thanks to the aggressiveness of their successors. Today we hardly face any "end of history," because no civilization—excepting Soviet socialism, or, as some prefer, communism—is being relegated to the scrap heap of history. There will still be great conflicts, although they will not necessarily be "clashes of civilizations." No new civilization will be born during the next few generations. However, the planetary ethnic-cultural melting pot will evolve through the interpenetration and blending of diverse values.

In some sense, of course, there already is a new civilization. How lucky we are to have a global economy, worldwide finances and electronic money, transoceanic jets and mass international tourism, the Internet, and satellite television thanks to which more than a billion people could watch the landing on the moon or the World Cup finals. We have wireless communications and mass culture, and people can buy more copies of a book—the latest volume in the Harry Potter series—in a single day than all the libraries in the world held 500 years ago.

The pursuit of material values dominates this civilization to a large degree, although spiritual values are beginning to count for more, just as they did in antiquity. The shifting of social priorities on this level could have enormous consequences for the way we do business, and the issues of economic dynamics. Stagnation and output growth, development and the lack of development may be seen in new ways. Individuals can develop "horizontally," thanks to spiritual growth and a deeper experience of nature and culture, as well as "vertically," by climbing the career ladder and amassing possessions. Something analogous could occur in models of social development, with more attention paid to the verb "to be" than the verb "to have," and the latter seen not merely in terms of "the more, the better." Of course, in order to be, you must first have at least the minimum, but there is no reason that the growth of the state of possession need necessarily outstrip experiential development. Such changes would look different in poor countries, because the priority there must be an increase in output to ensure at least a chance of satisfying the elementary material needs. A reevaluation of consumer preferences may take place. Poor countries will not uncritically replicate the patterns of rich countries, not only because objective physical barriers may rule this out in some places, but also because doing so will not seem worthwhile. The world is not going to become one big North America, but it is not going to become one big Bhutan either. It will be somewhere in the middle, between these two extremes.

In the new civilization, working together, coexisting, and tolerance exist side by side with conflicts, marginalization, and ruthlessness. This civilization is developing to an increasing degree through cooperation and coordinated action, and to a decreasing degree through dominating others. It is more a civilization of a multiplayer game than of people struggling against each other. Games must always have rules, but struggles often have none. This aspect of things will be increasingly important in terms of the cultural conditioning of development processes. An increasing level of global regulations will be negotiated among the players in the game, rather than being imposed on the weaker by the stronger. There will be a fundamental value shift in the direction of the democratization of economic processes. Economic growth itself will contribute to this, because there is a positive correlation between the level of development and the advancement of democracy.

The world is not democratic. Moreover, even if democracy triumphed in all countries—something we are closer to than ever before—the sum of national democracies would not equal planetary democracy. Recent events at the United Nations illustrate how far we are from such democracy. A record number of countries, 182, voted in the General Assembly in 2005 to condemn the U.S. trade embargo against Cuba. Voting against were only the United States, its faithful ally Israel, and two small island states from the Pacific, Palau and the Marshall Islands. The United States took no notice, because it is not some world quasi-democracy that should decide what is right, but rather the caprices of a group of old-school politicians. This will change, and it will happen before our eyes.

Until these qualitative changes occur, countries can focus on the bottom line when voting. Interesting research by two Harvard economists proves that the American government corrupts some countries. They found that fifteen countries that served as rotating members of the U.N. security council received 59 percent more foreign aid when they held voting rights in that body than before or after.[4] This enhanced level of aid is maintained during the two years they have seats on the council, after which, as soon as they give up their seats, the level of foreign aid drops back to its previous level. This is called democracy in action.

A system of feedback relationships and mutual influences between regulation and democratization in a multipolar world is now taking shape. It will be more supportive of increased output and the sensible division of this output than the world that was divided between two opposing camps in the second half of the twentieth century, or the world that was dominated by a single superpower at the beginning of the twenty-first century.

A multipolar world must find a way to govern itself. Perhaps it would be better to say that it must find a way to steer processes with global consequences that must be supervised but that exceed the supervisory capacity of even the most powerful individual country. This is not a call for a world government, which would be the height of naïveté. However, there is a need for institutionally simple solutions, namely, coordinated action and international agreement. Institutions of this type, coordinating policy on a global scale in order to control events, will become increasingly common. In the coming decades, they will have more impact than technological change on the way things are run.

More of a sense of justice in distribution and less action from a position of economic strength, less ignorance about the cultures of other countries and deeper mutual understanding, more formally equal rights and genuine respect for partners—these are the cultural traits that have a chance to develop in the coming decades. It is worth doing everything possible, because this is the way to have fewer conflicts, disputes, and wars, and more cooperation and development.

However, we should not have illusions or encourage them in others. The twenty-first century will be a time of cultural confrontations, but not the same as in previous epochs. This is the result of the overlapping of various phenomena and processes in science, technology, economics, and politics. Technology will force the desired cultural changes no less than politics, and the economy will benefit. Politics will interfere, spoiling things at times but encouraging development at other times. If we manage the great feat of coming up with knowledge-based politics, then policy will be more of a catalyst than a roadblock to balanced growth.

In evaluating growth and development, we will rely less and less on the inadequate category of gross domestic product, which still dominates the thinking of economists and the actions of politicians. It will be replaced by new concepts and measures. We can hope that one of them will be the ISI—the Integrated Success Index, which I proposed earlier. It offers an all-around reflection of the complexity of socioeconomic progress. This is not so much a matter of changing the way we measure the scale and rate of economic change as of doing it the right way.

The third compass point on our horizon is the increasing need for policy on a planetary scale, capable of dealing creatively with the interdependence characteristic of the contemporary economy. We face a fairly stark choice: the institutionalization of globalization versus increasing chaos and lack of coordination. The birth of a new institutional order will be painful, and it will be slow. The pain will come because the powerful feel pain when they give up any of their power. They are used to applying the principle of *divide et impera*, divide and rule, in the old style, but new times have arrived. There will have to be a somewhat different way of ruling, and it will be impossible to keep creating divisions in as unjust a way as heretofore. The birth will be slow because it will not be designed from the top down, although that is theoretically possible. Instead, it will have to come about through a laborious learning process. It has never proved possible to design an institutional order intelligently, and in advance, on the basis of the canonical knowledge in management, economics, sociology, and psychology, and then to put it into practice. Things like this have always emerged, instead, from the interplay of interests. Academic knowledge plays, at best, the role of prompter in the theater of real life.

The desire to rebuild American hegemony into a position of permanent world leadership is a symptom of naïveté underlain with nostalgia, and megalomania, but most of all it is a waste of time. The exceptional American position as a superpower that could largely dictate and condition the rules of the game, including the economic game, has been short-lived: less than two decades, from the disintegration of the U.S.S.R. to the end of the current decade. In his book *Second Chance*, Zbigniew Brzezinski, a great spokesman for the American cause, tried to make the case that if it had not been for mistakes by the last three presidents, and especially those that George W. Bush committed in his two terms, the United States could have held on to its dominant position. Perhaps—but only on the condition that it had been inclined to share power, just a little, with the rest of the world. Unfortunately, it was not so inclined and, even worse, it is still not so inclined. Brzezinski believed that there continued to be a chance for a *Pax Americana*. All it would take, he said, was for Americans to elect the right president in 2008, and for that president, in turn, to choose the right values and the right way of running world affairs. He added that there would be no third chance. Brzezinski was wrong; despite what some people wished for, there was not even a second chance. The position of the United States in the twenty-first century may change, as did that of Spain in the seventeenth. Spain too was a world superpower, but its industry did not have to manufacture much because the country could buy everything it needed with the gold and silver that it brought home from its colonies—up to a point. Its situation was very similar to the unique position of the United States and the dollar. Is this a good thing, or bad?

It depends. The world might be better without American leadership, or it might be worse. We got along fine without Spain, because England emerged as the powerhouse. What will happen this time around? Not so long ago at all, the United States had the kind of exceptional influence over world affairs that no one ever had before. It could have chosen to set up better institutions, more pro-development and conciliatory, to run the world. However, it ran things too much with an eye to its own particular interests. Furthermore, it ran things badly—shortsightedly, without vision, more as a mentor than as a partner. Along the way, it wasted its second and final chance to dictate a planetary institutional order, and left us in chaos. This was not a good thing.

It also, however, represents a chance, and it's always a good thing to be in with a chance. It is not a second chance for American world leadership, but rather a chance to arrange things in a sensible new way.

There must be an order based on peaceful coexistence rather than wars either hot or cold, and on an imperative for the efficient functioning and development of a globalized economy.

New institutions, functioning in suitable organizational frames, must therefore ensure a relatively stable financial basis for macroeconomic reproduction. A great deal can be accomplished by curbing the unfettered movement of speculative capital, which must be brought under more stringent control than at present. Taxation is an instrument that must be used to cool the excesses.

The fact that the United States, Britain, and perhaps some other countries oppose such measures, and will continue to do so for a long time, disqualifies them as sensible world leaders, just as much as their occupation of Iraq or uninvited efforts to impose the neoliberal system.

An effort should also be made to limit the number of national currencies and support efforts to create more common currency zones, not only as instruments of regional integration, but also as stepping-stones to a world currency, which just might come into being someday.

The World Trade Organization has a large role to play. It is the best of the big international economic organizations, in part because it is the least undemocratic. The institution of free trade can do more than almost anything else to maintain a high growth rate for the poor countries, without harming the rich ones. However, it must be authentically free, without nontariff barriers or subsidies that are either overt or concealed in the manipulation of currency rates.

In creating a new institutional order that is up to the challenge of the world economy and the contemporary multicultural civilization, it will be necessary to delegate successive prerogatives of authority to international structures, regional integration groups, and international governmental and nongovernmental organizations. Before they can play their role, international organizations, and especially the United Nations and the Bretton Woods system, will have to go thorough democratization. They were designed for the institutional architecture of the divided world that emerged after World War II, and later modified to only a modest degree after the end of the Cold War.

Among the markets emerging from both the former Third World and the postsocialist transformation, the position of the poorer countries must be shored up significantly. China, India, Russia, and perhaps Brazil and Indonesia are capable of looking after themselves and getting what they deserve. Others need to be helped, rather than hindered, in making their voices heard. Stronger regional structures can play a role in this.

The twenty-first century will belong not only to China, but also to the European Union. This epochal experiment in bringing together nations that fought and slaughtered each other more often than they cooperated over the last 2,000 years will be carefully monitored by others. If it succeeds, and there are many signs that it will, then other countries on other continents will have no choice but to draw their own conclusions. In wishing for the success of the European Union, we are wishing for the success of the world. The still-evolving institutional order of the European Union—which unfortunately has many flaws, especially where it permits excessive bureaucracy and the wasting of public money—can serve as a reference point for others. Local specifics notwithstanding, certain of the market economy institutions that function in a supranational context have universal import.

The new world institutional order must be meshed with the growth tendencies and component parts of the global economy, on the one hand, and evolving cultural values, on the other. It cannot follow a Western model, but must take account of the countries of the East and the aims that guide them. From this perspective, it is impossible to overstate the role of China in working out a new institutional model. It would be advisable for the European Union, the United States, and Japan, which together still account for half of world output, to consult China on all important issues, including those that do not affect it directly. Then there will be a better chance that China, when it is on top, will also consult others on matters of mutual interest.

We must be on our guard against the danger of losing our way on the road leading to the new institutional system that the globalized economy needs so badly. The United Nations was not up to the job, the United States got in over its head, and we have no idea where current trends are leading. Are we heading toward a new order or new chaos? If it is order, then the globalization process should accelerate, and it may show its human face. If chaos, it will be a drag on globalization and in turn on the development of the world economy as a whole. A new, progressive order will require the curbing of the economic and political ambitions of some of the players on the world stage so that things can be better for everyone. A new, regressive chaos will limit the possibilities for the entire world community while allowing the few to make money. This is the alternative.

_____

The fourth compass point on our horizon poses the question of the future interaction of globalization and the processes of regional integration. The integration of neighboring countries into regional groupings will continue. These groupings will take different forms and will be held together by bonds of varying strength. Their organizational structures and institutions will also differ. There is already a spectrum of such organizations. ASEAN, the Association of Southeast Asian Nations, has ten members.[5] Since Georgia quit, eleven post-Soviet republics, with Russia in the leading role, of course, make up the CIS, the Commonwealth of Independent States.[6] Mercosur, the *Mercado Común del Sur*,[7] is the common market of South America. NAFTA[8] groups countries in North America. The SADC is the Southern African Development Community.[9] There are fifteen members of ECOWAS, the Economic Community of West African States.[10] The South Asian Association for Regional Cooperation, or SAARC,[11] is grouped around India, Pakistan, and Bangladesh. Six countries from the Gulf area belong to the Gulf Cooperation Council.[12] Then there is the European Union,[13] the most advanced of all these players. Over 100 members of these various groupings account for almost three fourths of world output. More new groups will arise. Once an economic and currency union forms around China, Japan, and a unified Korea, we will have almost the entire world economy grouped in ten regional structures.

There are many fascinating sidelights here, because some of these regions overlap and there are ambiguities as to their scope and function. We do not know where we will have complementary, integrated neighboring structures, and where there will be rivalry. One group that bears watching is the Shanghai Cooperation Organization (SCO), founded in 2001. Still a loose structure, its significance should evolve in the coming years and crystallize in the coming decades. Its members include China, Russia, and the four post-Soviet Central Asian republics of Kazakhstan, Kyrgyzstan, Uzbekistan, and Tajikistan. India, Mongolia, Afghanistan, and Iran, which aspires to full membership, have observer status. The member countries have a billion and a half people, and the number rises to almost 2.9 billion if we throw in the observers— over 40 percent of humanity. The integration of the core of the CIS with the core of the SAARC, with China as the linchpin, could completely change the shape of the global economy. Many politicians see this as a tactic for outmaneuvering the West, and that is exactly what it is, and what it will continue to be.

There are three ways of looking at the evolving relationship between regional integration and globalization. Regional integration processes can be seen as

- An antidote to globalization.
- An alternative to globalization.
- A vehicle for further globalization.

The first variant sees globalization as a process that is irrational from the practical point of view. Local integration is a refuge against domination by a single planetary order that is not fully logical in economic terms. Globalization is inevitable, but encouraging and accelerating the formation of regional structures can cushion its impact.

The second variant, which sees regional integration as an alternative to globalization, is sharper. Instead of a strongly interdependent but weakly regulated world economy, we would have many organizations of countries that are close to each other both geographically and culturally. Globalization should be blocked and regionalization favored because it is more rational. The question is, "Would the sum of all this local rationality make the world as a whole less irrational?"

The third variant would treat regional integration processes as relatively safe and convenient vehicles for moving globalization on to the next, higher level of institutional maturity. This view sees regional structures as safe because they could aim for pragmatic local solutions without sacrificing the economies of scale, while at the same time avoiding the conflicts of interest inherent in the more differentiated world market. They also offer a chance to try out institutional innovations on a more limited scale, rather than on the world as a whole. Once more, the value of the European Union can be seen. If something does not work in the E.U., then it probably won't work on the scale of the entire planet. What works in Europe might, but need not necessarily, work for the world. The convenient part is that the actors in the next, intensified stages in world integration would not be some 200 national economies that are highly differentiated in cultural, economic, and institutional terms, but rather a dozen or so regional bodies. They would do the hard work of compensating for gross inequalities, coordinating levels of production, and bridging cultural gaps.

This third option, treating regionalization as a safe, convenient vehicle for sensible globalization, embodies the attributes of the coincidence theory and the new pragmatism. It would make globalization more sensible by limiting the scope for irrationality. We would speak in terms of "trans-regional" rather than "trans-national." Fewer entities would have to coordinate their decisions and actions, and this should be more effective. Isn't there a saying that correlates the number of cooks and the quality of the broth?

———————

The fifth compass point on our horizon involves the potential for modifying the process of globalization, especially where it bears on the environmental, social, and cultural aspects of development, through the growing role of nongovernmental organizations. There are huge numbers of them, and that is both the problem and the hope. Some of them will never amount to anything, but others have already made a positive impact. The way some people bristle at the very name of these organizations shows that the NGOs interfere in matters that governments, global corporations, and international organizations would prefer to keep to themselves.

Organizations like Greenpeace, Oxfam, Jubilee 2000, Amnesty International, Transparency International, Médecins sans Frontières, and Reporters Without Borders play no small role in matters connected with fair development and authentic concern for its human consequences. These movements and structures will have a growing role in shaping the new planetary institutional order, where political, cultural, and technical considerations interpenetrate and overlap.

Oxfam and Jubilee 2000 lobbied effectively for the rich countries to write off the debts of the poorest countries. Transparency International and Reporters Without Borders keep the spotlight on corruption. Amnesty International and Médecins sans Frontières monitor the humanitarian treatment of political refugees. All of these efforts benefit from the synergy of technical, political, and cultural progress and transformation. The all-seeing eye of Big Brother, which Orwell warned us about, can also work for the good. Today almost everything can be seen everywhere, not just on the metropolitan streets or in the government offices of the democratic countries, but also in Chechnya, Darfur, Abu Ghraib, or Guantanamo. This is true both figuratively and literally, because still and video images find their way so effortlessly onto the Internet. NGOs help in this, and they can quickly bring issues to the world's attention.

The role of NGOs, especially the global ones, extends beyond lobbying and pressure tactics. It also includes worthy actions that governments and profit-oriented businesses aren't interested in, or aren't good at. The whole twenty-first century will inevitably throw up challenges for social organizations, mostly in education and culture, but also in environmental protection, social welfare, and health, especially preventive medicine. Nongovernmental economics experts will have their hands full. They will advise the governments of countries with emerging and less-developed markets about how to foster enterprise, and they will do so more frequently and better than the orthodox advisers from the Bretton Woods organization or the lavishly paid emissaries of the governments of countries that are concerned primarily with protecting their own interests.

Amidst this plethora of issues, NGOs must refuse to allow themselves to be burdened with tasks that remain the responsibility of states and markets. It is not the job of NGOs, from the local to the international level, to do government bureaucrats' jobs for them, or to meet their responsibilities to the public. Nor can NGOs allow business to shift onto them the tasks that should be paid for by the taxes on business, such as aid for the socially marginalized or excluded. NGOs cannot agree to be left to clean up after business, especially in areas like environmental protection.

Public finance, the fundamental intermediary institution between the state and the market, must continue to play its essential role and must do so to a greater degree than ever on an international or even global scale. NGOs are not surrogates for either commercial or governmental and intergovernmental entities; instead, they stand alongside these entities as the third pillar of the contemporary economy. This is how they must be seen in the global perspective.

As a result, humanity will start to resemble a worldwide civic society, in a positive-feedback relationship with the advancing global market economy and the slowly emerging global democracy. Coordinating these megatrends is the greatest task facing the human race over the next few centuries. In our lifetimes, we are already in a position to make our own contribution.

———————

The sixth compass point on our horizon will feature intense competition for dwindling natural resources in the shadow of intensified debates about the state of the natural environment. The two are intertwined, and the public awareness of the feedback loop connecting these issues will grow. Every so often, a grand assessment on the order of the memorable Millennium Ecosystem Assessment[14] will appear. There will be recurring questions about the limits of growth and the admissible level of material- and energy-intensiveness in the world economy.[15] Questions will also recur about the limits of environmental contamination. From this perspective, things do not look rosy. Supplying the materials necessary for life is a far different proposition when we compare the needs of almost 7 billion people, and 9 billion in the near future, with the situation not so very long ago when there were 2 or 3 billion of us. It is becoming increasingly difficult to dispose of everything left over from the production and consumption of these goods. GDP will mean less and less, while the world quotient of trash becomes increasingly significant.

Against this background, the twenty-first century and the centuries that follow will be kaleidoscopic. At times, the emphasis will fall on the need to reduce the use of raw materials, and at others on new technology and the implementation of advances in materials engineering. We will concentrate on extracting resources from previously inaccessible places, before shifting the focus to the value of "being" rather than "having." Conciliation and negotiation will characterize certain periods, whereas conflicts and wars will dominate others. This continuously shifting kaleidoscope will help to undermine some barriers and bring others down entirely—but not all barriers. In certain fields, things can only get worse.

In the face of all this, change will be multidirectional, as it has been in the past. Half a century ago, declining supplies, on the one hand, and the explosion of new capabilities being developed by the chemical industry, on the other, led to a situation in which, boosted by clothing retailers, artificial materials took the place of natural fabrics. Women rushed to buy nylon stockings, and men proudly showed off their permanent-press shirts. People looked longingly at rayon coats, naugahyde jackets, and polyester suits (not to mention leisure suits and pants suits) that they wouldn't be caught dead in today. It turned out that breakthroughs in agribusiness (encouraged by clothing retailers) made it possible for vastly greater numbers of people to go back to natural fabrics, so that we now proudly wear silk, linen, cotton, and wool varieties from cashmere and Shetland to the mohair associated in the Polish imagination with the knit berets popular among the dowdy audience of talk-and-prayer radio.

There will be more and more well-dressed people and quality merchandise. Not so long ago, in parts of the world that are developed today, people went around barefoot, in their one raggedy shirt. Today hundreds of millions of people, perhaps even a billion of them in the least-developed countries, do not have a change of clothes. They are the ones who should be complaining to anyone in earshot that they don't have a thing to wear. Yet we are more likely to hear this lament in the developed countries, even from people whose dresser drawers and closets are so jam-packed that they don't know what's in them. We can be sure that our grandchildren will be singing the same tune, and so will their grandchildren in the twenty-second century.

The changes dictated by fashion or the appearance of new gadgets are insignificant compared with the adjustments we will have to make as our stocks of raw materials decline and become exhausted. The trouble is that we know that these resources exist, and we know that they are limited, but we don't actually know how much is left.

Skirmishing goes on all the time, especially over small, local issues. The greater crises and conflicts in the Middle East, the oil-bearing regions of Africa, or on the continental shelf off the south and east shores of Asia ostensibly concern other principles, but when we take a good, hard look, we see that it's about access to oil. There's a danger that it could run out. The traditional fields of conflict will be joined by new ones, like the Arctic. Energy resources, especially petroleum, are only a single factor in the supply of the world economy, no matter how crucial. Other resources that are nonrenewable within the historical time frame will also start running out, and the geological time frame is not an option.

Petroleum is problem number one for the twenty-first century in resource and energy terms. The hope is that, on the one hand, the supply is greater and the stocks will last longer than the scare stories in the media, and, on the other hand, that we will be able to make increasing use of alternate sources. If we keep consuming at the present rate of about 80 million barrels a day, according to one frequently cited forecast, the supply will run out around 2040. Recent estimates by British Petroleum speak of a forty-year supply. As far as natural gas goes, we are said to have sixty years left. Is this the way it will be? If not, then why not? Where is the truth, where is the ignorance, where are the mistakes, and where are the lies?

Things are far more complicated than they seem to be at first glance. Here too we are dealing with the deliberate manipulation of public opinion, including garden-variety falsehoods packaged as expert analysis. The aim is to scare politicians and the general public badly enough that they will swallow the bitter pill of rising prices for gasoline, natural gas, and electricity without complaining too much. In addition, everything can be blamed on the Chinese, for adding to demand and driving up the prices of raw materials by buying more. Of course, anyone with any sense at all sees that the Chinese are not the perpetrators, but simply additional victims, because they are paying as much as everybody else.

The game will go on. The great transnational corporations from the energy complex will continue to corrupt politicians, while the politicians try to manipulate the corporations. The corporations and the politicians join in frightening consumers through the subservient media. All it takes is a pseudo-expert analysis or a political declaration, and the journalists do the rest, quickly and obediently.

As always, politicians may try to mete out justice, but they also find themselves on the receiving end. Sometimes they're wrong, and their heads roll. Along with national security and the financial markets, energy policy is the biggest minefield for politicians, on both the domestic and the global scale. Some have made great careers for themselves, but a lot of blood has also been shed, and this will continue to be the case in the future.

An important consulting firm in the energy sector recently forecast that 2005 would mark the peak of petroleum extraction; every sign on earth and in the heavens indicates that this was utter nonsense. However, there are people who will commission such nonsense, because "prognoses" of this kind are perfect for inducing fever on the market and driving up prices. At the other end of the scale, you can find experts who claim that the peak will never arrive, so that even if we cannot go on increasing output and consumption forever, we can at least hold them at the present level. These too are lies.

Everything that we know indicates that "peak oil," the point after which the level of extraction can only fall, will come in this century. Serious experts disagree over exactly when this will happen. They mention the years from 2020 to 2040 most frequently, and that's practically tomorrow. On the basis of a range of expert forecasts, an authoritative report prepared by the U.S. General Accounting Office, which many regard as independent, suggests that the peak could come in any given year from now until 2040.[16]

The uncertainty about when comes from the fact that it is hard to judge the reliability of the data. Experts in the field warn that the private interests of producers and distributors may distort estimates about the size of present and future oil fields. There are political pressures, and knowledge in the field of petroleum geology is far from complete. Unexpectedly, or so it would appear, optimistic news keeps coming in about vast new deposits in Ghana or Brazil. There are many unknowns. The way that political disturbances can complicate things is seen these days in Iraq, the Niger Delta, Sudan, and thereabouts. Tomorrow problems will crop up in some other place.

It is plain to us that the question of when extraction begins to fall will depend on the coincidence of several circumstances. We also know what those circumstances will be—namely, the physical and political accessibility of the deposits and the profitability of extraction, the speed of the transformation to technology that is not based on petroleum and its byproducts, and the scope of technical progress in energy conservation. We should not be under any illusions that the progress we have been making in this field is sufficient. Over the last third of a century, the consumption of petroleum per unit of income generated in the wealthy G-7 countries has fallen by 55 percent, but the level of income on a world scale is rising so rapidly that we would have to reduce energy consumption per unit by a factor of more than 10 in order to solve the problem, and that is not going to happen.

The specter of a cataclysm is haunting the world—the specter of the catastrophic warming of the earth. This would seem to be the only thing that could force a political reevaluation and greater interest in the search for alternative ways of meeting humanity's energy needs. This is the point at which the wealthy United States learns from still-poor Brazil that it is possible to rely on biofuels on a mass scale. Things look rosy because the sources of biofuel—corn, sugar cane, and rapeseed—are renewable. Once again, our good old Polish beetroots come into play, the very ones that helped end the abomination of slavery. However, soaring demand for these crops means instant price pressure on the food products made from them. Once again, things can flip around, and the price of food could outstrip that of fuel in the future; it wouldn't be the first time. This is the way things happen, because many things happen at the same time.

Less promising are specific, ecologically friendly sources of energy, such as water, wind, and solar, which is potentially the largest. By the nature of things, the supply of these apparently cheap sources of energy does not occur where the greatest demand is. Mountain rivers, tides, and strong winds seldom appear next to large urban agglomerations or industrial centers. The cloudless blue sky and strong sunshine are attributes of the Mediterranean, the Caribbean, or the Bay of Bengal, where the need for heat energy is vestigial in comparison to the Baltic, Hudson Bay, or the Sea of Japan. To find widespread use, energy from these sources would have to be cheap enough to offset the cost of transport. Wind energy shows that radical progress is possible. The cost of generating a kilowatt-hour fell from $2.00 in 1970 to between $0.05 and $0.08 at present. By comparison, energy from burning coal costs between $0.02 and $0.04. We're close to the point where wind power will pay, as long as the wind blows.

This will happen in California before it happens in the Central European lowlands. There, and everywhere, we are going to have to grit our teeth and go nuclear. This is the only option that can be available everywhere on a mass scale, with fuel resources assured for several more centuries. It will be safe enough. For a long time now, it has been cheap and clean, and safer than the dirty energy from burning coal and some kinds of petroleum.

The only drawback to atomic energy is the irrational fear of it. This is a perfect example of dissonance among technology, culture, and politics. It will take decades to solve this problem. Is humanity ready? Absolutely not! Smoothing over this supercrisis in the energy sector will require many long years of complex, costly, and difficult work on numerous fronts. Afterward, people will look back and wonder what all the fuss was about.

Afterward? When will that be? Before the crisis of peak oil, which we will not be prepared for, or after? Peak oil will mean a gigantic recession caused by structural shortages of energy. This will lead not only to a drastic regression in the human standard of living, but also to wars, because it will escalate far beyond threats and skirmishes. Reasonable anticipation could prevent all this.

If we want humanity to close the stable door before the horse has bolted, we should undertake all possible means, in terms of technology and public education, to neutralize conservative politicians and combat the special interest groups and their media mouthpieces. We have to start now, during the present generation. Peak oil will not come until 2040, or even 2070, but there is much less time to undertake the action that will avert the economic and political shocks.

With the most optimistic assumptions about the adaptive ability of the world economy, and its specific societies and industries, effective adjustment to the anticipated collapse of oil production will take a minimum of twenty years. I think it will take even longer. To be realistic, it will be at least forty years. What about the fact that we were already being warned forty years ago that we were reaching an energy-based limit to growth? Those warnings were not wrong, only the time frame. This time we are not wrong, because the first forty years have passed, and the next forty will pass quickly, and our planetary stocks are being run down the whole time. Moreover, at the end of those eighty years there will be more than three times as many people on earth. Documented reserves in the middle twenty-first century will not be any larger, even counting in the estimates for the Sahara, the Arctic, and the Antarctic.

Sometimes analyses and forecasts extrapolate on the basis of models that are simple, or even too simple. This is a mistake. The American Energy Information Association forecasts in its annual report, which assumes the continuation of present policy, that world energy use will grow by 57 percent to 2030. If the price of petroleum remains stable, then coal will again become the most widely used source of energy. The results for environmental warming and the condition of the atmosphere would be lamentable.

To transform attitudes about the environment and the consumption of resources at this stage in our history, we will need the appropriate economic mechanisms. Although changes in mentality and the social approach to these issues should not be downplayed, we need more than the right intentions.

The subject of the role of the state and public sector, on the one hand, and capital and the private sector, on the other, will keep coming back in new permutations. We are already being told that private business can solve this problem best. Business knows how to pollute the environment and make money while doing so, but the best way to overcome the difficulties is through public-private partnership.

However, little can be accomplished without getting business on board. A clean environment and rational, rather than pillage-based, management of nonrenewable resources must simply be made to pay. It will do so to an ever-increasing degree. Competition in the context of growing ecological consciousness will produce positive results. The newest airliner from the international Boeing Company, the 787, with its beautiful name, Dreamliner, is advertised not as the fastest or most comfortable passenger jet, but the most environmentally friendly, because it pays to advertise it this way. That's the heart of the matter. How can we make it pay? And for whom should it pay? For everyone?

As on the issues of development or the struggle against poverty, neoliberalism will promise much but deliver little. Partly out of fear of regulation and partly in the hope of high profits, it is already making promises. Profits are the most important thing. For things to work out in social terms, there must be action from above, through policy that creates institutions and imposes market regulations that force private capital to behave in an environmentally friendly way, and from below, taking advantage of the eternal love of profits. Once, companies in England were brought under a simple regulation that required them to draw water from rivers downstream from the sites of their factories. This quickly induced them to clean their waste water before discharging it, because otherwise the water would have been contaminated with their own pollutants, slightly diluted, when they drew it from the river. A simple procedure like banning the use of car horns in built-up areas saves us many decibels. Of course, this only works where institutions and culture are strong, so that rules are respected. We also know countries and places where people toss litter out the car window and never take their hand off the horn for long.

It is doubtful that anyone will come up with a better solution than imposing a tariff on those who emit carbon dioxide and other greenhouse gases. This will have to be done internationally, because the instrument must be applied on a global scale. According to the Intergovernmental Panel on Climate Change, the special U.N. expert group, a fee of $20 to $50 per ton of carbon dioxide emissions, levied from 2020 to 2030 on, should bring about a stabilization at the level of 550 parts per million, or p.p.m., which is the measure of gas concentration, by the end of the century. This is regarded as a safe level.

A $50 fee in the United States, the world's largest polluter, would raise the price of gasoline by about 15 percent, and of electricity by about 35 percent. This is not much, considering that other factors have caused much greater price rises, and above all in view of the good it could do. Progress is greater, and more visible, in Europe, but Europe alone cannot save the planet. Even getting the United States to join Europe in the campaign would not be enough, but it would be an essential factor in inducing the largest future polluters, China and India, to sign on. Only when all these powers act together can things start to change for the better.

The IPCC estimates that stabilizing carbon dioxide at 550 p.p.m. would reduce the rate of growth in the average global temperature by 0.1 percent per year. In other words, if we had begun applying this instrument in the twentieth century, then the average temperature of the surface of the earth would have increased by only 89.5 percent of its actual rise—that is, by some 0.66° Celsius (1.19° Fahrenheit), rather than the actual figure of 0.74° C (1.33° F)—plus or minus 18 percent, as the IPCC estimates. Over the long run, such fractions of a degree will have critical significance for the fate of the earth and humanity.

On the subject of global warming, there is not even consensus among reliable, honest experts. If the IPCC experts state that "it is extremely likely" that the rise in the earth's temperature is the result of human activity, there are those who immediately point out that the IPCC did not say "for certain." Perhaps it is simply a weather anomaly or, as other experts suggest, mere transient warming, the sort of thing that happens from time to time, and man is only having an incremental effect on a global phenomenon that arose on its own and will go away on its own.

Perhaps there is something to this view. After all, we are now in a long phase known as the "minor warming period," which followed the "little ice age" that began around the middle of the thirteenth century. That period ended about 1780, when it was possible for the last time to walk on the ice from the eastern shore of Chukotka to the western shore of Alaska. (The land bridge between Asia and America existed until about 30,000 or 40,000 years ago.) Since then, we have been in the minor warming period. It will last until around 2300, or even into the second half of the twenty-fourth century. Then it will get colder again, although it will probably remain warmer than it is now, since the starting point will be warmer, and the temperature will fall until the end of the millennium. In the fourth millennium, in turn, we will enter another minor warming period. A thousand years from now, people may well be talking about a similar problem, except that mankind's theoretical knowledge and practical capacity for influencing the temperature of the earth will be taken for granted by then.

Even if this is the case—if human activity is not responsible for the warming of the earth and all the dire consequences—it is nevertheless correct to reach the practical conclusion that we must do something to cool down the climate. Bringing about this specific public good is one of the most significant and difficult tasks facing humanity in the twenty-first century, and afterward. It is a global problem *sui generis*.

In pragmatic terms, it does not matter what the cause is. The effects are what count, and it is becoming harder and harder to live with them. How much harder we do not know. The problem is even more complex because, regardless of overall warming, the frequency of heat waves in various parts of the world has doubled since 1880. We feel this every summer in an increasing number of places. In the summer of 2007, about a thousand people died because of the extreme heat waves in Central Europe.

There are various definitions of a heat wave. For example, the definition used in the United States is three successive days when the temperature exceeds 90°F (32.2°C). Other countries have definitions based on their own typical weather—or rather, average weather, for who can say what is typical? The World Meteorological Organization defines a heat wave as five successive days when the temperature exceeds the normal maximum temperature by 5°C. The local average for the years 1961–1990 is taken as average, which corresponds to the subjective feelings of many people: things were normal then, but they're not normal now.

Heat waves occur in places where they used to be unknown. I once visited Moscow in May, normally the most pleasant month, except that there was a heat wave and the thermometer stood at 36.7°C (98.1°F), the normal human body temperature, but too hot for Moscow. The heat wave made the news around the world, but the same temperature would have been normal in Djibouti. When I was in Djibouti not long afterward, the thermometer reached 47°C (116.6°F), which was no news at all, but I was drinking five liters of water per day.

The IPCC forecasts an increase in the average temperature by 0.3°C (0.54°F) from 2004 to 2014. This is a concrete indicator, and it is a big jump for a decade. In turn, the forecast for the end of the century envisions a rise in temperature somewhere within a wide range from 1.8° (3.24°F) to 4.0°C (7.2°F). These figures could have quite different effects on the world in 2100, and on policy today. If the temperature rises by only 1.8°C (3.2°F), then it will be a matter of life, rather than death. If the average temperature is as high as 18.5°C (65.3°F)—the record 14.5°C (58.1°F) of 1998 plus 4°C (39.2°F)—then life will be impossible in many places.

In some places, there will be more and more devastating heat waves and droughts, and in others there will be destructive rains and floods. It will be either too hot or too dry. Or there won't be anything, because the shores of the world's oceans will rise. If this is the case, then we must act now, and take a range of steps that the voters will not like. And politicians don't like it when the voters don't like something. It's better to put things off until the next generation than to lose the next election. That's the unfortunate thing about democracy: There's always a next election.

This is what makes it worthwhile to fight for a universal tariff, on a global scale, to stabilize the level of atmospheric carbon dioxide at a safe level. If it is going to be 1.8°C (3.24°F) warmer within three generations without that tariff, then a reduction in the rate of increase in the global average temperature by 0.1 percent a year, as mentioned earlier, would reduce the additional warming to about 1.5°C (2.7°F), which would probably be bearable. However, if it is going to be 4.0°C (7.2°F) warmer, then reducing the increase to 3.0°C (5.4°F) will not save us. We should start sooner, go further, act more radically, and do more.

In the fight for the natural environment, we must achieve an epochal consensus of states, acting in the general interest, and private capital, which cares more about its shareholders than its stakeholders. The hard part is to make it all happen now, on a scale that is international and, at times, thoroughly global.

It might be unfair to characterize private capital as being completely uninterested in the side effects of its actions, especially those with negative social consequences. However, it would also be naïve in the extreme to trust capital to take steps to protect the environment out of its own free will. That would be like leaving the wolves in charge of the sheep. However, you can tame a wolf and, slowly, turn it into an acceptable sheepdog. We could accomplish something similar with private capital, and much more quickly. With the right policy, institutionalization, and culture, there is a chance to harness private capital to the general good in the future. Then the wolf would be sated and the sheep safe.

Spending on the environment and nature resembles spending on armaments and war. It is similar in that the effect on the economy of public (state) appropriations for the military and wars is analogous to that of appropriations for environmental protection. In the short term, a billion yuan for air filters can give the same effect as an identical expenditure on a squadron of new fighter planes. A billion dollars for the utilization of industrial waste sets in motion a chain of effective demand within the American economy that is the same as spending the same billion dollars on another aircraft carrier. A billion rubles spent on cleaning up contaminated rivers in the industrialized European part of Russia yields the same amount of production, employment, and return budget revenue as an identical sum pumped into the military radar tracking system.

In the longer term, apart from the immediate effect of stimulating production and employment through the creation of additional aggregate demand, there are also beneficial structural effects, including scientific-technical progress with all its advantages. It is understandable that this enormous conversion of production requires many years and enormous political determination. The postsocialist countries demonstrated what is possible in this field by converting their armaments sectors to peacetime production over the course of more than a decade. Such conversion requires, above all, a change in the value system and the assurance of world peace by means other than saber rattling.

If only the United States had spent as much on combating the greenhouse effect as it spent on the occupation of Iraq, we could all feel a bit more secure. If other countries shifted resources from arms and the upkeep of their militaries to the purchase of equipment for environmental protection and the employment of qualified specialists, economic performance in those countries and in the countries that supplied environmental equipment would improve, and the climate, in both the literal and figurative sense, would be far more conducive to development.

It should also be more pleasant for capital to make profits on something that can be praised in public, like the Boeing 787, than to go on lying about the benefits of arms production. Then the production of the Dreamliner and other pro-ecological goods and services would be just as profitable as the building of the B-2 Spirit strategic bomber was for Boeing's competitor, Northrop Grumman, or services that consist of sending young soldiers off to die.

All of this is too little. We need a revolution—another tax revolution. Leaving aside the venerable idea of tax breaks for income derived from environmentally friendly production, businesses and households by the turn of the next century will pay less and less on income tax (and even less on property), and more and more on their contribution to energy use and pollution. Countries as a whole, and regional groupings, will pay taxes of this kind into a joint planetary treasury, a global ecological budget into which no one will want to pay but from which everyone will want to benefit. We will have accurate ways of determining, on an ongoing basis, who is performing deleterious activity, and this will be the basis for levying the taxes. Along with changes in public consciousness, this will lead to a comprehensive metamorphosis of the means of production and patterns of consumption, resulting in the desired transformation of the relationship between humankind and Mother Earth.

The appreciation of the seriousness of the situation has been increasing rapidly of late, and not only as a result of active political campaigns organized by groups that are aware of the scale of the threat. Science fiction books and TV programs, and horror and catastrophe films make an impact too and are sometimes more effective than cold scientific arguments at forcing politicians to act. People react to the books and movies that scare them, and politicians react to the fear in the electorate. Apparently, irrational foreboding can sometimes do more than rational arguments. Over the last four years, the number of Americans who see cause for "great concern" has jumped from 28 to 41 percent. Amazingly enough, almost half of registered Republicans, under the influence of neoliberal economics, state that everything is fine with the environment. Only 9 percent of Democrats feel this way, so viewing and reading habits obviously differ. It's a good thing that the Democrats will govern the United States from 2009 to 2017 and, with luck, even longer.

None of this—more effective policies at the national level, better transnational coordination, cultural changes, and, above all, more perfect economic and financial mechanisms and more effective administration—can give us additional resources to a degree that would permit the world as a whole to consume energy and raw materials on the same scale as North America or Western Europe, either in the foreseeable future or at any subsequent point. That would require the resources of two additional earths. In the long term, however, we can imagine progress in the form of conservation and a new technological revolution involving nanotechnology, materials engineering, and biotechnology, that might give us the equivalent of one additional earth. The power of the human intellect is not unlimited, but its limits are distant and still unexplored.

The seventh compass point on our horizon is population. According to the newest U.N. demographic forecasts, in the blink of an eye—in 2050—there will be 9.3 billion of us. Some of us will still be alive then, but we will be in the minority. There will be thirty times as many people as there were a thousand years ago, but it won't be the end of the world. On my first birthday, there were 2.5 billion of us; when I finished writing this book, there were 6.6 billion. When I reach the end of my earthly journey, there will be almost 3 billion more.

There's a lot of meaning in these billions. Multidirectional demographic changes are a big problem for the future. Aside from the constantly rising overall total, the picture also includes

- The extreme differentiation of natural growth.
- The overpopulation of certain regions.
- The aging of the population.
- Great migrations.

Each year, almost 80 million people come into the world—the equivalent of the population of Germany, Turkey, or Egypt. The population increases at different rates in different places. It is rising fastest in sub-Saharan Africa, in the Middle East, and in Southeast Asia; it is somewhat slower in Latin America; and slowest of all in Europe and North America. At present, 80 percent of humanity lives in less-developed countries; at mid-century, it will be 90 percent.

The changes are fundamental. In 1900, three times as many people lived in Europe as in Africa (408 and 133 million, respectively). This will be reversed in 2050, with 1.766 billion in Africa and 628 million in Europe. Another 100 years down the line, the ratio will be nearly 5:1 (2.308 billion and 517 million, respectively), despite the fact that, in the meantime, far more Africans will have moved to Europe than the reverse. The total share of the "Old World" and the "New World" in the world population will fall from 28.5 percent in 1950 (21.7 percent in Europe and 6.8 percent in North America) to 9.4 percent in 2150 (5.3 and 4.1 percent, respectively).

The United Nations forecasts that the human population will hit 7 billion as early as 2013. Then we will have to wait another fourteen years to reach 8 billion. We achieved 6 billion in 1999. There will be 8 billion in 2027. We will reach 9 billion around 2050, depending on the forecast. Some say it will happen in 2046, and others only in 2054, if it makes any difference. Afterward, things will be completely different.

The population should grow only one tenth as rapidly as at present in the second half of the twenty-first century and throughout the twenty-second. There will be stagnation, with growth of only 6 to 7 million per year. According to these prognoses, we will need 150 years to add another billion people. There should be slightly more than 10 billion of us in 2200, and then the number of people will stabilize. Fifteen years ago, the United Nations was predicting stabilization after 2200 at about 11.6 billion, but a few things happened in the meantime. Many more things will happen before then, and many of them will happen at the same time.

The overall rate of population growth is decreasing. This is good news. There are more and more of us, but the world population is growing more slowly. The average annual rate of growth has declined from a very high 2.2 percent in the 1960s to 1.2 percent in 2005. This is excellent, because, at a rate of 2.2 percent, the population would double every thirty-two years. But it is also very bad news, because it will double every fifty-eight years at a rate of 1.2 percent. The earth cannot bear it. It is therefore imperative to lower this rate even more. Furthermore, the reduction must vary significantly from one place to another. This is another unprecedented challenge for the twenty-first and succeeding centuries.

The tendency reversed in that special year, 1989. Until then the absolute annual population growth had been increasing constantly (to 87.7 million). Afterward, it began falling somewhat and has stood at around 77 million since 2007. The U.S. Census Bureau predicts that the absolute rise in global population will hold more or less steady until about 2015, oscillating between 76 and 78 million annually. Then it will decrease systematically, to about 46 million per year at mid-century.

If this average resulted from a regional breakdown that was advantageous in social and economic terms, then we could take heart. However, this is not the case. There are places where the population is increasing terrifyingly quickly, and others where it is beginning to decline in absolute terms. These divergent tendencies are functions of several variables, above all birth rate, infant mortality, and life expectancy. These demographic processes, in turn, are functions of living conditions and expectations of change in the future. They all show enormous disparities. Furthermore, migration must be taken into account. Things will go on in a similar way in the future.

The distressing fact is that the most children are being born in the least-developed countries, where it is hardest to feed, house, and educate them. This is very bad news. It is socially and culturally conditioned. The economic consequences are lamentable. The lack of development shows in low incomes, and shortages of food and basic health care. Some of these children die in infancy and others before their fifth birthday. Those who survive are fated to a miserable existence.

Four of the countries with the highest birth rates—Afghanistan, Somalia, Burundi, and the Democratic Republic of Congo—are also among the ten poorest in the world, with annual per capita incomes below $800 by purchasing power. Somalia and three more of the poorest countries—Mali, Niger, and Angola—are also among the bottom ten in terms of infant mortality. Angola and Sierra Leone have the worst infant mortality rates in the world, at 184.4 and 158.3 deaths per thousand live births, respectively. In Mali and Niger, women give birth to an average of 7.4 children. The figure in Afghanistan is 6.6, and in Yemen it is 6.5. On average, at least one child dies in each of these families. Five of the ten countries with the highest birth rates are, as a direct result, also among the ten countries with the highest population growth according to the U.N. estimates for 2005–2010: Burundi (3.9 percent), Afghanistan (3.85), Niger (3.49), Congo (3.22), and Mali (3.02). The highest rate of population growth, a record-breaking 4.5 percent, has recently been achieved in Liberia. Other countries and territories high on this list include Western Sahara, East Timor, Eritrea, and Palestine. It is striking how many of these countries have recently been involved in armed conflict and are reacting in some degree to those nightmarish times.

When you travel around these countries, you can feel the prevailing social climate, and see with your own eyes that, if the vicious circle is not broken—poverty contributing to the excessive growth of the population, which in turn perpetuates the misery that can provoke armed conflicts, which are additionally spurred by ethnic divisions—then there is no chance of breaking free of structural stagnation and entering on the road of development. Not so long ago, China was poverty-stricken. If that country had not adopted draconian birth-control measures (women give birth to an average of 1.75 children and the rate of population growth is 0.58 percent), it would be the most populous vale of misery in the world today, rather then the greatest success story in development policy.

At the other extreme, we have countries where women give birth to barely a single child on the average, or only slightly more. The most drastic cases, which have no global significance in relative terms, are Taiwan, Singapore, and Hong Kong, with birth rates of 1.12, 1.07, and 0.98, respectively. The larger countries near the bottom of this list include Japan (1.23), Ukraine (1.24), Russia (1.39), and Germany (1.40). There is an international list of 222 countries and territories, on which the bottom ninety-six have birth rates below 2.1—the so-called replacement rate, which sustains the current population (not counting migration).

By coincidence, the United States opens the lower division of this list in 126th place, with a birth rate of 2.09. Poland comes in 206th, very near the bottom, with a rate of 1.26, just below Italy, Spain, South Korea, and Lithuania, and just above Slovenia, Moldova, Ukraine, and Bosnia-Herzegovina. It is striking that, of the twenty countries with negative rates of population growth, sixteen are European postsocialist countries, including Russia, Georgia, and Armenia. The other four are Germany and Japan, where the rate is still falling, and the statistically marginal Dominican Republic and Guyana. Thus, although there will be more and more people, there will be increasing numbers of people (too many) in some countries but decreasing numbers (too few) in others. It is clear that this demographic imbalance cannot help but intensify the already powerful migration movement.

It is estimated that more countries will dip below the population replacement threshold by 2050. All twenty-seven countries of the European Union are already there. When the foundations of the present Union were laid in 1957, all these countries had birth rates above 2.1. Now the rate ranges from 1.86 in Ireland to 1.21 in Lithuania. In this context, prognoses call for a decline in the population of Europe from the present level of 730 million—but there is no agreement as to how low it will go.

Some predict a decline of barely 1 percent, or about 7 million people, whereas others, who significantly include the U.N. experts, say that it will be no less than 10 percent, or more than 70 million people. In this variant, Europeans would not constitute 11 percent of humanity as they do today, but a mere 7 percent, because the population on other continents will be growing rapidly. Only in North America will it remain below the world average, yet the population of the United States itself will rise by 100 million from the present figure of 302 million (which does not include more than 10 million illegal immigrants, whose deportation is favored by a third of the legal residents). However, things might turn out differently, in view of the *reconquista* and increasing waves of immigration from South and Central America to California, New Mexico, Arizona, Nevada, and Texas. Some of these immigrants have at least some Native American blood, but this time it will be impossible either to exterminate them or confine them to reservations.

In any case, all demographic forecasts evoke numerous doubts and reservations, even more than strictly economic forecasts. Every forecast starts with assumptions. The margin of uncertainty increases as the time frame lengthens, and demographic forecasts are long-term by nature. All sorts of things can happen in the meantime that are now unforeseeable, or even unimaginable. We know from experience that forecasting is a very risky business. Demographic forecasts are on especially shaky ground in terms of predicting rates of birth and death in less-developed countries, as well as the net results of great migrations.

When we see forecasts that the population of Russia will decrease from the current level of 140 million to 104 million in 2050, we must ask if this is possible or if we are looking at some sort of distortion. If it is the latter, as we suspect, then the question is whether it is intentional. It seems wrong to extrapolate over future decades the trends from recent years, when Russia experienced an acute demographic crisis that was, in part, a side effect of the abortive attempt to transform the system according to the neoliberal model and in part the result of environmental contamination and an unhealthy life-style.

The logic of development processes suggests a rise, rather than a fall, in the population of Russia over the next two generations. People will immigrate to Russia, rather than emigrate. This scenario anticipates an improvement in the Russian political and economic situation, even as the opposite stereotype is being promoted in the West: a country that still does not have a functioning market economy or full-blown democracy but that does have a xenophobic population. Nevertheless, about 50,000 people moved back to Russia from Israel in the years 2001–2003. The returns continue. The remedy for a demographic crisis is not immigration, but tangible development and optimistic sentiment about the future. These things are connected.

We do not know whether Russia will repeat the progress that it made in the nineteenth century, but the signs are there. In the lives of two generations, from 1860 to the "real" end of the nineteenth century in 1914, Russia rose to the rank of the world's sixth-largest industrial power. In 2007, Russia's overall output surpassed that of Italy. In 2008, it passed France. In 2009, it is catching up with Britain. Once again, Russia would be the sixth-largest economy in the world, with the difference that this time, in addition to the United States, Germany, and Japan, the countries ahead of it in the pecking order would be not France and the United Kingdom, but China and India.

While some societies expand numerically, others will shrink. The population of Sudan is predicted to rise from 39.4 million at present to 73 million in 2050, while that of Poland falls from 38.5 to barely 30.3 million (the same as in 1962). Thus, a ratio of 1:1 will change to 5:2. The number of Pakistanis is set to rise from 164.7 to 292.2 million, whereas the number of Japanese will fall from 127 million today to 102.5 million. Thus the ratio of 13:10 will more than double, to 28:10. There are now 20.4 million Australians, and in two generations there will be 28 million. Across the Indian Ocean, poor Mozambique now has the same population as wealthy Australia, but it will have 39.1 million people in 2050. The ratio will swell from 1:1 to 7:5.

Here, there, and everywhere, populations will grow older, just like people, with the difference that populations do not pass away. This has cultural, social, political, economic, and financial consequences. They do not pass away, but some individuals move away by migrating from their country of birth. Then all the forecasts go out the window. It may well be that many of the people living in Australia in mid-century will be first- and second-generation descendants of people from East Africa, or that millions of Japanese will have Pakistani roots—and that the streets of Poland will be far more colorful than at present.

The wealthiest societies will age fastest. For example, about 30 percent of the population of Germany will be over sixty-five in 2030. In thirty years, there will be as many people in America over eighty-five as there are under five. This process can now be seen not just in the statistical tables, but on the Florida beaches. Around Naples, the average age of the "gals" sunbathing is about seventy. Countries on the way up are also getting older, because increased longevity is one of the effects of economic development.

The average age of humanity rose only from 23.5 to 26.5 years in the second half of the twentieth century, but is forecast to jump to 37.8 in the first half of the twenty-first century. The number of people over sixty will rise from 10 percent to about 22 percent. Right now, about one fifth of the people in highly developed countries are over sixty. In 2050, it will be about one third. In the world as a whole, the average lifespan will rise by ten years, from sixty-six to seventy-six.

Averages always blur and oversimplify things. A given average can represent completely different situations and processes. Average longevity is something that must be approached with particular caution. The mortality of small children brings it down drastically. When a child in an African village is taken from its mother at the age of four and the mother goes on to live out the world average of sixty-six years, the two of them together have an average lifespan of thirty-five years. This accounts for the shocking statistics on longevity, or rather the brevity of life in poor countries, especially in Africa. The social and economic consequences of such an average are completely different in a situation where both mother and child live no more than thirty-five years. This too can happen, especially in the countries decimated by the plague of HIV-AIDS, such as Swaziland, where the average lifespan is 32.2, or Zambia, where it is 38.4.

What do you see when you travel around these countries? A multitude of children and young people, quite a few of the elderly, but very few in the prime of life—and this is precisely the part of the population that determines economic activity and, as a consequence, the standard of living. That standard is bound to decline when there are few capable of working and many who must be kept because they are not at work yet or are no longer at work. Paradoxically, this is a reason to have numerous progeny: As expensive as they are to raise, they can be put to work young as cheap labor. Later, if the parents manage to live those sixty-six years, they can always find someone from among the young folks to look after them.

These societies have an hourglass profile, wide at the top and bottom and narrow in the middle. Broadening the middle while narrowing the base is an important task for social policy in the fight against poverty. The campaign against HIV-AIDS is also crucial, because the disease devastates the occupationally active part of society most of all. This must be changed in the future; otherwise, there will be vast areas of the earth where many are born, many die, but few work.

Europe too can expect significant changes in its age structure. Forecasts call for a serious dip in the college-age population. In some cases, such as Italy or Spain, it will be an outright collapse. Around 2045, the number of people between twenty and twenty-four is expected to fall by more than 40 percent in the former country and almost 50 percent in the latter. In France, the corresponding decline is estimated at more than 8 percent. What can be done? How should we react? Where will the army recruit? If there is less potential cannon fodder, perhaps there will be fewer senselessly destructive wars. However, it will be necessary to worry about human capital in the middle run and its replacement in the long run. Universities cannot be closed, and bringing in students from China and India will not solve the problem. Above all, this is the age group that most frequently marries and starts families. There might not be a lot of children being born now, but at least there are some. When there are no parents, where will the children come from? The stork won't solve this problem, and neither will the invisible hand of the market.

It is not easy to influence the birth rate, but population policy must be applied. By its nature, it is long term and therefore requires special instruments. However, even when there is success at shaping the age structure of the population through the use of cultural and social-policy measures in the form of special budget allocations, family payments, free child care, universal schooling, and tax deductions, the effects appear only much later.

Migration can serve as a vent for growing tensions, especially on the labor market, where they have a negative impact on economic functioning and growth. The idea, of course, is not for older people to go away, but for younger ones to come in. The ethnic and cultural composition of the population changes as a result, but that is a separate matter, and another problem. There will be more and more changes of this type.

History has varied lessons for us. The direction of the migration of peoples does not change as dramatically as in literary fiction, and is not always a one-way street leading to America. Surprisingly enough, in the quarter century from 1899 to 1925, fully one third of the Polish immigrants to America returned home. The lack of adaptive capacity was decisive; it was not easy adjusting to the demands of American industrial culture, with all its competition.

More recently, in another context, more Poles returned to their homeland than left it in 1996–1997, when average annual growth remained above 6 percent for several years. That was because they had a more optimistic vision of their future in Poland, and this is the decisive factor. People do not choose the direction of migration so much because of the present state of affairs wherever they are, as because of their outlook and expectations. These expectations are always a function of the present state to a degree, but they are also derivatives of the way people imagine the future at two different points on the map. Migration is a matter of both leaving somewhere and arriving somewhere.

We should be under no illusions: the twenty-first century will be a century of Great Migrations. About 200 million people are now living permanently outside the country of their birth, and this number will rise dramatically. There are regions where immigrants already comprise the majority of the inhabitants, even though they are denied citizenship and many elementary rights. This is the case in those Arab countries that attempt to enhance the prosperity of their citizens by exploiting both rich deposits of oil and gas, and a copious influx of cheap labor. Half of the fewer than 9 million residents of the United Arab Emirates, Kuwait, Qatar, and Bahrain are immigrants, mostly from Bangladesh, Pakistan, India, Sri Lanka, the Philippines, and, recently, Vietnam. There are also considerable numbers of educated specialists from Europe and North America. Immigrants make up about one third of the people in Bahrain and the majority in Qatar and Kuwait. Only 20 percent of the 4.5 million people in the United Arab Emirates are citizens. The elites in these countries boost their own standard of living by exploiting immigrant labor in a ruthless way that sometimes borders on slavery, but they are laboring under a delusion when they imagine that they will easily rid themselves of this mass of guest workers when they no longer need them. They won't. The majority will stay, rotating in the meantime, just as millions of Africans and their descendants stayed in America after the abolition of slavery, or as Hindus settled permanently on Fiji. They came there to work the sugar plantations on quasi-voluntary indentures, usually amounting to five years, that bore a strong resemblance to feudal servitude. They should have gone home when they had worked off their indentures, but many decided to stay. Today we can see that about half the people on Fiji have Indian roots.

Many of the immigrants in the Middle East who are totally bereft of rights today will win citizenship and other privileges. Some of them, with good reason, already feel at home.

The time has come for one more epochal migration. It is plain that its main trails will continue to lead, as they already do, from poorer to richer countries. The process will only intensify. Attempting to stop it by force is a symptom of political folly. Selective policies that shut some people up in camps and deport them while inviting others to immigrate are proof of the cynicism of the affluent countries. The former people are usually unqualified, poor barbarians who should be kept outside the gates, whereas the latter are experts, educated somewhere else at the expense of another country's taxpayers, who are supposed to balance the local labor market by adding supply.

In a single year, 2003, Britain granted more than 10,000 visas and work permits to qualified medical and nursing personnel from Africa, including 5,880 from South Africa, 2,825 from Zimbabwe, 1,510 from Nigeria, and 850 from Ghana. Almost a third of the doctors practicing in Britain were educated in the countries they left behind. Forty-one percent of Tanzania's university graduates have emigrated and are working in highly developed OECD countries. The figure for Angola is 57 percent, and for Fiji it is 62 percent. In Haiti, which is even poorer, the percentage is 79, and in Jamaica it is 81.

This is a typical brain drain, but it is something more; it smacks of apartheid. Whereas the needed personnel are practically begged to come in without a thought for the havoc wrought on the professional staffs in their home countries, others are cast aside even when they manage to set foot inside their destination. The countries that suffer this drain of qualified workforce should be compensated for their education no less generously than they must pay for the services they import. This is not a matter of personal migration, because such transfers of human capital have far-reaching internal consequences for the entire process of macroeconomic reproduction. It goes without saying that this has a multidirectional influence on the competitive capacity (and thus the development potential) of the countries that lose and gain sought-after, highly qualified workers.

Migration should not be viewed simply from the utilitarian and cultural point of view, and nor through the prism of its economic consequences. It is shameful that people are still denied the right to move about freely in times of such advanced globalization, when the world, including its poorest areas, has been forced to accept the free transfer of goods and capital. When we rose up off of all fours and became bipeds, we achieved the first of the human rights: the Right to Movement. Migration is movement. In the twenty-first century, this right will increasingly come to the fore. It cannot continue to be suppressed under the flimsiest of pretexts. The time of barriers and roadblocks, walls and fences, and barriers and barbed wire should already be in the past, rather than returning to haunt us. Sermons about democracy and human rights become a mockery when people are denied the right to move around. This is what life and the world are for. There are those who treat passports and visas as a way of shackling people to the land, as a kind of contemporary feudal obligation or apartheid, except that now the village is global. Visas cannot be abolished like feudal labor obligations, but they should be radically limited in the future. In the long run, in the supranational and planetary dimension, this would be a great advance for development.

The response to the challenge that migration poses to the globalized economy must rest on complex, comprehensive action by the richer part of the world community. It must act as a catalyst for the economic development of the poorest part of that economy, on the one hand, and must create a broad cultural, institutional, and political framework for the absorption of streams of immigrants, on the other. The quicker the rich countries are ready to transfer a part of their GDP to the poor ones in a sensible way, the less GDP they will have to transfer within their own national budgets to finance the growing masses of legal and illegal newcomers from all over the globe.

The combination of low birth rates, extended longevity, and mass migration will put unprecedented, almost unbearable stress on health care, the retirement system, and social services. This will probably lead to mutinies, revolts, and revolutions. These upheavals will take one form in rich countries with better-developed social market economy institutions, and other forms in countries that have not yet become rich and that have placed insufficient emphasis on the imperative to create the appropriate financial and organizational underpinnings to meet these challenges. Norway will manage, but will Portugal? Japan has a chance to deal successfully with this syndrome, but what about France? It will be easier for Spain than for Poland, but both of these countries will have big problems—not as monstrous as those of Mexico or Indonesia, but bad enough to spark unrest.

Relative peace, including control of human migration, can only be assured when the rate of population growth in low-income countries is substantially reduced. In purely formal terms, each reduction per mille—one tenth of 1 percent—in the rate of population growth (assuming that the absolute quantity of output remains unchanged) automatically yields a growth in output per capita of that same per mille. If the population of Brazil had risen by 0.51 percent instead of 1.01 percent, then—as long as nothing else changed—GDP per capita would have grown by 4.1 percent instead of 3.6 percent in 2007. This is a small change in a single year, but over the course of ten years it results in a per capita GDP that is 7 percent higher, and over two decades it yields 20 percent more. These are significant differences, of the kind that can determine qualitative improvements in development. Attempts to lower population growth are therefore no less significant than efforts to increase the overall level of economic growth. Both are crucial to improving the material situation of the population. How many of us there are has a lot to do with how we live.

As we keep surveying the horizon of the future, the eighth compass point that commands our attention is poverty, misery, and social inequality. The specialist literature on "inequality and the struggle against poverty" would already fill a huge library. The more economists write about inequality, you might say if you wanted to be nasty, the more of it there is. Of course, there is no such correlation. However, there is another connection: For more than a few experts, community organizers, journalists, and politicians, not to mention bureaucrats, writing about inequality and its consequences has become a good way of making a living. Research and consulting on poverty and inequality have become a cottage industry. When you take account of the aid money devoted to the issue, it is a multi-billion-dollar industry. Some authors have written in this context about the neocolonialism of international organizations in the field.[17]

A future statesman or stateswoman—and the earth will still produce some great ones—might well ask what to watch out for, how to diagnose the situation, and what therapy to apply to avoid the outbreak of the next Great Revolution. The answer should be: Aside from changes in the natural environment and demographic movements, beware of poverty, social inequality, and their consequences. No revolution has ever broken out in the name of inequality. Nor would any reasonable person ever demand total equality, which is bound to be more unjust than some forms of inequality. The danger lies in the injustice of excessive inequality. That's when it's time to act—before it's too late.

Orhan Pamuk, the Turkish writer who is neither an economist nor a sociologist but who won the 2006 Nobel Prize in literature, writes in *Snow* that, "It's not enough to be oppressed, you must also be in the right! Most oppressed people are in the wrong to an almost ridiculous degree."[18] A Marxist would say that life, no matter how miserable, hasn't yet managed to form their consciousness. It is a fact that many of the poor have allowed themselves to be misled or, if you prefer, to be made fools of. Many of them do not even know that they are oppressed. Today, however, news spreads fast, especially bad news. Before long, mumbo jumbo like TINA—"There Is No Alternative"—will be yesterday's newspapers. The dilemma for the future is this: Should we reduce the ranks of the oppressed or wait for them to stop being fools and start developing their own revolutionary consciousness?

Classical economics, including its neoliberal variant, suggests possibilities for reducing income inequality. This should supposedly occur as a result of the free flow of capital (while human capital, it is understood, would remain subject to limitation). The theory assumes the full mobilization of the factors of production. This should lead to the allocation of capital where rates of return are highest. Its transfer to relatively less-developed countries would stimulate growth there. We know all too well that the theory has failed the test, not only because we observe an increase in capital transfers from some poorer countries to richer countries, but above all because the neoliberal assumption of convergence has not worked out in practice. Poorer countries were supposed to automatically develop more quickly than richer ones, but it simply hasn't happened.

Even given the most extreme liberalization, the factors of production in themselves, without intervention, are mobile only to the degree that it pays. It turns out that a whole range of places where the hunger for capital is greatest are the very places where it doesn't pay to invest. Without the appropriate intervention on a supranational or even global scale, we should therefore not expect any significant change. It is thus hardly surprising that, even when huge swathes of the world have been reshaped on the neoliberal model, there is not the slightest indication that the poor and the rich, the less developed and the more developed, are drawing closer to each other. The difference between income (a flow) and wealth (a stock of assets) is greater than ever before.

The question is this: "Will it continue to grow?" If so, what are the limits to the differences in living standards between nations, and between the particular social groups within those nations? Or has the world already hit the wall, and is it imperative to put a halt to the growing inequality right now, and then go on to reverse the unfavorable tendencies?

Without getting into arguments about tenths of percentage points, it seems to be a reasonable conclusion that slowing the growth of the disparity of incomes, and speeding up development in poorer countries, as well as facing the challenge of excessive inequality in certain rich countries, would be in the best interests of humanity and the global economy. This applies to the GDP of whole countries and to the incomes of the populations of those countries. We know that this will take a change in values first of all, followed by strategies and policies that result from those values. We also know all too well that this will not necessarily happen. Greed and folly can easily get the upper hand over moderation and forethought.

There may not be sufficient moderation and forethought to produce development policy based on the new pragmatism. Policy, instead, may continue to be redolent of old dogmas and domination by special interests. If this is so, then we will face antagonistic tensions on a world scale before long. This means that the problems will be overcome in a tumultuous way, through revolts and conflicts, and uncontrolled migration and redistribution. This will bring growth to a halt in the richer countries, but in this case the limitation of growth will be a side effect of the disturbances, rather than a strategic measure to forestall them.

Many politicians and a few economists like to go around saying, "It can't go on like this." It can. Strategic inequalities, the kind that replicate themselves from one generation to another, are decisive, and will continue to be so, as is shown clearly by this whole interpretation of history and the contemporary world—up to a point, a point in time. There is no way at this moment to predict when that will occur, but it will not be on the scale of historic time. At the most, it will be on the time scale of a generation. The boundaries of human patience and social tolerance for this scale of inequality and the associated degree of social exclusion, including poverty and misery, will continue to be tested. Whether they will be tested to the breaking point or whether common sense will step in while there is still time is something we will just have to wait to learn. We know—someone, somewhere knows—what should be done to make things better, but no one knows whether it will be done. Even worse: There are grounds for suspecting that it will not be done.

One swallow does not make a spring, they say. When swallows are singing all around, however, spring has arrived. President Lula da Silva of Brazil has spurned the whispers of the neoliberal prompters. If the things that Brazil has done under his presidency could be done in all the less-developed regions of the world, then we would be saved. For now, we can only wait and see where the Brazilian road leads. Are we looking at a structural trend or mere transient, limited change?

The Brazilian government is implementing a nonorthodox, pragmatic economic policy at significant variance with the Plano Real that preceded it. In the preceding decade, the Plano Real concentrated on combating inflation, and this was correct at the time. However, it was naïve to expect this in itself to improve the lot of the poor masses. Far from declining, the Gini coefficient soared to 0.596 in 2001. This was one of the factors that brought the leftist government of Lula da Silva to power in democratic elections.

Lula's social policy, combined with fiscal discipline, brought the Gini coefficient down to 0.567 in 2005. During the president's second term, it has continued to fall. This is happening because wise interventionism and economic policy are coordinating various determinants of development to guarantee that the lowest incomes grow faster than the highest. Over the four years from 2002 to 2006, the share of income obtained by the poor half of the population rose from 9.8 to 11.9 percent, while the share received by the highest decile on the income ladder fell from 49.5 to 45.8 percent. This is still a gigantic disproportion. It impedes balanced development and makes it more difficult to recoup lost time, but at least it represents the tangible reversal of the disastrous earlier tendencies. If the trend can be maintained, it will be a great success. The outlook for Brazil will be good.

Of particular significance is the successful Zero Hunger (*Fome Zero*) program, which provides direct budgetary subsidies to the poor. These are modest subsidies, amounting to 60 real ($31 by the exchange rate or $53 by PPP) for the poorest families, and 120 real to households with children under fifteen, on the condition that those children are in school. All recipients must also receive vaccinations, which are documented in a special booklet. These are straightforward measures (although the logistics are far from simple, given the terrible state of the infrastructure and the service sector), but they can do a lot of good.

This costs money, but where does the money come from? The cost, in fact, is a tiny fraction of what many countries spend on armaments or wasteful, overgrown bureaucracies, so there are savings to be made. The international community could easily help as well. The additional payment to poor countries of a mere per mille—one tenth of 1 percent—of the GDP of the G-7 and European Union for such purposes would amount to about $33 billion, and this could change the face of the world. It would not necessarily make it a human face overnight, but at least it would be a more enlightened face, less distorted by the grimace of hunger. Applying the Brazilian standards could induce half a billion families around the world to send their children to school and vaccinate them against various diseases. Could there be a better prescription for development and the fight against poverty than a healthier and more educated younger generation?

Big numbers are impressive, but small numbers tell us more. What would this per mille mean to those who are expected to contribute it? In the United States, it would amount to $4.00 per month per person. In Poland, it would work out to about 2.50 zloty, or less than one dollar. It takes resolve, and people with the qualities of the president of Brazil. More specifically, it takes a theoretical concept, political will, and practical skill at solving developmental problems. This is the point where we can stop saying, "It can't go on like this," and start expecting that it won't.

It is amazing how little gets done, despite

- The vast knowledge about development economics.
- The abundance of positive experience in the practical conquest of barriers to growth.
- The achievements to date in limiting the scale of poverty.
- The general level of wealth and capital accumulation in some parts of the world.

People must understand, want to do something, and have an authentic motivation to act. Some must be willing to stump up those four dollars or two and a half zloty, and others must be willing to organize the transfer of the resulting millions and billions. The recipients must make an enormous effort to prevent the aid from being wasted. Solving problems requires the coordination of values, institutions, and policies. The skilful application of the coincidence theory of development can be invaluable, but at times, in small matters, all it takes is some common sense and elementary honesty. A lack of these things is the greatest hurdle in the fight against poverty and antidevelopmental inequalities.

———————

Progress in education and research, and the creation of new bridge-heads for the information-based economy and society, have great significance in shaping the future. They represent the ninth compass point on our survey of the horizon. Expanding the scope of education and freeing it of restrictions will give billions of the earth's inhabitants access to information and knowledge that are valuable in themselves and are also priceless instruments for economic progress. To an increasing degree, human economic activity will rely on knowledge, and this will change the way society functions.

Hegel and his follower Marx taught us that life determines consciousness, but the opposite is also true. The impact of consciousness, especially the cultural stratum, on the economy and its development, and thus on the material conditions of life, is far from trivial. There is a strong feedback mechanism that will make this cause-and-effect relationship even stronger in the future, because the role of knowledge in production processes is growing all the time. Science, research, and knowledge have been treated for decades as direct factors of production, and their importance is increasingly prominent. Knowledge is one of the crucial elements of consciousness. "I think, therefore I am." It is also true to say, "I know, and therefore I can."

Some theoretical approaches regard knowledge, alongside land (natural resources), capital, and labor, as deserving of separate treatment as one of the variables that determine output growth. This depends on how we conceive of capital. If we treat it in a nontraditional but up-to-date way, as including not only real and financial capital, but also human and social capital, then there is no justification for treating knowledge separately. It is better and methodologically clearer to regard knowledge in the broad sense as a separate determinant of output growth and socioeconomic development. It is a variable that ought to be taken into consideration as an independent category in multifactorial growth models. This is the way the coincidence theory treats it. As for the future, we must understand that, even as it grows increasingly prominent, the role of knowledge as a crucial segment of human capital will become differentiated.

It is a good thing to maintain one's distance to all the chatter about building a knowledge-based economy. Someone might ask the simple question, "What is the opposite of a knowledge-based economy—an ignorance-based economy?" No matter how little people know, at least they know something, right? There is no such thing as an ignorance-based economy. All business, like all civilization, is based at its deepest level on knowledge. The difference today is that there is more knowledge than ever before. Decent high school or college students today know more than some Nobel Prize winners of a century ago. They know, but they don't necessarily understand, and there lies the difference. Not only will the store of knowledge keep growing in the future, and at an exponential rate, but the understanding of the essence of things will also be more widespread. At every level of the economy, from the micro level in companies to the macro level in national economies and the mega level on a global scale, the ability to make creative use of gigantic stores of knowledge to multiply material and spiritual values will be increasingly important.

The concept we are dealing with here is fuzzy by definition, and so it will remain. In a utilitarian vein, we might define a knowledge-based economy as one in which the arrangement of the factors of production is such that people who know more will contribute to growth to an increasing extent. There can be no doubt that the economy and the society through which it functions will get better and better at using knowledge to produce growth. That much we can say. Yet we will still have to sow and harvest, hunt and dig, load and carry, grind and mine, cut and sew, and so on. However, the army of people doing these things will be smaller, and the ranks of those who spend most of their time thinking will swell. To be sure, the saying "thinking has a future" is not new. Einstein added the adjective *colossal*, but even the ancients knew it. It had a future back then, and it will have even more of a future in the future.

We must be wary of special pressure from various corners of the academic community, who simply treat the idea of a knowledge-based economy as a pretext for advocating the improvement of their own material situation. I have nothing against higher salaries for professors.

However, the fact that they earn more, either directly or through grants, does not mean that we have more of a knowledge-based economy, unless their higher salaries automatically translate into greater stores of knowledge. There is no such simple relationship. For that to come about, a few other things will have to happen in culture, institutions, and policy.

The places where there is greater public funding for research are not necessarily the places where the economy will become more knowledge-intensive. However, this will surely happen where companies emphasize the use of knowledge to improve their competitiveness through innovative and inventive products, professional management, permanent career development for their employees, and the hard financing of research, and especially applied research. Basic research will continue to be financed publicly in large part, although the spread of the institution of public-private partnerships will become increasingly promising. Only the mightiest global companies, along with some particularly well-endowed foundations, will be able to fund private basic research.

Economically successful countries demonstrate clearly that a higher rate of development is achieved where the manufacturing sector demands technical and organizational innovation. Unfortunately, we cannot expect to see this in the countries that need rapid growth the most, that is, in the poor countries. A knowledge-based economy is a luxury that wealthy countries can afford, where companies have abundant capital, and where the state can afford to co-finance research and implementation, and has the will to do so.

Poorer countries, in turn, must work at gradually improving their educational and public-information systems. No one should encourage the illusion that they can leapfrog the stages of development and start producing things that it took richer countries a long time to begin making. Brazil can manufacture regional jets because it knows how to do so, and other countries are impressed. However, the things that these other countries should copy are not the jets, but rather programs like *Fome Zero*. A knowledge-based economy can be built where the structural problems of human capital have largely been solved through the elimination of illiteracy and the achievement of a critical level of technical civilization. The majority of countries still have a great deal of work to do in this regard.

Building a knowledge-based economy—or perhaps it is better to talk about an economy based to an increasing degree on knowledge—

requires the correct sequencing and gradation. In any given economy, there are sectors that play a leading role, and others that join in. Over time, an increasing proportion of business activity will create added value, to an increasing degree, through the use of human intellectual resources rather than the physical resources of the earth. Some of the countries in this world are leaders and others play catch-up. Over time, more and more of them will exhibit more and more signs of economic growth based on domestic human capital rather on than real capital. Financial capital will always be important, if for no other reason than the fact that it is required for investment in the cultivation of human capital. Knowledge costs money.

A knowledge-based economy is a little bit like a pond when someone throws a stone in. The initial energy input results in wider and wider rings of ripples. In the economy, knowledge applied in one place spreads throughout the immediate vicinity, and then to new companies, industries, and sectors. As long as the initial impulse was strong enough, the ripples keep coming—like other countries and regions joining in, thanks to the dissemination of knowledge, and especially research and implementation.

What does this mean from the point of view of the wealth of nations? The countries at the peak of the world pyramid will make the largest contribution to the knowledge economy through inventions. Below them is the more numerous group of countries at a medium level of development, which will mostly contribute innovation. Finally, there is the largest group, consisting of relatively poor countries that seek to improve their situation through imitation, most of all. This "3I" model—invention, innovation, and imitation—will drive the whole world economy forward. It will enhance overall effectiveness and may help less-developed countries to make up some of their arrears, although it need not necessarily do so.

Much will depend on institutional and financial solutions regarding licenses, patents, recipes, patterns, trademarks, and copyrights. If we look at a world map showing intellectual property rights, we see that they are even more concentrated than energy reserves. For a long time now, they have been more valuable. As early as 1938–1939, France received as much for a dress sewn by a leading designer as it paid for the import of 10 tons of coal and could exchange a liter of perfume for 2,000 liters of gasoline. Now it is not only a matter of technology, but also of trademarks, which can sometimes cost more than the materials and labor that go into making the product. The owners of these rights, like the profits derived from them, tend to be gathered in the rich countries, not because of a caprice of nature, as in the case of raw materials, but thanks to the creativity of the human intellect.

If we could somehow draw up a map of talent, we would see that it is more evenly distributed around the world than raw materials or intellectual property. Yet talent alone, without knowledge and financial support, amounts to little. For understandable reasons, the rich countries are not necessarily eager to share their knowledge and skills with others. What rich counties really want is not only to be rich, but also to stay richer than everybody else. Maintaining their scientific and technical predominance is the surest way to do this. The rivalry in these areas will intensify over the coming decades and centuries. Clashes of interests that could result in conflicts have already arisen over technologies connected with the military complex, as well as a range of other products such as pharmaceuticals. This will lead to wars that are bloodless but genuine, and usually silent because intelligence agencies, rather than armies, will fight them.

On the one hand, as knowledge expands into new realms, the scope of the economic activity that can be called knowledge based will broaden in every country, including the most highly developed ones. On the other hand, the number of countries where this kind of activity takes place will also increase. The portion of the GDP attributable to the knowledge-based economy will grow rapidly all over the world, but it will grow most during the next few decades in the countries that are already highly developed. The GDP will weigh less there. It can be weighed, because part of it is embodied in various products that weigh something. Over the last two decades, the weight of the American GDP has declined by about 20 percent. We notice the same phenomenon, on a smaller scale, in less technologically advanced countries.

The development gap separating the rich countries, with their relatively "light" GDP, from the poor and less-developed countries may continue to grow, at least where its breadth is determined by the shortfall in education and the quality of human capital. In the longer perspective, when the foundation necessary for the rapid enhancement of that capital has been laid—the elimination of illiteracy, universal secondary education, adequate tertiary education, and a research-and-development base—it will be possible to go beyond dreaming of creating a knowledge-based economy to the point where one actually exists.

What new things will the future bring? Will it simply be a matter of perspiring less and thinking more? No, it will be much more than that. Knowledge is like all other resources: It is important not only to have it, but also to know what to do with it. Success will belong to the sectors, professional groups, countries, and regions that can create knowledge and that, more important, know how to use it. All the knowledge of English-speaking Nigerian and Kenyan computer programmers will lead nowhere as long as they keep working as hackers. All the professional skill of Iranian and North Korean physicists will be misapplied until it is harnessed by sensible policies that place scientific and technical progress at the service of development. All the knowledge put into creating the next American antimissile defense system and yet another Russian anti-anti-missile system will fail to improve international security, and will be detrimental to development, because it is a waste of rare capital. Knowing more is not enough to guarantee a knowledge-based economy. You must know how to use that knowledge. Policy should also rely more on knowledge.

The tendency to expand the scope of economic activity as a result of the eruption of knowledge, and especially of scientific knowledge, has been apparent since the late nineteenth century. We still talk about necessity being the mother of invention. In fact, this is changing, because inventions frequently create new necessities. If you take a good look around, from kitchen gadgets to banking services and from computers to talking cars, you see that we did not invent these things because we needed them, but that we need them (some of them, at least) because we invented them.

The "knowledge-based economy" is intensifying this phenomenon. In the non-knowledge-based economy, experiments came before theory. Intellectual progress consisted of creating a better instrument, tool, machine, formula, technology, or final product, but this was achieved through experiments, through trial and error. Now the theory comes before the application. First, we know why something works or happens, and only afterward does it happen.

It is hard for economists to refrain from asking whether this is also true of their own discipline. To an increasing degree it is, although not completely. This is for reasons that we presented at the beginning of this tale. If there is less ideology and more pragmatism, if economics is to be a science, then yes, it will be so. In the case of more and more problems, we will first know how (and therefore why) something happens, and only later will it happen. It is one of the paradoxes of the present day, and perhaps of the future, that even in the age of the knowledge-based economy, economic policy is not necessarily or always based on knowledge and the findings of the science of economics. Until it is, we cannot really speak of a knowledge-based economy. Much work remains to be done.

———————

In disciplines other than economics, there will be more scientific and technical progress. The nature, dynamics, and consequences of this progress comprise our tenth compass point as we survey the horizon of the future. What can we expect, and what should we fear? History offers a mixed lesson. We know full well that the human intellect has frequently served evil causes. Our first task for the future is to ensure that science and technology promote progress, rather than destruction. The fact that science has great potential for shaping a creative, developed, and peaceful future is no guarantee that it will be so. It could be, but not necessarily. If the triad of culture, institutions, and policy functions properly, it may well be so.

Will the twenty-first century provide us with an Eighth Great Invention, to follow standing erect, fire, the wheel, money, print, electricity, and the Internet? Or will we have to go on waiting? What will it be? Never before in history have we had so much advance knowledge. When Gutenberg printed his first Bible in 1454, he could never have dreamed that someday there would be millions of people reading the Bible by electric light. When Edison switched on the first light bulb in 1879, he could never have imagined that the Bible could be summoned up with one click through the wireless Internet. Only in the most recent instance, that of the World Wide Web, did anyone know what was coming. Even then, things were not clear from the outset. In 1989, when Tim Berners-Lee, today Sir Timothy, presented a proposal for a website at CERN, the particle physics laboratory outside Geneva, which I've mentioned already, his boss wrote "vague but exciting". In 1994, there were about 10,000 websites. In 2007, there were more than 100 million. Before long, people will stop counting. They'll simply be universal. It's more exciting than its creators could have dreamed.

Do we know what the next epochal invention could be, or even have a general idea? In human history, only the first five Great Inventions were possible without previously accumulating vast amounts of knowledge and laying the theoretical groundwork. All they required was curiosity, boldness, repeated trials, a spontaneous process, and a brilliant idea.

There are numerous signs that we know what's coming. Things have changed and, since the late nineteenth century, it has been necessary for the theory to be in place and the information collected before a great invention could take place. Science conceives of something that is then created in the real world; the essence and mechanism of the invention is already completely understood, or nearly so. The theoretical concept and the scientific interpretation precede the actual technical step forward. Technology is a transmission belt between scientific ideas and cultural and economic practice. There is a lot going on, and the next big thing will come along sooner or later, and probably sooner. It will likely have to do with manipulating the beginnings and the course of life, including sickness and longevity. This will result from research progress in physics, chemistry, genetics, and biology, assisted by the computational and modeling power of computers. Yet again, the most interesting things will happen at the points of contact between the disciplines. Interdisciplinary studies have indeed a colossal future.

We know in retrospect that, in the twentieth century, it was physics that gave humanity two monumental accomplishments, although some say that we have a tendency to exaggerate when we evaluate the significance of new technology.[19] The first of these accomplishments was an advanced ability to control the forces of nature. Some of them have been harnessed, although not always in a way that encourages us to sleep soundly at night. We have lived more than half a century in the shadow of the atomic mushroom cloud. The second accomplishment makes the twentieth century different from everything before and after—the ability to move people, merchandise, and information around with a completely new order of quantity, speed, distance, and comfort. These innovations, from the car and the airplane to the computer and the Internet, have changed the face of the world forever.

Today, looking ahead, we do not know, or rather, we are not sure that biology will play a similar role in the twenty-first century. Right now it looks similar to the situation with physics 100 years ago—not in terms of the specific problems to be solved or the particular innovations waiting around the corner, but rather in terms of the sense that these advances must lead to a future that is as fascinating as it is mysterious. Physics was seen in exactly the same terms.

In 100 years we will know the answers. Furthermore, the things that are exciting and wrapped in the clouds of the unknown today will have become mundane. Great leaps forward can be seen only in context. If we trace the changes in cars over the last 100 years, we see that the alterations from one model year to the next were apparently minor. Yet if we compare a Model T Ford to the latest Toyota Prius, we are in two different worlds. Each has four road wheels and one steering wheel, but that's about it. This is what a 100-year retrospective looks like. At first, the changes are so numerous and continual that not much seems to be happening, and it seems to be happening slowly. In fact, lots of things are changing, and they are changing fast. Take people—they look the same as they did 100 years ago, but now they are educated differently, they work and take time off differently, they receive different medical treatment, and they will die differently.

Which changes should we welcome, and which should we reject? There is much controversy in medicine, genetics, biology, and even physics. Genetic engineering and biotechnology will be crucial in the coming decades. This is not certain, but it is highly likely. The 1997 British experiment in cloning that produced the world's most famous sheep, Dolly, was the symbolic opening of a new era. It had begun earlier, but that was the moment that launched us on a new trajectory into the future.

Simple procedures in genetic engineering have become routine. What was science fiction in the early 1990s is now part of the real world. The first patents have been taken out on artificial living organisms, or rather on living organisms created in a nonnatural way under laboratory conditions. The fact that this is possible—and I am talking about both the creation of the organism and the legal procedure bringing it under intellectual property rights—is still inconceivable to most people. Yet it will end up benefiting them, in ways that include the prolongation of their lives. Or so we hope.

The issues at stake here are not merely intellectual. More than ever before, they have an ethical dimension. They are impeded or blocked by formal policy instruments, administrative prohibitions, and public opinion brought to bear in an organized way by special pressure groups and a broad range of religious denominations and churches, seconded as always by the dutiful media. This is hardly the Inquisition or burning at the stake. Nevertheless, it resembles the irrational attempts to block or deny things that we accept as obvious facts today, such as the movement of the heavenly bodies or human descent from apes. Copernicus's heliocentric theory and Darwin's theory of evolution only became accepted after a great deal of turmoil. Some inventors and discoverers had to endure torture before the truth became true. This is not something we should gloss over. The only tenable reaction is to keep debating the merits of the issue and weighing up the rational arguments and real threats at scholarly symposia and in the forum of public opinion.

On the one hand, given the lack of experience and proven regulatory mechanisms in such a new field as genetic engineering, some misgivings are inevitable. There is a lot to think about. DNA from one organism can be introduced into another. This breaks down the age-old boundaries between individuals, and even between species. Genetic modification, in itself, is nothing new in nature, yet many regard it as counter to nature or, if you prefer, in violation of divine law.

On the other hand, these blocking maneuvers are only temporary. If something can be created, it will be created. Someday, far in the future, all of this will seem normal, just as it now seems normal that man evolved rather than being created by God, or that the earth revolves around the sun rather than the opposite. I have no doubt of this, although it may not come to pass even in the times of our grandchildren's grandchildren. Nor do I doubt that some potential or real advances will have to be kept under lock and key, just as humanity does at present with such products of the human intellect as the ABC weapons—atomic, biological, and chemical.

This is how it will be. We do not run the risk, as humankind did fifteen centuries ago, of forgetting many of the skills and achievements of the ancients and having to wait 1,000 years until some of them, like Chinese printing, could be reintroduced during the Renaissance. This fate does not threaten us for many reasons. Once, only a narrow circle of scholars, artists, and artisans knew such things; now huge numbers of people know them. Although the most advanced knowledge is concentrated in certain places around the world, there are a great many such bright points on the map, and there will be more and more of them.

Fukuyama writes that, "The ultimate question raised by biotechnology is, 'What will happen to political rights once we are able to, in effect, breed some people with saddles on their backs, and others with boots and spurs?'"[20] Yet isn't this already the case? Some people are born in sheds on the sands of the Kalahari in Botswana or in half-abandoned collective farms on the plains of Russia, while others are born into the families of educated bureaucrats in Gaborone or newly rich entrepreneurs in Moscow. Some people's parents belong to the Paris financial establishment and other people's parents are immigrants housed in a suburban *banlieue*. Isn't it true that some children (a multitude of them) spend their childhoods in the misery of the slums of Mumbai, and others among that city's business elite? The former are indeed born "with saddles on their backs" and the latter "in boots and spurs."

The fact that we are already formed in this way when we enter the world for our longer or shorter lives is not the realization of some futurological prognosis bordering on science fiction. We are shaped from birth as a result of the prevailing economic relations, social structures, and political alignments. People will continue to be born with saddles or in spurs, not because of undesirable genetic manipulation, but because of a shortage of the desired economic and political manipulation.

New academic disciplines are emerging as a result of the high rate of scientific and technical progress and of the growing interdisciplinary trend. Progress in research and innovation will lead to further specialization, and some theoretical and applied subjects of particular importance to development will become autonomous. The megatrends at the intersection of nature, society, technology, and the economy mean that university websites will feature new departments, just as they have added ecology, biotechnology, genetic engineering, nanotechnology, space science, and molecular biology in our lifetimes. Global Studies will be a new, independent field focusing on the interdependence of ecology, culture, politics, and economics in the context of the world system. It could just as aptly be called Applied Planet Studies, or APS, because it is the science of our earth.

In some of the areas where great progress will be made, necessity remains the mother of invention, especially in relation to new energy sources and new energy-intensive technologies. Nonrenewable resources will run out and the energy crisis will grow more acute. Much will happen in materials engineering and nanotechnology, a discipline so new that many computer spell checkers still highlight its name as a mistake. New terminology will keep springing up to describe the progress in technology and organization.

Management is a word to bear in mind, because the management of flows and assets—human, real, financial, and informational—is tremendously significant, especially in the countries that lag behind. They can make great strides in organizing the processes of production and distribution, and in managing personnel and companies. This is what was once referred to as noninvestment progress, which gave the misleading impression that the situation could be improved without putting anything into it. Nevertheless, these kinds of changes can enhance efficiency at less cost than creating new production capacity or implementing new technology.

When you wait hours or days for a rickety bus or truck in Benin or Eritrea, you find yourself bursting to improve the management of the transport system, which is a bottleneck to economic expansion, and you sometimes forget that the lack of management is itself a mode of management. People there still need to learn that time counts. In the most technically advanced societies, time counts for more than money, and the situation is reversed. Making use of the growing resources of free time, which can be spent—or wasted—on consumption, education, culture, entertainment, recreation, or sport, is a looming management challenge.

Many things will happen in electronics. Some innovations will enhance the quality of life, whereas others will be senseless gadgets. An MP3 player or iPod, or whatever their successors are called, with sufficient memory could store more music than anyone could listen to in a lifetime. Devices of a similar size will receive hundreds of TV channels, although no one can say what the purpose of this might be. In a quarter of a century, the computers in homes and offices will be able to match the performance of today's supercomputers. This progress remains incomplete, however, because there is no prospect of moving sidewalks to deliver pupils to my old school.

———————————

The Internet will be everywhere, all over the planet and beyond. It is our eleventh compass point as we survey the horizon of the future. It is also the most perfect instrument ever invented for observing our planet, the things that happen, and why they happen, in both the figurative and, to an increasing degree, the literal sense.

The Internet will soon make it possible for us to see everyone, or at least to know where everyone is. It's like Skype, where we can keep track of everyone who makes their profile visible. As I write these words, there are 21.4 million users. In thirty or forty years, it will only take one mouse click to locate everyone, and to establish wireless contact with almost everyone. Of course, the world has been wireless throughout almost its entire history. You could contact anyone, as long as they were within shouting distance.

The computer revolution of the latter twentieth century has been referred to, with good reason, as the information age. Many still lack both the key and the door that it was supposed to open, but there is no doubt that this revolution has added greatly to the wealth of large parts of the globe. It centers on digitalization—the use of numerical codes for text, images, and sound—and the unprecedented ease of storing, processing, and using all kinds of information in education, science, technology, culture, and the economy.

The coming decades will see the wireless revolution, a continuation of the information revolution in a new phase. Wireless data transmission will make it possible to access digital information about almost everything at costs so low that, in marginal or growth-related terms, they will be practically insignificant.

There are parallels between the present and forecast introduction and dissemination of wireless technology and the wide application of electric motors in devices ranging from coffee grinders to sewing machines to elevators in the first half of the twentieth century, and of computers on a mass scale in devices ranging from radios to streetlights to aircraft in the second half of that century.[21] The analogies are a guide. Knowing what has already happened tells us a lot about what will happen.

What will the consequences be? Most of them will be beneficial, some will be horrific, and all will come as a shock at first. In Poland, we once had a single telephone booth for a whole housing project. In addition, the wires were sometimes cut. Compare that to the universal prevalence of cell phones in every home today, and the fact that no one worries about wires (although there may be occasional problems with cellular coverage). In parts of the world many homes still do not contain even a cell phone, but new services, particularly in relation to personal finance, are springing up even where wireless communication is still a novelty. In Africa, cell phones help make up for the inadequacy of the banking system. Quasi-banking services are available by cell phone in South Africa and even in the Congo. Subscribers can key in short text messages that enable them to check their accounts, open new ones, make transfers, and pay some bills. In Kenya, only about 3 million people have bank accounts, but a million use the wireless M-PESA payment system. In Botswana, 17 percent of the people who do not have bank accounts have cell phones. Wireless technology can play an increasing role in overcoming the limitations of the hard infrastructure and the unavailability of traditional services. This will have a positive impact on economic efficiency and living conditions.

The results of the coming "revolutions" will be diverse, depending on the usefulness of wireless data transmission in production, distribution, and consumption. Generally speaking, improvements in the quality of management will help to raise efficiency by making operations less material- and energy-intensive, while streamlining inventory management and optimizing the use of human resources. Sectors of the economy aspiring to the status of knowledge-based will make rapid progress. However, there will also be much to learn. Just as it is possible to flounder under piles of paper containing superfluous information, it will also be possible, and much easier, to find oneself swamped by unneeded words, figures, responses, and images in digital form. This theme will continue to appear in comedy films, and we will laugh in 2036 the way people laughed at Chaplin's *Modern Times* in 1936, even if the director is not Chaplin. Great filmmakers will still come along every once in a while.

Some devices will communicate with each other constantly and exchange information to improve their functioning. We will not have to carry documents around, because they will go wherever we go. We will still have to walk to school, but the bookbag will be lighter, or transmitted wirelessly. As we shop, our refrigerator will inform us what we are out of, and the store shelves will place orders with the wholesalers, who in turn will inform the manufacturers on a running basis about which products are in demand. Doctors will know the answer to the question "How are you?" before we enter their offices, but whether patients will feel any better is another question entirely. Many people will furnish themselves with gadgets, now available only to the best-equipped armies, that allow them to monitor events and communicate in real time. No cats or dogs will ever get lost, because we will always know where they are.

It will also be difficult for people to get lost, and this will come as a relief to some and an annoyance to others. The explosion of wireless data transmission of all kinds will alter our approach to ethical quandaries. Intimacy, privacy, and the protection of personal information will not be the same. Even today, when the police stop a drunk driver on the Helsinki-Turku highway, they can immediately find out not only how much alcohol he has in his blood, but also, through a wireless connection, how much he earns. A portable device uses these parameters to issue a ticket on the spot, reflecting both the gravity of the offense and the miscreant's ability to pay. This places three familiar entities—the traffic code, the cop, and the ticket—in a new light. Now people decide in the presence of other people to furnish, process, and make use of information. What will happen when devices communicate with each other, omitting the human intermediary? Who will watch the watchers—other devices? We can see how much there is to do in terms of technology and logistics, and of institutions and politics.

Like fire, Google is a powerful instrument given to humanity free of charge. It is far more than a search engine. It combines satellite photography and satellite navigation systems to make it possible to locate every street and lane in larger cities, and to an increasing degree in hamlets and bergs as well. Before long, we will be able to check who is out in their backyard, in the same way that villagers used to check to see whose chimney had smoke coming out of it. Special programs use satellite imaging to track ice shelves and the effect of their dimensions on global warming. We can monitor refugee camps in Darfur, on the border of Chad and Sudan, which is important for bringing public and political pressure to bear on the international community to force the government in Khartoum to do something about the humanitarian crisis.

We already take for granted the useful applications that Google calls "gadgets." New ones are being added all the time, and some of the names indicate how incredible they are. Not long ago, they would have been something out of a fairy tale. Once people scanned the horizon to see what the weather was going to be like. Now 3D Weather Globe informs us in real time about the current conditions, and even the forecast for the next few days. This is useful for frequent travelers. There is also a global clock that tells us where it is night, where the sun has risen, and where it hasn't set yet. Sitting in front of the computer, we can glance to the left and see what the weather is like on the campus in Aarhus, and then glance right to check whether the sun has come up in New Zealand yet, and whether we should send that e-mail.

In the old days, people would go out onto the front porch to "have a look around." Now more and more people do the same thing as they sit in front of their computers and surf the net. This is no substitute for actually traveling and taking in the complexities of a place, but it is a far cry from running your finger over the map, which is all that most people could do in bygone centuries. Paradoxically, owing to nonlinear development, young people in some parts of the world where education is limited have seen a computer, but have never seen a map. It is hard to believe, but up to 25 percent of the people on earth still do not know what their planet looks like, because they have never seen either a map or a globe.

The really surprising thing is not the rate at which new applications appear on the Internet, but how quickly we take them for granted. It is still hard for many of us to imagine that while the students of the coming generation are sitting in the lecture hall, they will have all the world's knowledge at their fingertips, thanks to wireless devices. Within a few decades, everyone will take that for granted. What was impossible on a mass scale even a few years ago is now run-of-the-mill, like watching movies on YouTube or downloading songs on iTunes. Innovations in both the official and the illegal sectors make it all possible. Now there are eMule or Morpheus, which let users download "anything that can be stolen"—music, movies, TV shows, computer programs, and games. The net has become the horn of plenty.

Through the Internet, committed nongovernmental and supragovernmental organizations will militate for specific political actions. This kind of pressure will escalate and come to hold an increasingly powerful position relative to governments. Not controlled by governments, parties, or capital, the world-wide net will call the tune for governments and companies on a planetary scale, the same way that countries reacted in the last century to the demands of rebellious populations. If Victor Hugo had published *Les Misérables* 200 years later, in 2062, it would surely contain descriptions of the Internet as well as the street barricades. Since Hugo won't be around, someone else will have to write the book. Great writers will still come along every once in a while.

There will be a lot of books. The Internet will no more drive them off the market than television eliminated movies, or film superseded the theater. However, people will have less time to spend reading because they will be spending more time online, especially in the more highly developed countries, where the danger of being swamped by digital information will be greatest. There will be more and more words, but images will have more impact in relative terms. In societies on the way up, including those just shaking off illiteracy as they overcome poverty, reading will flourish. The book will have a second birth, and the Web will be a help, rather than a hindrance.

The Internet has already changed the lives of millions, to the point where many cannot imagine existing without it. For better or for worse, some are so absorbed in the Web that they cannot see the world beyond it. Or rather, they see the world almost exclusively through the Web, which is like food or air to them. Or perhaps like a narcotic—although the Internet is not the worst thing a person can become addicted to.

Over the next few decades, the Internet may change the lives of billions, rather than mere millions. If the dream of the "$100 computer" comes true, then vast numbers, especially the young, will have access in Africa, Asia, and Latin America. Students in schools and universities will go on-line, and others will follow. The most important thing is that the Internet will mean that there are more students, because it will be a powerful educational instrument in countries that will fully deserve the appellation "developing."

If conservative political circles in rich lands and the ossified bureaucrats and experts in international organizations feel that additional aid to poor countries is a waste of money, there is one more way to prove them wrong. Supporting the development of the Internet in less-developed countries is a great challenge, but also a great opportunity. It would drive up demand for hardware and software, most of which originates in more-developed countries, and the sales would stimulate additional growth there. The project is worth one more per mille, a tenth of 1 percent, of the GDP of the advanced countries. That would make a total of $8.00 per month—not much at all, but it adds up to a lot.

Unfortunately, the Internet also remains a playground for hackers and other pranksters who use it in ill will. The aggression sometimes includes the theft of private data, or simply its blind destruction. A single intrusion can result in the larceny of a mother lode of data, as happened to the Monster.com job-search site. Every user is prey to constant attempts at hacking by way of malware distributed over the Web. At this very moment, I have received an e-mail with a malicious-looking attachment from one Johann Brookes, who for all I know may be sitting in Nairobi or Nizhny Novgorod, or even Warsaw. The subject line reads, "What's happened last night." What happened? I spent last night writing about the Internet. Large-scale Internet crises do occur, and they threaten the functioning of information and shipping systems, companies, and even whole countries. This is a completely new aspect of security, which will become more important as our reliance on the Web grows. Mass attacks, capable of paralyzing the network, will grow more common, and protection against them will cost more. Some hard terrorism will turn into soft terrorism. Actually, it has happened already.

We will have to learn how to deal with this abuse, and we will have to pay the price. This is another example of what happens when knowledge is not rooted in the proper cultural, institutional, and political soil. You have to know something to create malware, put other users at risk, and establish yourself up as a hacker, gangster, or terrorist on the Web. Some experts sit up all night trying to figure out how to deal with the new threats, whereas others sit up writing new viruses or trojans. The Internet security company Sophos estimates that more than 8,000 new trojans are released into the wild every month. This is how knowledge and practical skills can serve undesirable ends. We are all going to have to learn new forms of online personal hygiene if we want to stay clean, safe, and healthy.

The Internet is wonderful, but it is hardly a wonder cure for all our ills in this world on the move. Lenin was wrong when he said that communism is Soviet power plus the electrification of the whole country. The enthusiasts of the "new economy" are just as wrong if they think that market liberalism plus the power of the Internet equal perfect capitalism—which is something that does not exist and never will.

Conflict and security, war and peace—these words could describe the whole history of humanity. There has never been a year without conflicts and battles somewhere that, at least from the individual or local point of view, constituted wars. There have also been long periods that were relatively more peaceful, when there was less fighting and more security. From this point of view, we—the overwhelming majority of us who came into this world in the middle of the twentieth century or later—have been lucky. What about the future? That is the final, twelfth compass point on our survey of the Twelve Great Issues for the Future.

We have managed, for these last sixty years and more, to avoid thermonuclear total war, even without the world government that Einstein said, this time erroneously, we needed. More surprisingly, the outbreak of a nuclear conflict was regarded during the presidency of Ronald Reagan as more likely than the collapse of the Soviet Union. In the 1980s, there was not a single serious scholarly work dealing with the economic consequences of the fall of the USSR, but Washington used taxpayer money to finance interdisciplinary research on the economic aftermath of nuclear war. As a result, we now have some fascinating works[22] on the specific kind of economic development that begins from zero.

The fact that we have made it this far does not at all guarantee that our luck will hold. Nevertheless, the odds are close to negligible. People aren't that stupid. However, if terrorists obtain atomic weapons, they will use them. People can be pretty stupid.

For the foreseeable future, this is the greatest threat, as long as there are terrorists and as long as there are ABC weapons, the weapons of mass destruction. Those weapons will exist forever, so the question is: "How long will terrorists be around?" Not forever, we may hope, but they will not leave us alone during our lifetimes, and quite possibly for a few generations yet to come. Before there are fewer terrorists, there will be more. There are already far more of them than there were in 2001, although no one knows how many.

I was in New York right after the tragic events of September 11, 2001. At the time, no one there realized what the long-term consequences of the attack on the World Trade Center would be. No one thought that the misguided American response to this enormous crime would lead to an intensification of the terrorist threat. Success in protecting the territory and citizens of the United States from this barbarity has not ensured the same safety at other points scattered around the world. If this is what the aggressors wanted, then they have been successful.

Aside from the fact that millions of people around the world have been terrified, the costs of operating a range of enterprises, delivering many services, and governing countries have risen. These costs are sometimes invisible, but they are staggering. Politicians and journalists, who sometimes act in their pursuit of sensation as if they were the unwilling spokespersons of the perpetrators, have done more than the terrorists themselves to keep whole societies in a state of fear. They threaten and blackmail people into irrational behavior. All of this has a negative impact on business, and thus another point on the probable terrorist agenda has been achieved.

The response to terrorism must rely above all on comprehensive, globally coordinated, long-term action to remove the causes, rather than armed combat against the symptoms and effects. Action against the effects is also needed, but it cannot solve the problem, even if that action were far more adroit than it is in reality.

In 2005, on the anniversary of the attack on Atocha station, the international association called the Club de Madrid held a conference on *Democracy for a Safer World*. The king of Spain, Juan Carlos, headed the list of experts and heads of governments. Madeleine Albright, President Bill Clinton's secretary of state, told me that America's reaction to the threat had unquestionably made world terrorism worse. Zbigniew Brzezinski elsewhere also claims this to be true.. Both of them, indeed, served under Democratic presidents, whereas the "War on Terror" was declared by a Republican president. Nevertheless, most serious analysts and independent academic experts shared their views.

Some markedly partisan political scientists showed considerable obstinacy in campaigning to insert a passage in the declaration issued by this influential assembly to the effect that poverty is not a factor that encourages international terrorism. It took a concerted effort to prevent this explicit assertion from appearing at the very beginning of the economic section of the declaration. The incident tells us a great deal.

No one has come up with a better form of preventive action than balanced economic development on a global scale. If it did not weaken the resolve of the terrorists themselves, it would at least undercut their social support. Development shortfalls are surely some of the strongest inducements to international terrorism. Less injustice in sharing the spoils of growth, less social exclusion, liberalized migration and cultural absorption of ethnic minorities, and international relations founded on a basis of partnership all have great significance.

This may not be a totally effective antidote to the pathology of extreme religious fundamentalism and nationalism, but it would go a long way toward undermining the rigid social and political attitudes that encourage organized terrorism. Terrorism itself has gone international, and perhaps even global. It makes use of science and the Web. It cannot be defeated by force, because it is different in scale from the Baader-Meinhof Gang and Red Brigades of the past, or the dwindling power of the Sendero Luminoso, the IRA, and ETA. It must be fought using methods that require us to understand that poverty is public enemy number one for humanity, including the wealthy. We should declare war on poverty around the world, in order to avoid another world war.

There is no doubt that the greatest institutional threat we have inherited from the previous century is the denationalization or privatization of war. The demon has slipped the leash of state control. Just as it is always a problem to get the genie back into the bottle, we are left wondering what to do about this most real of all our problems. It does not occur in highly developed countries with strong institutions and adult cultures. In those countries, the state keeps the army under control and finances it from tax receipts. It is increasingly rare for armies to take over and install undemocratic regimes, as they frequently did not long ago in the less-developed states of Africa and Latin America.

One of the most flourishing places in Central America today is Costa Rica. That country has abolished its army but does not feel insecure. One of the least flourishing countries in Southeast Asia is Burma, where a dictatorial military junta controls the state and the economy. Burma is not secure. Things are worst where the institution of the state itself is in disarray or collapse, as was the case in Afghanistan until recently, in Nepal for a time, and in Somalia all the time. Security requires a strong state and, above all, strong institutions. A lot of effort will have to be put into reinforcing the state and its institutions in numerous countries.

Quasi-local conflicts have not only a negative impact on regional security, but also the potential to spread like cancer through the entire world organism. Things can be kept under control when the countries involved are relatively small, but if the countries are larger, like Pakistan or Nigeria, then the consequences for world peace are more dire. We see interdependence, one of the prime traits of globalization, at work here. To avoid big wars, we must constantly prevent small ones.

What makes things more difficult is the fact that, against the background of the general neoliberal euphoria over trade liberalization, the armaments trade has been deregulated to an irrational degree. The dismantling of the state monopoly may be irrational, but it has been lucrative for the lobby concerned. The production of and trade in military equipment and ammunition have been privatized. The removal of the state institutions that supervised these matters is an impediment to coordinated international action. The illegal arms trade is flourishing, despite the fact that manufacturing tanks, antitank weapons, and machine guns is not the same as counterfeiting and smuggling Gucci handbags, Nike shoes, or Lanvin ties.

Paradoxically, things are more dangerous when democracy is flourishing than when it was restricted. Instead of one state-run cold war, we have a plethora of privatized mini-wars. It will be all the harder to remedy this situation because there are more actors on the scene, the lines of conflict are less clear, and the issues are less transparent. It is no surprise that a militarily powerful Russia finds itself unable to deal with the Chechens, and the assembled might of NATO, with the superwealthy United States in the vanguard, cannot finish off the Taliban in grindingly poor Afghanistan.

The sooner we reverse the proportion between expenditures on armaments and war (including the numerous "peacekeeping missions," of course), and appropriations to co-finance the development of the poor lands, the sooner the root causes of these smoldering or blazing armed conflicts will begin to disappear. This will not be easy, but it is possible. We can find the examples we need in Central America and Indochina.

Having no illusions is a good thing. The powerful military-industrial complex and the associated political lobby (not to mention, once again, the generously sponsored media) are not something dreamed up by pacifists and populists, but hard facts. This sector's special interests are also hard. What would happen if peace broke out? If there were no threats and conflicts, there would be no demand and no sales, no income and no profits. We need to remain fully aware of the political economy of potential and real wars. For societies and humanity, they are a nightmare. For the death merchants, they are business. The nightmare is business. The conundrum cannot be fully removed in a generation or five generations or, in all probability, ever. Believing otherwise would be utopian. However, the harmfulness of the syndrome can be alleviated, and we must strive to do so in the decades and centuries to come.

Therefore, we have reasons to be afraid, but we should not go mad. Will we be taking off our shoes at airport checkpoints until the end of time? Type *terror* into Google and you get 87 million links. Type in *peace* and you get 189 million. Type in *war* and you get 532 million. It is interesting, and also a little sad, to see how many synonyms for war we have created in all our languages over the centuries, and how few for peace. It will be interesting to observe which of these two lexical families, *war* or *peace*, expands the most during the coming century. I think that it will be peace, in the end. Economic development will play a crucial role. The dilemma of war and peace will remain indissolubly connected to the dilemma of stagnation and development.

———————

All of this can be seen, clearly or as if through the fog, on the horizon of the future. The essence lies in the fact that, as we edge forward over time, we see something new, something different, each day. The face of this world on the move will keep changing. The way we live will also change, but not as rapidly as it has in our time. Haven't we been lucky! The changes in life style over a mere two generations connected with the increase in longevity, the doubling of the population, urbanization, the ubiquity of air travel, the car, TV, the telephone, the computer, and above all the explosion of the Web, have been epochal. Never before has so much changed in such a short time, and it will probably never happen again—at least not on such a mass scale, so universally, and so powerfully felt day in and day out.

A hundred years from now, the political map of the world will look pretty much the way it looks today. The things that had to change have, for the most part, already changed. There won't be any caliphate, the unitary Islamic state. That's another pipe dream. Some countries will break up—Iraq soonest of all, followed by a few in Africa and South Asia. Others may shift their borders, mostly in Africa as a way of correcting the political legacy of colonialism and adjusting in a more sensible way to the dispersion of ethnic groups, rather than continuing to follow the old imperialist straight lines that carved up the land like pieces of a cake. Most of these corrections will be handled through negotiation and territorial compensation.

Few states will merge into new entities. It might happen in some parts of the Middle East, where the success story of the United Arab Emirates is a model, and perhaps among some of the African countries that feel themselves strongly bound together in cultural terms. There will be new federations, and the regional integration groups will be far stronger than at present, especially the Asian economic community and the South American alternative to North America's NAFTA. Australia and New Zealand, looking back nostalgically on the times when they were, first, the remote antipodes and, later, pro-Western allies of the United States, will be drawn into the orbit of Asia, and more specifically of China and Japan. Those two countries will continue their peaceful rivalry. The United States will still be a superpower, trying to keep up as China and Europe pull away.

Human migration will continue on a larger scale. Many Asians from the south and east of the continent will settle in the territories of the Russian Far East, in the Primorsky Krai (which, surprisingly, had several times the present population density 2,000 years ago) and above all Siberia, where life will become increasingly tolerable. When I asked the rector of the university in Birobijan, the capital of the Jewish Autonomous Oblast in the Russian Far East, whether English was popular in his foreign language department, he said that two different languages were particularly in demand: Hebrew among those who had made up their minds to leave, and Chinese among those who had made up their minds to stay.

Far from causing wars, migration, such as the great migration from Africa and the Middle East to Europe, will be a key way of avoiding them. Europeans will also be on the move, and in every conceivable direction. They will even be going to Siberia—voluntarily, for a change. Although it will still not be *Paradis*, millions will move to Africa, and especially the regions with attractive natural surroundings, just as today's city dwellers move to the country because logistics have improved and their jobs no longer tie them to the inconveniences of urban life.

Culture will become more heterogeneous. As a result, there will be far more tolerance for the values of the people who are moving around the world in such numbers. Personal contact will foster this tolerance, and so will the media. Contacts will be a vehicle for cultural and economic progress, and a factor that blurs cultural traditions. We can already see this today, when many local cultures, often referred to as "folk," are slowly receding into oblivion, or being cultivated by amateur groups and as tourist attractions. This is what has happened with the Highlanders in Scotland and the Gypsy caravans of Central Europe, with the Turkish villages and in Tibet. It will happen everywhere.

It will be brighter, especially at night. There will be much more light, although it won't necessarily be the *"Mehr licht!"* that Goethe called for on his deathbed. Almost everywhere, electrification will be more intense than it is today in heavily populated areas. Evenings will last longer in places where they now end when the sun goes down. One of the things that strikes you most when you travel around today is the intensity of the electric lighting in North America, and its absence in

Africa. When your airplane is approaching LAX, everything is lit up. The urban agglomeration beneath you uses up several times as much electricity as the populous country of Ethiopia, where the descent to Bole airport takes place in nearly total darkness. There will be fewer and fewer places where you can admire total darkness even for a brief moment. The vast majority of people living in affluent countries have never experienced it, and they never will unless they happen to find themselves in the vastness of the Sahara, the Australian Outback, the Mongolian steppes, the Siberian tundra, or the middle of the Pacific, the places where there is not a single light bulb or a single campfire for 100 or more kilometers around, and where all the notebooks and satellite phones are turned off.

For several years, the Bortle Dark-Sky Scale has used scores from 1 to 9 to measure the degree to which artificial lighting and its reflections impinge upon the darkness.[23] Copernicus and his contemporaries all over the world could wonder at a sky with a score of 1, as can the Barre family in Niger today. New Yorkers have a sky with a score of 9. On a clear night in Manhattan, you can see less than 1 percent of what the Wappinger Indians saw there almost 400 years ago, before they sold the island to the Dutch for 60 gulden. Aside from distant parts of Alaska, it is never darker than 2 anywhere in the United States. Even the most remote mountain meadows in Poland are 3 or brighter because of reflected urban light, the glow over small towns, or the glare from village homesteads.

A hundred years from now, 95 percent of humanity will never see what our forebears saw every day, or rather every night, and which some people are still lucky enough to see, even though they may not even be aware that it is possible not to see what "everybody can see." While vast areas of the earth 100 years from now will not be as brightly illuminated as the United States is today, the great majority of the earth's inhabited space will fall between 5 and 9 on the Bortle scale. Only rarely will it be 2 to 4, and expeditions to enclaves with a score of 1 will rank among the greatest of tourist attractions.

This is a matter not only of losing the chance to see something that is absolutely beautiful, but also of understanding the psychophysiological consequences of a state of affairs that upsets the natural biological rhythm of life. Turn out the lights in your room and see what you can see. It's not dark, even when you're asleep, and people sleep far better in total darkness.

A hundred years from now, some species of animals and plants will have disappeared, and so will some ethnic groups and languages. Languages will vanish especially quickly. The linguists who say that we lose two languages a month and that the only ones left in the future will be English, Chinese, Spanish, and Arabic[24] are exaggerating, perhaps deliberately, as a way of making people aware of the problem. However, it is a fact that some languages and dialects are now spoken only by a handful of people.

A favorite anecdote among travelers relates how the great German explorer Alexander von Humboldt was wandering through the South American jungle when he reached the village of Maypures on the banks of the Orinoco. He heard words from a language he did not recognize— it turned out that a parrot was chattering away. Humboldt asked the Indians what language that was, and they replied that it was Atures, but that only the bird spoke it. The last people from that ethnic group had died several years before Humboldt arrived in 1800.

Today only 1,500 Karo people live on the banks of the Omo in southwestern Ethiopia. The last words in the Kerek language will be uttered before long on the Bering Sea in Chukotka, because fewer than thirty of those who speak it are still alive. There are villages in Papua New Guinea where only a dozen or so of old people gossip around the fire in their mother tongue. The same is true in the highlands along the border between Laos and Vietnam, or in the jungles of Borneo. Three Aborigines who speak the Mati Ke language are said to be alive on the northern coast of Australia. Before long, like the last tree on Mauritius, the last member of another tribe will be gone, and there won't be any parrot to come to the rescue.

Ludwik Zamenhof (1859–1917) envisioned a beautiful utopia in which everyone communicated in the simple, global language of Esperanto. That dream will never come true, but the effects of the divine retribution for the human intrusion into heaven are slowly being reversed. We built the Tower of Babel and had our tongues confounded, but the number of languages we speak is on the decline. At the same time, more and more people will speak English, although that language will never become the McLanguage that some people fear. It will grow even more dominant, however, especially because it has finally won the long war with French over the right to be the planetary *lingua franca*. Above all, it has become the language of business, and science and technology, including economics. Millions of people will know their native language, but also regard English as their own, just as they can regard the world as their own.

There will be fewer languages but more words. The interpenetration of cultures, and above all the progress in science and technology, will enrich language. In the Renaissance it was mainly literature—poetry and drama—that gave birth to new words. (Shakespeare is credited with introducing more than 2,000 new words to English.) Now, this is the role of science. Thousands of words will come into use that can be found in no dictionary today. In economics, most of them will have to do with finance and management. These words do not exist yet because the phenomena and processes they will describe do not exist yet, or are not known.

The basic data and analyses will still be categorized by country, but more and more of them will refer to new profiles that cut across the traditional national breakdown. New measures of economic progress and social prosperity will emphasize nonmaterial values and the increasing worth of the natural environment.

Some countries will rank among the most highly developed even without growth in output or migration, because they have a clean environment, something that cannot be transferred like physical goods and some services. These countries will become wealthy without having to undergo environmentally destructive industrialization or create a knowledge-based economy that, in the present sense of the concept, is more than they can afford. Their asset will be their attractiveness to tourists. There are triads of these countries: Ecuador-Peru-Bolivia, Namibia-Botswana-Zambia, and Laos-Cambodia-Burma. Mongolia will also be wealthy. It will be the first country in history to become a national park in its entirety, or perhaps rather a park for all humanity.

Although the value of world output will be many times greater, it will weigh less and less in the literal sense. Similarly, our output today would weigh less, if it could be placed on some sort of cosmic scale, than the output of a few decades ago. One reason for this is the decreasing material-intensity of production and the growing share of services in GDP, but even more important is the fact that value comes from the knowledge built into products, rather than the material processed to make them. A 136-gram iPod is worth more than five tons of coal. A 2.5-kg. MacBook Pro costs as much as 25 tons of cement. The "heavier" the knowledge, the lighter the GWP (Gross World Product), and the higher the GNH (Gross National Happiness) and GWH (Gross World

Happiness), at least to the degree that these indexes reflect education and the level of cultural attainment.

There will be new common-currency zones. Now we have four of them basically—two in Africa, one in Europe, and one in America. A century from now, there may be more than a dozen, including a zone in Central and South America that uses the dollar. The American currency will be the world's third choice. The main reserve currency will be the yuan, which will also circulate in several other Asian and African countries. The euro will be in second place. Not only will it last out the century, but it will circulate in more than fifty countries in Europe, Asia, and Africa. The global, our world currency, will still be on the drawing board because the world economy won't yet be rational enough for it. That day may never come, for the same reason that Esperanto never really caught on.

The world economy will be far more integrated than at present, but it will still not make up a fully integrated organism on the model of the classical national economies. Nevertheless, more and more business will be done across borders that are so invisible that people are no more aware of crossing them than they are when they drive from Belgium into the Netherlands today. Yet there will still be borders marked with barbed wire and guard towers where armed sentries keep watch.

The world institutional order will be different, but still far from perfect. We will still complain about how it doesn't meet "the challenges of the modern world." However, the world will be more balanced from the point of view of political and economic forces, and the influence of countries or groups of countries on the course of events.

The far more functional entities that emerge after the liquidation of the World Bank and the International Monetary Fund will be based on more democratic and pragmatic development economics, instead of using high-sounding slogans while serving the political interests of the wealthy states. The new headquarters will be in Asia, above all because that is where one of the centers of economic thinking, especially of the theories of growth and development regarded as the mainstream, will be. China will use part of its reserves as seed capital, and as an inducement for others to join the new organizations.

World public opinion will count for much more, not that this will necessarily be to the liking of the national politicians who trumpet their love of democracy. However, the power of nongovernmental organizations and the technical capabilities of the wireless network will simply make it easier to ask people what they think. It will no longer be possible to ignore this voice, the way today's rulers do. We will still be a long way from a true planetary democracy on the principle of one person, one vote, because those votes will continue to be tabulated, at least informally, within the context of material status. On the global scale, we will be closer than ever to universal suffrage, but we won't be there yet.

The world will re-enact the twentieth-century American longevity explosion, which took the country from life expectancies of 48.3 years for men and 46.3 for women in 1900 to 74.2 and 79.9, respectively, in 2000. The average planetary life expectancy will be about eighty years, and in the richer countries it will be more than ninety. Will personal and collective happiness keep up?

"May you live 100 years" will go from a conventional but sincere wish in some countries to a hard-headed short-term prognosis. There will be more retirees in the postproductive phase of their lives than children and young people in the preproductive phase. If three German women continue to give birth to four children between them, then that country, chosen here as an example, will be unable to sustain its level of population without relying on increased inward migration, especially from the Islamic countries, with their pro-procreation attitudes. This will have far-reaching consequences for models of consumer behavior, on the one hand, and public finances and the savings market, on the other. The Swiss may ban minarets from their Alpine landscapes because they regard them as unsightly, but they will be unable to vote down the higher Muslim birth rate. They will end up having to accept mosques with minarets disguised to look like church spires.

We will treat cancer with tablets and regard it the way we regard tuberculosis today—being diagnosed with TB was once a death sentence. AIDS will have the status that syphilis has today—syphilis once decimated whole populations. When we catch cold, the standard treatment will still involve aspirin and a week in bed. Medicine will be very expensive. A healthy lifestyle—preventive medicine, treatment, and all the varieties of active tourism, recreation, and sport, not to mention healthy food—will be one of the biggest items in domestic budgets in affluent countries.

Unfortunately, new diseases will appear, and they will be terrible. We cannot even imagine how or when they will attack us. Preparedness for outbreaks will cost as much as keeping the peace, but it will be worth paying for, because this is a matter of life and death.

We will work four days a week, although those who wish will try to work seven. Getting to work will take twice as long as it does today. Fewer people will commute, because more will work at home. Good urban and suburban mass transit will be back in favor. There will be less leisure time on working days, but more in the week as a whole. Because leisure time is consumption time, it's a good thing that people will have more money to spend. We will earn four times what we earn today. An average annual pay rise of 1.4 percent, in real terms, will do the trick, or 10 percent every seven years. It works out the same over 100 years.

We still won't be able to satisfy our needs, which will outstrip income. A long-term development strategy should not only worry about creating conditions for a steadily rising level of output, but also take into account a realistic appraisal of consumer appetites. There comes a time when those appetites must stop escalating. The wealthy and even the middle class will count their money differently—evaluate it differently, in fact—once they learn to factor in the monetized value of free time. Today it is hard to get a reliable answer when you ask how much an hour of free time—free of work or commuting to work—is worth. In the future, everybody will know the answer.

In 100 years, we will react to the water bill the same way we react to soaring electricity bills today, because water will be more and more expensive. Climate tariffs will go from being symbolic to commercial and will constitute an important source of revenue for localities with green grass and clean water. The taxes that pay for public goods will be viewed correctly as expenses for essential services that the private sector cannot supply. An awareness of the necessity of such services will go hand in hand with greater acceptance of the way they are paid for— through taxes. Politicians and commentators will still see the fiscal system as profitable, at least for themselves.

An enormous part of our household budgets will continue to be wasted on covering the cost of advertising, which makes up part of the price of everything we buy. On the macroeconomic scale, there will be controversy over whether advertising should be treated as a cost of production or as part of what is produced. Perhaps a portion of this expenditure, as evidently wasteful, should be deducted from indexes of well-being, if not from GDP. We will also pay more for analyses prepared by companies that monitor advertising in order to help save consumers from being buried under the marketing avalanche. Like advertising today, in some ways, consumer protection will be both a great line of work and a powerful political force. A hundred years from now, people will be amazed at the things that ad agencies used to get away with, just as we shake our heads over the fact that the faithful used to pay good money for indulgences in the Middle Ages.

Nationalism will not disappear from economic policy, although patriotism will contain relatively more cosmopolitanism than protectionism. "Motherland" will count for less among the social values, and "children's land" for more. That is, the rising generation will count for more than nostalgia for the past. Investing in education will seem more important than providing social welfare for the elderly, who will have to look after themselves through the highly developed system of private insurance. The young, in turn, will save more for the whole of their long old age and less for their series of brief vacations. They will have more time to save, because the average retirement age in developed countries will be closer to seventy than to sixty. Nevertheless, retirement will last longer and be healthier, and therefore happier, than today.

The data in the statistical annuals and economics textbooks will be updated on demand, wirelessly, and it will no longer be necessary to get up from the armchair where one is reading to check definitions on the Internet, look something up in an atlas, or compare the statistics in the book with the latest original sources. Access to all information from every point on the face of the earth will be technically feasible.

As individuals and societies, people will have a qualitatively different approach to questions of pollution and environmental destruction. Everyone will agree with the need to clean up the environment, and there will be powerful, almost unanimous pressure for action. Attitudes to smokers changed rapidly in the course of a few decades, and polluters will be seen the same way in the future. We can already see things starting to happen, but the changes will be epochal before long. Today most of us would find it unthinkable to dump garbage in our backyards, up against the neighbor's fence. Over time, individuals and more and more nations will regard it as equally inconceivable to contaminate the environment anywhere, in any way. This is a cultural change that will have far-reaching cultural and economic implications.

Bringing the climate under control to a certain extent will help ward off the danger of natural disasters, but the poorest regions, especially in sub-Saharan Africa, will be even more vulnerable than at present to shortages of water caused by meteorological anomalies. The effects of climate change that we are beginning to feel today will be coming under partial control. To the satisfaction of some, however, the changes wrought by warming will make it possible to exploit resources that were previously inaccessible. In particular, the dissolution of the north polar icecap will make it possible, and profitable, to extract resources from the Arctic Sea. The United States Geological Survey estimates that up to one fourth of the undiscovered energy reserves lie there.

Just to be safe, Russia carried out a bold, technically impeccable operation in which it deployed the two *Mir* deep submergence vehicles (*mir* means in Russian both "peace" and "the world") to the bottom of the ocean, 4,200 meters beneath the North Pole, where members of the Russian team planted a titanium national flag, just as the Americans planted the Stars and Stripes on the moon in 1969. The difference is that no one will be bringing any raw materials back from the moon even 100 years from now, because there are not enough of them there to make economic sense, and above all because it will still be technically impossible.

It will take an hour and a half to fly from Moscow to San Francisco. Getting to the airport and going through security will take longer than the flight across two continents and the ocean that divides them: a five-to-six hour trip, with only ninety minutes spent in the air. Instead of credit cards or passports (which will still exist, and have more importance than ever), we will simply have to touch a finger to a screen or look deeply into one of the electronic eyes that follow us everywhere. People in uniform will frisk us, and specially trained dogs will sniff at us. There will be electronic dogs too. They might be better at sniffing, but not at anything else.

It will not be necessary to write text messages or e-mails. All we will have to do is say what we are thinking, and the message will reach its recipient, who will immediately hear or see us. At home, we will be able to watch every movie ever made and listen to concert performances of every conceivable musical work, merely by choosing from a list on the digital console. We won't even have to touch anything if we don't want to. Saying the title out loud will be enough. Say "Haydn's *The Creation*, with John Eliot Gardiner conducting the English Baroque Soloists" and you will be listening to it. Say "Antonioni's *Il deserto rosso*" and you will be watching it. Say "Pink Floyd's *The Wall*" and you will be seeing and hearing it. The fee will be automatically deducted from your online bank account, so you can cherish the illusion that it doesn't cost anything.

All of this is only for some. The rest will live in poverty. Even if it looks, in some places, like today's middle-class existence, it will still be poverty. Many people will continue to subsist in abject misery and only live half as long as the average in the richest countries, despite significant declines in infant and child mortality. They will have no safety net to protect them if they cannot find a job, fall ill, or grow old. Relatives and kindly neighbors will still bear the entire burden. Neither hunger, nor epidemics, nor illiteracy will go away. Great numbers of people will be unable to speak English or the regional *lingua franca*, always vital for business and especially trade, like Swahili in East Africa, Hausa in Nigeria and the adjacent countries, French in the Sahel, or Hindi in the Indian subcontinent. They will not even know how to read in their own language.

For great contingents of humanity, the standard and style of life will change not at all, or only to a minimal, imperceptible degree: simple, total reproduction. As it was, so it will be. Many people today stand in the same relationship to their own forebears of several generations ago. The physical and biological clocks are running, but the hands of the cultural and economic clocks remain immobile.

A significant portion of humanity will have neither the need nor the financial means to gain access to the information that exists. The need must be stimulated, and the means created. Therefore, the distance separating this segment of humanity from the most highly developed societies will be greater than at present, despite all the progress lying before us. The "$100 computer" exists, with its tremendous potential for qualitative change in the poorest countries, but it cannot overcome the lack of roads and power lines, or inadequate education and hygiene.

Although some slums will disappear, others will arise. Some metropolises will thrive and others decline. The face of this world will change, literally. Its more developed part, the "north," will be more and more colorful. Many cities will look like Los Angeles, a megalopolis where "people of color" already account for over half the population. This ethnic blending will enhance the cultural landscape, and may well enrich the social fabric (although it could also lead to antagonism). This is the great unknown: How will all these people choose to function? Will it be like Odessa a century and a half ago, before the shock and shame of the first pogrom, or like contemporary Western cities—certain incidents notwithstanding—such as Amsterdam or Copenhagen? Or will there be new fodder for the proponents of the "clash of civilizations"? The American model of cultural mixing seems most promising. Although there are also shadows looming over this model, as shown in recent disturbances in Los Angeles and some other cities, it still has an enormous amount to teach the rest of the world, including Europe. The greatest of these lessons is mutual understanding and tolerance, where minorities melt into the mainstream culture while enriching it with their own.

We will manage to dodge the Very Big War, which could kill 300 million people in a single day—equal to the entire human population a thousand years ago. Nevertheless, small wars will break out here and there every few years, on all continents, although things will be worst where there is poverty in terms of output and wealth in terms of resources. After all, some use must be found for the weapons that the rich countries produce; the best solution is to sell them, and test them from time to time, in the poor countries that will be able to afford this idiotic expenditure for the next century, and the centuries after that.

Even if all this comes true, who among us today cares what the world will be like in 100 years, since we won't be here? A hundred years ago, who cared what the world would be like a century onward—in other words, today? Few, if any, cared. Yet everything happens so fast. The next "now" comes along faster than a frame in a film. This is the pulsating reality of our lives. Some among us remember grandparents born as much as 150 years ago. The grandchildren of the youngest among us will read these words 150 years from now. That's three centuries! You only have to focus your vision and your thoughts in one direction and the other, and you start to see everything. It is like being on all fours again—such a stable posture, but so uninteresting—and then standing up straight and having a good look around the horizon. There really is a lot to see.

It's always better to see than not to see. To understand more, rather than less. To imagine things accurately, rather than not at all. So many mistakes in the future can be avoided, just as our forebears could have saved us so much trouble. They weren't up to it. They didn't do it, and the price had to be paid. They didn't think in a comprehensive, long-term way. They didn't make comparisons. They didn't move around enough in time and space. If they had been better at doing that, we could have had it better. If we're better at it, then they—those generations to come—will have it better, and will have less to complain about. It won't matter if they don't put up any monuments, but it will be nice if they don't have any reasons to curse us.

———————

And then, there will be less dung, and many more flowers.

A Letter

To My Granddaughter's Granddaughter

Warsaw, 2010

My Dear Girl,

You were born in the *fin de siècle*, at the end of the 21st century; I was born in the middle of the 20th. I graduated from high school in 1967, and you in 2107. It's hardly strange that the questions on the final exam were different. There's been a lot of water under the bridge, and look how quickly it flowed! Time separates us, and it connects us.

The future is the past. The past is the future.

In the years that are your past, but that still remain my future, a good many of the things that could have happened did happen. The reason it turned out this way, and not otherwise, is explained by my coincidence theory, the theory of development that is no longer something new in your time, but rather something obvious. However, many of the things—good and bad—that could have happened, didn't. This is the difference between us. We have a completely different relation to before and after.

Things could have happened, but didn't. This means that one of the critical elements, from the blend of circumstances that determine what happens, was missing. Sometimes this was just a matter of luck, but deliberate human action was decisive more often. In any case, words were always important. They have meaning, a great deal of it.

It's amazing how many things were supposedly impossible but happened anyway. In my day, we didn't have enough imagination. With unpredictable things, imagination makes more difference than knowledge, because we don't have any knowledge to go by yet.

All of us, including you, are the outcomes of a future that might well not have happened. As you can see from your viewpoint, we took advantage of most of our chances, but we missed a few. You live in a completely different world that's still on the move, but that could have been even happier, more beautiful, and richer. There must be a lot of flowers, but there could have been even more, couldn't there?

When I gaze far into the future, I see—because I know—how much is possible. When you peer into the past, in turn, you surely see—because you know so much more, even though you're not majoring in economics—how many chances were missed. The loss is irreversible, or at least it will remain so for another hundred years.

But it doesn't matter. The next hundred years will pass. Write a letter to your granddaughter's granddaughter (maybe she'll study economics). Tell her to read *Truth, Errors, and Lies: Politics and Economics in a Volatile World* and check to see where we were right and where we were wrong. And tell her to be sure to send us an e-mail, or whatever they call it then, in 2210.

I'm glad that you're majoring in APS. I always said that interdisciplinary studies have a colossal future. You'll understand a lot, and see even more, and you'll have a chance to help development along. Everybody should do all they can.

At the beginning of the 20th century, Albert Einstein said that a scientist tells himself a story and then uses an experiment to check whether it is true or not. In physics, an experiment can verify the correctness of a hypothesis—although not all hypotheses—at once. Some were not confirmed beyond question until the early 21st century, and even in the early 22nd century some will surely be comprehensible to only the very few. Development economics can only be verified on the historical scale, and this has sometimes been very costly. Remember: it's better to be right while there's still time.

I've told my story. You've read this book, and you have all the facts verified, classified, and interpreted at a touch, or a click, or a voice command, so check for yourself! I hope that you'll be happy when you see that I was right.

Being right is just as nice as being lucky.

I hope that you and all those around you will be right, and that even more so, you'll be lucky!

Always and eternally yours,

gwk

P.S. I'm enclosing a thousand euro, because something tells me you haven't got a thing to wear. Buy yourself something nice!

:-)

Notes

1. The World, Words, and Meaning

1. See, for instance, Kazimierz Łaski, "The Stabilization Plan for Poland," *Wirtschaftspolitische Blätter*, 5 (1990): 444–58. See also Mario D. Nuti, *Crisis, Reform, and Stabilization in Central Eastern Europe: Prospects and Western Response* [in] *La Grande Europa, la Nuova Europa: Opportunità e Rischi* (Siena: Monte dei Paschi di Siena, 1990). The author of the present work has published extensively on this issue in scholarly journals since 1989. See also a polemic with Jeffrey Sachs, who had powerful influence on the Polish minister of finance and other high government officials at the time: Grzegorz W. Kołodko, "Patient Is Ready," *The Warsaw Voice*, Dec. 4, 1989.

2. Carl Sagan, "The Fine Art of Baloney Detection," *Parade*, Feb. 1. 1987.

3. Michael Shermer, *Why People Believe Weird Things: Pseudoscience, Superstitions, and Other Confusions of Our Time* (New York: W. H. Freeman, 1997).

4. Francis Wheen, *How Mumbo-Jumbo Conquered the World: A Short History of Modern Delusions* (London: Harper Perennial, 2004).

5. Francis Fukuyama, *The End of History and the Last Man* (New York: Free Press, 1992).

6. Isaac Getz and Alan G. Robinson, "Innovate or Die: Is That a Fact?" *Creativity and Innovation Management*, 12, no. 3 (2003): 130–36. www.black well-synergy.com.

7. For more on the great postcommunist systemic changes see Grzegorz W. Kolodko, *From Shock to Therapy. The Political Economy of Postsocialist Transformation* (New York: Oxford University Press, 2000)

8. The author of the present work joins with other authors in considering the lessons to be learned from the Polish transformation—what worked and what didn't—and its applicability for other countries in the process of complex

systemic change in *The Polish Miracle: Lessons for the Emerging Markets* (Burlington, VT: Ashgate, Aldershot, 2005).

9. Joseph E. Stiglitz, *Globalization and Its Discontents* (New York: W.W. Norton, 2002).

10. Robert Gwiazdowski, "Stiglitz: falszywy prorok" [Stiglitz—a false prophet], *Forbes* [Polish edition], Dec. 2006, p. 144.

11. Andrew Reynolds, introduction to Victor Erofeyev, *Life with an Idiot*, trans. Andrew Reynolds (London: Penguin, 2004), pp. xx.

12. Wisława Szymborska, "List," translated by Stanisław Barańczak and Clare Cavanagh, *Monologue of a Dog* (Orlando, FL: Harcourt, 2006), pp. 83–87.

13. Jeffrey D. Sachs, *The End of Poverty: How We Can Make It Happen in Our Lifetime* (New York: Penguin, 2005).

14. Montaigne, *Essays*, Charles Cotton translation (1877), I, 9.

15. See, for instance, Paul Ekman, *Telling Lies: Clues to Deceit in the Marketplace, Marriage, and Politics* (New York: W. W. Norton, 1985), and Chris Thurman, *The Lies We Believe* (Nashville: Thomas Nelson, 1989).

16. David Harvey, *A Brief History of Neoliberalism* (New York: Oxford University Press, 2005).

17. John R. Lott and Kevin A. Hassett, "Is Newspaper Coverage of Economic Events Politically Biased?" Social Science Research Network, 2004, www.ssrn.com.

18. Christopher Andrew and Vasili Mitrokhin state that the KGB managed to place no fewer than 1,980 articles in the Indian press in 1976, and 440 in the Pakistani press in 1977. These are only examples of a form of information manipulation that was practiced universally and, of course, by both sides during the Cold War. *The World Was Going Our Way: The KGB and the Battle for the Third World* (New York: Basic Books, 2005).

19. Janos Kornai, *By Force of Thought: Irregular Memoirs of an Intellectual Journey* (Cambridge, MA: MIT Press, 2006).

20. World Bank, *The State in a Changing World* (New York: Oxford University Press, 1977); Janos Kornai, *The Role of the State in a Post-Socialist Economy: Distinguished Lecture Series* (Warsaw: Leon Kozminski Academy of Entrepreneurship and Management, 2001), www.tiger.edu.pl; Joseph E. Stiglitz, *Making Globalization Work* (New York: W. W. Norton, 2007); Fukuyama, *State-Building: Governance and World Order in the 21st Century* (Ithaca, NY: Cornell University Press, 2004).

21. Wei-Bin Zhang, *Economic Growth Theory: Capital, Knowledge, and Economic Structures* (Burlington, VT: Ashgate, Aldershot, 2005); Elhanan Helpman, *The Mystery of Economic Growth* (Cambridge, MA: Harvard University Press, 2004). Mathematical formulas take precedence over words and dominate the discourse in the former book. The latter book, containing no formulas at all, represents one of the best studies of the issues of economic growth.

22. Albrecht Fölsing, *Albert Einstein: A Biography* (New York: Penguin, 1998), p. 457.

2. How Things Happen

1. Jim Crace, *The Pesthouse* (London: Picador, 2007).
2. Cormac McCarthy, *The Road* (New York: Vintage International, 2007).
3. Tobias Buck reports in an article dated March 5, 2007, that "The European Union's economic development is only now reaching the level achieved by the US more than two decades ago. . . . The US reached the EU's current level of gross domestic product per capita in 1985, according to [a] report by Eurochambres, the pan-European business lobby." "EU Economy Is 20 Years Behind US, Says Study." http://www.ft.com/cms/s/0/9ebc7f02-cb3e-11db-b436-000b5df10621.html (accessed July 31, 2009).
4. The Fespaco (Festival Panafricain du Cinéma et de la Télévision de Ouagadougou) has been organized in Burkina Faso every two years since 1969, and has become a cultural event of significance for the whole continent and an engine for the emergence of the young African cinema onto the world scene. At the twentieth anniversary festival in February-March 2007, the Nigerian film *Ezra* by Newton Aduaka won the grand prize, the Yenneng Golden Mustang. The film recounts the fate of a boy soldier in the Sierra Leone civil war, which has left the country one of the poorest in the world, with a per capita GDP of about $900 by purchasing power parity, which equated to a mere $200 at the exchange rate in 2007, enough to pay for one night's stay at the best hotel in the war-ravaged country's capital, Freetown.
5. Louis Armstrong, *Black and Blue* in *The Louis Armstrong Collection*, vol. 2 (St. Laurent, Quebec: Excelsior-St. Clair Entertainment Group, 1995).
6. Barack Obama, *Dreams from My Father: A Story of Race and Inheritance* (New York: Crown Publishers, 2007).
7. Purchasing power parity, or PPP, is frequently used in international comparisons. It takes account of the wide differentials in price structure and level as a way of indicating the amount of goods and services that can be purchased in the local currency. For instance, if the same representative "shopping basket" of consumer goods could be purchased in China for 2 yuan as could be bought with $1.00 in the U.S., then $1.00 would be worth 2 yuan by PPP, rather than 8 yuan by the official exchange rate. This example is close to reality, since the GDP of China calculated by PPP is about four times higher than when it is calculated by the official exchange rate. The Chinese GDP is in fact equal to 78 percent of that of the E.U., instead of 18 percent by the official exchange rate. In the case of Poland, the ratio is about 1.5 to 1.

8. "Fit at 50? A Special Report on the European Union," *The Economist,* March 17, 2007.

9. William Faulkner, *Requiem for a Nun* (New York: Random House, 1959), Act I, Scene III.

3. A Brief History of the World and What We Can Learn from It

1. Zygmunt Bauman, *Wasted Lives. Modernity and Its Outcasts* (London: Polity Press, 2004).

2. Although this book devotes very little space to alternative history, it is worth consulting a collection of essays by leading Western historians, Robert Cowley (ed.), *What If? Eminent Historians Imagine What Might Have Been* (New York: Putnam, 2001).

3. See Jacques Attali, *1492* (Paris: Fayard, 1991).

4. *Tango na głos i orkiestra* [Tango for vocal and orchestra], words and music by Grzegorz Tomczak, vocal by Maryla Rodowicz, Antologia 3 (Polygram Polska, 1996).

5. The queen's award of a knighthood to Salman Rushdie led to international tensions, even between such allies as Pakistan and the U.S. Rushdie is the author of the controversial The Satanic Verses (London: Viking, 1988), which led to the subsequent fatwah by orthodox Islamists calling for his death. The Iranian authorities lifted the fatwah in 1998, but the affair flared up again when Rushdie reappeared on the international scene, now as Sir Salman, in June 2007.

6. See the survey of leading futurologists in Joseph F. Coates and Jennifer Jarratt, *What Futurists Believe* (Bethesda: World Future Society, 1989).

7. Angus Maddison, *The World Economy: A Millennial Perspective* (Paris: OECD, 2001). This is the most frequently cited study of estimated output changes over the last 2,000 years. Maddison estimates per capita GDP in Western Europe in 1000 CE at about $400, which was $50 less than a thousand years earlier. The estimate uses 1990 prices. If the intervening inflation is taken into account, these values would be almost $710 and $800, respectively, at 2007 prices.

8. Some people think that the inhabitants of India are "Indians," who are also sometimes erroneously referred to as "Hindus." Hindus, regardless of where they live, profess the world's oldest religion, Hinduism; there are at least a billion of them.

9. There were about 300 million people in the world in 1 CE and about 310 million in 1000 CE, according to estimates by John D. Durand, *Historical Estimates of World Population: An Evaluation* (Philadelphia: University of Penn-

sylvania Population Studies Center, 1974), http://www.indianngos.com/issue/
population/statistics/statistics9.htm. Maddison, *World Economy*, p. 28, estimates
population growth in the first millennium as about 16 percent (with an almost
imperceptible annual rate of 0.02 percent), from about 231 to 268 million. See
also Massimo Livi Bacci, *A Concise History of World Population* (Oxford, U.K.:
Blackwell, 2006). Palmer C. Putnam, *Energy in the Future* (London: Macmillan, 1954) estimates world population at 275 million in 1 CE, 295 million in
1000 CE, and 300 million only in 1200 CE.

10. Our great-great-great-great-grandfather is our grandfather's grandfather's grandfather, and our great-great-great-great-grandson is our grandson's
grandson's grandson.

11. Samuel P. Huntington, *The Clash of Civilizations and the Remaking of
World Order* (New York: Simon and Schuster, 1998).

12. The indicator for economic growth, in conformity with the methodology and nomenclature used in International Monetary Fund statistics, includes 15 European countries: Albania, Bulgaria, the Czech Republic, Croatia,
Estonia, Hungary, Lithuania, Latvia, Macedonia, Malta, Poland, Romania,
Slovakia, Slovenia, and Turkey. Malta and Turkey are usually not considered
to be part of "East-Central Europe." On the other hand, it does not include
the European members of the post-Soviet CIS—Belarus, Moldova, and
Ukraine—despite the fact that these countries are clearly part of East-Central
Europe.

13. In these estimates, *Western Europe* means the twelve of the fifteen highly
developed old members of the E.U. that belong to the eurozone. This excludes
E.U. members Britain, Sweden, and Denmark, as well as Iceland, Norway,
Switzerland, and the statistically insignificant Andorra, Liechtenstein, Monaco, and San Marino. This does not affect the statistical picture, since these
countries have GDP rates similar to those of the E.U. members. From 1998 to
2007, the rate of GDP growth in Britain, at 2.4 percent, was 0.6 percent
higher than that in the eurozone at the exchange rate. This means that the
GDP growth in Western Europe as a whole was about 0.1 percent higher.

14. See Michael Shermer, "The Chaos of History: On a Chaotic Model that
Represents the Role of Contingency and Necessity in Historical Sequences,"
Nonlinear Science, 4, 1993, pp. 1–13.

15. On the meanderings of economic development in Eastern Europe as
compared with Western Europe, see Ivan Berend, *History Derailed: Central
and Eastern Europe in the "Long" 19th Century* (Berkeley: University of California Press, 1997), and *An Economic History of Twentieth-Century Europe: Economic Regimes from Laissez-faire to Globalization* (Cambridge: Cambridge University Press, 2006).

16. These data are expressed in purchasing power parity at 2007 prices, assuming that they are about 75 percent higher than the 1990 prices used by

Maddison. Data for the quartile groups based on Maddison, *The World Economy: Historical Statistics* (Paris: OECD, 2003). See also the estimates in 1990 prices made by the International Monetary Fund, *World Economic Outlook* (Washington, DC, 2000).

17. This is the title of the lovely book by Lapierre, which served as the basis for the later, less-than-lovely film adaptation. A major character in the book is a Catholic priest from Poland, Stephan Kovalski, but his place is taken in the film by an American nurse, and not because of some possible association with Mother Teresa, but rather for commercial reasons. Dominique Lapierre, *The City of Joy* (New York: Warner Books, 1985); the 1995 film is directed by Roland Joffe.

18. So it has been at least since the publication in 1776 of Adam Smith's *An Inquiry into the Nature and Causes of the Wealth of Nations*.

19. See David S. Landes, *The Wealth and Poverty of Nations: Why Some Are So Rich and Some So Poor* (New York: W. W. Norton, 1998).

4. Globalization—and Then What?

1. As pointed out by Vincent Cable, *Globalization and Global Governance* (London: Royal Institute of International Affairs, 1999).

2. David W. Pearce, ed., *The MIT Dictionary of Modern Economics* (Cambridge, MA: MIT Press, 1992).

3. V. I. Lenin, *Imperialism, The Highest Stage of Capitalism*, www.marxists.org.

4. Kwame Nkrumah, *Neo-Colonialism: The Last Stage of Imperialism* (London: Thomas Nelson & Sons, 1965).

5. It should be "goods and services," not "merchandise and services." Merchandise is the product of human labor intended for exchange (sale) and can be either a good (material) or a service. Therefore, "merchandise and services" is a tautology, because it literally means "goods and services and services."

6. Karl Marx and Friedrich Engels, *Manifest der Kommunistischen Partei* (London, 1848); the "Communist Manifesto" was first published in German. www.marxists.org

7. See Federico Mayor et al., *The World Ahead: Our Future in the Making* (London: Zed, 2001), p. 136.

8. Thomas L. Friedman, *The World Is Flat: A Brief History of the Twenty-first Century* (New York: Farrar, Straus, and Giroux, 2005).

9. For the functioning of the global financial market, its impact on the real economy, and the benefits and risks of the globalization of finance, see *Financial Globalization: The Impact on Trade, Policy, Labor, and Capital Flows* (Washington, DC: International Monetary Fund, 2007).

10. Christopher Andrews and Vasili Mitrokhin provide a fascinating account of this historical moment in the second volume of their inside account

of the KGB, *The World Was Going Our Way: The KGB and the Battle for the Third World* (New York: Basic Books, 2005).

11. *Globalization, Growth and Poverty: Building an Inclusive World Economy* (Washington, DC: World Bank, 2002).

12. On the relationship between globalization and the postsocialist transformation, see Grzegorz W. Kolodko, *The World Economy and Great Postcommunist Change* (New York: Nova Science Publishers, 2006); and Saul Estrin, Grzegorz W. Kolodko, and Milica Uvalic (eds.), *Transition and Beyond* (New York: Palgrave Macmillan, 2007).

13. Lester C.Thurow, *The Future of Capitalism: How Today's Economic Forces Shape Tomorrow's World* (New York: William Morrow, 1996), p. 115.

14. *World Economic Outlook: Spillovers and Cycles in the Global Economy* (Washington, DC: International Monetary Fund, 2007), and especially chapter 5, "The Globalization of Labor," pp. 161–192.

15. Joseph E. Stiglitz, *Making Globalization Work* (New York: W. W. Norton, 2007).

16. Jeffrey Frieden, *Will Global Capitalism Fall Again? Bruegel Essay and Lecture Series*, June 2006.

17. John Man, *Genghis Khan: Life, Death, and Resurrection* (London: Bantam Books, 2004).

18. Jung Chang and John Halliday, *Mao: The Unknown Story* (London: Jonathan Cape, 2005), especially chapter 5, "Maoism Goes Global," pp. 478–489.

19. The CFA franc is used in fourteen countries, including twelve former French colonies, as well as Guinea Bissau (formerly Portuguese) and Equitorial Guinea (formerly Spanish). The total population of the zone is about 120 million. The CFA was pegged first to the franc and, since 1999, to the euro at 1 to 655.957. In fact, there are two separate legal tenders at this peg, the West African franc (XAF) in Benin, Burkina Faso, Guinea Bissau, Mali, Niger, Senegal, Togo, and Côte d'Ivoire, and the Central African franc (XOF) in Chad, Gabon, Equitorial Guinea, Cameroon, Congo-Brazzaville, and the Central African Republic

20. The East Caribbean dollar (XCI) has been used since 1965 in the eight OECS countries, with their population of 600,000, plus Anguilla and Montserrat. The British Virgin Islands, an OECS country, uses the U.S. dollar. The XCI is pegged at $1US to 2.7 EC$.

21. Of the twenty-seven E.U. member states, sixteen belong to the Eurozone: Austria, Belgium, Cyprus, Finland, France, Germany, Greece, Ireland, Italy, Luxembourg, Malta, the Netherlands, Portugal, Slovakia, Slovenia, and Spain. Slovakia and Slovenia are the only two postsocialist countries in the group. The sixteen countries have a total of some 330 million residents. All the other E.U. members states are under an obligation to join the eurozone upon meeting the strict fiscal and monetary convergence criteria set by the

Treaty of Maastricht. The only exceptions are Denmark and the United Kingdom, which negotiated opt-out agreements. Aside from the CFA, the exchange rates of at least six currencies, including the Pacific franc (XPF), are pegged directly to the euro, and eight others have pegged floats (meaning that their values can fluctuate within fixed bands in relation to that of the euro); www.ecb.int.

22. Robert A. Mundell, *International Economics* (New York: Macmillan, 1968), especially chapter 12, "A Theory of Optimum Currency Areas," pp. 117–186; www.columbia.edu.

23. Robert A. Mundell, *The International Financial Architecture. The Euro Zone and Its Enlargement in Eastern Europe, Distinguished Lectures Series* [Warsaw: Leon Kozminski Academy of Entrepreneurship and Management (WSPiZ), 2000], www.tiger.edu.pl; *One World Economy, One Global Currency? Distinguished Lectures Series* (Warsaw: Leon Kozminski Academy of Entrepreneurship and Management (WSPiZ), 2003); www.tiger.edu.pl.

24. There is no shortage of either apologists or critics. The apologists include Johan Norberg, *In Defense of Global Capitalism* (Washington, DC: Cato Institute, 2003); Martin Wolf, *Why Globalization Works* (New Haven: Yale University Press, 2004); Jagdish Bhagwati, *In Defense of Globalization* (New York: Oxford University Press, 2004). As for the critics, see Will Hutton and Anthony Giddens (eds.), *Global Capitalism* (New York: The New Press, 2000); Naomi Klein, *No Logo: Taking Aim at the Brand Bullies* (London: Harper Collins, 2001); Manfred B. Steger, *Globalism: The New Market Ideology* (Lanham, MD: Rowman & Littlefield, 2002); and Joseph E. Stiglitz, *Making Globalization Work.* The controversy has also elicited contributions by Polish economists, sociologists, political scientists, and philosophers. The author of the present work has joined this debate on numerous occasions, both in works published in Polish and in those that have appeared in English, including *Emerging Market Economies. Globalization and Development* (Aldershot, UK: Ashgate, 2003), which focuses on the positive implications for development, and Grzegorz W. Kolodko (ed.), *Globalization and Social Stress* (New York: Nova Science Publishers, 2005), which examines the downside.

5. The World As It Is

1. On the staggering scale of Dürer's contribution to art, see Paul Johnson, *Creators* (New York: Harper Collins, 2006).

2. For additional remarks on the methodology and calculation of data related to disparities in income distribution around the world, see Bob Sutcliffe, "Postscript to the Article World Inequality and Globalization," *Oxford Review of Economic Policy*, Spring 2004, siteresources.worldbank.org.

3. On the methodology used to construct the Human Development Index, as well as the full figures and their components for individual countries, see *World Development Indicators 07* (Washington, DC: The World Bank, 2007) and *Development and the Next Generation: World Development Report* (Washington, DC: The World Bank, 2007).

4. See World Health Organization, *The World Health Report 2007. A Safer Future: Global Public Health Security in the 21st Century* (Geneva: WHO Press, 2007), http://www.who.int/whr/2007/en/index.html.

5. Armartya Sen, *Development as Freedom* (New York: Alfred A. Knopf, 2000).

6. Freedom House provides methodological explanations and detailed data at its website, www.freedomhouse.org.

7. Similarly, the Heritage Foundation features detailed information at www.heritage.org.

8. Bjørn Lomborg, *The Skeptical Environmentalist: Measuring the Real State of the World* (Cambridge: Cambridge University Press, 2001).

9. *Ecosystems and Human Well-being: Current State and Trends* (Chicago: Island Press, 2005), www.millenniumassessment.org.

10. www.cia.gov.

11. Official reserve assets at the end of January 2008 were 46.2 billion euros, equal to $68.6 or 167.8 billion Polish zloty.

12. Parikshit K. Basu, "Financial Globalisation and National Economic Sustainability," *Global Economic Quarterly*, 3, no. 2 (2002): 145–62; Dipak Dasgupta, Marc Uzan, and Dominic Wilson, eds., *Capital Flows Without Crisis? Reconciling Capital Mobility and Economic Stability* (London: Routledge, 2001).

6. The Withering of Neoliberalism and Its Tattered Legacy

1. Among those proclaiming this view is the 2004 Nobel Prize winner Edward C. Prescott, in his "Nobel Lecture: The Transformation of Macroeconomic Policy and Research," *Journal of Political Economy*, 114, no. 2 (2006): 203–35.

2. U.K. Chancellor of the Exchequer Ian MacLeod (Conservative) introduced the concept into the political and economic idiom as early as 1965, but it rose to prominence later, in the 1970s, when the analysis of the stagflation process served as the basis for Gottfried Haberler's economic theory. See *Economic Growth and Stability: An Analysis of Economic Change and Policies* (Los Angeles: Nash Publishing, 1974), and *The Problem of Stagflation: Reflection on the Microfoundation of Macroeconomic Theory and Policy* (Washington, DC: American Enterprise Institute for Public Policy Research, 1985).

3. János Kornai, *Economics of Shortage* (Amsterdam: North-Holland, 1980).

4. Grzegorz W. Kolodko and Walter McMahon, "Stagflation and Short-ageflation: A Comparative Approach," *Kylos*, 40, no. 2 (1987): 176–97.

5. One of the most famous curves in the history of economic thought, the Phillips curve, illustrating the inflation/unemployment relation, was sprung upon the world by the New Zealand-born economist Alban W. Phillips in an article published in a British journal in 1958: "The Relationship Between Un-employment and the Rate of Change of Money Wages in the United Kingdom in 1861–1957," *Economica*, 25, no. 100 (1958): 282–299.

6. Edmund S. Phelps, *Inflation Policy and Unemployment Theory* (New York: W.W. Norton, 1972). The announcement of the award of the Nobel Prize em-phasized the fact that Phelps's work had led to a deeper understanding of the relationship between short- and long-term economic policy. Phelps also wrote about optimizing the distribution of national income (global output) and capital accumulation (the so-called golden rule of accumulation).

7. David Harvey, *A Brief History of Neoliberalism* (New York: Oxford Uni-versity Press, 2005), pp. 62–63.

8. Views in favor of or opposed to the "Washington Consensus" are sur-veyed in Grzegorz W. Kolodko, *Post-Communist Transition and Post-Wash-ington Consensus: The Lessons for Policy Reforms*, [in] Mario I Blejer and Marko Skreb, eds., *Transition: The First Decade* (Cambridge, MA: MIT Press, 2001), pp. 45–83. Joseph E. Stiglitz subjects the Consensus to a thoroughgoing cri-tique in *Making Globalization Work* (New York: W.W. Norton, 2007).

9. John Williamson coined the term *Washington Consensus* in the late 1980s. For the theoretical underpinnings and the interpretation of this concept in eco-nomic policy, as well as an interpretation of these interpretations by the man who invented the term, see his *Differing Interpretations of the Washington Consen-sus* [in] *Distinguished Lectures Series No. 17* (Warsaw: Leon Kozminski Academy of Entrepreneurship and Management [WSPiZ], 2005), www.tiger.edu.pl.

10. On the basis of his own experience, John Perkins writes about the delib-erate forcing of poor countries into the debt trap and the methods used along the way in *Confessions of an Economic Hit Man* (San Francisco: Berrett-Koehler, 2004).

11. There is already an extensive literature on the issue, including Olivier Blanchard, *The Economics of Post-Communist Transition* (New York: Oxford University Press, 1997); Marie Lavigne, *The Economics of Transition: From Socialist Economy to Market Economy* (Chatham, Kent: Macmillan Press, 1995); Kazimierz Poznański, *Poland's Protracted Transition: Institutional Change and Economic Growth* (Cambridge: Cambridge University Press, 1995); and Vladi-mir Popov, *Shock Therapy versus Gradualism Reconsidered: Lessons from Transi-tion Economies After 15 Years of Reforms, TIGER Working Paper Series 82* (War-saw: Leon Kozminski Academy of Entrepreneurship and Management, 2006), www.tiger.edu.pl.

12. Professor Kazimierz Laski of the Vienna Institute for International Economic Research (WIIW) issued a particularly chilling critique of "shock therapy" in "The Stabilization Plan for Poland," *Wirtschaftspolitische Blätter*, 5 (1990): 444–58), where he warned that industrial production would fall by 25 percent in the first year, 1990, causing mass unemployment. Unfortunately, he was right.

13. Then, after the successful implementation of the program known as "Strategy for Poland," the author of this book for the first time had stepped down from the Polish government. He was deputy prime minister and minister of finance in four governments in 1994–97 and 2002–03.

14. The Dutch researcher Donald Kalff, who also has real-world business experience, dispels the idea that the American model of capitalism and management offers any sort of qualitative advantages and considers the implications of this fact for competitiveness and the growth of production in *An Un-American Business: The Rise of the New European Enterprise Model* (London: Kogan Page, 2005).

15. For the negative impact of excessively unequal income distribution on the rate of economic growth, see Vito Tanzi, Ke-Young Chu, and Sanjeev Gupta, eds., *Economic Policy and Inequality* (Washington, DC: International Monetary Fund, 1999).

16. Bernt Bratsberg et al., *Non-linearities in Inter-generational Earnings Mobility* (London: Royal Economics Society, 2006); *American Exceptionalism in a New Light* (Bonn: Institute for the Study of Labor, 2006).

17. For the results of this Gallup poll, see "Testing Muslim Views: If You Want My Opinion," *The Economist*, March 10, 2007, p. 63.

18. I reflected on tensions in relations between the United States and Iran in a two-part article, "Triggering the Next Iranian Revolution," *The Globalist*, March 14 (part one) and March 15 (part two), 2007. www.theglobalist.com.

19. Results of a representative survey conducted by the BBC. See "Latin America and the United States: Spring Break," *The Economist*, March 3, 2007, p. 49.

20. Francis Fukuyama expresses some impassioned views on this subject in *America at the Crossroads: Democracy, Power, and the Neoconservative Legacy* (New Haven: Yale University Press, 2006). See also the comparative analysis of the presidencies of George H. W. Bush, Bill Clinton, and George W. Bush in Zbigniew Brzezinski, *Second Chance: Three Presidents and the Crisis of American Superpower* (New York: Basic Books, 2007).

21. At the end of 2007, the World Bank shocked and astonished a good many people by revising its previous estimates downward and announcing that the Chinese GDP, by purchasing power parity, was no less than 40 percent lower than previously estimated. This would mean that it hovered in the region of $6 trillion, rather than $10 trillion. The GDP of India was "marked down"

on an even greater scale, which meant that it was not slightly larger than that of Japan, but rather about half as large. This radical rewriting of the estimates did not cast the authors in the best light. How could they have been so wrong? And how could we know that they hadn't gotten it wrong again? Understandably, GDP according to PPP will always be an approximation, at best. Taking into account all the methodological reservations, I have decided to stick to the original estimates, which seem to reflect reality more accurately.

22. With fertility rates so high in these extremely poor countries (GDP per capita in Niger and Mali amounted to $1,000 and $1,200, respectively, by PPP in 2007), infant mortality below the age of five is 249 per thousand in Niger and 219 per thousand in Mali. By comparison, it is 31 in China and 4 in the most highly developed countries—Finland, Japan, and Sweden. In Poland, it is 8. See *Development and the Next Generation* (Washington, DC: World Bank, 2006), pp. 292–293.

23. Brzezinski, *Second Chance*, p. 64.

24. David Sater, "The Rise of the Russian Criminal State," *Prism*, September 4, 1998; Janine R. Wedel, *Collision and Collusion: The Strange Case of Western Aid to Eastern Europe 1989–1998* (New York: St. Martin's Press, 1998); and "The Harvard Boys Do Russia," *The Nation*, June 1, 1998, pp. 11–16.

25. I published extensively on the subject at the time, even in the *New York Times* ("Russia Should Put Its People First," July 7, 1998), *The Economist* ("Don't Abandon Russia," Feb. 27, 1999), and the World Bank's new research series ("Ten Years of Post-socialist Transition: The Lessons for Policy Reforms," *Policy Research Working Paper 2095*, April 1999). See also my major book *From Shock to Therapy: The Political Economy of Postsocialist Transformation* (Oxford: Oxford University Press, 2000). Earmath's plea nevertheless remains relevant, because the truth has not yet come out decisively on top—if it ever will.

26. See "The Challenger," *The Economist*, Dec. 11, 2004.

27. Peter Mandelson quoted in a story on the BBC News website: "EU-Russia Relations at Low Ebb," April 20, 2007, news.bbc.co.uk.

28. Cf. the 2007 *CIA World Factbook* (Washington, DC: Central Intelligence Agency), www.cia.gov.

29. Justin Yifu Lin, appointed chief economist and senior vice president of the World Bank in 2008, is also a member of the Academic Board of the TIGER Research Center, where he has visited and lectured. See *Lessons of China's Transition from a Planned to a Market Economy* [in] *Distinguished Lectures Series No. 16* (Warsaw: Leon Kozminski Academy of Entrepreneurship and Management [WSPiZ]), available at www.tiger.edu.pl.

30. See Vito Tanzi and Ludger Schuknecht, "The Growth of Government and the Reform of the State in Industrial Countries," *IMF Working Papers* 95/130 (1995).

7. What Development Is and What It Depends On

1. See Nic Marks, Saamah Abdallah, Andrew Simms, and Sam Thompson, *The Happy Planet Index* (London: New Economics Foundation, 2006). Richard Layard also writes about the category of happiness as perceived from the economic perspective in *Happiness: Lessons from a New Science* (London: Penguin, 2006).

2. Press release: "University of Leicester Produces the First Ever World Map of Happiness: Happiness Is Being Healthy, Wealthy and Wise," www2 .le.ac.uk; Adrian White, "World Map of Happiness," *Psych Talk*, March 2007.

3. A mathematical formula for calculating the degree of the human poverty gap can be found in the study *Indicators for Monitoring the Millennium Development Goals: Definitions, Rationale, Concepts, and Sources* (New York: United Nations, 2003), p. 9; mdgs.un.org.

4. *Development Goals Report 2007: Statistical Annex* (New York: United Nations, 2007). The relevant information is available at mdgs.un.org.

5. Questioning the assumption about diminishing returns from capital, Paul Romer, in particular, contributed to creating and developing an endogenous model of economic growth. See his "Increasing Returns and Long-Run Growth," *Journal of Political Economy*, 94, no. 5 (1986): 1002–37.

6. See Robert E. Lucas, "On the Mechanics of Economic Development," *Journal of Monetary Economics*, 22, no. 1 (1988): 3–42.

7. See George Mavrotas and Anthony Shorrocks, eds., *Advancing Development: Core Themes in Global Economics* (New York: Palgrave Macmillan, 2007), a daunting tome (803 pages) rich in a variety of themes relevant to contemporary development economics and containing as its Chapter 28 my text, *Institutions, Policies, and Economic Development*, pp. 531–54.

8. Stagnation and Development—Institutions, Policy, and Culture

1. John Seabrook, "Sowing for Democracy," *The New Yorker*, Aug. 27, 2007.

2. Statistical data cited in "Caught in the Middle, As Usual," *The Economist*, Nov. 12, 2005, p. 49.

3. See Andres Åslund, *How Russia Became a Market Economy* (Washington, DC: The Brookings Institution, 1995).

4. See Max Weber, *The Protestant Ethic and the "Spirit" of Capitalism*, translated and with an introduction and additional selections by Peter Baehr and Gordon C. Wells (New York: Penguin, 2002).

5. The 1996 film explains more about the essence of economic populism, and not only in its Peronist variant, than some scholarly studies of the subject.

6. Elhanan Helpman writes about the meanderings of economic growth and the complexities of its interpretation in a work that is both interesting and accessible to an exceptional degree, the aptly titled *The Mystery of Economic Growth* (Cambridge, MA: Harvard University Press, 2004).

9. The Coincidence Theory of Development and the New Pragmatism

1. *Our Posthuman Future: Consequences of the Biotechnology Revolution* (New York: Farrar, Straus & Giroux, 2002), p. 66
2. Dani Rodrik, *Let a Thousand Growth Models Bloom*, www.project-syndi cate.org; *Rethinking Growth Strategies* [in] *WIDER Perspectives on Global Development* [(Houndmills, Hampshire, and New York: Palgrave Macmillan, 2005), pp. 201–223.

10. The Uncertain Future

1. See National Intelligence Council, *Mapping the Global Future: Report of the National Intelligence Council's 2020 Project. Based on Consultations with Nongovernmental Experts around the World* (Washington, DC, Nov. 2004), www .foia.cia.gov.net.
2. William Easterly, *The Elusive Quest for Growth: Economists' Adventures and Misadventures in the Tropics* (Cambridge, MA: MIT Press, 2002); *The White Man's Burden: Why the West's Efforts to Aid the Rest Have Done So Much Ill and So Little Good* (New York: Penguin, 2006).
3. Paul Collier, *The Bottom Billion: Why the Poorest Countries Are Failing and What Can Be Done About It* (New York: Oxford University Press, 2007).
4. Ilyana Kuziemko and Eric Werker, "How Much Is a Seat on the Security Council Worth? Foreign Aid and Bribery at the United Nations," *Journal of Political Economy*, 114, no. 3 (2006): 413–51.
5. The members of ASEAN, the Association of South East Asian Nations, are Burma (Myanmar), Brunei, Cambodia, Indonesia, Laos, Malaysia, The Philippines, Singapore, Thailand, and Vietnam.
6. All but one of the former Soviet Republics are in the loosely affiliated CIS (Commonwealth of Independent States), with the exception of the three Baltic States—Estonia, Latvia, and Lithuania—that have joined the E.U. Georgia left the grouping after the recent military conflict with Russia. The members of the CIS are Armenia, Azerbaijan, Belarus, Kazakhstan, Kyrgyzstan, Moldova, Russia, Tajikistan, Turkmenistan, Ukraine, and Uzbekistan.

7. The member states of Mercosur are Argentina, Brazil, Paraguay, Uruguay, and Venezuela. The affiliated members of the associated free-trade zone are Bolivia, Chile, Colombia, Ecuador, and Peru.

8. The members of NAFTA, the North American Free Trade Agreement, are Canada, Mexico, and the United States.

9. The Southern African Development Community has fifteen members: Angola, Botswana, the Democratic Republic of Congo, Lesotho, Madagascar, Malawi, Mauritius, Mozambique, Namibia, The Seychelles, South Africa, Swaziland, Tanzania, Zambia, and Zimbabwe.

10. The members of ECOWAS, the Economic Community of West African States, are Benin, Burkina Faso, Cape Verde, Gambia, Ghana, Guinee, Guinee Bissau, Ivory Coast, Liberia, Mali, Niger, Nigeria, Senegal, Sierra Leone, and Togo.

11. In 2007, Bangladesh, Bhutan, India, the Maldives, Nepal, Pakistan, and Sri Lanka were joined as members of SAARC (The South Asian Association for Regional Cooperation) by Afghanistan.

12. The Cooperation Council for the Arab States of the Gulf (CCASG), usually referred to as the Gulf Cooperation Council, groups together Bahrain, Kuwait, Oman, Qatar, Saudi Arabia, and the United Arab Emirates.

13. The member states of the E.U. are Austria, Belgium, Bulgaria, Cyprus, the Czech Republic, Denmark, Estonia, Finland, France, Germany, Greece, Hungary, Ireland, Italy, Latvia, Lithuania, Luxemburg, Malta, the Netherlands, Poland, Portugal, Romania, Slovakia, Slovenia, Spain, Sweden, and the United Kingdom. Croatia and Turkey, negotiating their accession, have associated status.

14. See *Ecosystems and Human Well-Being: Scenarios* (Chicago: Island Press, 2005), www.millenniumassessment.org.

15. Thirty years after the first, best-known work on the resource-related limits to growth, we have a new work by the redoubtable authorial team of Donelli H. Meadows, Dennis Meadows, and Jorgen Andrews, *The Limits to Growth: The 30-Year Update* (London and Sterling, VA: Earthscan, 2004).

16. See General Accountability Office, U.S. Congress, *Uncertainty About Future Oil Supply Makes It Important to Develop a Strategy for Addressing a Peak and Decline in oil Production* (GAO-07–283), Feb. 2007.

17. The cynicism and moral turpitude of the donors of "economic aid" to the poorest countries form the subject of a provocative and highly concrete book by Graham Hancock, *Lords of Poverty* (Nairobi: Camerapix Publishers International, 2004).

18. Orhan Pamuk, *Snow* (New York: Knopf, 2004), p. 240.

19. David Edgerton, *The Shock of the Old: Technology and Global History Since 1900* (London: Profile Books, 2006).

20. Fukuyama, *The End of History and the Last Man* (New York: Free Press, 1992). pp. 9–10.

21. See "A World of Connections: A Special Report on Telecoms," *The Economist*, April 28, 2007.

22. Jack Hirshleifer writes about ways of overcoming the economic consequences of thermonuclear war in *Economic Behavior in Adversity* (Brighton, UK: Wheatsheaf Books, 1987).

23. In 2001, John E. Bortle, the retired fire chief of Westchester, New York, proposed a system for measuring the darkness of the night sky on a scale of 1 to 9, which has gained acceptance among amateur astronomers. Bortle is a columnist for *Sky & Telescope* magazine, www.shopatsky.com.

24. See Mark Abley, *Spoken Here: Travels Among Threatened Languages* (Montreal: Vintage Canada, 2004).

Index